THE COMPLETE
MAHABHARATA

Bhishma Parva

THE COMPLETE MAHABHARATA

Volume 5

Bhishma Parva

Anjuli Kaul

RUPA

Published by
Rupa Publications India Pvt. Ltd 2013
7/16, Ansari Road, Daryaganj
New Delhi 110002

Sales centres:
Allahabad Bengaluru Chennai
Hyderabad Jaipur Kathmandu
Kolkata Mumbai

ISBN: 978-81-291-2929-1

10 9 8 7 6 5 4 3 2 1

The moral right of the author has been asserted.

Printed at Repro Knowledgecast Limited, India

Contents

CANTO 1

JAMBU-KHANDA NIRMANA PARVA

AUM! Having bowed down to Narayana, and Nara, the most exalted of Purushas, and also to the Devi Saraswati, I invoke the spirit of *Jaya!*

Janamejaya asked, "How did those heroes, the Kurus, the Pandavas and the Somakas, and the great kings assembled together from various countries, fight?"

Vaisampayana replied, "O lord of the earth, hear now how those heroes, the Kurus, the Pandavas, and the Somakas fought on the sacred plain of Kurukshetra. Seeking victory, the mighty Pandavas, along with the Somakas, advance against the Kauravas. Accomplished masters of the Vedas, they take great delight in battle. Eager for success, they and their legions face the war.

Approaching the army of Dhritarashtra's son, those invincible warriors and their troops station on the western part of the plain, facing the east. Yudhishtira, the son of Kunti, has thousands of tents erected beyond Samantapanchaka. The whole earth seems then to be empty, divested of horses and men, destitute of chariots and elephants, with only the children and the old left at home.

That immense force has come from all of Jambudwipa over which the sun sheds his rays. Men of all races assemble together and occupy an area of many yojanas over plains, rivers, hills and forests. That bull among men, king Yudhishtira, orders excellent food and other things of enjoyment for all of them and their animals. He fixes diverse code-words for them so that anyone saying these would be known as belonging to the Pandavas, and also gives names and badges to all of them for recognition during the war.

Seeing the standard-top of Pritha's son, the great son of Dhritarashtra, with a white royal parasol held over his head, in the midst of a thousand elephants, surrounded by his ninety-nine brothers and allied kings, begins to dispose his troops against the son of Pandu. Seeing Duryodhana, the Panchalas, who take delight in battle, are filled with joy and blow on their booming conches and clash cymbals of sweet sounds.

Watching the happy troops, the hearts of Pandu's son and Vasudeva fill with joy. And those tigers among men, Krishna and Arjuna, seated together in one chariot, blow their celestial conches. And hearing the blast of the Panchajanya and the echoing blast of the Devadatta, the enemy soldiers are terrified, even as other animals are filled with fear on hearing the roar of the lion; many helplessly urinate and even defecate.

A frightful pall of dust arises and nothing can be seen, for, suddenly enveloped by it, the sun himself seems to have set. A black cloud pours a shower of flesh and blood over the troops all around. All this seems macabre and extraordinary. A wind rises, blowing along the earth numberless tiny stones, and harries the hundreds and thousands of fighting men.

Despite that, O king, both armies, filled with joy, stand keened for battle on Kurukshetra like two stormy seas. Indeed, that encounter of the two armies is wonderful, like that of two oceans when the end of the Yuga has arrived. The whole world is empty, having only the children and the old left at home, from that vast army having been mustered by the Kauravas.

O Bharatarishabha, then the Kurus, the Pandavas, and the Somakas make certain covenants, and agree on the laws governing the different kinds of combat. In order to fight fairly, men equally circumstanced must encounter each other. And if, having fought fairly, the combatants withdraw they should be able to do so without fear of being attacked. Those who engage in contests of words should be fought with words. Those that leave the ranks should never be killed.

A warrior in a chariot should be opposed by another such warrior; he on the neck of an elephant should have a similar adversary; a horseman should be met by a horseman, and a footsoldier, O Bhaarata, should be met by a footsoldier.

Guided by considerations of fitness, willingness, daring and strength, one fighting man should strike another, after giving notice. An unprepared or panic-stricken opponent must not be attacked. A soldier who is engaged with another, or is seeking refuge, or retreating, or one whose weapon is broken, or one unprotected by armour, should never be shot at or struck. Charioteers, animals yoked to chariots or bearing weapons, men engaged in the transport of weapons, drummers and blowers of conches, must never be assaulted.

Having decided on these rubrics of battle, the Kurus, and the Pandavas, and the Somakas gaze at each other in awe. After positioning their troops, the exhilaration felt by these powerful and high-souled men is reflected in their faces, which shine."

CANTO 2

JAMBU-KHANDA NIRMANA PARVA
CONTINUED

Vaisampayana said, "Seeing the two armies standing on the east and the west for the fierce and imminent war, the holy Rishi Vyasa, the son of Satyavati, learned in the Vedas, that grandfather of the Bhaaratas, trikalagyani, knower of the past, the present and the future, and seeing every time and everything as if they were before his eyes, says these words in private to the royal son of Vichitravirya, who is distressed and dejected, thinking of the evil policy of his own sons.

Vyasa says, 'Dhritarashtra, the day of reckoning for your sons and the other kings has arrived. Assembled for battle they will kill one another. O Bhaarata, their hour having come, they will all perish. Bearing in mind the changes brought on by time, do not grieve. O king, if you wish to see them fighting, I will grant you vision. Behold the war.'

Dhritarashtra says, 'O Maharishi, I would not like to watch the slaughter of kinsmen. I will, however, through your powers listen to the details of this battle.'"

Vaisampayana continued, "Upon his not wanting to see the battle but wishing to hear of it, Vyasa, that lord of boons, gives a boon to Sanjaya and he says to Dhritarashtra, 'O Rajan, Sanjaya will describe the war to you. Nothing in all the war will be hidden from his eyes. Endowed with celestial vision, Sanjaya will describe the fighting to you. He will have knowledge of everything.

Sanjaya will know everything: that which is manifest or concealed, occurring by day or by night, even that which is thought of in the mind. Weapons will not hurt him and exertion will not fatigue him. This son of Gavalgani will come out of the battle alive.

As for myself, I will spread the fame of these Kurus, and of the Pandavas. Do not grieve. This is destiny, O tiger among men. It does not become you to give way to grief. The war cannot be prevented. As for victory, it lies with the righteous.

There will be great slaughter in this war. I see numerous omens of terror. Hawks and vultures, crows and herons, together with cranes, alight on the tops of trees and gather in swarms. Delighted at the prospect of battle, these birds look down on the field before them. Carnivorous beasts will feed on the flesh of elephants and horses. Fierce herons, foreboding terror, and uttering merciless cries, circle across the centre of the field towards the south.

In both the twilights of every day, I see, O Bhaarata, the sun while rising and setting, covered by headless trunks. Tri-coloured clouds with their white and red ends and black necks, charged with lightning, and shaped like maces, envelop the sun at both dawn and dusk. I see the sun, the moon and the stars to be all ablaze, with no difference in their appearance at nightfall. I have seen this all day and all night. All of it forebodes fear.

On even the full moon night of the month of Kartika, the moon becomes invisible, or turns the colour of fire, the sky being of the hue of a lotus. Many heroic kings and princes, with arms like maces, will be slain and strewn upon the earth. Every night, in the sky I hear the fierce cries of battling boars and cats. The idols of the Devas and

Devis sometimes laugh, sometimes tremble; sometimes they vomit blood through their mouths, sometimes they sweat and sometimes fall down.

Drums, without being beaten, sound, and the great chariots of Kshatriyas move without being drawn by yoked horses. Kokilas, wood-peckers, water-cocks, parrots, crows, and peacocks utter fell cries. Here and there, cavalry soldiers, encased in mail, armed with weapons, shout fiercely. At sunrise, millions of insects fly everywhere in thick swarms. At both dawn and dusk, the four quarters of the earth seem to be on fire, and the clouds, Bhaarata, shower down dirt and flesh.

Arundhati, who is celebrated over the three worlds and applauded by the righteous, keeps her lord Vasistha at her back. The planet Sani appears to afflict the constellation Rohini. The sign of the deer in the moon has shifted from its usual position. A great terror is indicated. A dreadful roaring can be heard in the cloudless sky. The animals are all weeping, their tears falling fast."

CANTO 3

JAMBU-KHANDA NIRMANA PARVA
CONTINUED

Vyasa says, 'Cows are giving birth to asses. Men desire sexual pleasure with their mothers. The trees in the forests exhibit unseasonal flowers and fruit. Pregnant women, and even those who are not, are giving birth to monsters. Carnivorous beasts and birds live and feed together. Ill-omened beasts, some with three horns, some with four eyes, some with five legs, some with two sexual organs, some with two heads, some with two tails, some with fierce fangs, are being born, and maws agape, utter unholy cries. Horses with three legs and strange crests, with four rows of teeth and horns, are also being born.

O Rajan! Strange sights are seen in your city: the wives of many Brahmavadis are giving birth to eagles and peacocks, the mare is bringing forth a calf and the bitch jackals and cocks, while deer and parrots all screech inauspiciously.

Some women give birth to four or five daughters together, who begin to dance, sing and laugh as soon as they are born. The coarse laughing, dancing and singing of the lowest born portend dire events. Infants, as if drawn by death, fight each other with clubs and break down the little towns they built while playing.

Many kinds of lotuses and lilies grow on trees. Fierce winds blow and dust flies everywhere.

The earth trembles frequently and Rahu approaches the Sun. The white Ketu stays still, having passed beyond the asterism of Chitra. All these prophesy the destruction of the Kurus. A fierce comet rises, afflicting the constellation of Pusya. This great thing will bring calamity on both the armies.

Mars spins towards Magha and Brihaspati towards Sravana. Sani approaches the nakshatra Bhaga, afflicting it. Sukra, ascending towards Purva Bhadra, shines brilliantly, and wheels towards and faces the Uttara Bhadra arranging itself next to a smaller planet. Ketu blazing like fire mixed with smoke is stationary, having attacked the bright star of Jyeshta so sacred to Indra.

Dhruva burns strongly and turns to his right. Both the Moon and the Sun afflict Rohini. Ferocious Rahu has taken up his position between the constellations of Chitra and Swati. The red-bodied, fiery Mars orbits circuitously, staying aligned with the nakshatra of Sravana over-ridden by Brihaspati.

The Earth that produces crops each in their season is now covered with crops of every season. Every barley-stalk is graced with five ears, and every paddy-stalk with a hundred. When milked after their calves have suckled, cows, those best of creatures upon whom the universe depends, flow only blood.

Radiant beams of light emerge from bows, and swords shine brightly. It appears that the weapons can already see the war before them, as if it is already being fought. The weapons, the water, and the coats of armour all assume the colour of fire.

A great slaughter will take place. In this battle between the Kurus and the Pandavas, O Bhaarata, the earth will be a river of blood and the standards of warriors its rafts. The wild cries of animals and birds with blazing mouths are evil omens of dreadful outcomes. A fierce bird with but one wing, one eye, and one leg, hovering over the sky in the night, screams in such great anger, so as to make its hearers vomit blood.

It seems, O great king, that all weapons are now shining radiantly. The lustre of the Saptarishi mandala has been dimmed. Having approached the asterism of Visakha, Brihaspati and Sani, ablaze, have been still there for a whole year.

Three lunations twice meeting together in the course of the same lunar fortnight, the duration of the latter is shortened by two days. On the thirteenth day, therefore, from the first lunation, according to whether it is the day of the full moon or the new moon, the Moon and the Sun are afflicted by Rahu. Such strange eclipses, both lunar and solar, forebode a great carnage.

Overwhelmed by showers of dust, all the quarters of the earth look inauspicious. Predicting danger, angry clouds rain bloody showers during the night. Rahu of fierce deeds also balefully impacts the constellation of Krittika. Rough winds of evil omen are constantly blowing. All these will beget a war of numberless sorrows and untold grief.

The Nakshatras are of three types: the Deva, the Asura and the Manushya. A malignant planet casts its influence upon at least one of each, foreshadowing terrifying dangers. A lunar fortnight usually consists of fourteen, fifteen or sixteen days. Never have I known the day of new moon to fall on the thirteenth day from the first lunation, or the day of full moon on the thirteenth day from the same. And yet in the course of the same month both the moon and the sun have undergone eclipses on the thirteenth days from the day of the first lunation. These will result in a great massacre of the earth's creatures.

Though drinking blood in mouthfuls, the rakshasas are not satiated. The great rivers are flowing back to their sources, and their waters have become bloody. The wells are frothing and bellowing like bulls. Meteors, effulgent like Indra's thunderbolt, fall in showers with loud hisses. This night will be followed by direst evil.

People will have to light torches when they emerge from their houses to assemble and still be enveloped in the encircling thick gloom. Great Rishis have said that in such circumstances the earth drinks the blood of thousands of kings.

From the peaks of Kailasa, Mandara and Himavat thousands of explosions are heard and hundreds of great crags and peaks come crashing off their summits. Earthquakes swell the four oceans, which threaten to break their banks and sweep over the continents to drown the land.

Violent winds filled with sharp pebbles blow and mighty trees fall. In villages and towns both sacred and ordinary trees are struck by lightning and felled by savage winds. When Brahmanas pour libations onto the sacrificial fire, it burns blue, or red, or yellow. Its flames bend towards the left, giving off a vile stench and loud reports.

Touch, smell and taste, O king, have changed their very nature.

The flagstaffs of warriors tremble continually and emit smoke. Drums and cymbals shower coal-dust. And from the tops of tall trees all around, crows, wheeling in circles from the left, utter fierce cries of *paka! paka!* and perch upon the tops of standards for the destruction of the kings.

Demented wild elephants, their great bodies shaking in fear, dash here and there, spraying urine and dung. The horses in our stables are all melancholy, while our elephants wade into water. O Bhaarata, pay heed to all these omens, and do what needs to be done so that the world may not be completely destroyed.'"

Vaisampayana continued, "Hearing these words of his father, Dhritarashtra says, 'I think all this has been preordained. A great slaughter of men will indeed take place. If the kings die in battle observing Kshatriya dharma, they will be assured a place in those blessed regions where heroes go when they die and will find only happiness there. These great Purushavyaghras, who give up their lives in this battle, will win fame in this world and great bliss in the next.'

O great king, thus addressed by his son Dhritarashtra, that prince of poets, the Muni Vyasa concentrates his mind in supreme dhyana. After meditating for a short time, Vyasa says, 'Without doubt, O king of kings, it is Time that destroys the universe. It is Time also that creates the worlds. Nothing here is eternal. Show the path of dharma to the Kurus, to your kinsmen, relatives and friends. You have the power to restrain them. The slaughter of kinsmen has been declared sinful. Do not do that which is disagreeable to me.

Rajan, Death himself has been born in the guise of your son. Killing is never praised in the Vedas. It can never be beneficial. The members of one's race are as the limbs and organs of one's own body. Those limbs slay him that destroys them. Although you can well walk the righteous path of dharma, it is for the destruction of this race and of those kings of the earth that Time makes you deviate onto the evil path like one in distress.

O Rajan, your kingdom brings calamity upon you. Your virtue has been greatly diminished. Show your sons the meaning of dharma. You invincible one, of what value is that kingdom which brings sin upon you? Protect your good name, your virtue, and your fame. Then alone can you win heaven. Let the Pandavas have their kingdom, and let the Kauravas have peace.'

While Vyasa Brahmanottama is speaking, sadly, Dhritarashtra, the eloquent son of Ambika, once more addresses him, 'My knowledge of life and death is similar to yours and I know the truth of these things. Yet when a man's own interests are involved, he loses his discernment.

Father, I am like any ordinary man. I ask you to extend your boundless power to us. As a self-controlled soul you are our refuge and our guru. My sons do not obey me, great Rishi. I too am not inclined to commit this enormous sin. You are the cause of the fame, the achievements, and the inclination for virtue, of the Bhaaratas. You are the revered grandfather of both the Kurus and the Pandavas.'

Vyasa says, 'Royal son of Vichitravirya, tell me openly what is in your mind and I will remove your doubts.'

Dhritarashtra says, 'Holy one, tell me about all that happens to those that will be victorious in battle.'

Vyasa says, 'The sacred fire glows and its light ascends upwards. Its flame bends towards the right. It blazes up without being smoky. The offerings poured on it give out a sweet fragrance. It is said that these are the indications of future victory. The conches and cymbals emit deep, sweet sounds. The Sun and the Moon emanate pure rays. It is said that these are the signs of future success.

Crows, whether stationary or in flight, utter agreeable cries. Those that are behind them, encourage the warriors to advance; while they that are ahead forbid all advance. Where vultures, swans, parrots, cranes and woodpeckers utter delighted cries, and turn towards the right, the Brahmanas say that victory in war is certain there. Those armies whose ornaments, armour and standards shine so brightly that one cannot gaze upon them, and whose horses neigh melodiously, will always defeat their enemies.

The warriors who utter cheerful, energetic shouts, O Bhaarata, and whose garlands do not fade, always win in battle. Having penetrated the legions of their adversaries with cheerful cries, they who utter kind words, even to the enemy, and warn them before attacking, are victorious. The objects of the senses, not changing for the worse, become auspicious. Another indication of a victorious army is the joy among the soldiers at all times. Other signs of success include favourable winds, clouds and birds, while clouds and the rainbows bring beneficial rain.

This, O king, is what happens to the armies about to be crowned with victory, while the opposite happens to those that are about to be destroyed. Whether the army is small or large, the morale of the combatants is said to be a sure indication of victory.

One panic stricken soldier can cause even a vast army to take flight. And when this happens, it frightens even heroic warriors. If such an army is once broken and put to flight, it cannot be stopped, even like a frightened herd of deer or a powerful wave of water.

It is impossible to rally a mighty army once routed; why, seeing this, even those best fighters lose heart. Watching frightened and fleeing soldiers makes the panic spread in other directions, and soon the whole army is demoralised and scatters in all directions. And when an army is routed, even brave leaders cannot rally them.

Always exerting himself with activity, an intelligent man should strive to win success using peaceful means. It is said that the noblest success is that which is won through negotiation. That which is achieved by creating dissension in the enemy ranks is undistinguished. But the victory which is won by war is the worst.

There are many evils in battle, the first and greatest one being killing. Even fifty brave men who know one another, who are calm and determined, and free from family ties, can crush a large army. Even five, six, or seven men, who are unyielding, can achieve victory.

Vinata's son Garuda, O Bhaarata, did not ask for the help of many followers to defeat a great flight of birds. The numerical strength of an army is not always the reason for its victory. Victory is uncertain. It depends on chance. Even those who are victorious have to sustain losses.'"

CANTO 4

JAMBU-KHANDA NIRMANA PARVA
CONTINUED

Vaisampayana said, "Having spoken thus to Dhritarashtra, Vyasa departs. And Dhritarashtra, having heard those words, reflects in silence and soon begins to sigh repeatedly.

And then, Bharatarishabha, he tells the noble-souled Sanjaya, 'O Sanjaya, these kings, these lords of the earth, so brave and taking pleasure in battle, are in favour of striking one another with a variety of weapons. They are prepared to lay down their lives for the sake of owning the earth. Impossible to restrain, they are, indeed, killing one another to increase the population of Yama's kingdom. They are incapable of tolerating each other because of their desire to possess the earth and be prosperous.

Therefore, I believe that the earth must have many wondrous qualities. Tell me about these, O Sanjaya. Many thousands, millions, tens of millions, many hundreds of millions of heroic men have come together at Kurujangala. I want to hear in accurate detail about the locations and sizes of their countries and cities. Through the power of

Vyasa's boundless tejas, you are endowed with the light of divine vision and knowledge.'

Sanjaya says, 'Wise king, I will describe to you the merits of the earth according to my knowledge. You can see them with your eye of wisdom. I bow to you, O bull of Bharata's race.

Creatures in this world are of two kinds, mobile and immobile. By birth mobile creatures are oviparous, viviparous, and those engendered by heat and damp. Of these the foremost are the viviparous of which the leading ones are men and animals. There are fourteen species of animals, O king. Seven live in forests, and seven are domestic. Lions, tigers, boars, buffaloes, elephants, bears and monkeys are regarded as wild. Cows, goats, sheep, horses, mules, asses and men are the seven animals regarded as domestic by the learned.

These fourteen species of domestic and wild animals are mentioned in the Vedas, and sacrifices rest upon them. Of creatures that are domestic, men are foremost, while lions are the foremost of those that live in forests. All creatures support themselves by living upon one another.

Vegetables are said to be immobile; their five species include trees, shrubs, creepers, creeping plants living for only a year, and all stemless grasses. Thus there are a total of nineteen species of mobile and immobile creatures, and there are five of their universal constituents, the panchabhutas.

These twenty-four are described as Gayatri Brahman as everyone knows. He who truly knows these to be the sacred Gayatri, having every virtue, cannot be annihilated in this world. Everything comes from the Earth and everything, when destroyed, merges back into the Earth. Bhumi is the home and refuge of all creatures, and it is eternal. He who has the Earth, controls the entire universe with its mobile and immobile creatures. It is for this desire to possess the Earth, that kings kill one another.'"

CANTO 5

JAMBU-KHANDA NIRMANA PARVA
CONTINUED

Dhritarashtra says, 'O Sanjaya, so knowing of all things on the earth, the names of rivers and mountains, and its forests, and their dimensions, give me a detailed description of them all.'

Sanjaya says, 'Great king, since everything in the universe possesses the five elements, the wise deem all of them equal. These panchabhutas are space, air, fire, water, and earth. Their respective attributes are sound, touch, sight, taste, and smell. In addition to what is notably its own quality, each of these elements has the attribute or attributes of that or those coming before it.

The earth, say the Rishis, is the first among them all, possessing as it does the qualities of the other four, besides what is specially its own. Water has four attributes but not scent. Fire has three, sound, touch, and sight. Sound and touch belong to air, while space, akasa, has sound alone.

The existence of all living things depends, O king, on these qualities of the panchabhutas.

When the universe is held in balance, they exist in their natural state, separate and independent. When, however, they exist in conjunction with one another, then creatures with bodies spring into life. This is the unchanging order of things.

The elements are destroyed and the one succeeding merges into the one that precedes; and so also do they spring into existence, one arising from the one before it. All these are immeasurable, their forms being Brahman itself. In the world creatures consisting of the five elements can be seen. Men strive to discover their forms by using reason. However, inconceivable matters should never be sought to be understood by reason. That which is beyond human nature is an indication of the inconceivable.

But, O Kurunandana, I will describe to you the island of Sudarsana. This dwipa, Rajan, is formed like a wheel. Rivers and lakes cover it and its mountains look like a blur of massed clouds; it has many cities and delightful regions. It is also full of blossoming trees, which bear sweet fruit, varied crops, and other kinds of wealth. The ocean of salt surrounds it on all sides.

As a man can see his own face in a mirror, even so is the island called Sudarsana seen in the lunar disc. Two of its parts seem to look like a pipal tree, while two others appear like a large hare. It is surrounded on all sides with an assortment of deciduous plants. Besides these, the rest is covered by water. I will describe more to you in brief, and the rest later. Now listen to what I describe in brief.'

CANTO 6

JAMBU-KHANDA NIRMANA PARVA
CONTINUED

Dhritarashtra says, 'You are intelligent, O Sanjaya, and know the truth about everything. You have described the dwipa in brief. Now tell us about the island in detail. Tell me about the size of the expanse of land that looks like a hare. Then speak of the part resembling the pipal tree.'"

Vaisampayana said, "Sanjaya says, 'Stretching from east to west, between the two oceans, are six mountains of equal majesty. These are Himavat, Hemakuta, that most excellent mountain named Nishadha, Nila abundant with lapis lazuli, Sweta as white as the moon, and the mountain Sringavat made of many metals.

These six mountains are always the abodes of Siddhas and Charanas. A thousand yojanas lie between each of them, and many delightful kingdoms are situated there.

These divisions are called Varshas, O Bhaarata. Creatures of diverse species live in those kingdoms. The land where we are is in the Varsha named after Bharata. Moving northwards, the next is the Himavatvarsha. The land beyond Hemakuta is called Harivarsha. South of the Nila range and north of the Nishadha is a mountain called Malyavat that extends from east to west. Beyond Malyavat to the north is the mountain Gandhamadana.

Between these two lies the greatest mountain, called Meru, made of gold. Effulgent as the morning sun, it is like fire without smoke. Both its height and its depth measure eighty-four thousand yojanas. It stands bearing the worlds above, below and across.

Four islands are located near Meru: Bhadraswa, Ketumala, Jambudwipa otherwise called Bharatavarsha, and Uttara-Kuru which is the abode of men of dharma. The bird Sumukha, the son of Suparna, seeing that all the birds on Meru had golden plumage, thought that he should leave that mountain since no distinction could be made between the good, average and lowly birds. The luminous Sun, the Moon with its attendant nakshatras and Vayu the Wind-god all circle Meru.

The mountain, O king, is abundant in celestial fruits and flowers, and it is dotted with sparkling golden mansions. There, on that mountain, the heavenly beings, the Gandharvas, the Asuras, and the Rakshasas, accompanied by the Apsaras, frolic and play.

There Brahma, and Rudra, and also Sakra the king of the Devas, assemble to perform many kinds of sacrifices with bountiful gifts. Tumburu, and Narada and Viswavasu, and the Hahas and the Huhus, go there to praise them with sublime hymns.

The great-souled Saptarishis and Kasyapa, the lord of creatures, go there on every parva day. Upon its peak, Usanas, Sukra otherwise called the Kavi, sports with his disciples, the Daityas.

All the jewels and gemstones that we see and all the mountains abounding in precious stones are of Meru. A fourth part of this is enjoyed by the holy Kubera. Only a sixteenth part of that wealth is given to men. On the northern side of Meru is the lovely forest of karnikaras, extending over a range of hills and covered with the flowers of every season.

There the illustrious Pasupati himself, the creator of all things, resplendent with his three sun-like eyes, surrounded by his celestial ganas and accompanied by Uma, wears a chain of karnikara flowers on his neck, which reach down to his feet. Only the ascetic Siddhas can gaze upon him for they are truthful, steadfast and practise austere tapasya. Indeed, Maheswara cannot even be seen by evil men.

From the summit of that mountain, like a stream of milk, O ruler of men, the sacred and auspicious Ganga, Bhagirathi adored by the most righteous, gushes like a cataract, with a tremendous sound, falling headlong into the delightful lake Chandramas.

Indeed that sea-like sacred lake was formed by Ganga herself. While leaping from the mountains, Ganga, too turbulent to be supported by even the mountains, was held for a hundred thousand years by Siva, the bearer of the Pinaka, on his head.

On the western side of Meru, lie Ketumala and Jambukhanda, both great seats of humanity. There, O Bhaarata, the span of human life is ten thousand years. The men all have golden complexions, and the women are like Apsaras. They dwell in happiness without sickness or sorrow. The men born there are of the radiance of liquid gold.

On the summits of Gandhamadana, Kubera, the lord of the Guhyakas, with many Rakshasas and Apsaras, passes his time in joy. Besides Gandhamadana there are many smaller mountains and hills. The measure of human life there is eleven thousand years. There, O king, the men are most energetic, strong and full of good cheer; the women are all very beautiful, with the complexion of lotus flowers.

Beyond Nila is the Varsha called Sweta, beyond Sweta is Hiranyakavarsha, and beyond that lies Airavatavarsha, the vast. The last Varsha in the extreme north and Bharata's Varsha in the extreme south are both shaped in the form of a bow.

The five Varshas of Sweta, Hiranyaka, Elavrita, Harivarsha, and Himavatvarsha lie in the middle, and Elavrita is at the very heart of them all. Amongst these seven Varshas, the five already mentioned and Airavata and Bharata that which is further north surpasses the one to its immediate south in respect of the lifespan, stature, health, dharma, kama and artha of its inhabitants.

In these Varshas, O Bhaarata, creatures of diverse species co-exist.

Thus, is Earth covered with mountains. The majestic mountains of Hemakuta are otherwise called Kailasa where Vaisravana passes his time joyfully with his Guhyakas. Immediately to the north of Kailasa and near the mountains of Mainaka there is a large and beautiful mountain called Manimaya with golden peaks. Beside this mountain is a great, splendid lake with crystal-clear waters called Bindusaras with a beach of golden sand on its shores. There seeing Ganga, since called Bhagirathi after his own name, the Rajarishi Bhagiratha lived for many years in an awesome tapasya.

Numberless sacrificial stakes made of gems and the Chaitya tree made of gold can be seen there. It was there that Indra of a thousand eyes and great fame gained won spiritual triumph by performing a thousand sacrifices.

There the Lord of all creatures, the eternal Creator of all the worlds, Siva of supreme tejas, surrounded by his ghostly attendants, the ganas, is adored. There Nara and Narayana, Brahma and Manu, and Sthanu are ever present.

And there the celestial Ganga of three streams, issues out of Brahmaloka, and first shows herself; she then divides herself into seven streams, and becomes Vaswokasara, Nalini, the sin-cleansing Saraswati, Jambunadi, Sita, Ganga and Sindhu. The Supreme Lord himself arranged for the divine river, beyond human understanding, to flow from that place down into this world. It is there that since the beginning of creation, on thousands of occasions, the Devas and Rishis have performed sacrifices, after every pralaya, when creation begins afresh.

As for the Saraswati, in some parts of her course she becomes visible and in some parts remains hidden. This celestial sevenfold Ganga is renowned across the three worlds.

Rakshasas live on Himavat, Guhyakas on Hemakuta, and serpents and Nagas on Nishadha, while Rishis dwell on Gokarna. The Sweta mountains are said to be the abode of the Devas and the Asuras. The

Gandharvas always stay on Nishadha, and the regenerate Rishis on Nila. The mountains of Sringavat also are regarded as the resort of the gods.

Thus, O great king, is the world divided into the seven Varshas. Diverse creatures, moving and unmoving, are found in all of them. Both providential and human prosperity are seen in these realms. They cannot be counted. Those who want their wellbeing believe what I have now told you about this delightful land in the form of a hare about which you asked.

At the edges of that region are the northernmost and southernmost Varshas. I have described these as well. The two islands Naga-dwipa and Kasyapa-dwipa are the two ears of this great land shaped like a hare.

The beautiful mountains of Malaya, whose rocks look like plates of copper, are another prominent part of Jambudwipa whose shape resembles a hare.'

CANTO 7

JAMBU-KHANDA NIRMANA PARVA
CONTINUED

Dhritarashtra says, 'Tell me in detail, O wise Sanjaya, about the regions to the north and the east of Meru, as also of the mountains of Malyavat.'

Sanjaya continues, 'To the south of the Nila mountain and the northern side of Meru are the sacred Northern Kurus, O king, which are the home of the Siddhas. The trees there are always covered with sweet fruits and flowers. All the flowers are fragrant, and the fruits delicious. Indeed, some of the trees bear fruits according to the desire of the plucker.

Some other trees are described as milk-yielding. These produce milk and the six different kinds of food that taste of Amrita. They also provide cloth and in their fruits lie ornaments to be used by men.

The entire land is covered in fine golden sand. A part of the region has the radiance of gemstones like rubies or diamonds, or of the lapis lazuli. All the seasons there are pleasant and the land has no swamps.

The tanks are charming and full of delicious pellucid water. The men born there have descended from the Devas. All are of pure birth and extremely handsome. Of the fraternal twins the women resemble Apsaras in beauty. They drink the milk, sweet as Amrita, from those milk-yielding trees Of the twins born there, both men and women possess equal beauty, both are endowed with similar virtues, and both equally resplendent, grow up in love, like a couple of chakravakas.

The people of that province are always happy and free from illness. They live for tens of thousands of years and never abandon one another. A species of birds called bharunda, who have sharp beaks and great strength, lift them up when they die and throw them into mountain caves. I have just described to you, O king, the Northern Kurus briefly.

I will now describe to you the eastern side of Meru. Of all the regions there, the best is called Bhadraswa, where there is a large forest of Bhadra-salas, and a huge tree called Kalamra which always bears flowers and fruit. That tree is a yojana in height and is adored by Siddhas and the Charanas.

The men there are fair in complexion, and possess great energy and strength. The women have the colour of lilies, and are very beautiful to behold. White and radiant, their faces resemble the full moon; their bodies are as cool as its rays. All of them are skilled in singing and dancing. The life span of humans there, O Bharatarishabha, is ten thousand years. They remain young by drinking the juice of the Kalamra.

To the south of Nila and the north of Nishadha, stands a gigantic Jambu tree that is eternal. Adored by the Siddhas and Charanas, that sacred tree grants every wish. This realm has been named Jambudwipa after this tree. That prince among trees, a thousand and a hundred yojanas tall, touches the very heavens. The circumference of its fruit measures two thousand five hundred cubits, and it bursts open when ripe.

These fruit fall on the earth with a loud sound, and then pour out a silvery juice. That juice of the Jambu becomes a river, and encircling Meru, reaches the land of the Northern Kurus. If the juice of that fruit is drunk, it produces peace of mind. After drinking it, no thirst is ever felt again, nor the weakening effect of ageing.

A type of dazzling gold of the colour of Indragopaka insects called Jambunada, used for celestial ornaments, is found there. The men born there look like the morning sun.

On the summit of Malyavat, the fire called Samvartaka can always be seen, which blazes forth to destroy the universe at the end of the yuga. There are many small mountains towards the east on its peak, and Malyavat, itself, measures eleven thousand yojanas. The men born there have golden-coloured skins and these Brahmavadis are descended from the world of Brahma.

They perform the severest tapasya, drawing their vital seed up into their bodies. For the protection of creatures they all enter the Sun. Numbering sixty-six thousand, they fly before Aruna, surrounding the Sun's chariot. Heated by the sun's rays for sixty-six thousand years, they then enter the Moon.'

CANTO 8

JAMBU-KHANDA NIRMANA PARVA

CONTINUED

Dhritarashtra says, 'Tell me, O Sanjaya, the names of all the Varshas, and of all the mountains, and also about all those that live on those mountains.'

Sanjaya says, 'To the south of Sweta and the north of Nishadha, is the Varsha called Romanaka. The men that are born there are fair in complexion, of good parentage, and handsome. These men also do not have any enemies. And they live joyfully for eleven thousand and five hundred years.

To the south of Nishadha lies the Hiranmayavarsha where the river Hiranvati flows. There, O king, lives that great bird named Garuda. And the people there are all followers of the Yakshas, wealthy, and attractive in appearance. These men are endowed with great strength and happy dispositions. And they live for twelve thousand and five hundred years.

The mountains of Sringavat, O ruler of men, have three beautiful summits. One of these is made of jewels and gemstones; another, also made of all kinds of gems, is adorned with palatial mansions. There lives the self-luminous lady named Sandili.

From the north of Sringavat upto the sea is the Airavatavarsha, the most excellent of them all because of the presence of this jewelled mountain. The Sun gives no heat to this land and men do not age or decay. The Moon and the stars in the sky are the only source of light.

The men born there have the radiance, complexion and fragrance of the lotus; even their eyes resemble lotus-petals. With unblinking eyes, and an agreeable scent, they live without food and have mastery over their senses. Descended from the heavens, they are all without any sin. They live for thirteen thousand years.

To the north of the milky ocean, the Lord Hari of unlimited strength lives in his golden chariot. That vimana, with the speed of the mind, has eight wheels, with many supernatural creatures in it. It is the colour of fire, covered with Jambunada gold, and has a powerful energy.

Lord Hari is the Lord of all creatures, and enjoys great wealth. The universe merges into him at the moment of Pralaya, and it again emanates from him when the desire to create takes him once more. He is the principal actor, and the One who directs the actions of others. He, O monarch, is earth, water, space, air, and fire. He is Yagna embodied for all creatures, and Agni is his mouth.'"

Vaisampayana continued, "When Sanjaya says this, the great Dhritarashtra becomes absorbed in thought about his sons. Having thought deeply, and filled with energy, he says, 'Without doubt, O Suta's son, it is Time that ends the universe. And it is Time that again creates everything. Nothing here is eternal. It is the all-knowing Nara and Narayana that destroy all creatures. The gods speak of him as Vaikuntha, of immeasurable might, while men call him Vishnu, one that pervades the Universe!'

CANTO 9

JAMBU-KHANDA NIRMANA PARVA

CONTINUED

Dhritarashtra says, 'Tell me Sanjaya about this Varsha that is named after Bharata, where this senseless force has been collected, a land which I know both my son Duryodhana and the sons of Pandu want to possess. Tell me about this place; you are all-knowing.'

Sanjaya says, 'Listen to me, O king. The sons of Pandu do not covet this earth. It is Duryodhana who is greedy, and Sakuni, the son of Subala, and many other Kshatriya rulers who are inimical towards one another.

I will now tell you about Bharatavarsha. This land is loved by Indra, and also by Manu, the son of Vivaswat. It is the beloved of Prithu, of Vainya, of the high-souled Ikshvaku, of Yayati, of Ambarisha, of Mandhatri, of Nahusha, of Muchukunda, of Sibi, the son of Usinara, of Rishava, of Ila, of King Nriga, of Kusika, of the great Gadhi, of Somaka, and of Dilipa, and also of many other mighty Kshatriyas.

Let me describe to you that land as I heard of it. Listen to me, Rajan, as I tell you about what you have asked me. Mahendra, Malaya, Sahya, Suktimat, Rakshavat, Vindhya, and Paripatra, these seven are the Kala-mountains of Bharatvarsha. Besides these there are thousands of unknown mountains that are tall and mighty cloven with wondrous valleys. There are also many other smaller mountains inhabited by barbarous tribes.

Aryans and Mlecchas, O Kauravya, and many other races drink the waters of these rivers: the magnificent Ganga, Sindhu, and Saraswati; the Godavari, and Narmada and the great Yamuna; the Drishadwati, Vipapa, Vipasa and Sthulavaluka; the river Vetravati, and the Krishna-vena; the Iravati, Vitasta, Payosyini and Devika; the Vedasmrita, Vedavati, Tridiva and Ikshumalavi.

They also drink from the Karishini, Chitravaha, and Chitrasena; of Gomati, and Dhutapada and the mighty Gandaki, of Kausiki, Nischitra, Kirtya, Nichita and Lohatarini; of Rashasi and Satakumbha, and also the Sarayu; of Charmanwati, and Vetravati, and Hastisoma, and Disa; of the river called Saravati, and Venna and Bhimarathi; of Kaveri, Chuluka, Vina, and Satabala; of Nivara, and Mahila, and Suprayoga; of Pavitra, and Kundala, and Rajani, and Puramalini; of Purvabhirama, and Vira, and Bhima, and Oghavati; of Palasini, and Papahara, and Mahendra, and Patalavati, of Karishini, and Asikni, and the wide Kusachira; of Makari, and Pravara, and Mena, and Hema, and Dhritavati; of Puravati, and Anushna, and Saivya, and Kapi, O Bhaarata; of Sadanira, and Adhrishya, and the great stream Kusadhara; of Sadakanta, and Siva, and Viravati; of Vatsu, and Suvastu, and Kampana with Hiranwati; of Vara, and the mighty river Panchami, of Rathachitra, and Jyotiratha, and Viswamitra, and Kapinjala; of Upendra, and Bahula, and Kuchira, and Madhuvahini: of Vinadi, and Pinjala, and Vena, and the mighty Pungavena; of Vidisa and Krishna-vena, and Tamra, and Kapila, of Salu, and Suvama, the Vedaswa, and the mighty river Harisrava; of Sighra, and Pischala, and the river Bharadwaji, of the river Kausiki, and Sona, and Chandrama; of Durgamantrasila, and Brahma-bodhya, and Brihadvati; of Yaksha, and Rohi, and Jambunadi; of Sunasa and Tamasa, and Dasi, and Vasa, and Varuna, and Asi; of Nila, and Dhrimati, and the Parnasa; of Pomasi, and Vrishabha, and Brahma-meddhya, and Brihaddhani.

These they drink from, and many other great rivers, like the Sadonirmaya and Krishna, and Mandaga, and Mandavahini; and Mahagouri, and Durga, O Bhaarata; and Chitropala. Chitraratha, and Manjula, and Vahini; and Mandakini, and Vaitarani, and Kosa, and Mahanadi; and Suktimati, and Ananga, and Pushpaveni, and Utpalavati; and Lohitya, Karatoya, and Vrishasabhya; and Kumari, and Rishikulya and Marisha, and Saraswati; and Mandakini, and Supunya, Sarvasanga.

These rivers, O Bhaarata, are all mothers of the universe and confer deep punya. Besides these, there are hundreds and thousands of rivers whose names are not known. I have now recounted to you all the rivers I remember.

Now listen to the names of the peoples of the various kingdoms. They are the Kuru-Panchalas, the Salwas, the Madreyas, the Jangalas, the Surasena, the Kalingas, the Bodhas, the Malas, the Matsyas, the Saubalyas, the Kuntalas, the Kasi-kosalas, the Chedis, the Karushas, the Bhojas, the Sindhus, the Pulindakas, the Uttamas, the Dasarnas, the Mekalas, the Utkalas; the Panchalas, the Kausijas, the Nikarprishthas, Dhurandharas; the Sodhas, the Madrabhujingas, the Kasis, and the Ati-Kasis; the Jatharas, the Kukuras, O Bhaarata.

There are the Kuntis, the Avantis, and the further-Kuntis; the Gomantas, the Mandakas, the Shandas, the Vidarbhas, the Rupavahikas; the Aswakas, the Pansurashtras, the Goparashtras, and the Karityas; the Adhirjayas, the Kuladyas, the Mallarashtras, the Keralas, the Varatrasyas, the Apavahas, the Chakras, the Vakratapas, the Sakas; the Videhas, the Magadhas, the Swakshas, the Malayas, the Vijayas, the Angas, the Vangas, the Kalingas, the Yakrillomans; the Mallas, the Suddellas, the Pranradas, the Mahikas, the Sasikas.

There are the Balhikas, the Vatadhanas, the Abhiras, the Kalajoshakas; the Aparantas, the Parantas, the Pahnabhas, the Charmamandalas; the Atavisikharas, the Mahabhutas; the Upavrittas, the Anupavrittas, the Surashatras, Kekayas; the Kutas, the Maheyas, the Kakshas, the Samudranishkutas; the Andhras, and many hilly tribes, and many tribes living on lands in the foothills, and the Angamalajas, and the Manavanjakas; the Pravisheyas, and the Bhargavas; the Pundras, the Bhargas, the Kiratas, the Sudeshnas, and the Yamunas, the Sakas, the Nishadhas, the Anartas, the Nairittas.

There are the Durgalas, the Pratimasyas, the Kuntalas, and the Kusalas; the Tiragrahas, the Ijakas, the Kanyakagunas, the Tilabharas, the Samiras, the Madhumattas, the Sukandakas; the Kasmiras, the Sindhusauviras, the Gandharvas, and the Darsakas; the Abhisaras, the Utulas, the Saibalas, and the Valhikas; the Darvis, the Vanavadarvas, the Vatagas, the Amarathas, and the Uragas; the Bahuvadhas, the Kauravyas, the Sudamanas, the Sumalikas; the Vadhras, the Karishakas, the Kalindas, and the Upatyakas; the Vatayanas, the Romanas, and the Kusavindas; the Kacchas, the Gopalkacchas, the Kuruvarnakas; the Kiratas, the Varvasas, the Siddhas, the Vaidehas, and the Tamraliptas; the Aundras, the Paundras, the Saisikatas, and the Parvatiyas.

There are other kingdoms, O bull of Bharata's vamsa, in the south. They are the Dravidas, the Keralas, the Prachyas, the Mushikas, and the Vanavashikas; the Karanatakas, the Mahishakas, the Vikalpas, and also the Mushakas; the Jhillikas, the Kuntalas, the Saunridas, and the Nalakananas; the Kankutakas, the Cholas, and the Malavayakas; the Samangas, the Kanakas, the Kukkuras, and the Angara-marishas; the Samangas, the Karakas, the Kukuras, the Angaras, and the Marishas.

There are also the Dhwajinis, the Utsavas, the Sanketas, the Trigartas, and the Salwasena; the Bakas, the Kokarakas, the Pashtris, and the Lamavegavasas; the Vindhyachulakas, the Pulindas, and the Valkalas; the Malavas, the Vallavas, the further-Ballavas, the Kulindas, the Kalavas, the Kuntaukas, and the Karatas; the Mrishakas, the Tanavalas, the Saniyas; the Alidas, the Pasivatas, the Tanayas, and the Sulanyas; the Rishikas, the Vidarbhas, the Kakas, the Tanganas, and the further-Tanganas.

Among the tribes of the north are the Mlecchas, and the Kruras, O best of the Bhaaratas; the Yavanas, the Chinas, the Kambojas, the Darunas, and many Mleccha tribes; the Sukritvahas, the Kulatthas, the Hunas, and the Parasikas; the Ramanas, and the Dasamalikas. These countries are, besides, the abodes of many Kshatriya, Vaisya, and Sudra tribes.

Then again there are the Sudra-abhiras, the Dardas, the Kasmiras, and the Pattis; the Khasiras; the Atreyas, the Bharadwajas, the Stanaposhikas, the Poshakas, the Kalingas, and diverse tribes of Kiratas; the Tomaras, the Hansamargas, and the Karamanjakas. These and other kingdoms are on the east and on the north. My Lord, alluding to them briefly, I have told you all.

If the Earth's resources are properly used according to their qualities and nature, Bhumi is like an ever-yielding cow, which may be milked for its fruits of dharma, artha and kama.

Powerful kings who know of dharma and artha have become greedy for the Earth. They are restless in their craving for this wealth, for which they are willing to sacrifice their very lives in battle.

Bhumi is the home of both creatures with heavenly bodies and those with human ones. Wanting to enjoy the pleasures of Earth, the kings have become like dogs that snatch meat from one another. Their unbounded ambition cannot be satisfied.

It is for this that the Kurus and the Pandavas are striving for possession of Earth, by negotiation, creation of discord, bribery, and battle. If Earth is well nurtured, it becomes the father, mother, children, sky and heaven of all creatures, O Purusharishabha.'

CANTO 10

JAMBU-KHANDA NIRMANA PARVA

CONTINUED

Dhritarashtra says, 'Tell me, Sanjaya, in detail, about the lifespan, the strength, the virtues and vices, the future, past and present, of the people of Bharatavarsha, of Himavatvarsha, and also of Harivarsha.'

Sanjaya says, 'Bharatarishabha, the four yugas set in Bharata's Varsha are Krita, Treta, Dwapara and Kali. The yuga that comes first is Krita; next comes Treta; after Treta comes Dwapara; and at the very end, the Kali.

In the Krita Yuga, men live for four thousand years, while in the age of Treta they live three thousand years. At present in Dwapara, men live on Earth for two thousand years. In the Kali, however, there is no fixed measure of life, so much so that men sometimes die while still in the womb, or soon after birth.

In the Krita Yuga, men are born and have children, in hundreds and thousands. They have great strength and power, and are endowed with great wisdom, wealth and beauty. In that age Munis are born with the knowledge of asceticism and are naturally capable of great tapasya. They have great souls, are virtuous and truthful in speech.

The Kshatriyas born in that age are agreeable in appearance and able-bodied. Having great tejas, they are accomplished in the use of the bow, highly skilled in battle and brave.

In the Treta Yuga, all the Kshatriya kings are emperors ruling vast lands, which extend from sea to sea. They give birth to invincible warriors, who enjoy long lives, are heroic, and wield the bow in battle with great skill.

When the Dwapara sets in, all the four varnas born are energetic and ambitious, wishing to conquer one another.

The men born in the Kali Yuga have little energy, and are given to anger, greed and dishonesty. Jealousy, pride, anger, deception, malice and covetousness, O Bhaarata, are the qualities of the creatures in this age. A small part of the Dwapara Yuga remains before the advent of Kali.

With respect to all qualities the Varsha known as Haimavat is superior to Bharatavarsha, while Harivarsha is more excellent than Himavatvarsha.'

CANTO 11

BHUMI PARVA

Dhritarashtra says, 'Sanjaya, you have described Jambukhanda to me. Now tell me of its size and expanse. Tell me also, in detail and without omission, about the extent of the ocean of Sakadwipa, and Kusadwipa, of Salmalidwipa and Kraunchadwipa. Tell me also of Rahu, Soma and Surya.'

Sanjaya says, 'There are many islands, over which the Earth extends. I will speak of only seven islands to you, and of the Moon, and the Sun, and the planet Rahu.

The Jambu mountain spreads across eighteen thousand six hundred yojanas. The extent of the ocean of salt is said to be twice this size. That ocean is dotted with many kingdoms, and is adorned with precious stones and corals. It is also covered with mountains made of many metals. Thickly peopled by Siddhas and Charanas, the ocean is circular in form.

I will now speak to you of Sakadwipa; listen to me, O Bhaarata, as I describe it. That island is twice the size of Jambudwipa and the ocean is twice the extent of that island. Indeed, Sakadwipa is surrounded by the ocean on all sides. The kingdoms there are infused with dharma, and the men there live eternal lives. How can famine occur there? The people are all full of forgiveness and great tejas.

I have now briefly described Sakadwipa to you. What else, O king, do you wish to know?'

Dhritarashtra says, 'You have given me, wise Sanjaya, a brief description of

Sakadwipa; now tell me everything in detail.'

Sanjaya says, 'On that island, there are seven mountains strewn with jewels and have mines of gemstones. There are also many rivers whose names I will recount to you. Everything there is excellent and delightful.

The first mountain is named Meru. It is the home of the Devas, Rishis, and Gandharvas. The next mountain is called Malaya, stretching towards the east. It is there that clouds arise, and from there they scatter in all directions. The next one is Jaladhara from where Indra daily draws the finest water. It is from this water that we get seasonal rain.

Over the next high mountain called Raivataka, the constellation of Revati has been fixed in the sky. Brahma himself has done this.

To the north of this is the lofty mountain Syama. Its beautiful bright body is made brilliant by ascending clouds. And since those mountains are dark, the people living there are all dark in complexion.'

Dhritarashtra says, 'A great doubt arises in my mind because of what you say. Why do the people there have dark complexions?'

Sanjaya says, 'On all islands, there are fair and dark men, and those produced by a union of the fair and the dark races. But that mountain is called the Dark

Mountain because all its people are dark. Beyond this lies the great mountain called Durgasaila, and the next one is called Kesari. The breezes that blow from that mountain carry sweet fragrances. The height of each mountain is twice that of the one mentioned immediately before it.

O Kurunandana, the wise say that there are seven Varshas in that island. The Varsha of Meru is called Mahakasa; that of the water-giving Malaya is called Kumudottara. The Varsha of Jaladhara is called Sukumara: while that of Raivataka is called Kaumara; and of Syama,

Manikanchana. The Varsha of Kesara is called Mandaki, and that named after the next mountain is called Mahapuman.

At the heart of that Dwipa is a mighty tree called Saka equal in height and breadth to the Jambu tree in Jambudwipa and the people there always worship the Saka.

In the many delightful provinces of that island, Siva is worshipped, and it is there that the Siddhas, the Charanas, and the unearthly beings find rest and rejuvenation. The people are virtuous, and all the four varnas devote themselves to their svadharma. There is no theft. Freed from decay and death and gifted with long lives, the people grow as rivers during the monsoon rains.

The rivers there are full of holy water. Ganga herself, divided into many streams, is there, as are Sukumari, Kumari, Seta, Keveraka, and Mahanadi; so also are the rivers Manijala, Chakshus, and Vardhanika, O Bharatottama. There are other innumerable sacred rivers, from which Indra draws water for showering rain. It is impossible to recount the names and lengths of all these rivers. All of them are awesome and sin-cleansing.

There are four sacred provinces known to men on the island of Saka. They are the Mrigas, the Masakas, the Manasas, and the Mandagas. The Mrigas are largely inhabited by Brahmanas devoted to their svadharma. Amongst the Masakas are virtuous Kshatriyas who grant the Brahmanas their every wish.

The Manasas live by following the duties of the Vaisya order. They, too, have all their desires fulfilled; they are brave and steadfast in their devotion to dharma and artha. The Mandagas are all brave and upright Sudras.

In these lands there is no king, no punishment, indeed no person that deserves to be punished. They are all conversant with and diligently engaged in the practice of their respective duties and protect one another. This is what can be said about Sakadwipa.

To listen to the description of this great island also confers merit on the listener.'

CANTO 12

BHUMI PARVA CONTINUED

Sanjaya says, 'O Bhaarata, I will tell you about what is known of
the islands in the north. Listen to me. In the north, the first ocean
has waters of ghee. Then is the ocean whose waters are curds. Next
comes the ocean whose waters are wine, and then is another ocean of
water. The islands double in area as we proceed further north and these
oceans surround them.

In the centremost island is a lofty mountain called Goura made of
red arsenic; on the western island is the mountain Krishna, the favourite
abode of Vishnu. There celestial gemstones are found in abundance,
guarded by Kesava who, inclined to grace, bestows happiness on all
creatures.

Along with the kingdoms there, a field of divine Kusa grass in
Kusadwipa and the Salmali tree in Salmalika are adored.

In the Kraunchadwipa the mountain called Maha-krauncha is a mine
of precious stones and is worshipped by all the varnas. On the mighty
Gomanta, rich in all kinds of precious metals, lives the mighty Narayana,
endowed with wealth and eyes like lotus leaves, with those who have

attained moksha.

In Kusadwipa there is another mountain mottled with varicoloured corals and named after that island itself. This mountain is inaccessible and made of gold. O Kauravya, there is another splendid mountain there called Sumida. The sixth is called Harigiri.

These are the six principal mountains. The intervening space between these mountains doubles, moving further and further towards the north.

The first Varsha is called Audhido; the second is Venumandala; the third is called Suratha; the fourth is known by the name Kamvala; the fifth Varsha is called Dhritimat; and the sixth is Prabhakara; the seventh Varsha is called Kapila. These are the seven successive Varshas.

In these, Devas and Gandharvas, and other beings of the universe, sport and find their delight. The inhabitants of these Varshas are immortal. There are no robbers, nor any tribes of Mlecchas. All those who live there are almost white in complexion and very delicate.

As for the rest of the Dwipas, I will tell you all that I have heard. Listen with an attentive mind. In the Kraunchadwipa there is a towering mountain called

Krauncha. Next to Krauncha is Vamanaka; and next to Vamanaka stands

Andhakara. And next to Andhakara is that excellent massif Mainaka. After Mainaka lies the most wonderful of mountains called Govinda; and after Govinda is the mountain called Nivida.

Rajan, the spaces between these mountains increase twofold. I will now tell you about the lands that lie there. Listen to me.

The land near Krauncha is called Kusala; that near Vamanaka is Manonuga; that next to Manonuga is Ushna. After Ushna is Pravaraka; and after Pravaraka is Andhakaraka. The country after Andhakaraka is Munidesa. After Munidesa, in the land called Dundubhiswana live Siddhas and Charanas. The people there are almost white in complexion.

All these lands are inhabited by Devas and Gandharvas. In the island of Pushkara is a mountain by the same name, rich in jewels and gemstones. There dwells Prajapati himself praised and worshipped by all the Devas and Maharishis. A variety of precious stones from Jambudwipa is found there, and used for diverse purposes.

In all these islands the celibacy, honesty, discipline, health and lifespan of the inhabitants doubles as one moves northwards.

The land in those Dwipas, O Bhaarata, comprises but one country in which but one religion prevails. The Supreme Prajapati himself lives there; he holds the danda of chastisement and protects those islands. He is the king and the source of their bliss. He is the father, and the grandfather; he protects all creatures there, mobile or immobile.

Cooked food appears by itself and is enjoyed by the people.

Mahabaho, after these vast lands can be seen Sama, a starshaped land with four corners, and thirty-three mandalas. There, O Kauravya, live four grand elephants adored by all. They are Vamana, Airavata, Supratika and Sarvabhauma. All efforts to calculate the proportions of these four Diggajas are fruitless. Their length, breadth and width remain unknown.

In those regions winds blow irregularly from all directions and are caught by those elephants with the tips of their splendid trunks that have the colour of lotuses and can draw up everything in their path. They then exhale to release these winds which then arrive on Earth thus allowing all creatures to breathe and live.'

Dhritarashtra says, 'You have, Sanjaya, told me everything about the first subject in detail. You have also indicated the positions of the islands. Speak to me now about what remains.'

Sanjaya says, 'Indeed, O great king, the Dwipas have all been described to you. Listen now to what I tell you about the heavenly bodies and about the size of Swarbhanu. The planet Swarbhanu is large and round with a diameter of twelve thousand yojanas, and a circumference of forty-two thousand yojanas, according to the learned of ancient times.

The diameter of the moon is said to be eleven thousand yojanas while its circumference is declared to be thirty-eight thousand nine hundred yojanas of the illustrious planet of cool rays.

Anagha, sinless, it has been said that the great, swift, beneficent, and luminous Sun, is ten thousand yojanas across, and thirty-five thousand eight hundred around. These are the dimensions estimated here, O Rajan, of Arka.

The planet Rahu, on account of his great size, eclipses both the Sun and the Moon at regular intervals. I recount this to you briefly. I have now given you answers to all your questions. Let peace be yours. I have told you about the construction of the universe as indicated in the Shastras. Therefore, O Kauravya, pacify your son Duryodhana.

Having listened to this charming Bhumi Parva, a Kshatriya is endowed with prosperity, obtains the fruit of his desires, and wins the approval of the righteous. The king who listens to this on days of the full moon or the new moon, while carefully observing vows, finds enhancement in his lifespan, his fame and energy. The spirits of his ancestors are appeased. You have now heard of all the merits that flow from Bharatavarsha!'

CANTO 13

BHAGAVAT-GITA PARVA

Vaisampayana said, "Knowing the past, the present and the future, and seeing all things as if present before his eyes, Sanjaya rushes grief stricken into court from the battlefield. To Dhritarashtra, who sits lost in thought, he announces that Bhishma the grandfather of the Bhaaratas has been killed.

Sanjaya says, 'I am Sanjaya, O great king. I bow to you. Bhishma, the son of Shantanu and the grandsire of the Bhaaratas, has been cut down in battle. That foremost of all warriors, that Pitamaha of the Bhaaratas, is fallen. That greatest Kshatriya, who embodied the urjas of all archers, that grandfather of the Kurus, lies today on a bed of arrows.

That Bhishma, on whose strength your son relied as he played the game of dice, now lies on the battlefield felled by Sikhandin. That Maharathika who defeated all the kings of the Earth gathered together in a fierce contention at the city of Kasi, he who fearlessly fought Rama, the son of Jamadagni, oh, even he has today fallen to Sikhandin.

Resembling the great Indra himself in courage, and Himavat in firmness, like the ocean in gravity, and the Earth herself in patience, that invincible warrior with arrows for teeth, a bow for his mouth, and a sword for his tongue, that lion among men, has been brought to grief by the prince of Panchala.

That Parantapa, on seeing whom in battledress even the mighty army of the fearless Pandavas would tremble like a herd of cows facing a lion, having protected your army for ten nights and having accomplished mighty and well-nigh impossible feats, has set like the Sun.

He, who like Sakra himself, calmly shot arrows by the thousands, killed ten thousand soldiers every day for ten days, even he, slain by the enemy, lies, undeserving on the bare ground like a mighty tree felled by the wind, as a consequence, Rajan, of your evil counsels.'"

CANTO 14

BHAGAVAT-GITA PARVA CONTINUED

Dhritarashtra says, 'How has Bhishma been cut down by Sikhandin? How has my father, who resembled Vasava himself, fallen from his chariot? What has become of my sons, O Sanjaya, deprived of the support of mighty Bhishma, he who was like a divine being, and who led the life of Brahmacharya for the sake of his father? How do our warriors feel about the loss of that tiger among men who was filled with great wisdom, great power and great energy?

Hearing that that great leader of men, that unfaltering Kshatriya, is fallen, a terrible sadness pierces my heart. While advancing against the enemy, who followed him and who marched ahead? Who stayed by his side? Who moved alongside? What brave fighters followed protecting the rear of that Maharathika, that wonderful archer, that bull among Kshatriyas, while he penetrated into the ranks of the foe?

While attacking the enemy's divisions, which warriors opposed that great luminary of a thousand rays, who spread fear and destruction among their ranks like the Sun destroying darkness, and who accomplished near impossible feats in battle among the ranks of Pandu's sons?

How, indeed, Sanjaya, did the Pandavas stand up to the son of Shantanu, that invincible Kshatriya, when he attacked them? How did Kunti's son conquer the unconquerable one, who, though modest, was a tiger among men slaughtering the enemy's ranks with great ferocity, having arrows for his teeth, a bow for his mouth, and a terrible sword for his tongue?

Oh, how undeserving is he of such a fate, that fierce archer shooting raging arrows, mounted on this chariot, beheading his foes, that irresistible hero, irresistible as the fires at the end of the yugas, seeing who in readiness for battle made the great army of the Pandavas falter in its advance.

Having achieved great feats on the battlefield, destroying the hostile armies for ten nights, alas, that greatest of Kshatriyas has set like the Sun. He who, like Sakra himself, loosed an unending stream of arrows, and killed millions of soldiers in ten days, that descendant of Bharata's race, now lies on the bare ground, on the field of battle, a mighty tree uprooted by the winds, as a result of my evil counsels!

Seeing Shantanu's son, how could the army of the Pandavas succeed in striking him down? How did the sons of Pandu fight Bhishma? How is it that Bhishma fell when Drona lives? When Kripa was near him, and Drona's son Aswatthaman also, how could Bhishma, that foremost of destroyers be himself destroyed?

How could Bhishma who was an Atiratha and who could not be vanquished by the very gods, be defeated by Sikhandin, the prince of Panchala? He, who always regarded himself equal to the mighty son of Jamadagni in battle, he whom Jamadagni's son himself could not quell, he who resembled Indra in

valour, alas, O Sanjaya, tell me how that hero, Bhishma, born in the race of Maharathas, was brought down, for without knowing all the details I cannot regain my composure.

Which great archers of my army did not desert that glorious hero? What heroic warriors, at Duryodhana's command, stood protecting him? When all the Pandavas with Sikhandin in the vanguard moved against

Bhishma, did not all the Kurus stay by his side?

Hard as my heart is, surely it is not unbreakable, for why does it not break on hearing the news of the fall of Bhishma! In him lay boundless truth, intelligence, and political acumen. Alas, how was he slain in battle?

Like an imposing cloud, the twang of his bowstring its roar, his arrows its raindrops, and the sound of his bow for thunder, that Kshatriya shot his arrows at the Pandavas and the Panchalas and the Srinjayas who stood at their side; he struck hostile charioteers like the slayer of Bala smiting the Danavas.

Who were the heroes that resisted, like the shores of the surging sea, him that punished enemies, who was a terrible ocean of weapons, an ocean in which arrows were inexorable crocodiles and bows were the waves? Who resisted this limitless ocean, without an island, agitated and with no raft to cross it, in which maces and swords were like sharks, and horses and elephants like eddies, foot soldiers like fishes in abundance, and the sound of conches and drums like its roar?

Who resisted this Kshatriya, this ocean that swallowed horses and elephants and foot soldiers, an ocean that devoured enemy heroes and that seethed with wrath that constituted its Yadava-fire?

When, in Duryodhana's interests, Bhishma achieved great feats in battle, who were in his vanguard? Who were they that protected the right wheel of that tremendous warrior? Who were they that resisted hostile heroes who came from behind him with patience and vigour?

Who positioned themselves to guard him from the front? Who protected the fore-wheel as he battled the adversary? Who struck at the Srinjayas from beside his left wheel? Who were they that defended the irresistible advance troops? Who protected the flanks of that warrior who has made his last painful journey? And who, O Sanjaya, fought the enemy heroes in the general conflict?

If he was protected by our heroes, and if they were protected by him, why could he not then swiftly humble the army of the Pandavas, invincible though it may be? Indeed, how could the Pandavas succeed even in striking Bhishma who was like Siva Parameshti himself, that

Lord and creator of all creatures?

Sanjaya, you speak of the fall of Bhishma; that tiger among men, that mighty warrior, our refuge upon whom the Kurus were relying to fight the Pandavas, how was he slain by the enemy? In ancient times, all the Devas sought that Kshatriya's assistance to annihilate the Danavas. That foremost of sons filled with great tejas, on whose birth the famous Shantanu cast aside all grief, despair, and sorrows, how can you tell me that that celebrated hero, that great refuge of all, that wise and holy man who was devoted to his dharma and conversant with the truths of Vedic knowledge, has been slain?

Accomplished in the use of every weapon and imbued with humility, if the son of Shantanu, gentle, restrained, yet so intrepid, has been felled, then I regard the rest of my army as already destroyed. In my judgment, immorality has now become stronger than righteousness, for the sons of Pandu desire sovereignty even by killing their venerable elder! In olden days, Jamadagni's son Rama, who was acquainted with every weapon and who was superior to all, when fighting on behalf of Amvya, was defeated by Bhishma in combat.

You tell me that Bhishma, that greatest of warriors who resembled Indra himself in his feats, has been vanquished. What can bring greater despair to me than this? Suffused with great intelligence, he who was not slain even by that destroyer of hostile heroes, that Rama, the son of Jamadagni, who repeatedly defeated hordes of Kshatriyas in battle, he has now been laid low by Sikhandin. Surely then, Drupada's son Sikhandin, who has quelled that bravest and most skilful Kshatriya, who commanded the most powerful weapons, must be superior in energy and strength to the mighty Bhishma!

In that encounter, who were the heroes that accompanied that destroyer of enemies? Tell me how the battle was fought between Bhishma and the Pandavas. The army of my son, O Sanjaya, bereft of its hero, is like an unprotected woman. Indeed, that army of mine is like a panic stricken herd of cows lost without its herdsman. When he, who was braver than anyone else, was vanquished, what was the state of mind of my army? What power remains in our lives, when we have killed our all-powerful father, the most righteous of men in the world?

Like a man who wishes to cross the sea as he watches his boat sink in deep waters, my sons, I imagine, are weeping grievously on Bhishma's death. My heart must surely be hard that it does not tear apart even on hearing of Bhishma's fall. Endowed with vast weapons, intelligence, and insight, how could that invincible warrior have been quelled?

A man cannot free himself from death using weapons or courage, ascetic merit or intelligence, firmness or offerings. Indeed, time cannot be transgressed by anything in the world, when you tell me that Shantanu's son Bhishma is fallen. Consumed by grief because of my sons, indeed overwhelmed with great sorrow, I had hoped for relief from Bhishma. When he saw Shantanu's son lying on earth like the Sun fallen from the sky, what other refuge did Duryodhana seek?

Reflecting on this, I cannot foresee how this will all end, both for our allies and for our enemies as they range themselves in opposition to each other.

Sadly the duties of the Kshatriya varna as laid down by the Rishis are cruel; the Pandavas desire sovereignty even at the cost of the death of Shantanu's son, and we too crave it by offering up in sacrifice that great hero. The sons of Pritha and mine do all observe their Kshatriya dharma and, thus, incur no sin. This is the path of a righteous man in times of terrible calamity. The display of valour and great strength has been laid down among the duties of Kshatriyas.

How, indeed, did the sons of Pandu oppose my father Bhishma in battle? How were the troops arrayed, and how did he fight against those high-souled adversaries? How, O Sanjaya, was my father Bhishma cut down, and what did Duryodhana, Karna, the deceitful Sakuni, the son of Subala, and Dussasana say when Bhishma fell?

In the house of death that is war, where the chessboard is made up of the bodies of men, elephants, and horses, where arrows and javelins, mighty swords and darts kill and maim, who were those wretched gamblers, who staked their very lives? Who won in this game, who were defeated, who cast the dice successfully, and who have been killed, besides Bhishma, the son of Shantanu?

Tell me all, Sanjaya, for I am not at peace, hearing that Devavrata has been

slain, that father of mine, of great and terrible deeds, that jewel of battle, Bhishma! Anguish like a blade pierces my heart, born of the thought that all my children will die. As a fire blazes brighter when ghee is poured on it, you do deepen my sorrow.

My sons must even now be grieving, seeing Bhishma fallen, that great Bhishma celebrated in all worlds and who took upon himself a heavy burden. I will listen to all those sad outcomes of Duryodhana's terrible folly. Therefore, tell me everything that happened there, everything that happened in the battle, born of the folly of my wicked son. Confused or clear, tell me everything, Sanjaya.

Whatever was achieved in the war by the tejas of the great Bhishma who desired victory; tell me everything and in complete detail of how each battle between the armies of the Kurus took place.'

CANTO 15

BHAGAVAT-GITA PARVA CONTINUED

Sanjaya says, "You are deserving and this is a noble question. However, it does not befit you to blame Duryodhana. The man who incurs evil as the consequence of his own misdeeds, should not attribute the blame to others.

Great king, the man who injures others deserves to be killed for his sins. The upright and blameless Pandavas, along with their friends and counsellors, look up to you; they have endured their injuries, forgiven them, and lived peaceably in the forest.

Do not grieve as you listen to the grim stories of horses and elephants, and powerful kings I have seen by Yoga-shakti. For all this was predestined.

I have bowed before your wise and high-souled father, the Mahatman Vyasa, who has bestowed upon me the boon of divine understanding, a sight beyond the vision of the eyes, heightened hearing from a great distance, a knowledge of other people's thoughts and of the past and the future, a knowledge also of the origin of all those who transgress the sacred ordinances, the delightful power of coursing through the skies, and protection from all weapons in battle.

Now listen to me carefully as I narrate the romantic and awesome battle between the Bhaaratas, a battle that makes one's hair stand on end.

When the combatants were ready and arrayed by the rules of war, Duryodhana says to Dussasana, 'O Dussasana, let chariots be moved swiftly to protect Bhishma, and order our aksauhinis to advance.

I now recollect what I have been thinking for many years about the war between the forces of the Pandavas and the Kauravas. For us, nothing is more important than keeping Bhishma safe. If protected he will annihilate the Pandavas, the Somakas and the Srinjayas.

That pure-souled Kshatriya has said that he will not slay Sikhandin. Sikhandin was a woman in an earlier birth, and so Bhishma refuses to fight him. For this, Bhishma should be particularly well protected.

Let all my soldiers take up their positions, and be determined to kill Sikhandin. Also let the troops from all cardinal directions, skilled in the use of every kind of weapon, watch over the Pitamaha. Even the mighty lion, if left unprotected, may be slain by the wolf. We must not allow Bhishma to be slain by Sikhandin like the lion by the jackal.

Yudhamanyu guards the left wheel and Uttamauja the right wheel of Arjuna, and thus shielded, Phalguni himself safeguards Sikhandin. O Dussasana, ensure that Sikhandin, who is protected by Arjuna, and whom Bhishma will not attack, does not kill Ganga's son.'

CANTO 16

Bhagavat-Gita Parva continued

Vaisampayana said, "Sanjaya says, 'When the night passed, loud exclamations of the kings rend the air. The blast of conches and the sound of drums resembling the roars of lions, the neigh of horses and the clatter of chariot wheels, the noise of raucous elephants and the shouts, clapping of arm-pits, and cries of roaring combatants, all raise a thunderous noise.

The teeming armies of the Kauravas and the Pandavas, rising before dawn, complete all their deployments. When the Sun rises, the fierce weapons of attack and defence, the armour of your sons and the Pandavas, and the great splendid armies of both sides, are fully seen. Elephants and chariots, adorned with gold, look radiant like clouds streaked with lightning. The arrays of chariots look like cities.

Standing there, your father shines brilliantly like the full moon. And the warriors armed with bows and swords, scimitars and maces, javelins and spears, and other bright weapons of many kinds, take up their positions in the ranks. Resplendent standards, belonging to us and the enemy, are seen, hoisted by the thousands. Thousands of golden banners decorated with gemstones blaze like fire. They look beautiful even like the armoured heroes longing for battle.

Countless great Kshatriya commanders, wearing quivers, and with eyes big as those of bulls, and with hands cased in leather gloves, stand at the heads of their divisions, with shining weapons raised.

Subala's son Sakuni, and Salya, Jayadratha and the two princes of Avanti, Vinda and Anuvinda, the Kekaya brothers, Sudakshina the ruler of the Kambojas and Srutayudha the lord of the Kalingas, and king Jayatsena, Brihadbala, king of the Kosalas, and Kritavarman of the Satwata vamsa - these ten powerful tigers among men, whose arms resemble maces, these performers of sacrifices and givers of gifts to Brahmanas, stand each one at the head of an akshauhini of troops.

These and many other kings and princes, maharathikas all, knowers of statecraft, obedient to the commands of Duryodhana, all sheathed in mail, are seen at the head of their legions. All of them, wearing black deerskin, imbued with great strength, accomplished in battle, and cheerfully prepared, for Duryodhana's sake, to give up their lives and attain Brahmaloka, stand there commanding ten powerful akshauhinis.

The eleventh great division of the Kauravas, consisting of the Dhartarashtra troops, are positioned in front of the great army.

There in the vanguard of that division is Shantanu's son. With his helmet, royal parasol, and armour, all in white, we see the unfailingly mighty Bhishma looking like the risen moon. His standard bears the sign of a golden palmyra; he himself is mounted on a silver ratha. Both the Kauravas and the Pandavas gaze upon that hero, looking like the full moon encircled by white clouds.

On seeing Bhishma, the great archers amongst the Srinjayas, led by Dhrishtadyumna, look like little lesser animals looking at a mighty yawning lion. Indeed, all the warriors led by Dhrishtadyumna tremble in fear.

These, O Rajan, are the eleven splendid divisions of your army.

So also the seven akshauhinis belonging to the Pandavas are protected by the greatest Kshatriyas. Indeed, the two armies facing each other look like two oceans at the end of the Yuga agitated by fierce makaras, teeming with monstrous crocodiles. Never before did we see or hear of two such armies encountering each other like these of the Kurus.'"

CANTO 17

BHAGAVAT-GITA PARVA CONTINUED

Sanjaya says, 'Just as predicted by the holy Krishna-Dwaipayana Vyasa, the kings of the Earth gather in that manner for the great contention. On the day that the battle begins, Soma approaches the region of the Pitris. The seven great planets are ablaze as they appear in the sky.

The Sun, as he rises, seems to be split in two, and bursts into flames. Carnivorous jackals and crows, expecting to feed upon the dead, call out fiercely from all burning directions.

Every day the Pitamaha of the Kurus, and the son of Bharadwaja, rising from their beds in the morning, say with dhyana, "Victory to the sons of Pandu", while those mighty warriors are pledged yet to fight for your cause. Your father

Devavrata, aware of varna dharma, summons all the kings and speaks to them.

"Kshatriyas, the broad door into heaven is open to you. Pass through it to the region of Sakra and Brahma. The ancient Rishis have shown you this eternal path. Bring honour upon yourselves by fighting with alert minds. Nabhaga and Yayati, and Mandhatri, and Nahusa and Nriga, were triumphant in battle and attained bliss. It is a sin for a Kshatriya to die of sickness at home; to die in battle is his eternal duty."

Thus addressed by Bhishma, the magnificent kings, in their majestic chariots, move to the heads of their respective aksauhinins. Only Vikartana's son Karna, with his friends and relatives, puts aside his weapons for the sake of Bhishma. Without Karna then, your sons and their allies forge ahead, to the ten points of the horizon which reverberate with their leonine roars.

And their legions shine brightly with white sovereign parasols, banners, standards, elephants, horses, chariots, and foot soldiers. And the Earth fills with the sounds of drums and cymbals, and the clatter of chariot wheels. And the maharathas, bedecked with golden ornaments and with their bows streaked with gold, look as resplendent as hills of fire.

And with his large palmyra-standard, bearing five stars, Bhishma, the Senapati of the Kaurava army, looks like the radiant Sun himself. He orders your noble archers to take up their positions, which they do with alacrity.

King Saibya of the country of the Govasanas, accompanied by all the others, goes forth on a royal elephant graced with a banner on its back. And the lotus-complexioned Aswatthaman rides out prepared for every contingency, stationing himself at the very head of all the divisions, with his standard bearing the emblem of the lion's tail.

And Srutayudha and Chitrasena, and Purumitra and Vivimsati, and Salya and Bhurisravas, and that mighty maharathika Vikarna - these seven great archers mounted on their chariots and encased in excellent mail, follow Drona's son with Bhishma behind them. The lofty golden standards adorning their chariots shine brilliantly.

The standard of Drona, that most excellent of acharyas, bears the emblem of a golden shrine ornamented with a kalasha and a bow. That of Duryodhana, bearing a jewel-encrusted elephant, guides many hundreds and thousands of divisions. The rathas of Paurava, the king of the Kalingas, and Salya, are positioned in Duryodhana's vanguard.

The king of the Magadhas guides his aksauhini against the enemy on a bejewelled chariot with his standard bearing the image of a bull. The great force of the Eastern Kingdoms, protected by the chief of the Angas, Karna's son Vrishaketu, and the powerful Kripa, appears like the soft white clouds of approaching winter.

Stationed in front of his troops, with his silver standard bearing the emblem of the boar, is the splendid Jayadratha. A hundred thousand rathas, eight thousand elephants, and sixty thousand cavalry are under his command.

Commanded by the king of the Sindhus, that vast aksauhini in the forefront of the army with countless chariots, elephants and horses, is truly magnificent. With sixty thousand chariots and ten thousand elephants, the ruler of the Kalingas, accompanied by Ketumat, advances. His majestic elephants, looking like hills, and adorned with yantras, lances, quivers and standards, are strikingly beautiful.

The ruler of the Kalingas blazes forth with his lofty standard effulgent as fire, his royal parasol, golden cuirass, and the chamaras which fan him, all shining. Ketumat, riding on an elephant and holding a wonderful and beautiful goad, is also stationed in battle, O king, like the Sun in the midst of dark clouds.

And king Bhagadatta, fiery with energy and riding on his legendary elephant, goes out like the wielder of the thunder. And the two princes of Avanti, Vinda and Anuvinda, regarded as equal to Bhagadatta, follow Ketumat, riding on the necks of their elephants.

Thus arrayed by Drona and Bhishma, and by Drona's son, and by Bahlika and Kripa, the Kaurava vyuha, of numberless divisions of chariots, appears as if elephants form its body, the kings, its head; and the horses, its wings. Facing all sides, that fearsome vyuha seems to smile in readiness to spring upon the enemy.'

CANTO 18

BHAGAVAT-GITA PARVA CONTINUED

Sanjaya says, 'A loud uproar made by the fighting men in readiness for battle causes the heart to tremble. Indeed, the Earth seems to split in two with the sounds of conches and drums, the bellows of elephants and the clatter of chariot wheels. Soon the Sky and the Earth are filled with the neighing of chargers and the shouts of warriors.

O great Rajan, the troops of your sons and of the Pandavas both tremble when they face each other. There on that battlefield, elephants and chariots, decked in gold, are as beautiful as clouds flecked with lightning. And the standards of your allies, adorned with golden rings, glow like fire. And those standards of your side and theirs resemble the banners of Indra in his celestial mansions.

And the heroic warriors, all fitted out in golden coats of mail with the brilliance of the blazing Sun, themselves look like Agni or Surya. All the leading Kshatriyas amongst the Kurus, with magnificent bows, and other weapons ready, with leather gloves on their hands, and with standards, those mighty bull-eyed archers, stand lordly at the heads of their aksauhinis.

Protecting Bhishma from behind, among your sons are Dussasana, and Durvishaha, Durmukha and Dussaha and Vivimsati, and Chitrasena, and that maharatha Vikarna; also amongst them are Satyavrata and Purumitra, Jaya, Bhurisravas and Sala.

And twenty thousand maharathas follow them. The Abhishahas, the Surasenas, the Sibis, and the Vasatis, the Swalyas, the Matsyas, the Ambashtas, the Trigartas, and the Kekayas, the Sauviras, the Kitavas, and the dwellers of the Eastern, Western, and the Northern kingdoms, these twelve brave races are resolute in their determination to fight, heedless of their lives.

These protect the Pitamaha with an awesome array of chariots. And with a division of ten thousand war elephants, the king of Magadha follows that aksauhini. They who guard the wheels of the chariots, and they who protect the elephants, number a stupendous six million.

And the footsoldiers that march ahead, armed with bows, swords, and shields, number many hundreds of thousands. And they fight using also their nails and bearded barbs. And the eleven aksauhinis of your son, O Bhaarata, look like Ganga separated from Yamuna.'

CANTO 19

Bhagavat-Gita Parva continued

Dhritarashtra says, 'Seeing our eleven aksauhinis laid out in battle formation, how does Yudhishtira, the son of Pandu, with his smaller number of legions, make his counter-array? How does Kunti's son, Sanjaya, create his battle formation against that Bhishma who was a master of all kinds of vyuhas, Manushya, Deva, Gandharva, and Asura?'

Sanjaya says, 'Seeing Dhritarashtra's legions arrayed, Pandu's son of virtuous soul, Yudhishtira Dharmatma, says to Arjuna, "We have long known the wise words of Maharishi Brihaspati, that a small army must be made to fight by compressing its troops, while the large army may be stretched out at will. In encounters of the few with the many, the vyuha to be formed is the suchimukha, the needle-mouthed one. Our troops compared with the enemy's are few. Deploy our troops, Arjuna, in accordance with the precept of the great Rishi."

Arjuna answers Yudhishtira, "I will create for you an unshakeable and invincible vyuha known as the Vajra, designed by the very wielder of the thunder-bolt himself. He who is like the bursting tempest, he who cannot be defeated by the enemy in battle, Bhima that greatest of smiters, will fight at our head. That foremost of men, knower of all ayudhas, will be our leader at the front destroying our adversaries, shattering their very confidence.

Seeing Bhima, awesome in battle, all the enemy soldiers led by Duryodhana will retreat in panic like smaller animals upon seeing the lion; Bhima will protect us like a wall and dispel our fears like Indra who gives refuge to all heavenly beings. There is no living man who can even look upon Vrikodara of fierce deeds when he is angry."

Having said this, Dhananjaya moves to form his vyuha. He swiftly orders his troops into battle-array and advances against the enemy. And the mighty army of the Pandavas, seeing the Kuru army move, appears itself to look like the swelling, rushing and powerful current of Ganga. And Bhima, and Dhrishtadyumna blessed with great tejas, and Nakula, and Sahadeva, and king Dhrishtaketu, become the leaders of that force.

And king Virata, surrounded by this aksauhini, along with his brothers and sons, marches in the rear, protecting them from behind. The two radiant sons of Madri become the guardians of Bhima's wheels, while the five sons of Draupadi and the son of Subhadra, all blessed with tejas, protect Bhima from behind. And that maharathika, Dhrishtadyumna the prince of Panchala, with the valiant Prabhadrakas, protects those princes from the rear.

And behind him is Sikhandin, who in turn is guarded by Arjuna, and who advances with dhyana for the destruction of Bhishma. Behind Arjuna, to guard his wheels, rides the powerful Yuyudhana and the two princes of Panchala, Yudhamanyu and Uttamaujas, along with the intrepid Kekaya brothers, and Dhrishtaketu, and Chekitana.

Bhima, wielding his mace made of the sternest metal, moving with fierce speed on the battlefield, can dry up the very ocean. And there the sons of Dhritarashtra with their counsellors, stand looking at him. This, O Rajan, is what Bibhatsu says pointing out the mighty Bhima to Yudhishtira; while Arjuna speaks, all the gathered troops bow to praise and worship him.

King Yudhishtira, the son of Kunti, takes up his position at the heart of his army, surrounded by vigorous overpowering elephants which resemble moving hills. The high-souled and valorous Drupada, lord of the Panchalas, stations himself behind Virata with an aksauhini to fight for the Pandavas. And on the chariots of those kings are high standards bearing diverse emblems, decorated with beautiful ornaments of gold, and with the radiance of the Sun and the Moon.

Moving those kings to make space for himself, Maharatha Dhrishtadyumna, his brothers and sons around him, watches over Yudhishtira from behind. Transcending the lofty standards on all the chariots, yours and those of your opponents, is the gigantic Vanara on Arjuna's chariot.

Hundreds and thousands of foot soldiers, armed with swords, spears and scimitars, advance in front to safeguard Bhimasena. And ten thousand dauntless elephants, big as hills, emblazoned with golden armour follow the king like moving mountains. With temporal juice trickling down their faces, they resemble great rain clouds, and emit the fragrance of lotus flowers.

And the unconquerable Bhimasena, Mahatman, swinging his fierce mace that resembles a parigha surely looks as if he can easily crush the sprawling army of your son. Appearing like the Sun himself, and scorching the hostile army like fire, it is impossible for the warriors to even look at him.

This fierce and fearless Vajravyuha, facing all sides, and having bows for its lightning sign, is protected by the wielder of the Gandiva himself. Deploying their legions in this manner against your army, the Pandavas await battle. And protected by the Pandavas, that vyuha is veritably invincible in the world of men.

And as both armies stand waiting for sunrise, a wind begins to blow, gentle rain falls with no clouds in sight, and the roll of thunder is heard. Other dry winds blow showering the ground with sharp stones and a thick dust arises covering the world with darkness. Meteors begin to fall towards the east and, striking against the rising Sun, shatter loudly into fragments.

As the troops stand ready for battle the Sun rises without his customary splendour, and the Earth trembles and cracks open reverberantly in many places. The sound of thunder, O king, can be heard frequently on all sides and so thick is the billowing dust that nothing can be seen.

And the towering standards of the warriors, furnished with strings of bells, decked with golden ornaments, garlands of flowers, and rich cloths, graced with banners and like the Sun in splendour, are shaken by the wind, and jingle loudly like a forest of palmyra trees with a gale blowing lustily through.

Thus stand those tigers amongst men, the sons of Pandu, joyful in battle, having arrayed their legions against the army of your son, sucking as it were, the marrow of our warriors, with Bhima, mace in hand, stationed at their head.'

CANTO 20 .

BHAGAVAT-GITA PARVA CONTINUED

Dhritarashtra says, 'When the Sun rises, O Sanjaya, of my army led by Bhishma and the Pandava army led by Bhima, which, in joyful readiness for battle, approaches the other first? To which side are the Sun, the Moon and the Wind hostile, and against whom do the beasts of prey utter inauspicious cries? Who are those beautiful and daring young men? Tell me everything and in detail.'

Sanjaya says, 'Both armies look equally joyful and equally beautiful like blooming forests. Both armies abound in elephants, chariots and horses. Both are vast and terrible to behold, and hostile to each other. Both of them teem with outstanding warriors organised to conquer the very heavens.

The Kauravas stand facing the west, while the Pandavas face the east, ready to fight. The troops of the Kauravas appear like the army of the Danavas, while those of the Pandavas look like the army of the Devas. The wind begins to blow from behind the Pandavas against the face of the Dhartarashtras, and the predators howl against your son's legions. The elephants of your sons cannot bear the strong odour of the temporal juice emitted by the majestic elephants of the Pandavas.

And Duryodhana rides on a lotus coloured elephant, with rent temples, graced with a golden kaksha on its back, and protected by netted steel armour. He is at the very heart of the Kurus and is extolled by bards and singers. And a white sovereign parasol with a golden chain and moon-like brilliance is held over his head.

Sakuni, the lord of the Gandharas, follows, surrounded by his mountain men. And the revered Bhishma is at the head of all the troops, with another royal white parasol over him, armed with bow and sword, with a white helmet, a white banner atop his chariot yoked to white horses, looking altogether like a white mountain.

In Bhishma's legion are all the sons of Dhritarashtra, and also Sala of the Bahlikas; there are also all those Kshatriyas called Amvastas and Sindhus, and also the Sauviras, and the heroic people of the land of the five rivers.

And on a golden chariot drawn by red horses stands the valiant Mahatman Drona, bow in hand, the Acharya of almost all the kings, who remains behind all the troops, protecting them like Indra. And Saradwat's son Gautama, that frontline fighter, that high-souled and mighty archer familiar with all manner of warfare, accompanied by the Sakas, the Kiratas, the Yavanas and the Pahlavas,

takes up his position at the northern point of the army.

That immense force which is well guarded by maharathas of the Vrishni and the Bhoja vamsas, as also by the fighting men of Surashtra, well-armed and masters of weapons, and which is led by Kritavarman, goes towards the south of the army. Ten thousand chariots of the Samsaptakas, masterful warriors all, who were created for either the death or the fame of Arjuna, and who intend to stay close to and hunt Arjuna, all advance along with the brave Trigartas.

In your army, O Bhaarata, are a thousand magnificent war elephants to each of which are assigned a hundred chariots. A hundred horsemen are given to each chariot; each horseman has ten archers, each of whom is accompanied by ten foot soldiers armed with sword and shield. Thus does Bhishma lay out your legions.

As each day dawns, your great Senapati, Bhishma the son of Shantanu, sometimes moves your troops in the Manava vyuha, sometimes in the Deva, sometimes in the Gandharva, and at others in the Asura. Thronged with a large number of maharathas, and roaring like the very ocean, the Dhartarashtra army, disposed by Bhishma, stands facing the west for battle. Unbounded and dreadful as your army is, the army of the Pandavas, though smaller, appears to me to be colossal and invincible since Krishna and Arjuna lead it.'

CANTO 21

BHAGAVAT-GITA PARVA CONTINUED

Sanjaya says, 'Seeing the vast Dhartarashtra army ready for battle, king Yudhishtira, the son of Kunti, gives way to grief. Seeing that formidable vyuha formed by Bhishma and knowing it to be impenetrable, the king grows pale and says to Arjuna, "Dhananjaya, how will we fight the Dhartarashtras who have the Pitamaha as their Senapati?

How will we withstand the unshakeable and invincible vyuha which has been designed by that destroyer of foes Bhishma of transcendent glory, by the directions laid down in the scriptures? Parantapa, given the numbers of our troops we are doubtful of success. How, indeed, will we obtain victory in the face of this mighty formation?"

Arjuna answers Yudhishtira who is troubled by grief at the sight of your army, "Listen, O king, to how a few soldiers may defeat a vast army having many strengths. Since you are without malice, I will tell you the means by which we can triumph.

The Rishi Narada knows it, as do both Bhishma and Drona. Brahma himself in olden days during the battle between the Devas and the Asuras said to Indra and the other celestials, 'They who desire victory do not conquer by might and force so much as by truth, compassion, righteousness and vitality.'

Discriminating then between dharma and adharma, and understanding what covetousness is and what it is to fight without arrogance, victory lies with righteousness. Know, O Rajan, that victory is already assured to us in this war.

Indeed, as Narada says, "Where Krishna is, there is victory. Victory is inherent to Krishna, indeed it follows him. And as victory is one of his attributes, so is humility. Govinda possesses infinite energy. Even in the midst of uncountable enemies, he is without pain. He is the most eternal of Purushas. And victory surely lies where Krishna is."

Even he, indestructible and impossible to conquer with weapons, appearing as Hari in olden days, said clearly to the Devas and the Asuras, "Who amongst you would be victorious?" Even the conquered Devas replied, "With Krishna to lead us we will prevail." And it was through Hari's grace that the three worlds were conquered by the gods led by Sakra.

I do not, therefore, see any reason for you to be dejected, you who have the Sovereign of the Universe and the Divine Lord of the gods himself wishing you triumph.""

CANTO 22

BHAGAVAT-GITA PARVA CONTINUED

Sanjaya says, 'Then king Yudhishtira, laying out his own troops against the legions of Bhishma, urges them on, saying, "The Pandavas have now deployed their forces in counter array in keeping with the scriptures. Fight fairly, you sinless ones, who wish to enter the highest heaven!"

In the midst of the Pandava army is Sikhandin, and his troops are protected by Arjuna. And Dhrishtadyumna advances in the vanguard, protected by Bhima. The southern aksauhinis are guarded by that mighty archer, the handsome Yuyudhana of the Satwatas, who resembles Indra himself.

Yudhishtira is stationed on a chariot that is worthy of bearing Mahendra himself, adorned with an excellent standard, mottled with gold and glittering gemstones, and furnished with golden reins for the horses, in the midst of his war elephants. His sovereign white parasol with an ivory handle, unfurled over his head, is resplendent; and many great Rishis walk around him singing his praises.

Many priests, and regenerate Rishis and Siddhas, chant laudatory hymns, praying for the destruction of his enemies, with the help of japas and mantras, potent drugs, and a variety of propitiatory ceremonies. That Mahatman king of the Kurus, showering the Brahmanas with gifts of cows and fruit, flowers and gold, along with rich cloths, advances like Sakra, king of the Devas.

The chariot of Arjuna, with a hundred bells, the best Jambunada gold, having excellent wheels, possessing the effulgence of fire, and pulled by white horses, shines brilliant as a thousand suns. And on that chariot whose banner bears the Vanara emblem, whose reins are held by Krishna, stands Arjuna with the Gandiva and arrows in hand, peerless archer whom none can ever equal.

For crushing your sons' troops, the mighty Bhimasena Vrikodara, who assumes the most terrifying aspect, who without weapons and with his mere bare hands pounds men, horses, and elephants into the dust, that Mahabaho accompanied by the twins, is the protector of the heroic maharathikas of the Pandava army.

Seeing indomitable Vrikodara, like the towering leader of a herd of elephants, an enraged prince of sprightly lions, or like great Indra himself in earthly form, at the forefront of the army, the strength of your fighting men turns weak with fear, and they begin to tremble like elephants in mire.

And Krishna says to the valiant Arjuna standing in the midst of his troops, "There is the banner of Kuru's race, Bhishma, who scorches us with his wrath and stands rocklike in the midst of his forces. He who will attack our men like a lion, he who has performed three hundred Aswamedha yagnas, stands surrounded by great Kshatriyas who envelop his brilliance like clouds. Great Kshatriya, Purushottama, kill those troops and seek out that greatest of warriors, Bhishma Bharatarishabha!"'

CANTO 23

BHAGAVAT-GITA PARVA CONTINUED

Sanjaya says, 'Seeing the Dhartarashtra army approach ready for battle, Krishna says these words to Arjuna.

The Holy One says, "Purifying yourself, O Arjuna, on the eve of the battle, recite the hymn to Durga to achieve the enemy's defeat."

Thus addressed on the eve of battle by Krishna of fathomless intellect, Pritha's son Arjuna, alighting from his chariot, recites this hymn with folded hands.

Arjuna says, "I bow to you, O Mahayoginis, you who are Brahman, you who dwell in the forest of Mandara, free from decay and dissolution, O Kali, wife of Kapala, of a black and dusky hue, I bow to you! I submit to you, Mahakali, wife of Siva, the destroyer of the universe, you who bestow blessings on your devotees.

O exalted Durga, you who rescue us from danger, you who are blessed with every auspicious attribute, which has sprung from the Katas, you who deserve the most devoted worship, fierce one, giver of victory, victory's own self, you who bear a banner of peacock plumes, decked with every ornament, bear a terrible spear, hold a sword and shield, you who are the younger sister of the lord of cowherds, O Eldest, born amongst the Nanda cowherds, always fond of buffalo's blood, born in the race of Kusika, O Pitambara, you who, assuming the face of a wolf, have devoured Asuras, I bow to you who take delight in battle!

O Uma, Sakambhari, you who are white in hue, you who are also black, you who slew the Asura Kaitabha, O tawny-eyed and many-eyed, you who have eyes the colour of smoke, I venerate you!

You are the Vedas, the Srutis, and the highest virtue; you are auspicious to Brahmanas performing yagnas. O you who know the past, you who are ever present in the sacred shrines erected for you in the cities of Jambudwipa, I bow to you!

You are the Brahmavidya among sciences, and you are that slumber from which there is no waking. Mother of Skanda, who possesses the six noblest qualities, Durga, you dwell in the remotest corners of the Earth, and are described as Swaha and Swadha, as Kala, as Kashta, and as Saraswati, as Savitri, the mother of the Vedas, and as the Vedanta.

With inner soul cleansed, I praise you. Mahadevi, let me always be victorious on the battlefield, always minister to me through your grace on the field of war. You dwell in remote regions, where there is fear, in places of hardship, in the homes of your worshippers and in Patala. You always vanquish the Danavas. You are the mahanidra, the great sleep, the illusion, the modesty and the beauty of all creatures.

You are the twilight and the day, you are Savitri, and you are the Mother. You are contentment, you are sustenance, and you are light. It is you who supports the Sun and the Moon and make them shine. You are the wealth of the prosperous. The Siddhas and the Charanas look upon you in dhyana."'

Sanjaya continues, 'Understanding the depth of Arjuna's devotion, Durga, who is always graciously inclined towards mankind, appears in the sky, and in the presence of Krishna, the Devi says, "You will swiftly defeat your enemies, O

Pandava. Invincible one, you have Narayana on your side. You cannot be vanquished even by the Vajradhari Indra himself."

The boon-granting Goddess disappears. Having that boon from her, the son of

Kunti now regards himself as already victorious and mounts his magnificent chariot. And then Krishna and Arjuna, seated on the same chariot, blow their celestial conches.

The man who recites this hymn rising at dawn, does not fear Yakshas, Rakshasas or Pisachas. He can have no enemies; he does not fear snakes and any animal with fangs and teeth; nor does he fear kings. He is certain to be victorious in all battles, and if bound, he is freed from his shackles. He is sure to overcome all obstacles, is free from thieves, ever victorious in battle and has the blessings of Lakshmi Devi for eternity. In health and strength, he lives for a hundred years.

I know all this through the grace of Vyasa imbued with great wisdom. However, your evil sons, all entangled out of ignorance in the snare of death, do not recognise them as Nara and Narayana. Nor do they, ensnared by death, know that the hour of the end of this kingdom has arrived. Dwaipayana and Narada, Kanwa and the sinless Rama have all warned your son. But he does not accept what they say.

Where dharma is, there lie glory and beauty. Where modesty is, prosperity and intelligence are to be found. And in righteousness, there is Krishna; and where Krishna is, there is victory.'

CANTO 24

BHAGAVAT-GITA PARVA CONTINUED

Vaisampayana said, "Dhritarashtra says, 'There on that field, Sanjaya, which army first advances gladly into battle? Whose hearts are filled with confidence, and who are dispirited and downcast? In that war which makes the hearts of men tremble, who strikes the first blow, my forces or those belonging to the Pandavas? Tell me all this, Sanjaya. Among whose troops do the flowery garlands and balms emit fragrant scents? And whose troops, roaring fiercely, speak merciful words?'

Sanjaya says, 'The fighters of both armies are joyful and the flowery garlands and perfumes of both armies emit equal fragrance. Fierce is the collision that takes place when the tightly compacted ranks arrayed for battle encounter each other.

And the sound of musical instruments, mingled with the blast of conches and the noise of drums, and the shouts of brave warriors roaring fiercely at one another, reverberate all around. Terrible is the impact of the encounter of the warriors of both armies, filled with assurance and staring at one another, with the elephants uttering boisterous grunts.'"

CANTO 25[1]

SRIMAD BHAGAVAD GITA

Aum Sri Ganapatheyah namaha
Aum Sri Saraswatheyah namaha
Aum Sri Krishnayah namaha

Arjuna vishada yoga: the despair of Arjuna

"Dhritarashtra says:
'Upon the field of dharma[2], field of Kuru, gathered keened for war,
my force and the sons of Pandu, what did they do, Sanjaya?'
Sanjaya says:
'Seeing the Pandava army arrayed, Duryodhana then
his honoured master approaches; the king says these words:

---

1.   The translation of the Bhagavad Gita given here is a verse translation by Ramesh
     Menon from the original Sanskrit. It preserves the Sanskrit order of words, and tries
     to reflect the Sanskrit cadences. This is not a reworking of Ganguli's translation.

2.   truth; righteousness

"Behold this immense army, master, of the sons of Pandu,
deployed by Drupada's son, your brilliant pupil.
Here, heroes, mighty bowmen, of Bhima and Arjuna equals in war—
Yuyudhana and Virata, and Drupada maharatha[3];
Dhrishtaketu, Chekitana, and the valiant Kasiraja,
Purujit and Kuntibhoja, and the Saibya, bull among men.
And Yuddhamanyu the brave and the intrepid Uttamaujas,
Subhadra's son[4] and Draupadi's princes—surely, maharathas all.

Be aware, also, of the distinguished amongst us, O best of dvijas[5],
the commanders of my army—let me name them for you to know.
Yourself and Bhishma and Karna, and Kripa winner of wars;
Aswatthaman and Vikarna, and the son of Somadatta, as well.
And so many other heroes, too, willing to give their lives for me;
myriad weapons they wield, all of them masters of war.

Our army is invincible, defended comprehensively by the might of
Bhishma;
their force is inferior, guarded by Bhima's strength all around.
And positioned at every ingress, each at your station,
Bhishma alone you must all perfectly protect, surely, from every side."

To hearten him, the mighty Kuru ancient[6], the grandsire,
a lion's roar lets out and blows his conch reverberantly.
Then, conches and bugles and trumpets, kettledrums, horns
resound suddenly, all together: that sound was tumultuary.

When, from a magnificent chariot, white horses yoked to it,

---

3.   great (chariot) warrior
4.   Abhimanyu
5.   the twice-born, the two upper castes; in this case, the Brahmanas
6.   Bhishma

Madhava[7] and the Pandava[8], also, their divine conches sound.
The Panchajanya, Hrishikesa[9]; the Devadatta, Dhananjaya[10];
the great conch Paundra blows Vrikodara[11] of awesome deeds.
the Anantavijayam, the king, Kunti's son Yudhishtira;
Nakula and Sahadeva: the Sughosha, the Manipushpaka.
And the Kaasi, supreme archer, and Sikhandi, maharatha;
Dhrishtadyumna and Virata and Satyaki, the unvanquished.
Drupada and all the sons of Draupadi, O lord of the earth,
and Subhadra's mighty-armed son sound their conches, every one.
That clamour Dhritarashtra's sons' hearts pierces;
and sky and earth, also, that fierce uproar shakes.

Now, watching in formation the sons of Dhritarashtra, the monkey-bannered[12]
Pandava, when weapons are about to be loosed, raises his bow.
Then, to Hrishikesa he speaks these words, lord of the earth.

Arjuna says:
"Between the two armies, set my chariot, Achyuta[13].
So I can look at those arrayed against us, seeking war,
against whom I must fight—before battle begins.
The warriors let me see, that have come together here,
wanting to please Dhritarashtra's evil-minded son with war."'

Sanjaya says:

---

7.   Krishna
8.   Arjuna
9.   Krishna; Vishnu
10.   Arjuna; lit. 'winner of wealth'
11.   Bhima; lit. 'wolf-belly'
12.   Hanuman
13.   Krishna; immaculate one

'Asked this by Gudakesa[14], Hrishikesa, O Bhaarata[15],
drawing up that fine chariot between the two armies,
before Bhishma, Drona and all the rulers of the earth,
says, "Partha[16], look at these massed Kurus."

Then Partha sees standing there fathers and grandfathers,
masters, uncles[17], brothers, sons, grandsons and friends,
fathers-in-law and well-wishers—and in both armies, besides;
the son of Kunti looks closely at all those kinsmen deployed there.
By great pity overcome, stricken, he says this.

Arjuna says:
"I see my kinsmen, Krishna, gathered avid for war.
My limbs turn weak, my mouth is parched;
and my body trembles, and my hair stands on end.
The Gandiva slips from my hands and my skin burns;
and my anxiety I cannot control and the fierce whirling of my mind;
and omens I see, evil, Kesava,
and nor do I see what good can come from killing my kinsmen in
battle.
I do not want victory, Krishna, neither kingdom nor happiness;
for what a kingdom, Govinda, what for pleasures or even life?
Those for whose sake we want a kingdom, pleasures or happiness,
they are here for war, leaving their lives and wealth.
Masters, fathers, sons, and grandsires, too;
uncles, fathers-in-law, grandsons, brothers-in-law and other kinsmen;
I do not want to kill them even if they kill me, Madhusudana[18]:

---

14. Arjuna; curly-haired; conqueror of sleep
15. Dhritarashtra is a descendant of the ancient king Bharata, after whom Bharata
    varsha is named
16. Arjuna; Pritha's (Kunti) son
17. maternal
18. Krishna, slayer of the demon Madhu

not for lordship over the three worlds[19], what then of this earth?
Killing Dhritarashtra's sons, what joy will we get, Janardana?[20]
We will only find sin ourselves if we slay these sinners.
So we must not kill the sons of Dhritarashtra, who are our kin;
for, after killing our own, how can we be happy, Madhava?[21]
Even if these, their hearts ruined by greed, see no
atrocity in destroying the clan and no crime in harming friends,
why don't we realise that we must desist from this sin,
when we see clearly how heinous it is to exterminate one's race,
Janardana?

With the destruction of the clan, ancient family traditions are lost
forever;
when dharma is no more, evil takes all that race.
When adharma rules, Krishna, the women of the clan become loose;
when the women are depraved, Vaarshaneya[22], the varnas[23] become
mixed.
Crossbreeding only casts into hell those that ruin the clan, and the
clan, itself;
their manes surely fall, for the ritual of the offering of rice-balls and
holy water having disappeared.
Through the sins of these clan-destroyers, defilers of the varnas,
lost are sacred traditions[24] of caste and family, forever.
Men whose kuladharma has been destroyed, Janardana,
will live forever in hell, as I have heard.

Ah, what a great sin we have decided to commit:

---

19. Swarga, Bhumi and Patala; heaven, earth and the under-world
20. Krishna
21. Krishna
22. Krishna, scion of the Vrishnis
23. castes
24. dharma, spiritual

that from greed for the pleasures of kingdom, we are ready to kill our kinsmen.
While I am unarmed and unresisting,
let Dhritarashtra's sons kill me on the field of war—that I could still bear."'

Sanjaya says:
'Saying this, Arjuna sits down in the back of that chariot, in war; he casts aside his arrows and bow, his heart plunged in profound anguish.'

CANTO 26

SRIMAD BHAGAVAD GITA CONTINUED

Samkhya yoga: The way of samkhya[25]

Sanjaya says:
'Seeing him so, in the grip of pity, tearful, agitated,
grief-stricken, these words to him speaks Madhusudana.

The Gracious Lord says:
"From where has this stain come over you at this critical time?
This is the way of the base; it does not lead to heaven but fetches
infamy, Arjuna.
Do not go this cowardly way, Partha; it is beneath you;
abandon this vile faint-heartedness, and arise, O bane of your
enemies!"

Arjuna says:

---

25. see appendix for samkhya and yoga

"How will I attack Bhishma and Drona in battle, Madhusudana,
with arrows, when they are worthy of worship, Arisudana?[26]
Surely, without killing one's masters and noble elders, it is better to
live by begging alms in this world;
else, by killing our masters, if we enjoy wealth and pleasures we
shall enjoy
blood-stained spoils.
We do not know which of these would be better for us:
that we conquer them or that they vanquish us!
They whom killing, we would not wish to live—standing before us,
the
sons of Dhritarashtra.
The weakness of pity besieges my nature; my mind confounded about
what
dharma is, I ask you—
tell me what is unquestionably best for me. I am your disciple;
teach me, I submit to you.
Because I cannot see what can exorcise this anguish that withers my
senses,
not if I gained a thriving and unrivalled kingdom on earth, and even
lordship over the gods of light.[27]"'

Sanjaya says:
'Speaking thus to Hrishikesa, Gudakesa, scourge of his enemies,
says "I will not fight" and falls silent.

Then, Hrishikesa speaks smilingly, Bhaarata,
between two armies, to him who sorrowed, these words.

The Gracious Lord says:

---

26. slayer of enemies
27. the Devas

"You grieve for those not worth grieving over, and argue as if you were a wise man discoursing;

not for the dead or for the living do the wise grieve.

Surely, at no time ever did I not exist, or you, or all these kings;

and for sure, not in any future to come will any of us cease to exist.

Just as the indweller passes, in the body, through childhood, youth and old age,

the soul also assumes new bodies; the wise are not perplexed by this.

Contact between the elements alone, son of Kunti, causes cold and heat, pleasure and pain;

these come and go, they are evanescent; endure them, Bhaarata.

Whom these cannot perturb, the wise man, O bull among men;

who is the same in sorrow and joy, steadfast, is fit for immortality.

Never does the unreal exists, and the real never ceases to be;

of both these, surely, the end has been seen by seers of truth.

But, know, what pervades all this is immortal;

that everlasting being no one can destroy.

Mortal these bodies; eternal, it is said, the embodied soul;

It is immortal, ineffable—so, fight Bhaarata!

He that thinks of it as being a killer and he who thinks *This* is slain:

both do not know—it neither kills nor is slain.

This is not born nor ever dies, not in the past, present or future;

un-born, changeless, eternal it is, primeval; it is not killed when the body is slain.

Knowing this is indestructible, constant, un-born, immutable,

how does a man kill anyone, Partha, whom does he kill?

Even as a man abandons old, tattered clothes and puts on other fresh ones,

the indweller leaves old, worn bodies and enters other new ones.

Weapons cannot pierce *it*; fire cannot burn it;

water does not wet it, nor dry it, the wind.

Not pierceable, not burnable, not wettable, and also not dryable—
permanent, ubiquitous, abiding, invariable, eternal.
unmanifest, *it*; inconceivable, it; changeless, it, they say;
So, knowing it is such, you must not despair.
and if you think that it is constantly being born and continually dying,
even then, mighty-armed, you ought not to despair.
For he who is born death is certain, and birth is certain for who dies;
so, over what you believe to be ineluctable, you should not despair.
Unmanifest the source of beings, manifest their interim, Bhaarata;
unmanifest, too, their end; so why grieve for them?

As a miracle, some see it; and others say it is marvellous;
and others learn that it is ineffable; and some, after having learnt[28], still do
not know it.
This eternal spirit is unkillable, in every body, Bhaarata;
so, you must not grieve for any of the living.
And also, looking at your svadharma[29] you must not falter;
for, there is nothing higher for a Kshatriya than a war for truth.
Fortuitous and just, an open portal to heaven—
joyful are Kshatriyas, Partha, who find such a war!

But if you do not fight this battle of dharma,
then, forsaking your svadharma and your fame, you will find sin.
Besides, of your ignominy all men will tell forever,
and for the honoured, infamy is worse than death.
That out of fear you quit the battle these maharathas will think;
and in those that once held you in great esteem, you will find contempt.

---

28. one who knows, has studied, the Veda; knowing the scriptures
29. inherent caste duty, here as a Kshatriya warrior

And your enemies will malign you with vile slander,
scoffing at your prowess; what can be more painful than that?

Either being killed you will attain heaven, or, victorious, enjoy the earth;
so arise, Kaunteya, resolved to fight!
Pleasure and pain equally treat: gain, loss: victory, defeat;
then join battle—you will no sin incur.

I have told you about samkhya[30]; to the yoga of buddhi[31] now listen;
yoke[32] your intellect with this, Partha, the bonds of karma put to sword.
In battle, with this[33], there is no-one killed, no sin to consider;
even the least bit of this dharma preserves from great fear.
In the resolute soul, the mind is one, joy of the Kurus;
many-branched and unending are the thoughts of the irresolute.
With these memorised flowery words those of small vision
eulogise the panegyrics of the Veda, Partha, saying nothing else[34] exists.
Their hearts of desire, swarga their ideal, the rewards of births and rites they seek;
frequent, unvarying rituals, to have pleasure and power, they perform.
To pleasure and power attached, their thoughts beguiled by these;
with devoted mind to attain samadhi[35] they do not strive.
With matters of the three gunas[36] the Vedas deal; be without the

---

30.   system of philosophy founded by Kapila muni
31.   mind
32.   Yoga means to yoke; control, restrain, here
33.   Yoga of knowledge
34.   higher
35.   communion with God, liberation
36.   sattva, rajas and tamas

three gunas,

Arjuna:

free from duality; always established in sattva[37], unattached, serene.

As much use as in a well to a deluge of water everywhere:

so much in all the Vedas to a Brahmana of enlightenment.

You surely have the right to do your karma[38], not to its fruit, at any time;

the fruit of karma should not become your motive, nor be attached to sloth.

Steadfast in yoga, do your duty, renouncing attachment, Dhananjaya;

success and failure becoming the same: that equanimity is called yoga.

Far inferior is ritual to the yoked mind, Dhananjaya;

in wisdom seek refuge: pitiful are those driven by gain.

Mind yoked, you can be free here[39] of both good and evil;

so, to yoga devote yourself; yoga is genius at karma.

Performing karma, mind devoted, but its fruit renouncing, wise men, from the bondage of birth entirely freed[40], come to the place of no sickness.

When beyond this chaos of illusions your mind passes,

then you will arrive at indifference to what you have heard and what you will hear[41].

By the srutis confused:[42] when your mind becomes still, unmoving, in samadhi permanently, then you will find yoga."

Arjuna says:

---

37. the pure guna
38. natural duty
39. in this world
40. repeated birth, death and rebirth
41. srotasi refers to what you will hear in the Vedas, too
42. now confused

"How can you tell a man of resolution, who is founded in samadhi, Kesava?[43]

How does a realized one speak? How does he sit, how walk?"

The Gracious Lord says:
"When a man abandons all desires, Partha, which spring in the mind, and gratifies himself in just his soul, a man of unshakeable wisdom he is said to be.

Unaffected by adversity, whose mind, in fortune unmoved to desire; free of passion, fear and anger, a true muni is called.

Who everywhere is without affection; who, upon finding fortune or misfortune,

neither exults nor feels aversion, his wisdom is founded.

And when, like a tortoise completely retracts all its limbs, a man does his senses from their objects of desire, his wisdom is founded.

Through restraint the embodied can refrain from indulging the senses, but not from desire; even his desires disappear at the vision of *God*.

Of even, son of Kunti, a restrained man,
his turbid senses forcibly ravish his mind.

All the senses restraining, the sage sits intent on me;
for, one whose senses are tamed, his wisdom is established.

Dwelling on the objects of desire[44], a man becomes attached to these;
from attachment is born desire; from desire anger arises.

From rage comes upheaval[45]; from turmoil, the wavering memory;
after the loss of memory, destruction of the mind; when the mind is destroyed, he dies.

Emancipated from attraction and revulsion, but going among the

---

43. Krishna
44. sense objects; objects of sensuality
45. 'delusion' is the most common translation for sammohah

objects of the senses,
tamed by the Atman, ruled by the soul, he attains grace.
With grace, of all suffering the end comes;
the tranquil one's wisdom, surely, is quickly constant.
No wisdom for the wilful, and not for the reckless, faith;
and for the faithless, there is no peace; for the peaceless, from where joy?
Which ever of the ever-roving senses the mind yields to,
that bears his wisdom away, as the wind a boat on the sea.

So, he, Mahabaho, who withdraws completely
the senses from the objects of sensuality, his wisdom is profound.
When night comes for all creatures, is when the ascetic awakes;
what is waking for the rest, that is night for the visionary.
Always still, the ocean, though being filled by water entering into it;
equally, he who contains all desires entering him, acquires peace, not
he who submits to desire.
Leaving the things of desire, who roams the earth, unattached,
without 'mine', without 'I', he attains peace.
This is the Brahmi state[46], Partha; attaining to this, he is no more tempted;
abiding in this at his final hour, as well, he goes to Brahmanirvana."[47]

---

46. union with Brahman
47. Nirvana: absorption; eternal bliss; highest felicity; union; dissolution in; extinction; death; vanishment

CANTO 27

Srimad Bhagavad Gita continued

Karma yoga: The way of action

Arjuna says:
"If you think knowledge superior to action, Janardana,
then why to this ghastly deed do you commit me, Kesava?
With your seemingly ambiguous words, you only confuse my mind;
say one thing, decidedly, by which I can attain felicity."

The Gracious Lord says:
"In this world, two kinds of devotion were of old ordained by me,
O sinless—
the yoga of knowledge for samkhyas, the way of deeds for yogis.

By not doing his duty a man does not achieve freedom from karma;
nor by mere abstention is transcendent perfection attained.
Nor, certainly, can anyone even momentarily ever stay inactive;
because all are helplessly made to act by the Prakriti-born gunas.

He that restrains the organs of karma but continues to dwell in his mind
on the objects of sensuality, that foolish soul is deemed a hypocrite.
But he who, restraining the senses with the mind, Arjuna, engages
the organs of action in karma yoga, dispassionately—he excels.
You must always do your duty; because action is higher than inactivity;
besides, you will not succeed even in keeping your body through inertia.
All karma other than that done as an offering binds this world in rebirth;
for that, act, Kaunteya, free from attachment, consummately.

Together with sacrifice, creating men, of old Prajapati[48] said,
'By this, you will generate and multiply; let this be the yielder of your wishes.
Adore the Devas by this; let the Devas succour you;
by each other nourished, supreme felicity you will have.
Bound by the nurture of sacrifice, the gods will surely give you the pleasures you desire;
one who enjoys these gifts, without giving to them, he is certainly a thief.'

The saintly who eat the leftovers of a sacrifice are liberated from all sins;
but the sinful eat sin, who cook food just for themselves.
From food are born beings; from rain, food grows;
from sacrifice, come the rains; sacrifice from karma[49] springs.
Karma from Brahma arises, know; Brahma of the Imperishable is born;

---

48. Brahma, the creator; lord of the people
49. action, duty, caste duty, sacred duty

so, ubiquitous Brahma always abides in sacrifice.

Hence, this turning wheel, who does not live by it here[50],
lives in sin, indulging the senses—in vain, Partha, he lives.

But for him who is devoted only to the Atman[51], and remains
absorbed in the Atman, the man

who, also, is fulfilled only in the soul—for him no duty is ordained.

He surely has nothing to gain here, either by doing or by not doing;
nor does he, among all the living, seek any gain.

Thus, without attachment, always do your duty consummately;
for, by performing karma without attachment man attains the
Supreme.

Indeed, only through karma did in absolute perfection abide Janaka[52]
and others;

besides, also considering the good of the world, you must act.

Whatever a great man does: all that other men also do;
whatever norm he sets, that all the world follows.

Not for me, Partha, is there any duty in the three worlds,
nor anything to attain that is unattained; and I am always at work.

Surely, if ever I am not at my work, tirelessly,
my path would be followed by men, Partha, of every walk.

Plunged into ruin these worlds, if I did not do my work;
and I would be the cause of crossbreeding,[53] diminishing these
generations.

As the ignorant perform karma with desire, attachment, Bhaarata,
so must the knowing act, unattached, wanting the weal of the
world.

Not creating confusion in the minds of the unknowing attached

---

50. in this world
51. Soul; Self
52. the Rajarishi king Janaka, Sita's father, Sri Rama's father-in-law
53. varnasamkarasya: anarchy through mixing of the castes

to karma,
silently the wise man does all his work, yoked, absorbed.
Nature's essences perform karma, in every way;
he who is beguiled by egoism thinks, 'I am the doer'.
But he who knows the truth, Mahabaho, about the difference
between guna and karma—
the gunas act upon the gunas—so knowing, is not attached.
Those deluded by the gunas of nature become enmeshed in karma
born of the gunas;
those dull ones that do not know the *All*[54], a knower of everything
must not agitate.

To me all karma consigning, to the Atman your thought;
becoming desireless, dispassionate, do battle, leaving panic.
This my teaching, those men who always follow,
with faith, without derision, are also liberated from karma.
But they who slight this, do not follow my precept,
fools to all knowledge, are, know, lost, insensate.
In concord with his nature, acts even the wise man;
nature, beings obey▨what can inhibition achieve?
For the senses, attraction and revulsion towards the objects of
sensuality are inexorable;
no man must come under their sway, for they are his enemies.
Better in one's own dharma, flawed, than another's dharma
immaculately done;
death in one's own dharma is auspicious; another's dharma is
dangerous."

Arjuna says:
"Then what makes a man to commit sin,
even unwillingly, Vaarshaneya, with force as if coerced?"

---

54. the Truth, Brahman

The Gracious Lord says:
"It is desire, it is anger, arisen from the rajoguna[55]—
voracious, direly sinful, know this, here, for an enemy.
As fire is obscured by smoke and a mirror by dust,
as the womb hides an embryo, so is *it* hidden by that.
Shrouded, wisdom by this, of the wise the constant enemy,
with lust's form, Kaunteya, and an insatiable fire.
Senses, mind, intellect, its abode, it is said;
by these confounding, it shrouds the wisdom of the embodied.
So, your senses first control, Bharatarishabha;
kill this malignant thing, for this is the ruiner of knowledge and wisdom.
The senses are lofty, they say; higher than the senses is mind;
and beyond mind is intellect; but past intellect is *He.*
So, knowing what is beyond the intellect, stilling the self with the soul,
vanquish, Mahabaho, the enemy, lust-formed, unassailable."

---

55. the second guna, mode of Prakriti, of the essence of passion

CANTO 28

SRIMAD BHAGAVAD GITA CONTINUED

Gyana yoga: The way of knowledge

The Gracious Lord says:
"This yoga to Vivaswat[56] I revealed, immortal;
Vivaswan to Manu[57] taught it; Manu to Ikshavaku[58] imparted it.
So, by lineal tradition received, this the Rajarishis[59] knew;
after great time, here, the yoga was lost, Parantapa.
That very same have I to you today revealed, the ancient yoga:
for you are my devotee and my friend, because this is the secret
supreme."

---

56. the Sun god; Surya Deva
57. Surya's son Vaivaswata Manu: progenitor of the Manushyas or Manavas, humankind
58. Manu's son, great king, founder of the Suryavamsa, royal house of the Sun, into which Rama was born
59. royal sages, saintly kings

Arjuna says:
"Recent your birth, earlier the birth of Vivasvat;
so how do I comprehend this—you first taught him?"

The Gracious Lord says:
"Myriad births of mine are past, and yours, Arjuna;
these I know, every one; you do not know, Parantapa.
Though un-born, my soul immortal, the Lord of creatures though
being,
abiding in my own nature, I incarnate through my soul's maya.[60]
Whenever there is a decline of dharma, Bhaarata,
an ascendancy of adharma, then myself I manifest.
For the deliverance of the good and for the destruction of sinners;
in order to establish dharma, I come from age to age.
So, who my divine birth and deeds knows truly,
after leaving the body does not find rebirth; he finds me, Arjuna.
Gone, passion, fear, anger; absorbed in me, sheltering in me,
many, purified by wisdom's penance, have come to my being.
As they come to me, so do I cherish them;
my path men walk, Partha, on every path.

Those who wish for gain from karma sacrifice here to the gods;
for, speedily in the world of men gain attends on ritual.
The four varnas, my creation: by gunas, karma, divided;
its creator, also, know that I am act-less, immutable.
I am not by karma tainted; I do not desire the fruit of karma;
one who recognises me to be thus, he is not bound to karma.
This knowing, the ancients, too, performed karma, the seekers after
mukti;[61]
so must you do your duty, as the ancients did of old.

---

60. mysterious power of illusion
61. liberation; final salvation

What is karma, what is akarma? By this even the seers are baffled;
of that karma I will tell you, knowing which you will be saved from
every ill.
What karma is must also be understood, and what is forbidden
karma;
and what is not karma be known—deep is the way of karma.
Who in work repose sees, and in inactivity ado,
he is wise among men; he is a sage, all his duty done.
Whose every endeavour is without desire's intent;
whose deeds are burnt in wisdom's fire, him the wise call a sage.
Renouncing attachment for the fruit of work, always contented,
independent,
though incessantly at work, he does nothing at all.
Desireless, he of restrained mind, leaving all possessions,
just the body doing work, finds no sin.
With whatever chance gives contented, beyond duality, without envy,
and equable in success, failure—though doing, he is not bound.
Whose attachments are gone, who is free, mind founded in wisdom;
who acts only as a sacrifice—all his karma dissolves entirely.

Brahman the sacrifice, Brahman the oblation;
Brahman the fire into which Brahman makes the offering;
Brahman he surely attains through the devotion of Brahmakarma.[62]

Only with sacrifices to the Devas, some yogis worship;
into the fire of Brahman others sacrifice itself as sacrifice offer.
Hearing, the other senses, some into restraint's fire offer;
sound, the other objects of sensuality, others into the fire of the
senses offer.
All the senses' karma and the karma of life, others
offer into self-restraint's yogic fire, kindled by wisdom.

---

62. working for Brahman; serving Brahman

Material sacrifice; penance as sacrifice; with yoga, too, others sacrifice;
sacred study and knowledge, sacrifice the ascetics of stern vows.
Inhaling they offer into exhalation; exhaling into in-breath, as well,
others:
prana, apana's, movement stilling, those devoted to pranayama.
Others curb what they eat, into prana, prana offer;
all these, also, knowers of sacrifice: by sacrifice, their sins expelled.
Eating sacrificial remains, ambrosia, they go to eternal Brahman;
not this world is for the unsacrificing, much less any other, best of
Kurus.

So, many kinds of sacrifice are spread across Brahman's face;
karma-born, know, all these; so knowing, you will become free.
Better than sacrifice of wealth, the devotion of wisdom, Parantapa;
all karma, in entirety, Partha, culminates in wisdom.
That learn, through homage, by inquiry and service:
the wise, seers of truth, will teach you wisdom.
Which knowing, not again will delusion so torment you, Pandava;
with this, all creatures, without exception, you will see in yourself,
and in me.
Even if you, of sinners, of them all, are the greatest sinner,
all distress, by wisdom's boat, you will surely cross.
Just as its fuel of wood a fire makes ashes, Arjuna,
wisdom's fire all karma to ashes turns, as surely.
Nothing to equal wisdom in purity exists here;
that, of himself, one evolved in yoga, in time, within himself attains.
He of faith attains wisdom: absorbed, senses restrained;
wisdom gained, to supreme peace, also, he quickly comes.

The ignorant and the faithless and the doubting soul perishes;
not this world, not the next, nor happiness for the doubting soul.
Through yoga renouncing karma, with wisdom severing doubt,
a self-possessed one no karma binds, Dhananjaya.

So, cut away ignorance-born doubt seated in your heart, with
wisdom's soul sword;
turn to yoga—arise, Bhaarata!"

CANTO 29

SRIMAD BHAGAVAD GITA CONTINUED

Sannyasa yoga: The way of renunciation

Arjuna says:
"Renunciation of karma, Krishna, then again, yoga you extol;
which one of the two is better for me, say for certain."

The Gracious Lord says:
"Sannyasa and karma yoga effect liberation, both;
but of the two, doing karma is superior to inaction.

Know him as a constant renunciate, who neither dislikes nor desires;
for, detached from duality, Mahabaho, he is easily freed from bondage.
The callow say that samkhya and yoga are different, not the wise;
for, who is absorbed in one, of both enjoys the fruit.
The condition the samkhyas achieve, that yogis also attain;
and as one, who samkhya and yoga sees, he sees.
But sannyasa, mighty-armed, is difficult to attain without yoga;

the sage yoked to yoga, to Brahman swiftly comes.
Who is absorbed in yoga, pure soul, master of his mind, subduer of the senses,
who is the soul of all souls—though he does, he is not tainted.
'I do nothing' a yukta[63] thinks, a knower of truth:
while seeing, hearing, touching, smelling, eating, moving, sleeping, breathing,
speaking, emitting, ingesting, staring and blinking:
the senses in sensuality are engaged—in this awareness.

Resigning his karma to Brahman, without attachment, who works:
he is not stained by sin, as a lotus leaf by water.
With the body, with the mind, with the intellect, or merely with the senses,
yogis perform karma, leaving attachment—to purify the soul.
The yoked, sacrificing the fruit of karma, attains profound peace;
the unyoked, moved by desire, devoted to the fruit, is bound.
All karma with the mind relinquishing, dwells the restrained one, at ease,
in the city of nine doors[64], the embodied—surely, neither doing nor causing.[65]
Neither doer nor deed for the world, the Lord creates;
not union of work with its fruit; only nature acts.

Neither anybody's sin nor, indeed, their virtue does god assume;
wisdom is shrouded by ignorance; by this the living are deluded.
But whose ignorance is destroyed by knowledge of the Atman,
their sunlike wisdom illumines *that*, highest.
That their mind, that their soul, that their faith, that their devotion—

---

63. a yoked one, who is united with the divine
64. the body of nine inlets
65. anything to be done

they go to non-return, by wisdom their sins destroyed.

A Brahmana endowed with learning, humility; a cow, an elephant,
and even a dog and a dog-eater[66], the wise see as equal.
Even here, they conquer nature, whose minds are founded in
equalness;
because Brahman is immaculate, equal, so they abide in Brahman.
Not elated at getting the agreeable and not dejected upon finding the
unpleasant;
mind calm, undeluded, the knower of Brahman in Brahman dwells.
Who is detached from the outward touch[67], finds the bliss in the
Atman;
the one yoked in Brahman through yoga, he immortal bliss enjoys.
Surely, the pleasures of the touch of the senses, they are only wombs
of sorrow;
they begin and end, Kaunteya; not in them dwells a wise man.
Who can, even here, before leaving the body, endure
the lust- and anger-born rush, he is a yukta; he is the happy man.
Who joy within, rest within, and also light only within finds;
that yogi dissolution in Brahman, union with Brahman, attains.
Those rishis find Brahmanirvana, whose sins are exhausted,
doubts scattered, minds restrained: to the felicity of all beings devoted.
Freed from lust, anger, yatis, with minds restrained,
live subsumed in Brahmanirvana, those who know the Atman.
Outward objects of sensuality shutting out, and gaze fixed between
the brows;
making equal outward and inward breath, moving within the nose;
with restrained senses, mind and intellect, the sage devoted to
liberation,
who has departed desire, fear and anger, he is surely always free.

---

66. Chandala
67. of sensual contact, pleasure

Enjoyer of sacrifices and penance, great Lord of all worlds, friend to all beings—me, knowing, he comes to peace."

SRIMAD BHAGAVAD GITA CONTINUED

Dhyana yoga: The way of meditation

The Gracious Lord says:
"Not seeking karma's fruit, who does his ordained work,
he is the sannyasi and the yogi; and not one without the fire[68], and
not him without ritual.
So, what they call sannyasa, know that is yoga, Pandava;
for, without renouncing desire, no one becomes a yogi.
For the sage who aspires to yoga, karma is the way, it is told;
who has attained yoga, only for him is quiescence the way, they say.
Only when neither to the objects of sensuality attached,
he who renounces all desire is said to have attained yoga.
Raise yourself through the Atman; never abase yourself;
for, only you are your own friend; you alone, your own enemy.
His Atman is his friend only to him who has mastered himself;

---

68. who does not light the sacred fire

for the uncontrolled, his very soul is hostile like an enemy.

Who has conquered himself, who is tranquil, his soul is entirely composed,
in heat and cold, joy and sorrow, also, in honour and ignominy.
In knowledge and wisdom, fulfilled, unshakeable, master of his senses;
that yogi is said to be yoked for whom the clod of earth, a stone and gold are the same.
With the friend, the companion, an enemy, a stranger, an arbiter, an odious man, a relative,
as well as a saint and a sinner, he who is equal-minded, excels.

The yogi should constantly yoke himself: in seclusion,
alone, heart and mind controlled, without desire and possession.
In a clean place, setting his seat firm, himself,
neither too high nor too low, with kusa grass, cloth and deerskin, one over the other.
There, making his mind one-pointed, controlling his thought and senses,
sitting upon the seat, he should absorb himself in yoga, to purify his heart.
Aligning body, head and neck, keeping still and steady;
fixing his gaze on the tip of his nose, and not looking around;
serene, fearless, steadfast in the vow of celibacy;
mind controlled, intent on me, yoked, he sits devoted to me.
Thus yoking himself always, the yogi of subdued mind
to peace, supreme nirvana which abides in me, attains.

Not for one who eats too much is yoga, nor for him who overly fasts;
and not for him given to too much sleep, nor yet for the overly wakeful, Arjuna.
Who is restrained in food and pleasure, devoted in thought and deed;
moderate in sleep and waking, attains yoga, leaving sorrow.

When the restrained mind is founded exclusively in the Atman,
indifferent to every desire, then he is said to be a yukta.

As a lamp in a windless place does not flicker: similar, it is recorded,
is a yogi of restrained thought, engaged in the yoga of the Atman.
Where thought ceases, curbed by the practice of yoga;
and where, also, the mind sees the soul, and is fulfilled in the Atman;
in which infinite joy, through the intellect experienced, beyond the
senses,
he knows; and in which established, he surely does not move from
truth;
and gaining which, no other gain he considers as greater than that;
wherein founded, no grief, even the heaviest, shakes him:
that, know—the disunion from union with pain—to be absorption
in yoga;
this, with conviction, practise: yoga, with an undismayed heart.

Will-spawned desires, all, renouncing entirely;
with the mind, the host of senses surely restraining, on every side;
by degrees growing still, through firmly restraining the intellect;
in the soul having established the mind, let him not think of anything.
Wherever the restless and fickle mind strays, from there it must be
restrained,
brought back under the sway of just the Atman.
Who is of serene mind, only to this yogi the highest bliss
comes, his passion stilled, his spirit in Brahman, sinless.
Thus constantly devoting himself, the yogi, delivered from sin,
easily communes with Brahman, enjoys infinite bliss.

In all beings the Atman, and all beings in the soul:
the one absorbed in yoga sees everywhere the same.
Who sees me everywhere, and everything sees in me,
to him I am never lost, and he is not lost to me.

As abiding in all beings, who worships me, founded in oneness,
whatever his life, he is a yogi and lives in me.
In the image of himself, who everywhere sees the same, Arjuna,
be it in pleasure or in pain, he is deemed the highest yogi."

Arjuna says:
"This yoga you have said to be sameness, Madhusudana,
for this I see no enduring stability—out of restlessness.[69]
Fickle, surely, is the mind, Krishna, turbulent, strong, obstinate;
to control it, I think, is so difficult—like[70] the wind."

The Gracious Lord says:
"Doubtless, Mahabaho, the mind is difficult to control, unsteady;
but with practice, Kaunteya, and dispassion, it is restrained.
For the unrestrained, yoga is difficult to attain, I agree;
but the restrained soul, striving expediently, can attain it."

Arjuna says:
"Who cannot control himself, though he has faith, whose mind strays
from yoga,
without attaining consummation in yoga, to what end, Krishna, does
he come?
Does he not, from both fallen,[71] and like a rent cloud, surely perish,
unstable, Mahabaho, confounded along the path of Brahman?
This my doubt, Krishna, you must dispel entirely;
none but you, for sure, can effect the undoing of this doubt."

The Gracious Lord says:
"Partha, neither here nor hereafter, does he find harm;

---

69. of mind
70. controlling
71. devotion and yoga

for never does any good man, my friend, come to evil.

Having attained worlds of the righteous, living there for countless years,

into a home of the pious and the prosperous, the one fallen from yoga is nobly born.

Else, born even into a family of yogis of wisdom;

though rare indeed in the world is such a birth.

Thereupon, the evolution of his past life he recovers;

and, with that, strives again for perfection, Kurunandana.[72]

Also, that same previous practice bears him away, inexorably;

even a seeker after yoga transcends the Veda.[73]

But the yogi who strives with zealous mind, purified of all sin,

through many lives perfected, then comes to the supreme.

Than the tapasvin[74] greater the yogi; also greater than the gyani[75], regarded;

Than the karmi[76] greater the yogi—so a yogi become, Arjuna.

Of all yogis, even, who abides in me in his inmost soul,

who devotedly worships me, him I consider

the foremost yukta."

---

72. joy, child of the Kurus
73. Vedic ritual
74. ascetic
75. man of knowledge, wisdom
76. man of deeds, work

CANTO 31

SRIMAD BHAGAVAD GITA CONTINUED

Gyana Vigyana yoga: The way of knowledge and realization.

The Gracious Lord says:
"To me the mind cleaving, Partha, devoted in yoga, taking refuge in me,
without doubt, you will know me in full—listen how.
This knowledge to you, I, together with wisdom, will tell in full,
which knowing, nothing else here will remain to be known.
Among thousands of men scarcely one strives for perfection;
among these seekers, even among sages[77], hardly one knows me in truth.

Earth, water, fire, air, ether, mind, intellect and also
ego—this my differentiated nature, eightfold.

---

77. Siddhas: the perfect. a Siddha is also a semi-divine being of great purity, characterised by eight supernatural faculties, or siddhis

This is my lower nature; know my other transcendent nature—
the *Living Spirit*, Mahabaho, which supports this world.
These two are the womb of all beings, know;
I am all the world's source and its dissolution, as well.
Than me higher nothing else at all exists, Dhananjaya;
in[78] me all this is strung like so many jewels on a thread.

Taste am I in water, Kaunteya; light I am in moon and sun;
Aum in all the Vedas, sound in ether, manliness in men.
The pure fragrance in the earth I am, and brilliance in fire;
life in all beings am I, and austerity in ascetics.
The seed am I of all creatures, know, Partha—eternal;
the intelligence of the intelligent I am; the splendour of the splendid,
I.
And I am the strength of the strong; of lust, passion devoid;
in beings, legitimate desire am I, Bharatarishabha.
And whatever sattvik existences, of rajas and tamas there are:
from me alone they are, know—I am not in them; they are in me.

By all these, the three gunas' manifestations, this whole world,
deluded, does not know me, transcendent, supreme, immutable.
For, this divine, guna-comprised maya of mine is impenetrable;
only who in me refuge, they cross over this maya.
Not in me evil-doers, fools, refuge, lowest of men;
robbed by maya of wisdom, they yield to demonic ways.

Four kinds of men worship me, virtuous ones, Arjuna:
the distressed, the aspirant[79], the material seeker[80], and the wise man,
Bharatarishabha.

---

78. on *me*
79. after knowledge; the spiritual seeker
80. of wealth, gain

Of these the wise man, always in communion, of singular devotion, is
the best;
for, most dear to the wise man I am, and he is dear to me.
Noble are all these, surely, but the gyani I regard as my own self;
Because he, the yoked soul, is absorbed just in me, as his highest
refuge.
At the end of many lives, the wise man resorts to me:
'Because Vasudeva is all'—such a great soul is exceedingly rare.

Through desire they whose wisdom is swayed, worship other gods,
a myriad of rites observing, by their own natures compelled.
Whatever form, however, any devotee wishes to worship with faith,
in just that his faith I make firm.
He, to this faith yoked, *that*[81] to propitiate seeks;
and through that, obtains his wishes, which in truth by me alone are
granted.
But they have an end, the fruits of these small-minded ones;
to the Devas, the worshippers of Devas go; and my devotees come to
me.
The Unmanifest as reduced into manifestation: the ignorant regard
me;
my supreme nature not knowing—imperishable, unsurpassed.
I am not plain to all, being cloaked by my yogamaya;
this foolish world does not know me: un-born, immortal.
I know equally, Arjuna, past and present
and future beings; but me no one knows.
By desire- and aversion-arisen duality seduced, Bhaarata,
all creatures are born to ignorance, Parantapa.
But whose sins have come to an end, men of virtuous deeds:
they, from duality's delusion freed, worship me with unswerving
devotion.

---

81. form, deity

For liberation from decay, death, who strive, sheltering in me,
they the Brahman truly know, the Atman entirely, and all about karma.
As the Lord of creatures[82], master of gods, the support of sacrifice, me who know,
with absorbed minds they also know me even at the hour of death."

---

82. the elements, the material world

CANTO 32

SRIMAD BHAGAVAD GITA CONTINUED

Akshara Brahma yoga: The way of immortal Brahman
Arjuna says:
"What is that Brahman, what Adhyatma[83], what karma, Purushottama?
and what is called Adhibhutam, what said to be Adhidaivam?
Who is the Adhiyagna, and how: here in this body, Madhusudana?
And at the hour of death how are you known by the restrained soul?"

The Gracious Lord says:
"Deathless Brahman is supreme; nature is called Adhyatmam;
beings, souls, that which creates, sends forth, is named karma.
Adhibhutam is mortal forms, and Purusha[84], Adhidaivatam;
Adhiyagna even I am, in this body, O most excellent of the living.
And at the time of the end, only me remembering, while leaving the
body,

---

83. the Supreme Soul
84. the Cosmic Person

who departs, he comes to my being: of this there is no doubt.
Or else, of whatever thinking he gives up the body,
even to that he surely attains, Kaunteya, being ever absorbed in that thought.
So, at all times, think of me, and fight;
to me your heart and mind offered, to me you will surely come, without doubt.
Mind engaged in absorption in yoga, not straying,
who meditates, Partha, the supreme Purusha, divine, attains.
Who meditates on the Seer, the Ancient, the Ruler, smaller than the smallest,
the support of everything, of inconceivable form, Sun-coloured, beyond darkness,
at the hour of death, mind stilled, with devotion, yoked, and also, with the power of yoga,
prana fixed firmly between the brows—he, that supreme Purusha attains, divine.
That *Immortal* of which Veda knowers speak, which passionless sages enter;
wanting which, they practice brahmacharya—that condition to you briefly I will tell.

All inlets[85] restrained, and the mind confined in the heart;
in the head fixing the soul's life-breath, founded firm in yoga,
AUM, the one-syllabled Brahman, uttering, remembering me,
who departs, leaving the body, he goes to the highest destination.
Of nothing else aware, who ever remembers me, with constancy,
to him I am attainable, Partha, to the always yoked yogi.
Attaining me, to rebirth, house of sorrow, impermanent,
great souls do not return—the highest perfection they have reached.
Up to Brahma's realm, all worlds are subject to rebirth, Arjuna;

---

85. of the body, the senses

but upon me attaining, Kaunteya, there is no experiencing birth again.

A thousand yugas lasts Brahma's day, who know,
that his night lasts a thousand yugas, they are knowers of day and night.
From the Unmanifest all the manifest come forth at the advent of day[86];
at the coming of night, they then dissolve into that same, called the Unmanifest.
The host of beings, they the same which recur, dissolves,
when night comes, helplessly, Partha, comes forth, when day arrives.
But beyond this existence is another unmanifest unmanisfestation eternal:
He who, when all beings perish, is not destroyed.
This Unmanifest is said to be imperishable: this, which is called the supreme condition,
whom attaining, they do not return—that is my supreme abode.
He is the supreme Purusha, Partha, but through singular devotion can be attained—
in whom all beings dwell, by whom all this is pervaded.

Now the times of yogis not returning, and also returning,
when departing hence—those times I will tell you, Bharatarishabha.
Fire, light, day, the bright fortnight[87], the northern course[88]:
by these departing, those who know Brahman to Brahman go.
Smoke, night, also the dark fortnight, the six months of the southern course:
there, the lunar light, the yogi, obtaining, returns.

---

86. Brahma's day
87. when the moon waxes
88. the six months of the sun's northern course

The bright, the dark: surely these paths of the world are considered eternal;

going by one, he does not return; by the other he comes back again. Not, these paths, Partha, knowing, is the yogi deluded, ever;

so, at all times, yoked in yoga be, Arjuna.

By the Veda, by sacrifice, through penance, and also from charity what good fruits accrue—

the yogi transcends all that, and, this knowing, the supreme place attains, the primeval."

CANTO 33

SRIMAD BHAGAVAD GITA CONTINUED

Rajavidyarajaguhya yoga: The way of royal knowledge, the royal secret

The Gracious Lord says:
"Now to you, this deep secret I will reveal, O unenvious,
along with knowledge, wisdom—knowing which, you will be
delivered from evil.
The sovereign knowledge, sovereign secret, sacred, this, supreme,
directly perceived, righteous, most easily practised, immortal.
Men who are faithless in this teaching, Parantapa,
not attaining me, return to the path of this world of death.[89]

By me is pervaded all this world: in unmanifest form;
in me are all creatures, and not I in them situated.
And not in me are the creatures founded—behold my divine yoga!
The support of beings and not founded in the beings, my soul the

---

89. Samsara is also the world of illusions

beings' source.

As in akasa[90] is founded, ever, the great wind going everywhere,
even so do all beings in me abide, reflect.

All beings, Kaunteya, into Prakriti pass, mine,
at kalpa's[91] end;
again, these, at kalpa's beginning, I send forth.

In my own nature resting, I emit, again and again,
this entire host of beings, helpless, in Prakriti's sway.

And not me do these acts bind, Dhananjaya;
as one indifferent I remain, unattached amidst these works.

Under my rule, nature gives birth to all the moving and the immobile;
because of this, Kaunteya, the world revolves.

Fools mock me, who have assumed a human body:
my supreme nature not knowing—the Great Lord of beings.

Of vain hopes, of vain deeds, of vain knowledge, witless;
and also of Rakshasas' and Asuras' deluded nature partaking.[92]

But great souls, Partha, abiding in divine nature, me
worship, single-mindedly,
knowing[93] the source of beings, imperishable.

Always hymning me, and striving, with stern vows;
venerating me with devotion, ever yoked, they worship.

And through the ritual of wisdom yet others sacrifice, worship me:
as one, as apart, as many, universe-faced.

I am the ritual; I am sacrifice; the ancestral oblation, I; I, the herb;
the mantra, I; I alone the clarified butter; I, the fire; I, the offering.
the father, I, of this world, the mother, supporter, grandsire;

---

90.   space, sky, cosmic ether. The fifth element
91.   see appendix: note on time
92.   those that mock me
93.   I am

That which is to be known, the purifier, *Aum*, Rik, Sama and Yajus, also.
The goal, sustainer, lord, witness, abode, refuge, friend;
the origin, dissolution, the ground, the receptacle, the seed eternal.
I give heat; I withhold and send forth rain;
immortality and death, also, and reality and unreality—I, Arjuna.

Veda-knowers[94] who drink soma and are cleansed of sin, worshipping me with sacrifices, pray for the passage to heaven[95];
they attain the holy world of Indra, enjoy in heaven divine pleasures of the gods.
They that enjoy the vast world of swarga, when their merit is exhausted enter the mortal world;
thus, followers of the triune faith, seekers after pleasure, come and go.

With no other thought, they who worship me:
constantly, assiduously, their welfare I support.

Those, too, other gods' devotees, who sacrifice with faith,
they, also, only to me, Kaunteya, sacrifice; [96]not by ancient law.
For, I of all sacrifices am the enjoyer, and the lord, as well;
but they do not know me truly; so, they fall.
Deva worshippers go to the Devas; to the manes go adorers of the Pitris;
To spirits go spirit worshippers; and my worshippers come to me.
A leaf, flower, fruit, water, who, to me, with devotion offers:
that devout offering, of a pious soul, I accept.
Whatever you do, what you eat, that which you sacrifice;
whatever penance you perform, Kaunteya—that make an offering

---

94. knowers of the 3 Vedas. The Atharva is often not included in Vaishnava texts
95. Swarga
96. though

to me.

Thus from good and bad consequences you will be free, the bondage of karma;

to renunciation and yoga mind yoked, liberated, me you will attain.

The same, I, to all beings: none to me is hateful, none dear;

but those who worship me with devotion, they are in me and I, too, in them.

If even a most sinful one worships me, single-mindedly,

a saint he must be considered, for he has rightly resolved.

Quickly he becomes a righteous soul, eternal peace attains;

Kaunteya, know for certain, never does my bhakta perish.

For, in me, Partha, those who refuge, even they of sinful birth,

women, vaishyas and sudras, they also attain the supreme goal.

How much more then, pure Brahmanas and devout Rajarishis;

this impermanent, unhappy world having found—worship me.

Your mind on me; be my devotee; to me sacrifice; to me bow;

to me you will surely come, thus devoted, your mind on me intent."

CANTO 34

SRIMAD BHAGAVAD GITA CONTINUED

Vibhutih yoga: The way of Brahman

The Gracious Lord says:
"Yet again, Mahabaho, hear my supreme word,
which to you, I, holding you dear, will tell, wishing your weal.
Neither the hosts of Devas my origin know, nor the Maharishis;
for I am the source of the Devas and the Maharishis, in every way.
Who me, un-born and beginningless, Great God of the world, knows—
undeluded, he, among mortals, from all sin liberated.
Intelligence, knowledge, clarity, patience, truth, self-control, calm;
joy, sorrow; being, non-being; and fear and also fearlessness;
non-violence, equanimity, contentment, austerity, charity, fame, infamy—
born, these dispositions of beings, from me alone, of different kinds.

The great sages, the seven,[97] and the earlier four[98]; the Manus, also:
of my being, mind, born—from these, this world's progeny.
This power and work of mine who knows in truth,
he to unfaltering communion is joined—of this, no doubt.
I, of all the source; from me everything begins;
this knowing, me the wise worship, with devotion.
In me their thought, to me given their life, awakening one another;
and speaking of me always; and contented and joyful.
To them, always devoted, worshipping with love,
I give buddhi yoga, by which to me they come.
For these, out of tenderness alone, I their darkness of ignorance,
dwelling in my Self, dispel—with the lamp of wisdom, resplendent."

Arjuna says:
"The supreme Brahman, the highest abode, absolutely pure, you are,
the Purusha eternal, divine, the primeval God, un-born, immanent,
say all the sages, Devarishi Narada, too,
Asita, Devala, Vyasa; and you yourself tell me so.
All this I hold true, which to me you say, Kesava;
not, surely, Lord, your origin the Devas know, nor the Danavas.[99]
Only you yourself your soul, with your soul, know, Purushottama,
Source of beings, Lord of beings, God of gods, Lord of the world.
Surely, you alone can tell fully of the divine powers,
with which glories these worlds, you, pervading, abide.
How can I know, O Yogin, you, with constant contemplation?
And in which various forms are you, Lord, to be thought of by me?
Expatiate again on your power and might, Janardana;
for, I am not satiated hearing your words, like nectar."

---

97. Marichi, Atri, Angiras, Pulastya, Pulaha, Kratu and Vasishta
98. Sanatkumara, Sanatana, Sananda and Sanaka
99. demons, sons of Danu

The Gracious Lord says:
"Yes, I will tell you my divine manifestations,
only those which are main, best of the Kurus—there is no end to my
extent.
I, the soul, Gudakesa, in all beings' hearts dwelling,
and I the beginning and middle, and, also, the end of beings.
Of the Adityas I am Vishnu; of luminaries, the Sun, radiant;
Marichi of the Maruts I am; of stars I am the Moon.
Of Vedas, the Sama Veda am I; of Devas, I am Vasavah;[100]
and of senses the mind, I; in beings I am consciousness.
Of Rudras, Sankara I am; Vittesha[101] among Yakshas and Rakshasas;
and of Vasus I am fire; Meru among mountains, I.
And of priests, the chief, I, know, Partha: Brihaspati;
of generals, I am Skanda; of lakes, I am the ocean.
of Maharishis, Bhrigu, I; of speech, the single syllable[102];
of sacrifices the Japa yagna[103] I am; of mountains, Himalaya.
The Aswattha among all trees, and of Devarishis Narada;
of Gandharvas, Chitraratha; among Siddhas, Kapila muni.
Ucchaisravas among horses, know me to be, nectar-born;
Airavata among elephant lords, and among men, the king.
Of weapons, I, the Vajra; of cows am I Kamadhenu;
and among progenitors, I am Kandarpa[104]; of serpents I am Vasuki.
and Ananta I am among Nagas; Varuna of ocean-dwellers, I;
and of the manes Aryaman am I; Yama of regulators, I.
And Prahlada I am of Daityas[105]; Time, of reckoners;
and of beasts, the king of beasts, I, and Vainata[106] of birds.

---

100. Indra
101. Kubera
102. Aum
103. chanting god's names
104. Kama, god of love
105. demons, sons of Diti
106. Vinata's son, Garuda

The wind among purifiers I am; Rama of weapon-bearers, I;
and among fish the crocodile I am; among rivers I am Jaahnavi.[107]
Of creations, the beginning and end, also the middle, I, Arjuna;
metaphysics of sciences, the dialectic of debaters, I.
Of alphabets, the *a* am I and of compounds, the dual;
I alone, eternal Time; the Creator, I, facing everywhere.
And death, taking all, I, and the source of what is to be;
fame, fortune, speech of women, memory, intelligence, fortitude,
patience.
The Brihat Saman, also, of hymns, the Gayatri among mantras, I;
of months, Margasirsa, I; of seasons, the flower-mine.[108]
of deceivers, gambling I am; the splendour of the splendid, I;
victory I am; effort I am; the goodness of the good, I.
Of Vrishnis, Vaasudeva[109] I am; of the Pandavas, Dhananjaya;
of sages Vyasa, also, I; of poets, the poet Usana[110].
The rod[111] of punishers I am; the strategy I am of conquest seekers;
and the silence, also, I am, of secrets; the wisdom of the wise, I.
And, further, what is the seed of all beings—that, I, Arjuna;
which can exist without me: there can be no being, moving or
unmoving.
No end is there to my divine manifestations, Parantapa;
All this that I have said are [112] illustrative of my infinite glories.
Whatever existence is glorious, graceful or powerful, surely,
that, know you, from a portion of my splendour is born.
Anyway, of what avail all these knowing, to you, Arjuna?
I pervade all this with an iota of myself, support the Universe."

---

107. Ganga
108. Spring
109. Vasudeva's son, Krishna
110. Sukr
111. Yama's danda, rod of chastisement
112. merely examples

SRIMAD BHAGAVAD GITA CONTINUED

Viswarupa darshana yoga: The way of the vision of the Cosmic Form.

Arjuna says:
"To bless me, the supreme, secret, Adhyatmam, you revealed;
with these words that you spoke, my bewilderment has gone.
Indeed, of the appearance and passing of beings, I have heard
extensively
from you, Lotus-eyed; and also your greatness, imperishable.
It is just so: what you have said about yourself, Parameswara—
I want to see your Form Divine, Purushottama!
If you think *That* can be seen by me, Lord,
Yogeswara, then, to me show your Self Eternal."

The Gracious Lord says:
"Behold, Partha, my forms, hundreds and thousands,
of many kinds, divine, vari-coloured and -shaped.

Behold the Adityas, Vasus, Rudras, the two Asvins, also the Maruts;
many previously unseen wonders, behold, Bhaarata.
Here, as one, the Universe, whole, see now, moving and immobile,
in my body, Gudakesa; and whatever else you wish to see.

But you cannot see me with just these your eyes;
I give you divine sight—behold my Sovereign Yoga."'

Sanjaya says:
'So saying, then, my king, the Great Lord of yoga, Hari,
shows Partha his supreme Form Divine.

Countless mouths, eyes; countless amazing visions;
countless divine ornaments; countless divine weapons raised;
divine garlands, raiment, wearing; with divine perfumes
anointed;
of all wonders, refulgent; infinite, faces everywhere.
In the sky, if a thousand suns were together risen,
light like that might perhaps compare with the splendour of that
Great Being.

There, as one, the Universe, whole, of divisions manifold,
sees, in the God of gods' body, then, the Pandava.
Then, he, wonderstruck, horripilating, Dhananjaya,
bowing his head before *God*, with hands folded, speaks.

Arjuna says:
"I see the Devas, O God, in your body, and also all the myriad
hosts of
beings,
Brahma, the Lord upon lotus-throne seated, and all the Rishis and

Uragas[113] divine.

With countless arms, bellies, mouths, eyes: I see your infinite form everywhere;

neither your end nor middle, nor again your beginning, do I see, Lord of the Universe, O universe-formed.

With crowns, maces, and chakras, a mass of light, everywhere shining, I see you, hard to look at, on all sides with irradiance of fire, blazing sun—immeasurable.

You, the imperishable, the supreme, [114]to be known; you are the universe's ultimate basis;

you, the changeless guardian of everlasting dharma; the eternal Purusha, you, I believe.

Without beginning, middle, end; of infinite power; endless armed; the Sun, Moon, your eyes,

I see you, burning fire your faces, with your refulgence this universe searing.

This space between heaven and earth, surely, is pervaded by just you, and the dishas all[115];

seeing this your astounding, dreadful form, the three worlds are terrified, Mahatman.

Ah, you these hosts of Suras enter; some, in fear, hands folded, give praise;

Svasti![116], so crying, the Maharishi, Siddha hosts adore you with hymns of mighty praise.

The Rudras, Adityas, Vasus, and these Sadhyas; the Viswas, the two Asvins and the Maruts, and the Usmapas[117];

the Gandharvas, the Yakshas, the Asuras, Siddha hosts gaze at you

---

113. serpents
114. the thing to be known
115. the four quarters, directions of the sky
116. hail, peace!
117. manes, ancestors

in wonder, also, surely, all.

Your great *Form*, many-mouthed, -eyed, Mahabaho, of many arms, thighs, feet,

many bellies, many fangs, horrible, seeing, the worlds tremble, as also I.

Sky-touching, ablaze, countless-hued, mouth agape, huge blazing eyes:

seeing only you, my inmost soul quails; no stability do I find, nor peace, O Vishnu.

And seeing your fearful, fanged mouths, like time's fire flaming,

the directions I do not know, nor find joy—be merciful, Lord of gods, abode of the universe!

And Dhritarashtra's sons, all, with the hosts of kings;

Bhishma, Drona, and that Sutaputra[118], also, with our side's main warriors, too,

into your fearful jaws, terrible with fangs, rush;

some stick between the teeth; are seen, heads crushed.

As many rivers' swift waters just towards the ocean flow,

even so, those heroes of the world of men enter your fiery mouths.

As a burning fire moths enter, to perish swiftly,

even so, to perish, these men, also, fly into your mouths at great speed.

You lick[119], devouring on all sides the worlds, entirely, with mouths aflame;

your brilliance covers all the universe, you lustre terrible, searing, O Vishnu.

Tell me who you are, of dreadful form; salutations to you, best of gods, have mercy!

---

118. Karna
119. them up, while

I want to know you, the first, for I do not understand what you do."

The Gracious Lord says:
"Time I am, world-waster, ancient—the world to annihilate, here, my mission;
even without you[120], no future have all these, arrayed hostile, the warriors.
So, arise, glory gain: defeating your enemies, enjoy a thriving kingdom;
by me alone these have been killed already—the instrument, only, become, Savyasachin[121].
Drona and Bhishma and Jayadratha and Karna, as also other warrior heroes,
by me slain already, you raze; do not be afraid—fight, you will conquer in battle, the enemies.'"

Sanjaya says:
'Hearing these words of Kesava, hands folded, trembling, Kiriti[122]
bows, again, speaks to Krishna, falteringly, in terror, prostrating.

Arjuna says:
"Rightly, Hrishikesa, by your praises is the world enraptured and fascinated;
Rakshasas, terrified, flee in all directions, and the Siddha hosts pay homage.
And why not worship you, Mahatman, who are greater than Brahma even, the first creator;
O Infinite, Lord of gods, Abode of the universe, you are deathless; real, unreal; and what is beyond that.

---

120. killing them
121. Arjuna was ambidextrous
122. Arjuna, the crown-wearer

You, the first God, the ancient Purusha; you are the supreme home of the universe;

you are the knower and the known[123] and the final resort—by you the universe is pervaded, infinite-formed!

Vayu, Yama, Agni, Varuna, Sashanka, and Prajapati[124], the great Grandsire—you.

Hail, hail to you, a thousand times, and again, yet again, hail, hail to you!

Obeisance in front, also from behind, to you; obeisance to you on every side, O All!

Of endless prowess, boundless compass, you; everything you suffuse, so you are all.

'My friend', so thinking, rashly, whatever I said, 'O Krishna', 'O Yadava', 'O friend', thus,

not knowing *This* your greatness, out of my carelessness or out of love,

and whatever slight, in jest, was shown, at sport, lying down, seated, while eating,

alone or, Achyuta, in the presence of others—all that forgive me, O Incomprehensible.

The father you are of this world, of the moving, the unmoving; you are its adored and loftiest guru;

none is your equal, how then any greater, in the three worlds, as well, O unequalled power?

So, bowing, prostrating my body, I worship you, Lord adorable;

as a father his son, a friend his friend, a lover his beloved, you must, Lord, suffer me.

---

123. knowable, that which is to be known
124. the Gods Wind, Death, Fire, Sea, Moon, Brahma

The never-before-seen, seeing, I rejoice, and with fear my heart is
shaken so;
so, Lord, your other form show me—be merciful, God of gods,
home of the universe!
crowned, with mace, disc in your hands—I want to see you, just
as before;
that same form, four-armed, assume, O thousand-armed, universe-
bodied!"

The Gracious Lord says:
"By my grace, to you, Arjuna, this *Form Supreme* was shown, through
my divine yoga—
resplendent, universal, infinite, primal, which none but you has seen
before.
Not by the Veda, sacrifice, learning, not by charity, and not by rituals,
not by fierce penance,
in this form can I, in the world of men, be seen by anyone but you,
O Kurupravira.[125]
Do not be afraid, nor confounded, seeing this terrible *Form*, like
this, of mine;
free from fear, with a glad heart, again, then, the same, this my
form, see.'"

Sanjaya says:
'Thus to Arjuna saying, Vaasudeva his own form shows again,
and comforts that terrified, becoming once more the gentle, beautiful
Mahatman.

Arjuna says:
"Seeing this human form of yours, gracious, Janardana,
now, I become calm, return to myself."

---

125. great hero of the Kurus

The Gracious Lord says:
"Most difficult to see, this form which you have seen, of mine;
the Devas, even, always, this form to see are keen.
Not through the Veda, not by tapasya, not through daana, nor yet
by yagnas,
can I like this be seen, as you have seen me.
But through devotion, singular, can I like this, Arjuna,
be known, seen, and, in truth, also entered into, Parantapa.

Who for me does work; I his supreme; my devotee, of attachment rid;
without hostility towards any of the living, he comes to me, Pandava."

CANTO 36

SRIMAD BHAGAVAD GITA CONTINUED

Bhakti yoga: The way of devotion.

Arjuna says:
"Thus, always yoked, those devotees who worship you,
and, again, those who do the Imperishable, the Unmanifest—of
these, which have yoga?"

The Gracious Lord says:
"On me fixing the mind, who, ever absorbed, me worship,
with devotion supreme endowed, them, I the best yogis consider.
But who the Imperishable, ineffable, unmanifest, worship, the
ubiquitous and inconceivable, highest, unmoving, permanent,
restraining all the senses, everywhere even-minded,
they attain me, surely—to the weal of all beings devoted.
The travail greater of them, on the Unmanifest whose minds are set;
for, the way of the Unmanifest is painfully by the embodied attained.
But who all karma to me renounce, on me intent,

with singular yoga, me, through meditation, worship:
of them, I, the deliverer from death, samsara's[126] sea,
become, quickly, Partha—on me whose minds are set.

On me alone your heart set; in me let your mind dwell:
you will live in me, surely, thereafter, beyond doubt.

If your mind you cannot fix on me, steadily,
through the practice of yoga, then, me seek to attain, Dhananjaya.
Abhyasa[127], even, if you cannot do, let my work your highest be;
for my sake, even, work doing, perfection you will find.
If even this you cannot do, in performing yoga for me refuge;
all karma's fruit renounce, then, with subdued mind.

Better, surely, knowledge than routine; than knowledge meditation is
superior;
than meditation, the sacrifice of karma's fruit—upon renunciation,
peace follows.

Without aversion towards any creature, friendly and compassionate,
only,
without 'mine', without 'I'; equal in pain, pleasure; forgiving;
contended always, the yogi, self-controlled, of firm resolve,
to me given heart, mind—who is my devotee, he is dear to me.
By whom the world is not disturbed; and the world does not disturb
him;
from exultation, anger, fear, agitation who is free, he, too, is dear
to me.
Independent, pure, competent, indifferent, free from pain;
who all endeavour has abandoned—my devotee, he is dear to me.

---

126. the mortal world of delusion, transmigration
127. the exercise, practice of yoga

Who neither exults nor dislikes; neither grieves nor desires;
good, evil, abandons—that devotee, he is dear to me.
And alike with enemy and friend; also, to honour, dishonour;
in heat, cold, joy, sorrow, the same; free from attachment;
equal in blame, praise; quiet, contented with anything;[128]
Homeless, of firm resolve—my devotee, a man dear to me.
But who this immortal dharma, as told, follow,
with faith, me the[129] goal, those devotees are very dear to me."

---

128. which comes
129. their

CANTO 37

SRIMAD BHAGAVAD GITA CONTINUED

Kshetra Kshetrajna vibhaga yoga: The way of discernment between the field and its knower.

Arjuna says:[130]
"Prakriti and Purusha, also; kshetra and kshetrajna, too:
these, I wish to know; knowledge and the known, Kesava."

The Gracious Lord says:
"This body, Kaunteya, the field it is called;
this who knows, he is called kshetrajna[131], by those who know.
And the kshetrajna, also, me in every field, Bhaarata;

---

130. this verse is not included in many versions. If it is, the number of slokas in the Bhagavad Gita becomes 701, instead of 700. As in Radhakrishnan's translation, I have not numbered it here.
131. knower of the field

of kshetra, kshetrajna[132], the knowledge: that, true knowledge, in
my view.
and what that field is, and what its nature, and what its
transformations, whence arisen,
and what *He*[133] is, and of what origin—that, in brief, from me hear.
By the rishis, variously, sung, in chhandas[134], diversely, distinctly;
and also in Brahma sutra[135] passages, logical, decisive.
The mahabhutas[136], ego, intelligence, and also the unmanifest;
the senses, ten, and the one[137], and five sense pastures;
desire, aversion; pleasure, pain; the organism, consciousness,
fortitude—
thus, the field, in brief, is described, with examples.

Humility, integrity, non-violence, patience, uprightness;
serving the guru, purity, stability, self-control;
for the objects of sensuality, aversion; lack of egotism; and also,
in birth, death, old age, sickness—pain, evil, seeing;
detachment, no clinging to son, wife, home, the likes;
and, always, even-mindedness to desired,[138] unwanted happenings;
and for me, through exclusive yoga, devotion abiding;
to solitary places resorting; distaste for gatherings of men;
in spiritual wisdom, constancy; the knowledge of truth's end seeing—
all this gyana is called; ignorance, what is other than this.

That which is known, I will tell you, which knowing immortality
is gained;

---

132. Swami Vireswarananda: matter and spirit
133. the kshetrajna
134. Vedic hymns
135. aphorisms of Brahman
136. the five elements
137. mind
138. and

beginningless, *It*, supreme Brahman; neither being, *That*, nor un-
being, it is told.
Everywhere, hands, feet: that; everywhere, eyes, heads, faces;
everywhere, ears—in the world everything enveloping, it dwells.
all the senses' qualities reflecting, of all the senses devoid;
unattached and also all-supporting; without gunas and experiencing
the gunas.

Outside and within the living, mobile and unmoving, too;
being subtle, that, imperceptible; and far and near, that.
And undivided, in beings, also, seemingly, divided, exists;
and as beings' support that is known, devourer and creator.
Of lights, also, that the light, beyond darkness, said to be;
knowledge, the known, gained through knowledge, in the hearts of
all seated.
Thus, the field and also knowledge and the known, told in brief;
my devotee, this knowing, to my being attains.

Prakriti[139] and also Purusha[140], know, are beginningless, both;
and transformations and also gunas, know—of Prakriti born.
Effect, cause, instrument, agency—Prakriti, it is told;
Purusha, of joy, sorrow's, experience, the cause, it is said.
For, the Purusha, dwelling in Prakriti, enjoys the Prakriti-born gunas;
the cause, attachment to the gunas: of its birth in good, evil wombs.
Witness and sanctioner, lord, experiencer, great God,
and also the supreme soul, it's told—in this body, the Purusha
transcendent.
Who thus knows Purusha and Prakriti, with the gunas,
whatever his life, he is not born again.

---

139. nature, the feminine principle
140. soul, the masculine principle

Through meditation, the Atman see, some, in the Atman, with the
Atman;
others, through samkhya yoga, and by karma yoga, others.
Yet others, not thus knowing, hearing from others, worship;
and they also, surely, transcend death by devotion to what they
hear.[141]

Whatever being is born, motionless or mobile—
from kshetra and kshetrajna's union: that know, Bharatarishabha.

Equally in all creatures abiding, the Supreme God,
amidst the perishing, imperishable, who sees, he sees.
For, the same God seeing, everywhere, omnipresent,
he injures not the Atman with the Atman, so attains the final goal.
And only by Prakriti, karma is done, in every way,
who sees, also that the Atman is act-less, he sees.
When the diversity of beings as situated in the one, he sees,
and also, therefrom, their spread, the Brahman he then becomes.
Beginningless, without attributes, this Paramatman, immortal,
though dwelling in the body, Kaunteya, neither acts nor is tainted.
As, being subtle, the ubiquitous ether is not tainted,
so also, everywhere located, in the body, the Atman is not stained.
As one sun illumines this whole world,
so, too, the kshetri[142] illumines this entire kshetra[143], Bhaarata.

Between kshetra, kshetrajna, thus, the distinction, with eye of
wisdom,
and the deliverance of beings from Prakriti, who know, they attain
the Supreme."

---

141. Sruti is also the Veda
142. embodied soul
143. field, universe

CANTO 38

SRIMAD BHAGAVAD GITA CONTINUED

Gunatrai vibhaga yoga: The way of the division of the three gunas.

The Gracious Lord says:
"Again, the highest I will tell you, of wisdoms the best wisdom;
this knowing, the sages, all, to final perfection from here passed.
This wisdom resorting to, my nature attaining,
at creation, even, they are not born, and not during the dissolution
disquieted.
My womb great Brahma, into which the seed cast I;
to birth all beings, from that, come, Bhaarata.
In all the species, Kaunteya, whatever forms take birth,
of them, great Brahma the womb, I the seed-giving father.
Sattva, rajas, tamas, these gunas, Prakriti-born,
bind, Mahabaho, into the body the dweller imperishable.

Of these, sattva, being pure, is illumining, health-giving,
through attachment to happiness binds, and through attachment to

knowledge, O sinless.

Rajas has passion's nature, know, from craving, attachment, sprung;
it binds, Kaunteya, with addiction to action, the embodied.
But tamas, ignorance-born, know, deludes all the living;
through rashness, sloth, stupor, it binds fast, Bhaarata.
Sattva to happiness binds; rajas to activity, Bhaarata;
but, wisdom shrouding, tamas to rashness, it is told.

Rajas and tamas subduing, sattva prevails, Bhaarata;
Rajas, the same, over sattva and tamas; tamas, even so, over sattva
and rajas.

When through all doors[144] of this body, light radiates,
knowledge: then, know, sattva surely waxes.
Greed, activity, undertaking karma, disquiet, desire—
when rajas increases, these prevail, Bharatarishabha.
Darkness and inactivity, neglect and also delusion:
when tamas increases, these prevail, joy of the Kurus.

Now, while sattva waxes, if to dissolution[145] the embodied goes,
then, worlds of the highest sages, taintless, it gains.
In rajas, death finding, among those addicted to karma it is born;
and if dissolved during tamas, in dark wombs it is born.
Of virtuous karma, it is told, sattvik and pure the fruit;
while rajas' fruit is sorrow, and darkness the fruit of tamas.

From sattva arises knowledge; and from rajas only greed;
heedlessness, delusion, from tamas come, and also ignorance.
Upwards go those founded in sattva; midway remain the rajasas;
those steeped in the vile guna, go downwards, the tamasas.

---

144. of perception
145. death

No other agent than the gunas, when the seer sees,
and what is beyond the gunas knows, to my being he attains.
These gunas transcending, triune, which spring from the body, the embodied,
from birth, death, old age, pain, is liberated, immortality gains."

Arjuna says:
"What signs of one who these three gunas has transcended, Lord?
what his deportment, and how does he the three gunas transcend?"

The Gracious Lord says:
"Light and activity and, even, delusion, Pandava,
he does not shun, when they arise, nor, when they cease, long for.
As if indifferent seated, by the gunas who is not moved;
the gunas act: this knowing, who is still, unwavering.
The same in joy, sorrow, contented; equal[146] a clod, stone, gold;
the same to the pleasant, unpleasant; calm; equal to blame of himself,
to praise.
In honour, disgrace, the same; equal to a friend, an enemy;
all endeavours who has renounced—gone beyond the gunas, he is
said to have.
And me who, with unfailing yoga of devotion, serves,
he, these gunas transcends, for becoming Brahman is fit.
For, Brahman's abode I, immortal and imperishable;
and of eternal dharma, and absolute bliss."

---

146. for him

CANTO 39

SRIMAD BHAGAVAD GITA CONTINUED

Purushottama yoga: The way of the Supreme Person.

"Root above, branches below, the Aswattha[147], they tell of, imperishable, of which the chhandas are the leaves; who knows this, he is a Veda knower.

Below and above, extend its branches, guna-nourished,
sense-objects for twigs;
and below its roots stretch, binding in karma the world of men.
Not its form[148], either, is here perceived, not its end, nor beginning,
and neither its foundation.
This aswattha, deep-rooted, with the mighty sword detachment severing,
then, let that condition be sought, going where, there is no returning

---

147. peepul tree
148. true form

again;
only to that original Purusha surrender, from whom this ancient
world came.
Without pride, delusion; quelled, the sin attachment; spiritual always;
rid of desire;
liberated from the dualities, called pleasure, pain—the undeluded go
to that state eternal.

Not that, the sun illumines, not moon, not fire;
who go there do not return—that abode supreme, mine.

A mere particle of myself, a living spirit, eternal[149],
into the world of jivas the senses, mind the sixth, founded in nature,
draws.[150]
A body when assuming, and also when leaving it, the Lord
takes all these, leaving, even as the wind scents from their places.

Ears, eyes, and touch, taste, and also smell
dwelling in, and mind, he the sense-objects enjoys.
Departing or dwelling, as also experiencing, while associated with
the gunas,
the deluded do not see[151]; they see who have wisdom's eye.
Striving yogis also, *That* see, in themselves situated;
even striving, the unrestrained do not see it, unawakened ones.

That lustre of the sun, which the whole world illumines,
that in the moon, and that in fire—that light, know, is mine.
And the earth entering, creatures I support with energy;
and nourish all plants, the moon becoming, sapful.

---

149. becoming
150. to itself
151. the indweller; *It*

I the fire become, in creatures' bodies dwell;
prana, apana,[152] uniting with, digest food, the four kinds.
And, of all, I in their hearts am lodged; from me, memory, wisdom,
and their loss;
and in all the Vedas, I alone, the known; Vedanta's author, and also
the Veda-knower, I.

And two persons in this world: the mortal, and also the immortal;
mortal, all creatures; the unchanging, the immortal called.
But the highest being, another, Paramatman called,
who the three worlds enters, sustains them, imperishable *God*.

Because the mortal I transcend, and even the immortal surpass,
so, I am, in the world and in the Veda, known as Purushottama.[153]
Who, thus, undeluded, knows me, Purushottamam,
he, knowing everything, worships me with all his being, Bhaarata.

Thus, this most secret Shastra has been taught by me, O sinless;
this, understanding, wise he becomes; and all his duty done,
Bhaarata."

---

152. inward and outward breaths
153. the Supreme Person

CANTO 40

SRIMAD BHAGAVAD GITA CONTINUED

Daivaasurasampad vibhaga yoga: The way of the distinction between the divine and the demonic qualities

The Gracious Lord says:
"Fearlessness, essential purity, in wisdom's yoga steadfastness,
charity and self-control and sacrifices, sacred study, austerity, rectitude;
non-violence, honesty, without anger, renunciation, not critical, mercy
for the living, non-covetousness, gentleness, modesty, free of caprice;
vitality, forgiveness, fortitude, purity, without malice, without
hubris—
the wealth of one with divine nature born, Bhaarata.
Ostentation, arrogance and great conceit, anger, and also violence,
and ignorance—the endowments of those born, Partha, demonic.

The divine inheritance liberates, the demonic binds, it is thought;
grieve not: you to wealth divine are born, Pandava.

Two kinds of being in the world, the divine and also the demonic;
the divine at length have been spoken of; of the demonic, Partha,
from me hear.

Neither what to do nor what not to, they know, the demonic;
no purity and neither conduct, no truth, in them found.
Unreal, un-founded, they say, the world, *God*-less,
of continuing origin, nothing other than lust-begotten.
To this view cleaving, lost souls, of small minds,
come forth, of savage deeds, for the destruction of the world, its
enemies.
To lust surrendered, insatiable; by hypocrisy, arrogance, conceit,
possessed;
through delusion seizing fell designs, they act, sworn to evil.
And to cares boundless, ending in death, surrendered;
sensual enjoyment the highest[154]: that this is all convinced;
by desire's bonds, hundreds, bound; to lust, anger, yielded;
they strive, in order to gratify their desires, unscrupulously, great
wealth to amass.
'This, today, by me gained; this heart's desire I will satisfy;
this there is, and this, too, I will have[155]: more wealth.
By me [156]slain that enemy; and I will kill others, too;
the lord, I; I, the enjoyer; successful, I, strong, happy;
rich, well-born I am; who else is [157]like me?
I will sacrifice, give charity, rejoice!'—thus, by ignorance deluded.

By countless fancies confounded, in delusion's net ensnared;
addicted to satisfying lusts, they fall into foetid hell.

---

154. aim
155. in future
156. already
157. there

Smug with conceit, obdurate, with wealth's pride intoxicated,
they sacrifice,[158] in name sacrifice, with ostentation, disregarding precept.
To egotism, force, pride, lust and rage given:
me, in their own and other's bodies, hating, these envious ones.
These, haters vicious, vilest of men, in samsara,
I cast repeatedly only into inauspicious, demon wombs.
Fiendish wombs finding, the deluded, birth after birth,
me far from attaining, Kaunteya, then devolve to the basest state.

Triune, of this hell, the gates, which destroy the soul—
lust, anger and greed; so, these three abandon.
From these the man who is liberated, Kaunteya, gates to darkness, three,
does what is good for his soul, then reaches the supreme condition.

Who scriptural law forsakes, acts by desire's dictates,
he does not perfection attain, not happiness, not the highest goal.
So, let the Shastras[159] be your authority: what may be done, what is forbidden, to determine;
knowing what the scripture's laws declare, your karma you must do, here[160]."

---

158. only
159. scriptures: the Vedas, the Vedanga/Upanishads, the 18 great Puranas. The Ramayana and Mahabharata are traditionally only considered Itihasas, histories
160. in this world

CANTO 41

SRIMAD BHAGAVAD GITA CONTINUED

Sraddhatrai vibhaga yoga: The way of the divisions of the three kinds of faith

Arjuna says:
"Who scriptural laws forsake, but worship, with faith—
what is their condition, Krishna, sattva, rajas or tamas?"

The Gracious Lord says:
"Threefold is the faith of the embodied, of their nature born—
sattvik, rajasik and also tamasik; and hear about it.

In concord with his nature everyone's faith is, Bhaarata:
of his faith's nature, man—what his faith is, that indeed is he.

The sattvikas worship the Devas; the rajasas do yakshas and rakshasas;
pretas and other kinds of bhutas, tamasik men worship.

Not ordained by the shastras, violent austerities those men perform,
to pride, egotism yoked, by lust, passion's force possessed.
Torturing the elements in the body, the senseless,
and me, also, dwelling in the body—these, know, of demonic
resolve.

The food, too, by all liked, is of three kinds;
sacrifice, austerity, charity, as well; of the divisions of these, hear.
Longevity, vitality, strength, health, happiness, love, which augment;
succulent, soft, nourishing, tasty—foods dear to the sattvik.
Bitter, sour, salty, hot, pungent, harsh, burning—
foods by the rajasika liked: pain, grief, disease causing.
Cold, insipid, putrid, stale and what is
refuse and also unclean—food to tamasas dear.

By those expecting no reward, the sacrifice which by scriptural decree
is offered,
exclusively as a duty, mind absorbed, that is sattvik.
But aiming for its fruit, and also for display, what
is offered, best of Bhaaratas, that sacrifice, know, is rajasik.
Against law[161], where no food is given, without mantras, without
dakshina,[162]
of faith devoid, the yagna is tamasik, they say.

Of the gods, the twice-born, gurus, the wise, worship; purity,
rectitude,
continence and non-violence—bodily austerity is called.
Speech which no offence causes, and which is truthful, pleasant and
benign,
and also regular recitation of the Veda—verbal austerity is

---

161. scriptural
162. the fee paid to priests

called.
Mental calm, gentleness, silence, self-control,
purity of feeling, all these—austerity of mind are called.
With faith transcendent undertaken, this threefold penance, by men
who wish for no gain, devoted—sattvik is called.

For respect, honour, reverence, the austerity, and which with
ostentation
is performed, that, here, is deemed rajasik: fleeting, impermanent.
From foolish belief, the self torturing, the penance that is practised,
or to others meaning harm—that tamasik is said to be.

'To give is a duty': thus[163], to give charity, without[164] obligation,
and at a proper time and place—that charity is sattvik regarded.

But that which to be reciprocated, or aiming
for its fruit, in future,
and given grudgingly—that charity rajasik is considered.
at the wrong place, time: that charity given, and to the
undeserving,
without respect, contemptuously—that tamasic is told.

Aum tat sat—this is declared Brahman's triune name:
Brahmanas, by this, and the Veda and Sacrifice, were created of old.
So, *Aum*, thus uttering, acts of sacrifice, charity, austerity are
performed, scripture-enjoined, always by Brahmavadis.[165]
Tat: thus[166], without desiring their fruit, acts of sacrifice, penance
and various deeds of charity are performed, by liberation seekers.

---

163. thinking
164. expecting
165. expounders, followers of the Veda
166. they say

Reality and goodness, *sat* for these is used;
for laudable deeds, as well, the word *sat*, Partha, is used.
In sacrifice, austerity and charity, constancy—*sat* is called;
and also karma done for *that*, *sat*, indeed, is named.

Without faith, oblation[167], gifts[168], austerity performed, and whatever[169] done —
asat it is called, Partha, and is of no account hereafter nor here."

---

167. offered
168. given
169. else

CANTO 42

SRIMAD BHAGAVAD GITA CONTINUED

Moksha Sannyasa yoga: The way of renunciation, liberation

Arjuna says:
"Of sannyasa[170], Mahabaho, the truth I wish to know,
and about tyaga[171], Hrishikesa[172], separately, Kesinisudana.[173]

The Gracious Lord says:
"Desire-impelled karma abandoning, as sannyasa the seers understand;
all karma's fruit sacrificing, call tyaga, the knowing.

'Renounced as an evil, all karma,' say some thinkers;
'Acts of sacrifice, charity, austerity must not be abandoned,' and so

---

170. renunciation
171. relinquishment
172. Krishna
173. Krishna, Vishnu: slayer of the demon Kesin

say others.

Decisively hear from me about this tyaga, best of the Bhaaratas;
for, relinquishment, Purushavyaghra[174], of three kinds is declared.

Works of sacrifice, charity, these are not be relinquished but surely
performed;
sacrifice, charity and also austerity are purifiers of the wise.
But even these works done, attachment leaving and fruit,
as duty—this, Partha, my decided view, the best.
But with religious duty, the renunciation of [175]karma is not proper;
through delusion its abandonment, tamasik is declared.
Painful: so being, a duty; bodily suffering fearing, if it is
abandoned—
he, performing merely a rajasik relinquishment, surely does not
relinquishment's fruit gain.

When just because it ought to be, a prescribed duty is done, Arjuna,
leaving attachment, and also its fruit, that relinquishment is
considered sattvik.
Neither averse to unpleasant karma, nor to pleasant work attached—
the tyagi: of sattva possessed, intelligent, doubts dispelled.

Surely, impossible, for the embodied to renounce karma entirely;
but who the fruit of karma relinquishes, he a tyagi is said to be.

Unpleasant, pleasant and mixed: of three kinds karma's fruit,
accruing to non-relinquishers after death, but not to sannyasis,
ever.
These five, Mahabaho, causes, learn from me,
in the samkhya doctrine mentioned, for the accomplishment of all

---

174. best of men; tiger among men
175. such

karma.

The place and also the doer; and the various actions;
the many and different endeavours; and also destiny, the fifth of
these.
With body, speech, mind, whatever karma a man undertakes,
whether just or the opposite, these five are its causes.
This being so, who, yet, as the only doer himself
sees, from ignorance, he does not see: a foolish one.

Who no egotism has, whose intellect is not defiled,
though he kills these men, he neither slays nor is bound.[176]

Knowledge, the known, the knower: the triple impulse to karma;
the instrument, action, the agent, these the threefold conjunction of
karma.
Knowledge and action and agent, of three kinds only, the distinctions
of the gunas,
said to be, in the philosophy of the gunas; respectively, hear, of
these, also.

In all beings, the knowledge by which the *One*, imperishable, is seen,
undivided in the divided, that wisdom, know, is sattvik.
But separately, which knowledge, diverse entities, of various kinds,
perceives, in all creatures—that knowledge, know, is rajasik.
But what, as the whole, to one effect clings, illogically:
The unreal and trivial, that tamasik is said to be.

Which, ordained, without attachment, without attraction or aversion
is done,
by one not desiring its fruit, that karma is sattvik called.
But that karma, prompted by desire, or again, with egotistical

---

176. by what he does

motives,
done, with great strain, that is rajasik called.
For consequence, loss, violence: disregard, and for capability;
through delusion the karma undertaken, that tamasik is called.

Free from attachment, not egotistical, of fortitude, zeal, possessed;
by success, failure, unmoved—that doer is sattvik called.
Passionate, keenly wanting karma's fruit, greedy, violent-minded,
impure;
by elation, dejection moved—that agent rajasik is deemed.
Unstable, feral, obstinate, deceitful, spiteful, lazy;
morose and procrastinating—that doer tamasik is said to be.

To the divisions of intellect and also fortitude, according to the gunas,
threefold, listen,
told fully, separately, Dhananjaya.

Action and inactivity and what to do, what not to do, fear,
fearlessness,
bondage and liberation the intellect which knows, that, Partha, is
sattvik.
By which dharma and adharma, and what to do and also what not to,
is erroneously known—that intellect, Partha, rajasik.
Adharma as dharma that which regards, in darkness shrouded,
and all things perversely—that intellect, Partha, tamasik.

The fortitude by which one rules mind, life breaths, senses' functions,
through yoga unwavering—that firmness, Partha, sattvik.
But the fortitude by which to dharma, kama, artha one clings, Arjuna,
through attachment to the desire for gain[177]—that firmness, Partha,
rajasik.

---

177. the fruit of karma

By which sleep, fear, sorrow, dejection and also arrogance
a fool does not leave—that obduracy, Partha, tamasik.

But of happiness, now, the three kinds, hear from me,
Bhatarishabha—
long practice through which enjoyed, and sorrow's end attained.
That which at first like poison, at the end like amrita,[178]
that joy sattvika, it's told, of the soul's intelligence[179], serene, born.
From contact between objects of sensuality, [180]the senses, which arises,
at first like amrita,
but at the end is like poison—that joy rajasik is called.
And which joy, both at first and at the end, binding in delusion the
soul,
and which from sleep, sloth, heedlessness arises—that tamasik is
deemed.

There is not on earth or, again, in heaven among the gods,
a being that is free from these Prakriti-born three gunas.
Of Brahmanas, Kshatriyas, Vaishyas and Sudras, Parantapa,
their duties are divided, by their innate qualities.
Serenity, self-control, austerity, purity, forbearance, and also
uprightness;
knowledge, wisdom, belief in God—a Brahmana's duties, of his
nature born.
Valour, boldness, fortitude, skill, and even in war not fleeing;
generosity and lordliness—a Kshatriya's duties, of his nature born.
Farming, tending the cow, commerce—a Vaisya's karma, nature
born;
karma of the essence of service, a Sudra's, also of his nature born.

---

178. nectar
179. in the sense of realisation, enlightenment
180. and

Each to his own duty devoted, man attains perfection;
in his own karma absorbed, how perfection one attains, that hear.
From Whom beings arise; Who all this pervades:
through one's own karma Him worshipping, perfection a man
achieves.

Better in one's own dharma, imperfectly, than in another's dharma,
immaculately;
by one's naturally ordained karma doing, one incurs no sin.
The karma one is born to, Kaunteya, though flawed, one must not
abandon;
for, all endeavours by faults, even as fire by smoke, are clouded.

Unattached, his intelligence, everywhere; mind conquered; desire
gone;
to inaction's perfection supreme, through renunciation, he comes.
Finding this perfection, Brahman, also, how he finds learn from me,
in brief, Kaunteya, that consummation of knowledge, transcendent.
With intellect, pure, endowed, and firmly the mind restraining,
sound and objects of sensuality leaving, and likes, dislikes,
rejecting;
living in solitude, eating little, controlling speech, body, mind;
in dhyana yoga[181] absorbed, always, in dispassion sheltering;
egotism, force, arrogance, lust, anger, possessions,
forsaking, without 'mine', peaceful—to become Brahman, he is fit.

Becoming Brahman, clear-souled, he neither sorrows nor desires;
alike to all beings, for me devotion he finds, supreme.
Through devotion, me, he knows, how much and what I am, in
truth;
then, me truly knowing, he enters into me.

---

181. meditation

Even[182] all karma always doing, in me sheltering,
through my grace, he attains the eternal state, immutable.
Through thought, all karma to me renouncing; me the ultimate;
to buddhi yoga resorting, on me your heart constantly fix.

On me your thought[183], all difficulties by my grace you will cross;
but if you, from pride, do not listen, you will perish.
If, ego indulging, 'I will not fight', you think:
Vain this resolve of yours—your nature will compel you.
By your own nature-born karma, Kaunteya, bound,
what you do not want to do—being deluded—even that you will do,
helplessly.

God in all beings' hearts, Arjuna, dwells,
deluding[184] all creatures, as[185] upon a contrivance, with maya.
To Him alone for refuge go, with all your heart, Bhaarata;
by his grace, supreme peace you will find, the place eternal.

Thus, to you, has the wisdom, more secret than secrets, been told by
me;
reflect on it fully, and do as you wish.

Of all the most secret, again, hear: my supreme word;
since dearly loved you are by me, so I tell you, for your good.
[186]Mind on me; to me be devoted; to me sacrifice; to me prostrate;
to me you will surely come—truly, I promise you, who are dear to
me.

---

182. while; though
183. fixing your thought on *me*
184. whirling, spinning, turning around
185. if mounted
186. fix your

All duty abandoning, to me, the sole refuge, come;
I will liberate you from every sin, do not grieve.

This, you must not to the in-austere, nor the devotionless, ever,
nor one who has no wish to listen, tell, nor me who derides.
Who this supreme secret to my devotees teaches,
the highest devotion to me performs, to me surely comes, without doubt.
Nor is there among men anyone who to me does dearer service than he;
nor will there be than he, to me, another, dearer on earth.
And who studies this sacred conversation of ours,
through knowledge's sacrifice, by him, I adored will be—this, my view.
Faithful and without cavil, who just listens, that man:
he, too, liberated, to blessed worlds attains, of those of virtuous deeds.

Has this been heard, Partha, by you, with singular thought?
has your ignorant delusion been dispelled, Dhananjaya?"

Arjuna says:
"Dispelled my delusion, understanding gained, through your grace, Achyuta;
I stand firm, doubts gone; I will do as you say[187]."'

Sanjaya says:
'So, I, between Vaasudeva and Partha, great souls,
this converse heard, wondrous, making my hair stand on end.
Through Vyasa's grace heard I this secret, supreme
yoga, from the Lord of yoga, Krishna, directly, as he told it himself.

---

187. your bidding

O king, I remember, again and again, this wonderful conversation
of Kesava, Arjuna, sacred, and thrill with joy, over and over.
And as I repeatedly recall that *Form*, most awesome, of Hari,
great my astonishment, O king, and I tremble with joy again and
again.

Where the Lord of yoga, Krishna, where Partha the bowman:
there, fortune, victory, prosperity, eternal justice—this, my belief!'"

Aum shanti shanti shanti.
Hare Krishna.[188]

---

188. Appendix for the Bhagavad Gita at the end of this volume

CANTO 43

BHISHMA VADHA PARVA

Vaisampayana said, "Sanjaya says, 'Upon seeing Dhananjaya once again take up his arrows and Gandiva, the mighty Pandava maharathas utter a tremendous shout. And those heroes, the Pandavas and the Somakas, and those who followed them, filled with joy, blow their sea-born conches. And drums, and pesis, and karkachas, and cow-horns are beaten and blown together, to make a loud uproar.

And then there come the Devas, with Gandharvas and the Pitris, and the hosts of Siddhas and Charanas, wanting to witness the sight; and a host of most blessed Rishis accompany Indra of a hundred sacrifices leading them, to witness that great slaughter.

Then, seeing the two armies, that look like two oceans, ready for the encounter and restlessly moving, Yudhishtira Dharmaraja takes off his coat of mail and puts aside his excellent bow, and quickly alighting from his chariot, with joined hands, goes quietly on foot towards his Pitamaha Bhishma, facing the east, towards the direction where the enemy army stands.

Seeing this, Arjuna hastily alights from his chariot and follows

Yudhishtira, accompanied by his brothers. And Krishna also follows; and the chief kings of his army, filled with anxiety, also follow Yudhishtira.

Arjuna says, "What are you doing, O king, that abandoning your brothers, you go on foot, facing east, towards the enemy?"

Bhima says, "Where are you going, O king of kings, having cast off your armour and weapons, towards the enemy warriors, leaving your brothers?"

Nakula says, "You are my eldest brother, O Bhaarata; seeing you go this way, I am afraid. Tell us, where do you go?"

Sahadeva says, "When these vast and powerful forces are by our side ready to fight, where do you go, O king, in the direction of our enemies?"'

Sanjaya continues, 'Yudhishtira of restrained speech says nothing but walks on towards the enemy army. The high-souled, wise Krishna smilingly says to them, "I know his purpose. He will fight the enemy only after having paid his respects to all his superiors: Bhishma, Drona, Kripa and Salya.

It is heard in histories of olden times that he who fights against those that are his superiors, after having paid his respects, according to dharma, to his preceptors, those revered in years, and his kinsmen, is sure to be victorious in battle. This is my view as well."

When Krishna says this, loud exclamations can be heard among the ranks of Dhritarashtra's son, but the Pandava army remains perfectly still. Seeing Yudhishtira, the heroic warriors of Dhritarashtra's son speak among one another, "This one is a wretch of his race. It is clear that he is coming in cowardly terror to Bhishma's side. Yudhishtira, with his brothers, is seeking Bhishma's protection.

When Dhananjaya protects him, and Bhima, and Nakula, and Sahadeva also, why does the eldest son of Pandu come here in fear? Though renowned through the world, he could never have been born in the Kshatriya varna, for he is weak and his heart is filled with fear at the prospect of battle."

Then those soldiers all praise the Kauravas. Rejoicing with cheerful hearts, all of them wave their cloths. All the fighting men there then censure Yudhishtira and his brothers and Krishna too. The Kaurava army, having disdained Yudhishtira, becomes perfectly still. What would this king say? What would Bhishma say in reply? What would proud Bhima say, and what Krishna and Arjuna? What, indeed, has Yudhishtira to say?

Both the armies are filled with great curiosity. Meanwhile, penetrating the hostile vyuha bristling with arrows and spears, Yudhishtira, surrounded by his brothers, walks quickly towards Bhishma. Seizing his feet with his two hands, the royal son of Pandu speaks to Shantanu's son who stands there ready for battle.

Yudhishtira says, "I salute you, O invincible one. We will wage war against you. Grant us your leave to do so. Give us also your blessing."

Bhishma says, "Had you not thus come to me in this battle, I would have cursed you, O Bhaarata, to bring about your defeat. I am gratified, my son. Fight then and let victory be yours. O son of Pandu, whatever else you desire, may you obtain it in battle. Ask us also for any boon you want and if it is in my power to give, then you will not be defeated.

A man is the slave of wealth, but wealth is no one's slave. This is the truth and I have been bound by the Kauravas with their wealth. It is for this reason, Kurunandana, that I speak these words like a eunuch. Bound am I by the Kauravas with wealth. Beyond battle, what do you desire?"

Yudhishtira says, "Wise Pitamaha, keeping my welfare in mind, from day to day, look after my interests. Do battle, however, for the Kauravas. This is my prayer to you."

Bhishma says, "Rajan, what help can I give you in this? I shall, of course, fight for your adversaries. Tell me plainly what you have to say."

Yudhishtira says, "Bowing to you, I ask you, O Pitamaha, how shall we vanquish you who are invincible in battle? Tell me this for my benefit, if you see any good in it."

Bhishma says, "I do not, O son of Kunti, see the warrior who, even if he were the Lord of the Devas himself, can defeat me in battle when I fight."

Yudhishtira says, "My salutations to you, Pitamaha! And that is why

I ask you this. Tell us how your own death may be achieved by your enemies in battle."

Bhishma says, "I do not see the man who can quell me in battle. The time of my death has also not yet arrived."'

Sanjaya continues, 'Saluting him again, Yudhishtira accepts Bhishma's words with a bow of his head. And that Mahabaho, along with his brothers, goes towards the chariot of Acharya Drona amidst all the soldiers who watch him. Saluting Drona and walking around him in pradakshina, the king speaks to that invincible warrior.

Yudhishtira says, "With your leave, Acharya, I will fight with dharma, and thus permitted by you, O sinless one, I will defeat all my enemies."

He now goes to get the blessings of Acharya Kripa, who says, "If, having resolved to fight, you had not come to me, I would have cursed you, O king, for your complete overthrow. A man is the slave of wealth, but wealth is no one's slave. This is so true. Since I have been bound with wealth by the Kauravas, I must fight for them. I therefore speak like a eunuch in asking you: besides battle, what do you desire?"

Yudhishtira says, "Sorrowfully, I ask you, Acharya, to listen to what I say." Saying this, the king, greatly troubled and confused, stood silent.'

Sanjaya continues, 'Understanding, however, what he intended to say, Gautama Kripa says, "I cannot be killed, Rajan. Fight and triumph. I am gratified by your coming. Rising every morning I will pray for your victory. I say this to you sincerely."

Hearing Kripa's words, and paying him due respect, Yudhishtira goes to where the ruler of the Madras stands. Saluting Salya and walking around him in pradakshina he says to that invincible warrior, words that are for his own benefit.

Yudhishtira says, "With your leave, invincible one, I will fight without incurring sin, and so defeat my valiant enemies."

Salya says, "If, having resolved to fight, you had not come to me thus, I would have cursed you to be routed in battle. I am gratified and honoured by you. Let it be as you wish. I grant you leave: fight and be victorious. Speak, O Kshatriya, what do you need? What shall I give you?

Under these circumstances, beyond battle, what do you wish? A man is the slave of wealth but wealth is no one's slave. This is the truth. I have been bound with wealth by the Kauravas, and so I speak to you like a eunuch: I will grant you your cherished desire. Besides battle, what do you wish?"

Yudhishtira says, "Think daily of what is for my greatest good. Fight, according to your pleasure, for the sake of my enemy. This is the boon that I seek."

Salya says, "Given these circumstances, tell me how I can support you? I must, of course, fight for your enemy, having been bound by the Kauravas with their wealth."

Yudhishtira says, "O Salya, the boon I want is the one I sought during the preparations for the war: that you must weaken the energy of the Suta's son Karna during battle."

Salya says, "I grant you your wish, son of Kunti. Go, fight at your pleasure. I shall ensure your victory."'

Sanjaya continues, 'Having obtained the permission of his maternal uncle, the ruler of the Madras, Yudhishtira, surrounded by his brothers, comes out of that vast army.

Krishna goes up to Radha's son on the battlefield. And on behalf of the Pandavas, Krishna says to Karna, "I have heard, Karna, that because of your hatred of Bhishma you will not fight. Come to our side, O Radheya, and remain with us as long as Bhishma is not slain. After Bhishma is killed, you can fight for Duryodhana, if you have no preference for any of the sides."

Karna says, "I will not do anything that is offensive to Dhritarashtra's son, Kesava. Devoted to Duryodhana's good, know that I have offered up my life for him." Krishna stays silent, and rejoins the Pandavas.

Amidst all the fighting men, Yudhishtira loudly exclaims, "He who will choose us now shall be our ally!"

Seeing them, Yuyutsu says cheerfully to Yudhishtira Dharmaraja, "I will fight under your banner in war, against the sons of Dhritarashtra, if you will accept me, sinless one!"

Yudhishtira says, "Come, all of us will fight against your foolish brothers, Yuyutsu. Krishna and we all say to you: we accept you, Mahabaho, fight for my cause. It appears that both the thread of Dhritarashtra's line as also his funeral rites rest upon you. Splendid prince, accept us who receive you. The wrathful and evil-minded Duryodhana will cease to live.'"

Sanjaya continues, 'Yuyutsu, abandoning the Kauravas, your sons, crosses over to the army of the Pandavas, to the beating of drums and cymbals. Yudhishtira, again joyfully puts on his radiant coat of armour.

Those bulls among men mount their respective chariots and they organise their troops in battle formation as before. They cause hundreds of drums and cymbals to be sounded. They roar like lions. Seeing those tigers among men, the sons of Pandu, on their chariots, the allied kings, with Dhrishtadyumna and others, once more set up shouts of joy.

Observing the nobility of the Pandavas, who had paid due honour to those that were deserving of it, all the gathered kings praise them. And the kings talk with one another about the friendship, the compassion, and the kindness to kinsmen, displayed at the proper time by those high-souled ones. *Excellent! Excellent!* These are the words spoken everywhere, together with eulogies about those famed heroes.

As a result of this, the minds and hearts of everyone present are drawn to them. The Mlechchas and the Aryas there, who saw or heard of what the Pandavas had done, all weep, deeply moved. Those great warriors, of terrific tejas, cause large drums and pushkaras by the hundreds and thousands to be sounded; they blow their milk-white conches.'

CANTO 44

Bhishma Vadha Parva continued

Dhritarashtra says, 'When the legions of both my side and that of the enemy were thus arrayed, who strikes first, the Kauravas or the Pandavas?'

Sanjaya says, 'Hearing the words of his elder brother, your son Dussasana advances with his troops, with Bhishma at their head. The Pandavas, led by Bhima, also advance with joyful hearts, wanting battle with Bhishma. Leonine shouts, the noise of krakachas and the blare of cow-horns, and the sound of drums and cymbals, rise on all sides. The fighting men of the enemy assail us, and we too charge against them with loud shouts. The ensuing uproar is deafening.

In that terrible encounter, the vast armies of the Pandavas and the Dhartarashtras shudder for that reverberance of conches and cymbals, like forests shaken by the wind. The clamour of the hordes of kings, elephants and horses, rushing against one another in that evil hour, is as loud as that of tempestuous oceans.

And when that din, making one's hair stand on end, arose, Mahabaho Bhima begins to roar like a bull. Bhima's roars resound above the clamour of conches and drums, the grunts of elephants, and the leonine shouts of the warriors. Indeed, the shouts of Bhima transcend the neighing of the thousands of horses in both armies.

Hearing Bhima roaring like thunderclouds, his voice like the report of Sakra's thunder, your warriors are terrified. At those roars of that Kshatriya, the horses and elephants all urinate and excrete as other animals do at the roar of the lion. Thundering like a deep mass of clouds, and assuming an awful form, Bhima falls upon your sons.

Duryodhana, Durmukha and Dussaha, and that maharathika Dussasana, and Durmarshana, and Vivimsati, and Chitrasena, and the mighty maharatha Vikarna and also Purumitra, and Jaya, and Bhoja, and the valiant son of Somadatta, shake their splendid bows like masses of clouds streaked with flashes of lightning.

Drawing from their quivers long arrows resembling snakes that have just cast off their skins, they surround that mighty archer charging towards them, covering him with flights of arrows like the clouds shrouding the sun.

The five sons of Draupadi, and the majestic warrior Saubhadra, and Nakula, and Sahadeva, and Dhrishtadyumna of Prishata's race, attack those Dhartarashtras, rending them with arrows like mountain peaks with bolts of lightning. In that first encounter of the awe-inspiring twang of bowstrings and their flapping against the leather gloves of the fighting men, no warrior, on either side, retreats.

Bharatarishabha, I saw the lightness of hand of Drona's disciples, in particular those who, shooting countless arrows, always succeed in finding their target. And the sound of bowstrings is unceasing, and the blazing arrows flare through the air like meteors falling from the sky.

All the other kings stand as silent spectators witnessing that dread encounter of kinsmen. Those maharathikas remember the old injuries sustained at one another's hands, and wrathfully strive in battle, Bhaarata, always challenging each other aloud.

The two armies, of the Kauravas and the Pandavas, teeming with elephants, horses and chariots, look exceedingly beautiful on the battlefield like figures in a painting. The other kings all take up their bows. And the Sun himself is veiled by the dust raised by the soldiers.

They attack one another, at the heads of their respective troops, at the command of your son. The uproar of the elephants and the horses of those kings dashing into battle mingles with the leonine shouts of the warriors and the blast of conches and the sounds of drums. The tumult of that ocean, having arrows for its crocodiles, bows for its snakes, swords for its tortoises, and the bounding leaps of warriors for its gale, resembles a real surging sea. And kings in thousands, commanded by Yudhishtira, along with their forces, fall upon your son's legions.

The encounter between the warriors of the two armies is intense, and no difference can be seen between the men of the two warring sides, whether battling, or retreating in disarray, or rallying again to the fight. In that terrific and dreadful melee, Pitamaha Bhishma is most radiant, dominating that teeming host."

CANTO 45

BHISHMA VADHA PARVA CONTINUED

Sanjaya says, 'On the morning of that fateful day, the war that mangled the bodies of many kings begins. And the deafening shouts, the leonine roars of the Kauravas and the Srinjayas, both wanting victory in battle, resound through earth and sky. And a tumultuous pandemonium is heard mingled with the flaps of leather gloves and the blast of conches. Like roaring tigers, the men shout against one another.

The sound of bowstrings stretched by gloved hands, the heavy tread of foot soldiers, the furious neighing of horses, the falling of sticks and iron hooks on the heads of elephants, the clash of weapons, the jangle of the bells of elephants as they rush against one another, and the rumble of chariots like thunderclouds, mix to produce a clamour that makes one's hair stand on end.

And all the Kaurava warriors, reckless of their very lives and their intentions cruel, charge, with standards raised, against the Pandavas. Bhishma himself, taking up a bow that resembles the rod of Yama, charges Dhananjaya on the field. Arjuna of flaming tejas, seizes up the celebrated Gandiva, and rushes against Ganga's son. Both these tigers among the Kurus are determined to kill each other.

The mighty son of Ganga, despite a searing attack on the son of Pritha, cannot make him falter. And so also Arjuna cannot make Bhishma waver in battle.

The great archer Satyaki rides against Kritavarman. The battle duel these two is fierce and makes the hair of onlookers stand on end. With loud yells, Satyaki strikes Kritavarman, and Kritavarman smites Satyaki, and each weakens the other. Pierced all over with arrows, these maharathas shine like two blossoming kimsukas in spring bedecked with blood flowers.

The awesome young Abhimanyu battles Brihadbala. Soon, however, the ruler of Kosala cuts off the standard and kills the of Subhadra's son. Abhimanyu wrathfully pierces Brihadbala with nine arrows, and with two more that parantapa cuts down Brihadbala's standard, and with yet another, kills one of the protectors of his chariot wheels, and his charioteer as well. And the two continue to exhaust each other with vicious arrows.

Bhima faces your son Duryodhana, that maharathika, proud and pompous, who had so harmed the Pandavas. Both princes are tigers among men and maharathas. And on the battlefield, they cover each other with showers of arrows. And seeing these high-souled warriors fight, all are amazed.

Dussasana charges maharathika Nakula and pierces him with countless barbs which can pierce an enemy's very vital organs. Laughing, the son of Madri severs his adversary's standard and bow, and strikes him with twenty-five fine arrows. In the ferocious encounter, your powerful son kills Nakula's horses and cuts down his standard.

Durmukha assails the mighty Sahadeva, covering him with a storm of shafts. The heroic Sahadeva fells Durmukha's charioteer with a razor-tipped arrow. Both men, irrepressible in fight, attempt to strike terror into each other with vigorous shafts.

King Yudhishtira himself faces the ruler of the Madras, who breaks

Yudhishtira's bow in his hands. Throwing aside the riven bow, Kunti's son takes up a stronger bow and one that can loose arrows more swiftly. With wrathful cries and unerring aim, he covers the Madra king with deadly shafts.

Dhrishtadyumna, O Bhaarata, rushes against Drona in wrath, and the great Drona breaks the unyielding bow of the high-souled prince of Panchala that always finds its deadly mark. He looses a terrible shaft that is like the rod of Yama; this barb pierces the body of the Panchala prince. Swiftly snatching up another bow and fourteen arrows, the son of Drupada stabs Drona with a fluent volley. In high rage, they battle fiercely on.

The impetuous Sankha encounters Somadatta's son who is equally impulsive in battle and, asking him to stop and fight, shoots him in his right arm. The son of Somadatta strikes Sankha through the shoulders. The duel that follows between these two proud Kshatriyas soon becomes as ferocious as an encounter between the Devas and the Danavas.

Maharatha Dhrishtaketu of immeasurable soul and great wrath storms against Bahlika, himself an embodiment of rage. With a leonine roar, Bahlika draws blood from Dhrishtaketu with a shower of keen shafts. The king of the Chedis swiftly pierces Bahlika with nine savage arrows. Like two incensed elephants, they duel in thunderous rage.

They confront each other, appearing even like the planets Angaraka and Sukra.

The feral Ghatotkacha encounters the brutal and mighty rakshasa Alambusha like Sakra facing Bala in battle. And Ghatotkacha, O Bhaarata, pierces the rakshasa with ninety keen shafts.

Alambusha strikes Bhima's son copiously with his straight and wild wooden barbs. Lacerated, they shine like the mighty Sakra and the powerful Bala during the ancient Devasura yuddha.

Sikhandin rides against Drona's son Aswatthaman, only to be deeply wounded with a long arrow, making him tremble. Sikhandin also strikes Drona's son deep with an elegant shaft, and they continue in this vein with various kinds of barbs, plain and exotic.

Virata, the Senapati of a vast legion, swiftly advances to face Bhagadatta in battle, and covers Bhagadatta with a shower of arrows like the clouds showering rain upon a mountain breast. But Bhagadatta, that lord of the earth, swiftly envelops Virata with his own arrow cloud like thunderheads might the risen sun.

Kripa, son of Saradwat, rushes against Brihadkshatra, king of the Kaikeyas, and shrouds him in a barrage of arrows. Brihadkshatra also rains arrows down on the incensed son of Gautama. And having killed each other's horses and cloven off each other's bows, those two soon find themselves deprived of their chariots. In rage, they approach each other to fight with swords. And dreadful and unparalleled is the duel which ensues between them.

King Drupada wrathfully attacks Jayadratha, king of the Sindhus, who is cheerfully awaiting battle. Jayadratha stabs Drupada with three arrows and Drupada pierces him with a brace of barbs in return. And the battle between them, also, is awesome and fierce, and brings great satisfaction to all onlookers for it resembles a conflict between Sukra and Angaraka.'

CANTO 46

BHISHMA VADHA PARVA CONTINUED

S anjaya says, 'Bhaarata, I will now describe to you the clashes between hundreds and thousands of foot soldiers, who abandon all restraint. Here the son does not recognise the father, or the father the son of his loins; the brother does not acknowledge the brother, nor the sister's son his maternal uncle. The maternal uncle does not acknowledge the sister's son, the friend not the friend.

The Pandavas and the Kauravas fight as if possessed by demons. Some mighty warriors fall with their chariots shattered. The axle rods of chariots break as they clash against shafts, and the spikes of chariot yokes against spikes of chariot yokes.

And some warriors unite together to fight others that are similarly together, all wanting to kill. Some chariots, obstructed by other rathas, cannot move. Lofty elephants with rent temples fall upon other elephants, rending one another in many places with their tusks. Others encountering massive tuskers with arched howdahs and standards on their backs, and trained to fight with their tusks, scream in agony.

Disciplined by training and goaded by pikes and hooks, elephants not in rut attack those in demented musth. And some leviathans, encountering those in rut, run in all directions, screeching like cranes. Many towering mastodons, well-trained, and with juice trickling down from rent temples and mouth, lacerated by swords, spears and arrows in their vital parts, trumpet awfully and fall dead, shaking the earth. Some utter frightful cries and run in all directions.

The broad-chested, powerful foot soldiers that protect the elephants are armed with pikes and bows, and bright battle-axes, and with maces and clubs mounted with iron spikes, and short arrows, and lances, and brightly polished swords; they, too, charge in all directions seeming determined to kill each other. And the swords of brave fighters, steeped in human blood, shine brightly.

And the sound of the swords of Kshatriyas as they whirl and fall upon the vital parts of enemies is sickening. The heartrending wails of the hosts of fighting men, crushed with maces and clubs, and cut down with well-tempered swords, and pierced with the tusks of elephants, and grained by tuskers, calling upon one another, can be heard, Bhaarata, ah, like the cries of those cursed to hell.

Horsemen, on flying chargers with outstretched tails resembling the plumage of swans, dash against one another. And hurled by the riders, long-bearded golden barbs, polished and sharp, fall like snakes. Some heroic horsemen, on agile coursers, leaping high, hew off the heads of warriors in their chariots.

Here and there a maharatha, finding a host of cavalry within range, decimates them with arrows. Many incensed elephants bedecked with trappings of gold, and looking like newly-risen clouds, trample the horses underfoot to bloody pulp. Some elephants, struck on their frontal globes and flanks, and mangled by spears, scream horribly.

Massive tuskers, in the bewildering commotion, fling down and crush horses along with their riders; and some, overthrowing horses and riders with the points of their tusks, roam about smashing chariots with their standards.

Some majestic bull elephants, bursting with a surfeit of energy and gushing temporal juice, kill horses and their riders with trunks and legs. Nimble arrows, polished and pointed, so like snakes, fall upon the heads, the temples, the flanks, and the limbs of these great beasts.

And polished javelins, meteoric, hurled by noble arms, fall on all sides, piercing coats of mail in scarlet bursts and penetrating the bodies of men and horses. Many, drawing polished swords from sheaths made of the skins of leopards and tigers, cut down the enemy with fell strokes. Others, though themselves attacked and with gashed bodies, angrily fall upon their foes with swords, shields and axes.

Some tuskers, dragging down and hurling chariots and their horses with their trunks, begin to wander in all directions, exhorted by the cries of those behind them. The men, some pierced by spears, some dismembered by battle-axes, and some crushed by elephants and others trodden down by horses, and some slashed by chariot wheels, and others by axes, cry out plaintively to their kinsmen.

Some call out to their sons, and some to their fathers, and some to brothers and other kinsmen. Some call to their maternal uncles, and some to their sister's sons. And some call out to others, on this frightful battlefield.

Countless warriors lose their weapons, or have their thighs broken. Others with arms torn off or with gaping wounds, wail loudly, desperately wanting to live. And some, with a little remaining strength, tortured by thirst, and lying gasping on the field of battle, on the bare ground, beg for water. And some, soaking in pools of blood, O Bhaarata, censure themselves and your sons gathered for battle.

Brave Kshatriyas, who having injured one another, do not abandon their duels or cry out. Instead, lying on the battlefield, they roar with joyful hearts, and in great fury, they bite their own lips. They glower at one another with faces rendered fierce by the furrowing of their brows. And still others, enduring the pain caused by arrows and ghastly wounds, with strength and tenacity, remain perfectly still and silent.

Other maharathikas, deprived of their own chariots, and flung down and wounded by elephants, ask to be taken up on to the chariots of others. Many look glorious with their wounds like blooming kinsukas. In all the legions, countless cries can be heard, rising into the heavens.

And in this awful war that destroys Kshatriyas, the father kills the son, the son kills the father, the sister's son cuts down the maternal uncle, and the uncle the sister's son. Friend fells friend, and all kinsmen one another. Such is the slaughter in this conflict of the Kauravas with the Pandavas.

In that monstrous war of no mercy, the forces of the Pandavas, approaching Bhishma, begin to waver.

Mahabaho Bhishma, with his silver standard graced with the sign of the palmyra with five stars, sitting on his majestic chariot, shines like the full moon under Meru's peak.'

CANTO 47

BHISHMA VADHA PARVA CONTINUED

Sanjaya says, 'After most of the morning of that terrible day passes in that awesome engagement, so destructive of the most magnificent men, Durmukha and Kritavarman, and Kripa, and Salya, and Vivimsati, urged by your son, ride to Bhishma to protect him. Shielded by those five maharathas Bhishma penetrates the Pandava host.

The palmyra standard of Bhishma glides through the Chedis, the Kasis, the Karushas, and the Panchalas. With broad-tipped arrows, that Kshatriya razes the enemy, cutting off heads, and shattering chariots with their yokes and standards. Bhishma seems to veritably dance on his chariot as it courses along its path.

Elephants, struck by him in their vital parts, shriek dismally. Abhimanyu, mounted on his chariot yoked to excellent tawny steeds, charges at Bhishma's chariot in fury. With his standard adorned with a golden karnikara tree, he draws near Bhishma and the five maharathas who protect him. Abhimanyu strikes the standard of the palmyra-bannered warrior with a keen shaft, and hotly engages Bhishma and his defenders.

Piercing Kritavarman with one arrow, and Salya with five, Abhimanyu draws blood from the great patriarch with nine more. And with one shaft brilliantly shot from his bow drawn to its fullest stretch, he cuts off his adversary's gold standard.

With another barb, piercing through every defence, he severs the head of Durmukha's sarathy from his body; with another, he breaks Kripa's gold bedecked bow. With a flurry of jagged shafts, this young maharatha strikes so furiously, he also appearing to dance the while.

And seeing the lightness of his hand, the Devas are gratified. The deadly accuracy of Abhimanyu makes the other maharathas, headed by Bhishma, look upon him as being as much an archer as Arjuna himself. Sounding a twang even like that of the Gandiva, while stretched and re-stretched, his bow seems to revolve like a circle of fire.

Bhishma charges forward and pierces Arjuna's son with nine seething barbs; in turn, Abhimanyu burns the standard of that warrior of great tejas, while Bhishma strikes Abhimanyu's charioteer.

And Kritavarman, and Kripa, and Salya also, shoot Abhimanyu, but he stands before them like the Mainaka mountain. Though surrounded by these maharathas of the Dhartarashtra army, he continues to rain a ceaseless storm of arrows upon them.

He obstructs their mighty weapons with his tumult of arrows, and showering Bhishma with them, he sends up a joyful roar. And in this battle with Bhishma, the strength of Abhimanyu's handsome young arms is wonderful to see. Despite this prowess, Bhishma also looses his arrows at him. But Subhadra's son wards them off, and fells Bhishma's standard with nine arrows. And seeing that wondrous feat, the soldiers there set up a loud shout.

Bedecked with jewels, Bhishma's lofty silver standard, bearing the device of the palmyra, falls to the ground. Seeing this, the proud Bhima sets up a great roar to cheer on the son of Subhadra.

The irresistible Bhishma now invokes powerful devastras to appear. The Pitamaha of immeasurable soul envelops Abhimanyu with thousands of mystic arrows. Ten great archers and maharathas of the Pandavas swiftly advance in their chariots to protect the youthful hero - Virata with his son, and Dhrishtadyumna of Prishata's race, and Bhima, the five Kekaya brothers, and Satyaki.

As they recklessly fall upon him, Bhishma pierces the prince of Panchala with three sizzling shafts, and Satyaki with ten. And with one winged, razor like arrow, shot from his fully drawn bow, he cuts off Bhima's standard. That standard made of gold and bearing the device of a lion, plunges from Bhima's chariot. Bhima enraged stabs Bhishma with three arrows, Kripa with one, and Kritavarman with eight.

And Uttara, the son of Virata, seated on a tusker with upraised trunk, attacks the king of the Madras. Salya, however, succeeds in checking the unparalleled speed of that prince of elephants racing towards his chariot. Uttara wrathfully sets his leg upon the yoke of Salya's chariot, and kills his four magnificent horses.

Salya remains in that chariot, and hurls an iron spear like a venomous snake at Uttara. The lance pierces Uttara's coat of mail and he falls dead from his elephant's neck, with the hook and the lance loosened from his grasp. And Salya takes up his sword and, leaping down from his chariot, severs the enormous trunk of that mighty elephant. His coat of mail pierced all over with a torrent of arrows, and his trunk hacked, the elephant cries out and falls dead.

Salya hastily climbs into Kritavarman's splendid chariot. Seeing his brother Uttara slain and seeing Salya with Kritavarman, Virata's son Sweta blazes up in fury, like a fire on which ghee is poured. Stretching his majestic bow that resembles the bow of Sakra himself, the mighty Sweta rushes forward to kill Salya.

Surrounded on all sides by a host of chariots, Sweta moves towards Salya's chariot raining arrows at him. And seeing him charging like an incensed elephant, seven of your maharathas, Rajan, surround him on all sides, to save the king of the Madras from a certain death.

Those seven warriors are Brihadbala, king of the Kosalas, and Jayatsena of Magadha, and Rukmaratha, the gallant son of Salya, Vinda and Anuvinda of Avanti, and Sudakshina, king of the Kambojas, and

Jayadratha, lord of the Sindhus and the kinsman of Brihadkshatra. The stretched bows of these high warriors, decorated with many colours, look like flashes of lightning in the clouds. And they all rain unceasing arrows on Sweta's head like the clouds tossed by the wind that pour rain on the mountain breast at the end of summer.

That brilliant Kshatriya, enraged, strikes their bows with seven swift broad-headed arrows, and continues to assail them. And in the same moment as their bows are riven, they all instantly take up other bows. And they shoot seven arrows at Sweta.

And again that Mahabaho of immeasurable soul breaks these other bows with seven shafts. Their anger mounting, the maharathas whose bows have been riven, seize seven lances, roar loudly, and cast those seven javelins at Sweta's chariot. Those fiery spears, which course through the air like comets, with the sound of thunder, are all cleaved by seven uncanny shafts before they can reach that most excellent warrior, master of the most fearful astras.

Taking up a missile which can pierce every part of the body, he unleashes it at Rukmaratha. And this powerful weapon, with a force greater than that of a thunderbolt, pierces Rukmartha's body and he falls unconscious in his chariot. His charioteer fearlessly carries him away, unconscious, before the eyes of all.

Taking up six other arrows adorned with gold, Mahabaho Sweta cuts off the standard-tops of his six adversaries. That chastiser of enemies, piercing their horses and charioteers, and raining ceaseless barbs upon these six fighting men, moves towards the chariot of Salya. And seeing that commander of the Pandava forces moving swiftly towards Salya's chariot, a loud uproar of anxious cries rises up in your army, O Bhaarata.

Your valiant son, with Bhishma at the head of his forces, and supported by noble Kshatriyas and vast troops, advances towards Sweta's ratha, and rescues the Madra king from the jaws of death. A hair-raising battle erupts between your soldiers and those of the enemy, one in which chariots and elephants are all embroiled in bedlam. The old Kuru Pitamaha rains a flurry of arrows upon Abhimanyu and Bhima, and the maharathika Satyaki, and upon the ruler of the Kekayas, and Virata, and Dhrishtadyumna, and upon the Chedi troops.'

CANTO 48

BHISHMA VADHA PARVA CONTINUED

Dhritarashtra says, 'When that brilliant archer Sweta advances towards Salya's chariot, what do the Kauravas and the Pandavas do, Sanjaya? And also what does Bhishma do? Tell me, I entreat you.'

Sanjaya says, 'Rajan, hundreds and thousands of noble Kshatriyas, all brave maharathas, placing Sikhandin in the vanguard, and displaying their strength to your royal son, want to rescue Sweta. And they move swiftly towards Bhishma's chariot, bedecked with gold, to kill that meridian warrior. The battle that follows is hair raising to watch.

I will describe to you that astonishing and chilling battle between your troops and those of the enemy. Bhishma empties many chariots of their maharathas by sloughing off their heads with a barrage of arrows. Imbued with energy equal to that of the sun, he shrouds the very sun with his shafts; he eliminates his enemies that encircle him, like the rising sun dispels the surrounding darkness.

The son of Shantanu shoots hundreds of thousands of arrows that claim the lives of countless Kshatriyas. He cleaves the heads of countless valiant fighting men. Elephants cased in spiked armour fall like mountains peaks struck by lightning.

Chariots are seen entangled with one another. One chariot lies upon another chariot, and one horse upon another. And reckless chargers bear the corpses of daring young riders, hanging from their saddles with their bows still in their lifeless hands.

With swords and quivers as yet attached to their bodies, and loosened coats of mail, hundreds of men lie dead on the ground, sleeping on beds worthy of heroes. Charging against one another, falling down and rising up again, and charging once again, they fight hand to hand. Wounded deep by each other, they reel on the battlefield.

Incensed elephants rush in all directions, and hundreds of maharathas are slaughtered. Chariots and their riders are crushed on all sides. And they fall upon each others' chariots, and are killed by the arrows of another. A maharatha can be seen to plunge from a height, his charioteer also having been slain.

A thick pall of dust rises, and it is only by the twang of a hostile bow that the presence of an opponent is known to an embattled fighter. From the pressure upon their bodies, warriors gauge their enemies. And they fight on with arrows, guided only by the sound of bow-strings.

The very hiss of the arrows shot by the fighting men at one another cannot be heard. And so loud is the sound of drums that it seems to pierce the ears. In that tumultuous uproar making the hair stand on end, the name of the warrior called out as he shows his prowess, cannot be heard. The father does not recognise the son of his loins.

As a wheel breaks, or the yoke is torn off, or a horse killed, the maharatha is flung from his chariot, along with his sarathy. Many daring fighters, deprived of their rathas, are seen to take flight. Some are killed, while others are struck in their very vitals: but none escape unscathed, when dreadful Bhishma attacks the enemy.

In that burning, awesome fray, Sweta slaughters a vast number of the Kauravas. And he kills hundreds upon hundreds of noble princes with his inexorable arrows; in every direction, he smashes the bows and cuts off the heads of hundreds of great warriors, their arms decked with angadas.

Sweta annihilates maharathas and splinters chariot wheels, the chariots themselves, and shreds standards both small and large and precious, and numerous horses, and a multitude of men. As for me, fearing Sweta, and abandoning the magnificent Bhishma, I retreated from the battle and now stand before you, Rajan.

And all the Kauravas, though armed for war, desert Bhishma, and stand like spectators beyond the range of arrows. Joyful in the hour of widespread gloom, that tiger among men, Bhishma, alone stands unshakeable like Meru.

Melting the enemy, like the sun at winter's end, he stands in the shining radiance of his chariot like the irradiant sun. And that great archer shoots a tempest of arrows and mows down the enemy.

And being slaughtered by Bhishma in that fierce fight, the enemy warriors break ranks and flee from him, as if from a dire inferno. Encountering the prodigious Sweta, Bhishma alone stands calm and undaunted. Devoted to the cause of Duryodhana, he begins to ravage the Pandava warriors. Uncaring for his life, which is so precious to all men, he fearlessly destroys the Pandava army.

Seeing Sweta strike down the Dhartarashtra legions, your father Bhishma charges him. Sweta covers Bhishma with a fusillade of arrows. And Bhishma also cloaks Sweta in a shroud of shafts. And roaring like two bulls, they fall upon each other, like colossal maddened elephants or two raging tigers.

Thwarting each other's weapons with their own, those bulls among men, Bhishma and Sweta, fight, each to kill the other. In a single day the angry Bhishma can obliterate the Pandava army, if Sweta did not protect it.

Seeing Sweta holding off the Pitamaha, the Pandavas are filled with joy, while your son becomes despondent. Supported by his allies, Duryodhana garners his troops and wrathfully attacks the Pandava host.

Momentarily turning away from the son of Ganga, Sweta begins to energetically slaughter your son's forces like a violent wind uprooting trees. Beside himself with wrath, having routed your army, the son of Virata advances again towards Bhishma.

And those two high-souled maharathas, both blazing arrows, battle each other like Vritra and Vasava of old. Drawing his bow to the fullest stretch, Sweta pierces Bhishma with seven shafts. Bhishma swiftly checks his adversary like an incensed elephant curbing an angered rival.

Sweta, who delights the Kshatriyas with his prowess, strikes Bhishma, who in return stabs him with ten shining barbs. Yet that glorious warrior stands still like a mountain. Sweta gores Shantanu's son with twenty-five shafts, filling all those around them with wonder.

Smiling and licking the corners of his mouth, Sweta shatters Bhishma's bow into ten pieces with ten perfect arrows. Then aiming a plumed iron barb, he cleaves the palmyra on top of Bhishma's standard.

Seeing the standard of Bhishma cut down, your sons think that Sweta has killed the Pitamaha. The elated Pandavas, thinking the same, blow their conches. Seeing the palmyra standard of the great Bhishma laid low, a furious Duryodhana urges his troops into battle. And they all converge to protect Bhishma who was in danger.

To both his forces and to bystanders, the king says, "Either Sweta will die today, or Bhishma!"

Hearing Duryodhana, his maharathas swiftly advance to protect the son of Ganga. With great alacrity, Bahlika and Kritavarman, and Kripa, and Salya also, O Bhaarata, and the son of Jarasandha, and Vikarna, and Chitrasena, and Vivimsati surround Bhishma, and shower Sweta with a high storm of arrows.

That celebrated Kshatriya adroitly checks those angry opponents, displaying his own dexterity. Stopping them like a lion might a herd of elephants, Sweta smashes Bhishma's bow with a singing cloud of arrows.

Bhishma takes up another bow and pierces Sweta, Rajan, with feathered barbs. Sweta animatedly strikes Bhishma with numerous shafts before everyone's eyes.

Duryodhana is distraught seeing Bhishma, that most excellent Kshatriya, thwarted in battle by Sweta, and your whole army is alarmed.

And all who see great Bhishma, mangled by Sweta's arrows, believe him to be dead.

Enraged, seeing his standard fallen and the Dhartarashtra army checked, Bhishma looses a refulgent volley at Sweta. But Sweta, magnificent maharatha, wards off Bhishma's arrows, and once again rives the Pitamaha's bow with a thick and heavy shaft.

Beside himself, Bhishma flings aside that bow and takes up another bigger and stronger one. Aiming seven flat, whetted arrows, he kills Sweta's four horses with four, cuts down his standard with two, and with the seventh, provoked beyond all measure, cuts off his charioteer's head.

The stricken Sweta jumps down from his chariot. Bhishma attacks him from all sides with dense, relentless broadsides of arrows. Bleeding from many wounds, Sweta leaves his bow on his abandoned chariot and seizes up an occult golden lance.

Taking up that fierce astra which resembles the rod of Yama and could slay Death itself, Sweta furiously cries to Bhishma, "Stop and watch me, best of men!" And that great young hero hurls the serpentine lance, displaying his valour on behalf of the Pandavas. Loud exclamations arise among your sons, as they see that awesome missile in all its splendour. And launched by Sweta's arm, that ayudha like a snake that has just cast off its skin, falls like a meteor from the sky. Without the slightest quiver of fear, Bhishma cuts the shining thing that blazes through the air into nine fragments with eight winged arrows.

All your forces roar in jubilation. The son of Virata, seeing his lance of power desiccated, stands shocked, trembling suddenly, uncertain like one touched by the arrival of his final hour. But his rage still high, Sweta masters himself, and smiling, takes up a recondite mace to kill Bhishma. His eyes ruby red, and even more like a second Yama now, he assails Bhishma like a swollen river dashing against rocks.

So knowing of the strengths of others, knowing that Sweta's gada is impossible to thwart, Bhishma leaps down from his chariot to escape that sorcerous weapon. Sweta whirls the heavy mace in fury and casts it at Bhishma's chariot like Siva himself. And the mace, intended for Bhishma's destruction, reduces his chariot, its standard and its charioteer, its horses and its shaft, all to ashes. On seeing great Bhishma reduced to fighting on foot, many maharathas like Salya rush to his rescue.

Mounting another chariot and rather dejectedly stretching his bow, Bhishma slowly advances towards Sweta; he hears a celestial voice, an asariri in the skies, fraught with his own good, which says, "Mahabaho Bhishma, strive without losing a moment. This is the hour fixed by Brahma for your victory over this one."

Hearing those words spoken by the celestial voice, Bhishma joyfully moves towards Sweta to kill him. Seeing maharatha Sweta fighting on foot, many great Pandava warriors rush to his rescue: Satyaki, and Bhimasena, and Dhrishtadyumna of Prishata's race; and the five Kekaya brothers, and Dhrishtaketu and Abhimanyu of great energy.

And seeing them, Bhishma, along with Drona and Salya and Kripa, arrests them all like a mountain stopping the force of the wind. When all the high-souled warriors of the Pandava side are thwarted, Sweta cleaves Bhishma's bow with a sword. Throwing aside that bow, the Pitamaha, having heard the celestial message, decides it is time to slay Sweta.

Though baffled by Sweta's genius, maharatha Bhishma seizes up another bow, as splendid as that of Sakra himself, and instantly strings it. He advances towards Sweta alone, though the prince is surrounded by those tigers among men with Bhima at their head.

Seeing Bhishma near, Bhima pierces him with sixty shafts. But Bhishma checks Bhima, Abhimanyu and the other maharathas with awesome astras. He also strikes Satyaki with a hundred arrows, Dhrishtadyumna with twenty and the Kekaya brothers with five.

Holding up all those great archers with his own deadly fire, the Pitamaha advances purposefully towards Sweta. Invoking an inexorable weapon of Death, Bhishma sets it to his bowstring. And that winged shaft, imbued with the force of the Brahmastra, is watched by the Devas and Gandharvas, and Pisachas and Uragas, and Rakshasas at the moment Bhishma releases it.

In an eruption of blood, that blazing ayudha plunges cleanly through

Sweta's coat of mail and his body and passes into the earth, with a flash akin to lightning. Like the setting sun that divests the earth of light, the astra passes through Sweta, carrying away his life. Thus slain in battle by Bhishma, we see that young tiger among men fall to the ground like a crumpled mountain peak.

And all the maharathas of the Kshatriya race on the Pandava side lament. Your sons and all the Kauravas are elated. Seeing Sweta slain, Dussasana dances in joy on the battlefield to the loud music of conches and drums.

When that magnificent archer, that jewel of battle, is killed by Bhishma the other Pandava archers led by Sikhandin tremble in fear. Arjuna and Krishna slowly withdraw the men for the nightly rest. Bhaarata, the forces of both sides withdraw with frequent roars. And the Partha maharathas enter their quarters downcast, thinking of the dreadful slaughter of their splendid commander.'

CANTO 49

BHISHMA VADHA PARVA CONTINUED

Dhritarashtra says, 'When Sweta is killed, how do the Panchalas, those mighty archers, on the Pandava side, respond? Hearing that Sweta has been slain, what transpires between his comrades and his opponents that retreat before them?

Sanjaya, hearing of our victory, your words please me. My heart feels no shame in remembering our wrongdoing. The Pitamaha of Kuru's race is ever triumphant and devoted to us.

As for Duryodhana, having provoked war with that intelligent son of his uncle, on one occasion he looked for the protection of the sons of Pandu as he was anxious and afraid of Yudhishtira. At that time, abandoning everything, he was despondent. In view of the skill of the Pandavas, and thwarted and ensnared on all sides, Duryodhana for some time showed honourable behaviour, and placed himself under their protection.

Why, therefore, Sanjaya, has Sweta, who was loyal to Yudhishtira, been killed? Indeed, this magnificent prince has been hurled down to patala by a number of these despicable enemies of ours.

Bhishma does not support the war, nor does Acharya Drona; neither Kripa nor Gandhari likes it. Sanjaya, nor do I like it; neither does Krishna of Vrishni's race, nor Yudhishtira; nor Bhima, nor Arjuna, nor the twins, Nakula and Sahadeva, bulls among men. Always warned by me, by Gandhari, by Vidura, by Rama the son of Jamadagni, and by the high-souled Vyasa also, the depraved and corrupt Duryodhana, with Dussasana, always following the evil counsels of Karna and Subala's son, has behaved maliciously towards the Pandavas, and so great misfortune has fallen upon him.

After the killing of Sweta and the victory of Bhishma, what does the enraged Partha, with Krishna, do in battle? Indeed, it is Arjuna that I fear, and these fears cannot be dispelled. He is so very brave and powerful. He can decimate his enemies with his arrows. The son of Indra, and equal to Upendra, the younger brother of Indra, he is a warrior whose fury and intent are never futile. When you behold him on the field of war, what is your state of mind?

Valiant, familiar with the Vedas, resembling the Fire and the Sun in radiance, and owning knowledge of the Aindrastra, this Kshatriya of immeasurable soul is always victorious. His weapons always descend on his enemies with the force of the thunderbolt and he is blindingly quick in drawing his bowstring.

The formidable son of Drupada is also endowed with great wisdom. What does Dhrishtadyumna do when Sweta is killed? I am certain that the implacable hearts of the Pandavas burn for the injustices heaped upon them and the death of Sweta. Thinking of their wrath I am never at ease, by day or by night, on account of Duryodhana. How does the great war unfold? Tell me all about it, Sanjaya.'

Sanjaya says, 'Listen carefully, Rajan, to the account of your own wrongdoings. It is not fitting for you to attribute their outcome to Duryodhana. Your understanding is much like the construction of an embankment after the waters have disappeared, or like the digging of a well when the house is on fire.

With the passing of the morning, and the killing of Sweta by Bhishma,

Virata's son Sankha, that grinder of the enemy, always delighting in battle, seeing Salya stationed with Kritavarman on his chariot, suddenly blazes in anger, as does a fire when ghee is poured on it. Stretching his immense bow that is like the bow of Indra himself, he rides to kill the king of the Madras, supported on all sides by a legion of chariots. And Sankha shoots a torrent of arrows as he dashes towards Salya's chariot.

Seeing him come like an enraged elephant, seven of your maharathas surround Salya to save him from the jaws of death. Mahabaho Bhishma, thundering like the very clouds, and taking up a bow six cubits long, rides swiftly at Sankha.

And seeing great Bhishma charge, the Pandava host trembles like a skiff tossed in a storm. Arjuna swiftly places himself in front of Sankha to protect him from Bhishma. And the duel between Bhishma and Arjuna begins. Loud exclamations arise among the gathered. One army blurs into the other, and all are filled with wonder.

Salya alights from his great chariot, and savagely kills Sankha's four horses with his mace. Sankha jumps down from his chariot and, sword in hand, runs to Arjuna's chariot where he is safe, and mounts it. A dense cloud of arrows from Bhishma's chariot covers all the sky and the earth. The arrows that fall from that most excellent archer's deadly cloud annihilate the Panchala, the Matsya, the Kekaya and the Prabhadraka horde and rills of blood flow on Kurukshetra.

Leaving Arjuna Savyasachin, the perfectly ambidextrous bowman, Bhishma dashes towards Drupada, king of the Panchalas, surrounded by his forces. And he shrouds his beloved kinsman with a dazzle of arrows. Like a forest consumed by fire at winter's end, the troops of Drupada are obliterated.

Bhishma stands in that battle like a radiant smokeless fire, or like the sun himself at noon scorching everything with his heat. The Pandava fighting men are unable to even look at him. In terror, they look around for a protector, and seeing none, seem like a herd of trembling cows.

The Pandava forces, slaughtered or retreating dejectedly, lament dispiritedly while being pursued.

Bhishma, with bow always drawn in a circle, shoots fiery shafts like virulent poison, creating a continuous stream of arrows in all directions; that hero of rigid vows kills the Pandava maharathas naming each aloud as he picks them off one by one. When the Pandava troops have been routed and crushed, corpses askew strewn across the battlefield, the sun sets and nothing can be seen.

And then, Bharatarishabha, beholding Bhishma, proudly standing before them, the Parthas withdraw their forces for the night.'

CANTO 50

BHISHMA VADHA PARVA CONTINUED

Sanjaya says, 'When the troops have been withdrawn on the first day, and when Duryodhana is elated seeing Bhishma in full fury of battle, Dharmaraja Yudhishtira hastily approaches Krishna, accompanied by all his brothers and his allies.

Filled with great despair thinking of his rout, and seeing Bhishma's dominance, he says to Krishna, "See how Bhishma of terrible prowess consumes my forces with his arrows like fire consuming dry grass. How can we even look at that high-souled warrior who is sweeping through my men like flames fed with ghee?

Watching that purushvyaghra with his mighty bow, my men flee, excoriated by his barbs. Enraged Yama himself, or Indra armed with the Vajra, or even Varuna with Paasa in hand, or Kubera with his mace may be defeated. But maharatha Bhishma is impossible to overcome. I am drowning in the fathomless ocean called Bhishma, without a boat to rescue me.

Kesava, it is from my abysmal ignorance that I have Bhishma as my adversary in war. I want to quit this terrible massacre and take sannyasa in the forest. To live there is preferable to sacrificing these earthly kings to Death come hunting us in the form of Bhishma.

Bhishma is a master of the greatest astras, and he will annihilate my army. My fighting men are like insects rushing into a raging fire to their certain death. In fighting for a kingdom, I am being led only to sure destruction.

My gallant brothers also bear arrows for my sake, having lost both sovereignty and happiness for the love of me, their eldest brother. We regard life highly, and it is too precious to be so lightly sacrificed. During the rest of my days I will practise the severest tapasya. I will not anymore be the cause of the deaths of my friends and my kinsmen.

The resplendent Bhishma, with his divine weapon, ceaselessly thwarts thousands of my maharathas, the most excellent of great warriors. Tell me, Krishna, without delay, what should I do for my own good?

As for Arjuna, I see that he is an unmoved spectator in this battle. Only great Bhima, remembering Kshatriya dharma, fights with all his strength. With his mighty mace, this high-souled Kshatriya achieves the most difficult victories over foot soldiers and horses, chariots and elephants. But this hero cannot in fair fight destroy the enemy even in a hundred years. Only your Arjuna can achieve this with his Devastras.

He looks on indifferently as we are overpowered by Bhishma and Drona. The unceasing astras of Bhishma and Drona raze all our Kshatriyas. Unquestionably, the raging Bhishma and his allies will annihilate us. Krishna, go look for that great archer, that maharatha, who can extinguish Bhishma like rain clouds a forest fire. Then with your blessings, the sons of Pandu, their enemies defeated and their kingdom restored, will be at peace with their kinsmen."

Having said this, Yudhishtira, with a grieving heart and mind in turmoil, remains silent in reflection for a long time. Seeing the son of Pandu stricken with grief, Krishna lifts the spirit of the Pandavas saying, "Do not mourn, lord of the Bhaaratas. It does not befit you to lament, when your brothers are all brave archers renowned the world over.

I also am engaged in working towards your welfare, as are the revered maharathas Satyaki and Virata and Drupada, and Dhrishtadyumna of Prishata's line. All these kings and their legions honour you and are devoted to you. Maharatha Dhrishtadyumna, who commands your army, wants your welfare, as also Mahabaho Sikhandin, who is the one certain to kill Bhishma."

Hearing these words, before the assembled men and in the presence of Krishna, Yudhishtira says to Dhrishtadyumna, "You of Prishata's lineage, listen to my words which must not be violated. Approved by Vasudeva, you have been our Senapati. As Kartikeya was the Senapati of the divine forces, in bygone days, so also are you for the Pandava army.

Use your prowess, O tiger among men, and exterminate the Kauravas. I will follow you along with Bhima, and Krishna also, and the sons of Madri, all united together, the sons of Draupadi in full armour, and all the other valiant kings."

Dhrishtadyumna says, "Ordained by Shambhu himself, I am the proclaimed destroyer of Drona. I shall wage war against Bhishma, and Drona and Kripa, and Salya and Jayadratha, and all the proud kings on the Kaurava side."

When that most glorious of princes, that slayer of enemies, the son of Prishata, says this defiantly, the Pandava warriors are once more filled with great unyielding courage and heart, and roar loudly.

Yudhishtira says to Dhrishtadyumna, "Form the vyuha called Krauncharuma. This formation was the one advocated by Brihaspati to Indra in ancient days when the Devas and the Asuras fought, and it devoured enemy hosts. Unseen before, dazzle the Kauravas with its power."

Thus addressed by that god among men, Yudhishtira, like Vishnu by Indra, Dhrishtadyumna places Arjuna in the vanguard of the army at dawn. And Dhananjaya's standard, crafted by divine power at Indra's command, waves gloriously in the crisp morning air.

Decked with the colours of the Indradhanusha, the rainbow, that standard coursing through the air looks like an edifice of vapour which seems to glide along its chariot. And the bearer of the Gandiva, adorned with jewels, and that standard beside him, looks doubly brilliant, like Brahma with the Sun, and the Sun with the Self-created One.

King Drupada, surrounded by a host of fighting men, becomes the head of that vyuha. And the two kings Kuntibhoja and Saibya become its two eyes. And the ruler of the Dasarnas, and the Prayagas, with the Daserakas, and the Anupakas, and the Kiratas are its neck, Bharatarishabha.

Yudhishtira with the Patachcharas, the Hunas, the Pauravakas and the Nishadas, so also the Pisachas, with the Kundavishas, and the Mandakas, the Ladakas, the Tanganas, and the Uddras, and the Saravas, the Tumbhumas, the Vatsas, and the Nakulas, become its right wing. And Nakula and Sahadeva place themselves on the left wing.

On the joints of the wings are ten thousand chariots, and on the head a hundred thousand; on the back of the vyuha are a hundred million and twenty thousand rathas, and on the neck a hundred and seventy thousand. On the joints of the wings, and their tips move majestic elephants, like blazing mountains. And the rear is protected by Virata with the Kekayas, and the ruler of Kasi and the king of the Chedis, with thirty thousand chariots.

Forming this mighty vyuha, the Pandavas, eager for sunrise, await battle in armour. And their white royal parasols, rich and sparkling, as brilliant as the sun, bedazzle on their elephants and chariots.'

CANTO 51

BHISHMA VADHA PARVA CONTINUED

anjaya says, 'Seeing the awesome Krauncha vyuha, formed by Pandu's son of immeasurable energy, your son approaches Acharya Drona, and Kripa, and Salya, and Somadatta's son, and Vikarna, and Aswatthaman also, and all his brothers, led by Dussasana, and other mighty Kshatriyas gathered for battle, and speaks these judicious and pleasing words, "Armed with diverse weapons, you are all familiar with the shastras. Each of you maharathas is singly capable of decimating the sons of Pandu with their legions. How much more then we can accomplish when you are united. Our forces, protected by Bhishma, are beyond measure, while theirs, protected by Bhima, are limited.

Let the Samsthanas, the Surasenas, the Venikas, the Kukkuras, the Rechakas, the Trigartas, the Madrakas, the Yavanas, with Shatrunjayas, and Dussasana, and that admirable Vikarna, and Nanda and Upanandaka, and Chitrasena, along with the Manibhadrakas, protect Bhishma with their fighting men."

Then Bhishma and Drona and your sons form a mighty vyuha for resisting that of the Parthas. And Bhishma, surrounded by a vast fighting force, advances like the king of the Devas himself. And that mighty archer, the son of Bharadwaja, endowed with immense tejas, follows him with the Kuntalas, the Dasarnas, and the Magadhas, and with the Vidarbhas, the Melakas, the Karnas, and the Pravaranas also.

The Gandharas, the Sindhusauviras, the Sibis and the Vasatis with all their legions follow Bhishma, that ornament of battle; and Shakuni, with all his warriors, protects him. King Duryodhana, with all his brothers, with the Aswalakas, the Vikarnas, the Vamanas, the Kosalas, the Daradas, the Vrikas, as also the Kshudrakas and the Malavas, advances spiritedly against the Pandava army.

And Bhurisravas, and Sala, and Salya, and Bhagadatta, and Vinda and Anuvinda of Avanti, guard the left flank. And Somadatta, and Susarman, and Sudakshina, the ruler of the Kambojas, and Satayus, and Srutayus, are on the right flank. Aswatthaman, and Kripa, and Kritavarman of Satwata's race, with a very large aksauhini, are at the rear of the army. And behind them are the kings of many lands, Ketumat, and Vasudana, and the powerful son of the king of Kasi.

All the forces on your side joyfully await battle, blowing their conches with delight, and roaring like lions. Hearing these happy shouts the revered and powerful Bhishma also roars and blows his conch. Conches and drums, and many kinds of pesis and cymbals are sounded by others, setting up an upsurge of pulsating noise.

Krishna and Arjuna, both on a majestic chariot yoked to white horses, blow their beautiful conches decked with gold and jewels. Hrishikesa blows the Panchajanya, and Dhananjaya the one named Devadatta. Bhima of terrible deeds blows the enormous Paundra, and king Yudhishtira blows the Anantavijaya, while Nakula and Sahadeva blow upon the Sughosa and Manipushpaka.

The ruler of Kasi, and Saibya, and maharathas Sikhandin and Satyaki, and Dhrishtadyumna, and Virata, and that awesome archer, the king of the Panchalas, and the five sons of Draupadi, all blow their conches and set up leonine roars. And the great uproar of these Kshatriyas reverberates thunderously through the earth and the sky.

Thus, Rajan, the Kauravas and the Pandavas advance against each other eager to scorch each other in further battle.'

CANTO 52

BHISHMA VADHA PARVA CONTINUED

Dhritarashtra says, 'When the two armies stand ready in battle formation, how do those excellent warriors begin their attack?'

Sanjaya says, 'When all the forces are arrayed, the fighting men wait, in full armour, with their beautiful standards raised. And seeing the Kaurava army looking like the boundless ocean, your son Duryodhana, standing within it, commands his forces into fight.'

The soldiers, with savage intent, abandoning all caution, charge the Pandavas, with standards aloft. The battle is fiercely fought and makes one's hair stand on end. The chariots and elephants blur into each other. And vigorous, beautifully feathered shafts shot by maharathas rain down on the elephants and horses.

Mahabaho Bhishma of awesome prowess, encased in mail, takes up his bow, and approaching them, looses a torrent of arrows on the valiant son of Subhadra, and maharatha Arjuna, and the king of the Kekayas and Virata, and Dhrishtadyumna, as also upon the Chedi and the Matsya warriors.

And that mighty Pandava vyuha wavers at Bhishma's onslaught. Terrible is that encounter, terrible the Kuru grandsire. Horses and riders, and maharathas, fall swiftly. The Pandava chariot aksauhinis melt away.

Then that tiger among men, Arjuna, seeing the supreme Bhishma, angrily says to Krishna, "Press forward towards the Pitamaha. Bhishma incensed will annihilate our army for Duryodhana's sake. And this Drona, and Kripa and Salya and Vikarna, united with Dhritarashtra's sons headed by Duryodhana, and protected by this awesome archer, will slaughter the Panchalas. I must stop him."

Krishna cautions him saying, "Be careful, Dhananjaya, as I take you towards the Pitamaha's chariot." And he drives Arjuna's celebrated chariot towards Bhishma's.

With numerous banners waving, with handsome steeds resembling a flight of white cranes, with a raised standard bearing a roaring Vanara, Arjuna, the friend of friends, swiftly draws up on his chariot of sunlike radiance and the thunder of clouds, razing the Kaurava and the Surasena hordes.

Dashing like an incensed elephant he terrifies brave warriors felling them all round with his shafts, and encounters Bhishma, protected by the forces headed by Saindhava and by the fighting men of the East, and the Sauviras and the Kekayas. Who other than Bhishma, Drona and Karna can advance in battle against the bearer of the Gandiva?

Bhishma strikes Arjuna with seventy-seven arrows and Drona shoots him with twenty-five, and Kripa with fifty, and Duryodhana with sixty-four, and Salya with nine; and Drona's son, that purushvyaghra, with sixty, and Vikarna with three barbs; and Saindhava with nine and Sakuni with five. And Artayani pierces Pandu's son with three thick shafts.

Though pierced from all sides with sharp arrows, Mahabaho Arjuna does not falter; he is like a mountain struck by straws. In response, this Kiriti of immeasurable soul pierces Bhishma with twenty-five and Kripa with nine barbs, and Drona with sixty, and Vikarna with three shafts, and Artayani with three, and Duryodhana also with five.

And then Satyaki, and Virata and Dhrishtadyumna, and the sons of Draupadi, and Abhimanyu, all ride up, surrounding him for protection. The prince of the Panchalas, supported by the Somakas, advances towards the great Drona, who guards Bhishma.

Maharatha Bhishma swiftly stabs the son of Pandu with eighty fierce arrows, greatly pleasing your soldiers. Hearing the shouts of those maharathikas, Arjuna joyfully enters into their midst raining fire upon them.

Watching his troops struggle in battle against the son of Pritha, Duryodhana says to Bhishma, "This mighty son of Pandu, with Krishna, felling all our troops, cuts away our roots, even while you and Drona live. It is on your account that Karna has laid aside his weapons, and does not fight against the Pandavas. O son of Ganga, Arjuna must be killed!"

Bhishma Pitamaha saying, "Fie on this cruel Kshatriya dharma!" rides towards Arjuna's chariot. And all the kings, seeing both those warriors with white horses yoked to their chariots, roar like lions and blow their conches. Drona's son and Duryodhana, and your son Vikarna, encircle Bhishma and stand prepared; and so also do all the Pandavas, surrounding Dhananjaya. And the battle begins.

Bhishma pierces Arjuna with nine shafts; Arjuna strikes him in return with ten, probing his very vitals. With a thousand adroit missiles, Arjuna, famed for his archery, shrouds Bhishma in a net of arrows. Bhishma responds with a like mesh of his own. And both are pleased, and both delighting in battle, contend with each other without either gaining any advantage.

The flights of arrows from Bhishma's bow are dispersed by Arjuna's shafts. And so the torrents of arrows shot by Arjuna, cleaved by the arrows of Ganga's son, all fall tamely to the ground. Arjuna strikes Bhishma with twenty-five keenly whetted barbs. Bhishma strikes Partha with nine.

And these two glorious warriors, those Parantapas, sport with each other, piercing each other's chariots, horses, shafts and wheels. Suddenly Bhishma strikes Krishna squarely in his chest with three sizzling barbs, and Krishna bleeds red, Rajan, like a flowering kinsuka.

Infuriated at seeing Krishna wounded, Arjuna strikes Bhishma's sarathy with three searing arrows. Both maharathas strive against each other, without success. The dexterity of their charioteers allows them to display beautiful circles and advances and retreats with their chariots. They zealously seek any slight opening to strike, frequently changing positions.

Both Kshatriyas blow their conches echoingly, the boom of which mingles with their leonine roars; those maharathas twang their bows deafeningly. The resonance of their conches and the rattle of their chariot wheels agitate the very Earth, which begins to tremble and make cavernous sounds.

No one detects any weakness in either of them. Both are strong and courageous, and a match for the other. Guided by his fleeting standard, the Kauravas seek refuge in Bhishma; the Pandavas are inspired by Arjuna's moving banner. Seeing this stunning display of prowess, all present are filled with wonder.

No one, Bhaarata, observes any difference between the two, just as no one finds lapses in a man of dharma. At times, both become perfectly invisible in the prevailing clouds of arrows. At times, both are clearly seen.

The Devas with the Gandharvas and the Charanas, and the great Rishis watching this, say to one another, "These wrathful maharathas cannot be defeated by the Devas, the Asuras and the Gandharvas. This breathtaking battle will be held in awe in all the worlds. Indeed, such a war will never take place again.

Bhishma cannot be overcome by even brilliant maharatha Arjuna raining down arrows. So also Arjuna, who cannot be vanquished by the very gods, will not be defeated by Bhishma. As long as the world itself lasts, so will this battle continue without an outcome." We hear these words in praise of both embattled warriors.

While these two are engaged in displaying their magnificent dexterity, other soldiers of both armies kill one another with sharp-edged swords, polished battle-axes, innumerable arrows, and a variety of weapons. Brave fighting men continue to fell each other in the murderous war.

And the clash between Drona and the prince of the Panchalas is terrible too.'

CANTO 53

BHISHMA VADHA PARVA CONTINUED

Dhritarashtra says, 'Tell me, Sanjaya, how that great archer Drona and the Panchala prince of Prishata's race fight, each striving to put forth his utmost. I regard destiny to be superior to exertion, considering that Bhishma could not escape Arjuna in battle. Indeed, when enraged, Bhishma can destroy all mobile and immobile creation; then why can he not kill the son of Pandu?'

Sanjaya says, 'Listen attentively, Rajan, to the story of this awesome war. The son of Pandu cannot be defeated by the very gods led by Indra. With a range of arrows Drona pierces Dhrishtadyumna and fells his charioteer. He also strikes Dhrishtadyumna's four horses with four brilliant shafts. The daring Dhrishtadyumna strikes Drona's body deep with nine arrows and arrests him.

Bharadwaja's son, of great prowess and immeasurable soul, shrouds the wrathful Dhrishtadyumna with his arrows. And he takes up a forbidding missile, like a second rod of death, as powerful as Indra's Vajra. Seeing that astra aimed by Drona, fearful shouts arise among the fighting men.

We watch Dhrishtadyumna's prowess as he stands alone like a

mountain, adamant. He cuts down that blazing arrow flying towards him like his own death, and rains a storm of barbs on Drona. Seeing that incredible feat of Dhrishtadyumna's, the Panchalas with the Pandavas roar in delight.

Always seeking Drona's death, that fire prince hurls a spear at him, decked with gold and stones of lapis lazuli, like a thunderbolt. Drona smiles and cuts it into three slivers. Seeing his missile frustrated, Dhrishtadyumna looses a gale of arrows on Drona. Containing that squall, maharatha Drona smashes the Panchala prince's bow in his hands.

His bow riven, Dhrishtadyumna casts a mace weighty as a mountain at Drona. As it flies for Drona's life, we witness the astounding dexterity of Bharadwaja's son. By a nimble movement of his chariot, he avoids that golden arcane mace, in a wink, and looses shoots a clutch of inscrutable golden-winged shafts at Prishata's son. These pierce Dhrishtadyumna's armour drinking his blood.

The high-souled Dhrishtadyumna takes up another bow, and strikes Drona with five barbs. Those two bulls among men, both covered in blood, look quite beautiful, like two blossoming kinsukas in spring.

Drona again breaks Drupada's son's bow in his hands. That profound Kshatriya, the Acharya with arrows, like clouds lashing a mountain with rain. Roaring like a lion, he fells his enemy's sarathy and his four horses from his bay in the chariot; elegantly, fiercely he cuts away the leather glove that protects Dhrishtadyumna's right hand.

His bow broken, deprived of his chariot, his horses slain, and charioteer overthrown, the prince of Panchala begins to alight from his ruined ratha, mace in hand, ready to display great prowess. But before he can leap down, Bhaarata, Drona smashes his mace into fragments with arrows swifter than seeing. Ah, that was breathtaking to see!

The stalwart prince of the Panchalas, that Mahabaho, takes up a grand shield decked with a hundred moons, and a mighty sword, and dashes out, like a ravenous lion towards an incensed elephant, always, always to kill Drona. With lightness of hand and power, we see Bharadwaja's son curb Prishata's son with a spate of arrows.

Yet for all his great power, Drona cannot himself advance, for the maharatha Dhrishtadyumna stands resolute and unmoving, warding off those arrow clouds with his shield with unmatched skill. Bhima swiftly moves to help Dhrishtadyumna. He stabs Drona with seven arrows, and forces him to clamber on to another chariot. Duryodhana cries at the king of the Kalingas, with his large force, to protect Drona.

The fearsome Kalinga legion charges against Bhima at your son's command. And Drona, abandoning the prince of Panchala, faces Virata and Drupada together. Dhrishtadyumna advances to support Yudhishtira. A fierce fight breaks out between the Kalingas and Bhima, making one's hair stand on end; it quickly swells into an encounter that threatens to destroy the universe.'

CANTO 54

BHISHMA VADHA PARVA CONTINUED

Dhritarashtra says, 'How does the king of the Kalingas, that commander of a vast army, goaded by my son, fight Bhima of stupendous feats, that Kshatriya ranging over the field of war with his mace like Death himself?'

Sanjaya says, 'Driven by your son, the mighty king of the Kalingas, accompanied by a colossal force advances on Bhima's chariot. And Bhima, supported by the Chedis, charges that army, replete with chariots, horses and elephants, and bristling with powerful weapons, flying towards him with Ketumat, the son of the king of the Nishadas.

And Srutayus also, lively and armoured, followed by his troops in battle formation, rides with king Ketumat to assail Bhima. The lord of the Kalingas with thousands of chariots, and Ketumat with ten thousand elephants, and the Nishadas encircle Vayu's mighty son.

With Bhima at their head, the Chedis, the Matsyas and Karushas, along with others, plunge wildly at the Nishadas. A fierce and majestic battle erupts between Bhima and his enemies, all avid to kill one another, a terrific fray that resembles the clash between Indra and the host of

Diti's sons. The uproar of that horde reverberates like the booming ocean.

The fighting men fell one another, transforming the battlefield into a cremation ground strewn horribly with flesh, and flowing blood. The warriors, in their frenzy of killing, cannot distinguish friend from foe, and so man strike down their own. Ah, feverish is the encounter between the few and many, between the Chedis on one side, and the Kalingas and the Nishadas on the other.

After briefly displaying fierce valour, the Chedis abandon Bhima, and turn away. Unruffled by the desertion, the son of Pandu takes on the Kalingas single-handedly. The mighty Bhima stands unwavering, and inundates the Kalinga legions with torrents of arrows.

That mighty archer, the king of the Kalingas, and his son the maharatha Sakradeva, both strike Bhima painfully. Mahabaho Bhima fights back bravely, but his horses are felled by Sakradeva's volleys. Seeing Parantapa Bhima without a chariot, Sakradeva attacks him fervently with a gale like a cloudburst at the end of summer.

Bhima remains in his horseless chariot, and hurls an iron mace at Sakradeva. The son of the Kalinga king plunges to the ground, with his standard and sarathy, dead. Seeing his son killed, maharatha Srutayush surrounds Bhima with thousands of chariots.

Bhima discards his mace and takes up a sword. Crimson eyed with anguish and wrath, the great Kalinga rubs his bowstring, takes up an arrow deadly as a king cobra, and shoots it at Bhima. Bhima cleanly divides that coursing arrow in two with his imposing sword. And he roars in triumph, terrifying the soldiers.

In deranged fury, the Kalinga launches fourteen bearded stone-whetted shafts at Bhima, who in a blur smashes those arrows surging through the sky into bits with his sword. Bhima, husky bull among men, attacks Bhanumat. Bhanumat envelops Bhima withal shower of arrows, and makes the sky echo with a resounding shout. Bhima responds with strident roar after roar, like an angry tiger.

Hearing him roar so awfully, the Kalinga army grows fearful. That army suddenly sees Bhima as being more than a mere man. Levering himself by its tusks, Bhima, sword in hand, leaps onto the back of Bhanumat's elephant, and slices through Bhanumat with his magnificent sword, bisecting his trunk in a flash of scarlet.

Having killed that prince of the Kalingas, Parantapa Bhima dissevers the neck of his tusker which falls to the ground with a deafening bellow, like a cliff whose base has been eroded by the heaving sea. Leaping down from that dying elephant, the prince of Bharata's race stands once again on the ground, his mighty chest heaving, sword in hand and impervious as ever.

Destroying numberless elephants on all sides, he wanders across the battlefield, looking like a moving wheel of fire, decimating aksauhinis of cavalry, elephants, chariots, and hordes of footsoldiers.

And that lord among men, the mighty Bhima, moves hawklike, cleaving the bodies and heads of elephants and their riders with his keen-edged sword. On foot and furious, he strikes fear into his bravest opponents and baffles them singlehandedly, like Yama during the pralaya. Only the foolish dare challenge him rashly as he roams the battleground, sword in hand.

That hulking, terrifying Kshatriya smashes the shafts and yokes of chariots, also killing their warriors. Bhima displays all kinds of movements, so surprisingly agile and graceful for one of his bulk: he turns, and wheels, makes side-thrusts, jumps, runs, and leaps high. He races forwards and flies upwards. And some are mangled, struck by his sword through their very vitals, and others beheaded.

Many elephants, Bhaarata, some with their trunks and tusks severed, others with their temporal lobes slit open, deprived of riders, kill their own ranks and fall down with plaintive cries. And broken spears, and the heads of elephant drivers, and beautiful caparisons of elephants, and dazzling golden chords, and collars, and arrows and mallets and quivers, many kinds of war machines, and beautiful bows, short arrows with polished heads and hooks, and iron goads for driving elephants, bells of many shapes and tones, and hilts decked with gold, are seen tumbling to the ground along with horsemen past count.

And with elephants spread on the ground with parts of their bodies and their trunks cut, or killed, the field appears to be spread with fallen hills. That bull among men, having killed those majestic tuskers, moves on to raze the horses, and also fells their riders. Savage and ferine is the battle between him and them.

We see hilts and traces, and radiant golden saddle girths and covers for the backs of horses, and bearded shafts, and costly swords, and coats of mail, and shields, and beautiful ornaments scattered all around in that virile encounter. Bhima covers the earth with blood as if it were dotted with crimson lilies.

The mighty son of Pandu leaps high and dragging some maharathas down, fells them and their standards with his sword. Filled with entirely boundless energy, that Kshatriya sometimes lunges, or dashes on all sides, along many sudden paths; and the fighting men all look on in wonder.

And some he kills with his legs, and others he drags down, thrusting them into the earth. Some he strikes with his sword, and others he petrifies with his roars. Some men are thrown to the ground by the force of his thighs as he runs through them; others escape hastily, terrified to see him.

Yet again, the vast and vigorous force of the Kalingas rushes at the dreadful Bhima and surrounds him. Seeing Srutayush at the head of the Kalinga forces, Bhima charges him. The Kalinga king pierces Bhima's chest with nine whistling arrows. Like an elephant pierced with a goad, Bhima blazes up in anger, like a fire fed with ghee.

Ashoka, that most excellent sarathy, brings up a golden chariot for Bhima to mount. The son of Kunti swiftly climbs on and rides at the ruler of the Kalingas, calling out to him to halt.

The mighty, infuriated Srutayush looses a luculent volley at Bhima, flaunting his marvellous lightness of hand. Struck forcefully by nine shafts from Kalinga's bow, Bhima shivers like a snake beaten with a rod. With a growl he raises his bow and kills the Kalinga king with seven massive iron shafts.

With another two arrows he brings down the two powerful protectors of Srutayush's chariot wheels. He despatches Satyadeva and Satya to Yamaloka. Of immeasurable soul, Bhima has Ketumat's life with a mad flurry of arrow and spear. Supported by a force of many thousands, the Kshatriyas of the Kalinga country rise in incensed froth to confront the raging Bhima.

With spears and maces, swords and battle-axes, hundreds upon hundreds of the Kalingas besiege Bhima. Grandly foiling their torrents of missiles, the mighty one takes up his mace and again leaps from his chariot.

Bhima on his fresh rampage kills another seven hundred brave Kshatriyas; that Parantapa sends two thousand more Kalingas to their death. Ah, truly wonderful, even by his lofty norm, is his feat. Thus does Bhima of awesome prowess fell teeming bands of the Kalingas.

Elephants deprived of their riders by Bhima, and stricken with arrows, blunder frenetically across the battlefield, trampling their own men, with deafening roars, like masses of clouds driven by the wind. Mahabaho Bhima, sword in hand, triumphantly and stridently blows his conch.

And that blast makes the Kalinga forces tremble, all of them absolutely panic-stricken. The warriors and the animals quake in terror for Bhima charges down many paths, impetuously, in every direction, like a prince of tuskers, roaring, leaping high time and again. His enemies are flung into a trance.

The Kalinga army shudders in dread of Bhima like a vast lake agitated by a great crocodile. And seeing Bhima's wondrous feats, the Kalinga forces flee in all directions. When they rally again, the Pandava Senapati Dhrishtadyumna, Bhaarata, orders his own troops to fight.

Obeying their Senapati, many warriors of the Pandava army led by Sikhandin surge towards Bhima with their aksauhinis of consummate chariots. Dharmaraja Yudhishtira follows them with a grand elephant force the colour of clouds. Exhorting his men, the son of Prishata, surrounded by so many great warriors, takes upon himself the protection of one of Bhima's flanks.

There exists no one on earth who is more cherished by the prince of the Panchalas than Bhima and Satyaki; indeed he values them more highly than his life. As that Parantapa, the son of Prishata, watches Mahabaho Bhima rampaging among the Kalingas, he roars in exultation. He blows his conch and lets out a leonine roar. And Bhima, seeing the red standard of Dhrishtadyumna's chariot decked with gold and yoked with horses white as pigeons, is reassured. Soon enough he remounts his own chariot again.

Dhrishtadyumna of immeasurable soul advances to rescue Bhima beleaguered by the Kalingas. And both those Kshatriyas, Dhrishtadyumna and Bhima, of pulsating tejas, noticing Satyaki at a distance, furiously fall upon the Kalingas.

And that bull among men, Satyaki Yuyudhana, grandson of Sini, foremost of victorious warriors, swiftly rides to defend the flanks of Bhima and Prishata's son. Bow in hand, fighting ferociously, he devastates the enemy's ranks. Bhima lets flow a crimson river, a bloody current floating the shredded flesh of the Kalinga fighting men.

Beholding Bhima the men cry out, "This is Yama himself fighting against the Kalingas in Bhima's form!" Hearing those cries, himself encircled by armed adversaries, Bhishma breaks free of his encirclement and rides at Bhima.

Satyaki and Bhima, and Dhrishtadyumna rush at Bhishma's silver chariot decked with gold. And all of them surround Ganga's son and pierce him, each with three scathing barbs.

Bhishma pierces each of those mighty archers with three straight shafts. And checking those maharathas with thousands of arrows, loosed in moments, he kills Bhima's horses. Resplendent with golden armour and filled with tejas, Bhima stands firm on that horseless chariot and launches a spear at Bhishma's chariot, which the grandsire cleaves in two before it can reach him.

Bhima seizes a mighty mace made of Saikya iron and leaps down from his chariot. Dhrishtadyumna swiftly takes him into his own chariot and carries him to safety in plain view of all the soldiers.

Satyaki kills Bhishma's sarathy with a single arrow, and Bhishma is borne away from the battlefield by his horses with the speed of the wind. Bhima remains in the midst of his men, burning like a mighty fire consuming dry grass as he kills all the Kalingas. None of your warriors, Bharatarishabha, dare to oppose him.

And revered by the Panchalas and the Matsyas, he embraces Dhrishtadyumna and then Satyaki. In the presence of Dhrishtadyumna, Satyaki, tiger among the Yadus, of unthwarted prowess, gladdens Bhima by saying, "By our good fortune the king of the Kalingas, and his son Ketumat, and their kinsman Sakradeva, indeed, all the Kalingas, have been killed. With the strength of your arms alone, the vast legions of the Kalingas teeming with elephants, horses and chariots, noble Kshatriyas, and brave fighting men, have been decimated."

Having said this, the long-armed grandson of Sini, that Parantapa, climbs back into his chariot and embraces the son of Pandu. That maharatha begins to slaughter your forces vigorously augmenting Bhima's efforts.'

CANTO 55

BHISHMA VADHA PARVA CONTINUED

Sanjaya says, 'As the morning passes, and the destruction of chariots, elephants, horses, horsemen and footsoldiers and cavalry continues, Dhrishtadyumna engages with the three maharathas, Drona's son, Salya, and the high-souled Kripa.

And the valiant heir of the king of Panchala kills the celebrated steeds of Drona's son with a storm of arrows. Deprived of his animals, Aswatthaman climbs into Salya's chariot and showers him with his shafts.

Seeing Dhrishtadyumna battling Aswatthaman, the son of Subhadra rushes forward, loosing a tide of fire. He pierces Salya with twenty-five arrows, Kripa with nine, and Aswatthaman with eight. Drona's son retaliates, striking Arjuna's son with a fusillade of winged shafts; Salya stabs him with twelve, and Kripa with three fierce barbs.

Your grandson Lakshmana storms at Abhimanyu and a duel between them ensues. Duryodhana's vehement son covers Abhimanyu in a fury of arrows. His feat, O king, appears truly wonderful!

The magnificent Abhimanyu blithely shoots five hundred arrows at his cousin, in a flash. Lakshmana responds by carving up his adversary's bow in his hands, seeing which all the warriors send up a loud shout. That Parantapa, the son of Subhadra, discards his broken bow and seizes up another strong one.

The two young bulls among men defy each other ferociously, drawing rich, royal blood. Seeing his powerful son afflicted by Abhimanyu, Duryodhana himself rides to where the cousins fight feverishly. All the enemy kings surround the son of Arjuna with hosts of chariots. Invincible in battle and equal to Krishna himself in prowess, that resplendent Kshatriya remains unperturbed. Seeing Subhadra's son in the midst of fierce fighting, Arjuna rushes to rescue him. The kings allied to the Kauravas, led by Bhishma and Drona, with their chariots, elephants and horses, briskly attack Savyasachin.

A pall of dust, raised by footsoldiers and horsemen, horses and chariots, obscures the sky. Coming within range of Arjuna's arrows, those thousands of elephants and hundreds of kings cannot advance. All the creatures there wail loudly and darkness cloaks every direction.

The violation of the Kauravas assumes a fierce and dreadful mien. Neither the sky nor the sun, nor any of the cardinal points of the earth can be distinguished for Arjuna's tempest of arrows.

Many elephants have the standards cut down from their backs, and many maharathas their horses killed. Some commanders of chariot aksauhinis can be seen wandering purposelessly on foot, bereft of their chariots. And other maharathas, their arms graced with angadas, roam aimlessly with their weapons.

Fearing Arjuna, riders of horses and elephants abandon their beasts, and flee in all directions. Kings are felled by Arjuna's arrows or plunge to the ground from chariots and elephants and steeds. With his terrible volleys, Arjuna, fierce-faced, dissevers the upraised arms of warriors grasping maces and swords, or spears, quivers, arrows, bows, hooks, or standards.

Bhaarata, we see spiked maces shattered, and mallets, and bearded shafts, and short arrows, and swords, and sharp battle-axes, and spears and shields smashed into shards, and coats of mail and standards, and other weapons of all kinds, and parasols furnished with golden staves, and iron goads, and whips, and traces strewn across the battlefield in stacks.

There is no warrior who can face Arjuna in battle; whoever advances against him is killed. When all your fighting men scatter, Arjuna and Krishna blow their conches.

Bhishma sees the routed host and smilingly addresses the brave son of Bharadwaja, "The daunting, with Krishna in his chariot, frustrates all our forces. He cannot be overpowered today by any means; today he is like Siva at the end of the yuga and we cannot rally our legions, vast though they be.

Look how our forces scatter. The setting sun is about to reach that best of mountains, the sunset mountain Asta. Bharatarishabha, I think that the hour has come for us to withdraw our army. Our warriors are weary and panic-stricken and cannot fight anymore."

Having said this to Acharya Drona, Maharatha Bhishma orders the retreat of your army. And thus at nightfall, both sides withdraw.'

CANTO 56

BHISHMA VADHA PARVA CONTINUED

Sanjaya says, 'With the arrival of dawn, Parantapa Bhishma gives the order for the Kaurava army to prepare for battle. The son of Shantanu, eager for the victory of your sons, forms the Garuda vyuha.

And on the beak of that Garuda is Bhishma himself. Its two eyes are Drona and Kritavarman of Satwata's race. The famed Aswatthaman and Kripa, supported by the Trigartas, the Matsyas, the Kekayas, and the Vatadhanas, stand at its head. Bhurisravas and Sala, and Salya and Bhagadatta, and the Madrakas, the Sindhu-Souviras, and the Pancha-Noadas, together with Jayadratha, are placed on its neck.

And upon its back is Duryodhana with his followers. Vinda and Anuvinda of Avanti, and the Kambojas with the Sakas, and the Surasenas, Rajan, form its tail. The Magadhas and the Kalingas, with all the tribes of the Daserakas, encased in mail, form the vyuha's the right wing. And the Karushas, the Vikunjas, the Mundas, and the Kaundivrishas, with Brihadbala, are its left wing.

Arjuna, seeing this vyuha, forms another with Dhrishtadyumna to oppose it. The son of Pandu forms the commanding crescent moon vyuha.

Surrounded by kings of many lands, abundantly armed, stationed on the right horn, Bhima dazzles. Beside him are those maharathas Virata and Drupada; next to them is Nila bearing deadly weapons. After Nila stands the maharatha Dhrishtaketu, surrounded by the Chedis, the Kasis, the Karushas, and the Pauravas.

Dhrishtadyumna, and Sikhandin, with the Panchalas and the Prabhadrakas, supported by other forces, are stationed in the centre, Bhaarata, ready for battle. And there also stands Yudhishtira Dharmaraja surrounded by his aksauhini of elephants. Next to him are Satyaki and the five sons of Draupadi. Immediately beyond is Iravan. After these are Bhima's son Ghatotkacha and those maharathas, the Kekayas.

On the left horn of that vyuha stands that best of men, he whom Janardana, the preserver of the Universe, protects. It is thus that the Pandavas form their powerful vyuha to counter and destroy your sons and their allies.

Conches boom and the war between your forces and those of the enemy begins again. Chariots and elephants charge one another and blur on grim Kurukshetra. Hordes of elephants and hosts of chariots can be seen everywhere rushing wildly forward to effect the destruction of the enemy.

The roar of the chariots swiftly moving to either join the general fray or to fight individually is fused with the thunder of drumbeats. The shouts and yells of the dauntless warriors on both sides as they cut each other down reaches the very heavens.'

CANTO 57

BHISHMA VADHA PARVA CONTINUED

Sanjaya says, 'After the two armies have been disposed in battle formations, maharatha Arjuna wreaks great carnage on the commanders of the enemy's hosts of chariots with his arrows. Despite being slaughtered by him, who is truly like Siva at the end of the yuga, the Dhartarashtras persevere to fight the Pandavas.

Wanting to win blazing glory, unrelenting and absorbed in their task, scorning death, they break the Pandava ranks in many places and are also themselves broken. In places, Pandava and the Kaurava troops both briefly scatter and flee.

Nothing can be distinguished. A swirling dust arises and shrouds the very sun. The cardinal and subsidiary directions are a haze; the warriors are guided only by the indications of colours, passwords, names and tribal distinctions. Protected by great Drona, the vyuha of the Kauravas remains whole and steadfast. So also the formidable Pandava vyuha holds firm, defended by Arjuna and Bhima.

Chariots and elephants, in close ranks, and hordes of fighting men of both the armies, clash vigorously. In that savage fight, riders on horses kill one another with polished swords and long spears. Maharathas cut each other down with golden-winged arrows. And elephant-riders mow down others with broad-headed shafts and lances.

Hosts of doughty footsoldiers cheerfully slaughter others with short arrows and battle-axes. Maharathas kill elephants and their riders; and are in turn slain by the latter. Bharatarishabha, the horseman fells the maharatha with his spear, and is in turn flung down to the ground by the chariot warrior. In both the armies, the foot soldier kills the maharatha only to be razed by another rathika. Elephant riders fell horse riders, and horse-riders fell warriors on the backs of elephants.

All this seems all too awesome and so very bloody. Roars and screams of slayer and slain thicken the air and men quit their bodies in their thousands, each moment, and the air is a denseness of the shocked or bemused spirits of fighting men.

Everywhere foot-soldiers, elephant riders and horse riders despatch each other; and strewn with broken standards and bows, spears and housings of elephants, costly shawls and feathered barbs, maces and spiked clubs, kampanas and arrows, mottled coats of mail and kunapas, iron hooks, and polished swords, and golden winged shafts, the gore-slicked battlefield shines as if with floral wreaths.

The earth, mired with chunks of hewn off flesh and spilt blood, becomes impassable with the corpses of men and horses and elephants killed in that most dreadful war. Drenched with human blood, the dust settles, and the cardinal points become perfectly clear once again. Many headless bodies rise up in macabre pageant to intimate the end of the world. And in that fell and gruesome battle, maharathas can be seen escaping in all directions.

Then Bhishma and Drona, and Jayadratha, king of the Sindhus, and Purumitra, and Vikarna, and Sakuni the son of Subala, all leonine and invincible in battle, break through the ranks of the Pandavas. Bhima and Ghatotkacha, and Satyaki, and Chekitana, and the sons of Draupadi, supported by their allies, begin grinding down your forces and your sons, like the Devas razing the Danavas.

And those bulls among Kshatriyas, smiting one another, are awesome to behold; covered in blood, dripping blood, they glow like kinsukas. The foremost warriors of both armies, striking down their opponents, look like the luminous planets in the sky.

Your son Duryodhana, supported by a thousand chariots, storms at the Pandavas and Ghatotkacha the Rakshasa. The Pandavas, with a great host of fighting men, charge the Parantapas Bhishma and Drona.

The diadem-decked Arjuna furiously attacks all the foremost among the enemy kings. Abhimanyu and Satyaki ride against the forces of Subala's son Sakuni. A bloodthirsty encounter breaks out again between the two sides both of whom yearn for victory, a battle that makes one's hair stand on end.'

CANTO 58

BHISHMA VADHA PARVA CONTINUED

Sanjaya says, 'Then those kings, seeing Arjuna in battle, furiously hem him round with thousands of chariots and shroud him with a dark and dense cloud of arrows. And they hurl shining spears, and maces, and spiked clubs, and feathered barbs and battle-axes, and mallets and bludgeons at his chariot - braids of eerie lighting flashing.

With golden shafts Arjuna thwarts that shower of weapons coursing towards him like a flight of locusts. Watching the superhuman lightness of that hand, the Devas, the Danavas, the Gandharvas, the Pisachas, the Uragas and the Rakshasas cry out: "Magnificent, truly magnificent!"

The daring Gandharas, led by Subala's son with a vast force, encircle Satyaki and Abhimanyu. With diverse astras, Sakuni's warriors shatter the chariot of the Vrishni hero. Satyaki abandons his chariot and swiftly mounts Abhimanyu's. The two begin to slaughter the army of Subala's son.

Drona and Bhishma steadily dwindle the forces of Yudhishtira Dharmaraja with jagged shafts furnished with the feathers of the kanka bird. The son of Yudhishtira and his uncles, Madri's twins, now savagely raze Drona's legions in plain sight of both vast armies. That hair-raising battle can be likened to the one between the Devas and the Asuras in ancient times.

Bhima and Ghatotkacha achieve stupendous feats; until, riding up in fury Duryodhana thwarts them both. We see Hidimba's son displaying his prowess and even transcending his father. Enraged, Bhima shoots Duryodhana squarely through his chest, smiling the while. Duryodhana slumps onto the floor of his chariot and faints. His charioteer quickly bears him away to safety, and the forces supporting Duryodhana break rank and scatter.

Pursuing them, Bhima hunts the fleeing Kaurava army with inexorable archery.

Even before the eyes of Drona and Bhishma, blazing Dhrishtadyumna, foremost of warriors, thins their army with stunning flurries from his great bow. The Acharya and the Pitamaha together cannot stop your son's host from breaking ranks and fleeing from the terror that the Panchala prince brings.

When those thousands of maharathas have fled in all directions, Subhadra's son and Satyaki, that bull of Sini's race, together in the same chariot, attack the army of Subala's son. And Sini's grandson and that bull of the Kuru vamsa are radiant like the sun and the moon together in the sky after the last lunation of the dark fortnight.

Arjuna yet furiously rains down his remitless arrow storms on your army in mighty cloudbursts. Trembling like children, the Kaurava army flees his terror and his slaughter. Seeing their army run from battle, the enraged Bhishma and Drona move to stop its retreat.

Duryodhana himself comforts the fighting men and prevents a further flight of his unnerved forces. All the maharathas stop when they see your son. The common soldiers, seeing them halt, stop of their own accord; ashamed and wanting to display their courage to one another, Rajan, your army rallies like the surging sea at moonrise.

Seeing his legions revive, Duryodhana quickly rides upto Bhishma and says, "Pitamaha, whilst you are alive, and Drona, master of weapons, with Aswatthama and all our other friends, still alive, and that mighty archer Kripa, it is dishonourable that my army should take flight.

The Pandavas are not any match for you or for Drona, or for Drona's son, or for Kripa. Pitamaha, you are favouring the sons of Pandu by disregarding this massacre of my army. You should have told me before this war began that you will not fight against the Pandavas.

Had you and Drona said this, I would have reflected upon the course I should pursue with Karna. If I do not deserve to be abandoned by you both in battle, O bulls among men, fight with your full powers."

Hearing these words, Bhishma laughs and, rolling his eyes in anger, says to your son, "Many a time, I spoke to you in the interest of your good. As long as Krishna is with them, the Pandavas are invincible even against the Devas.

However, what my age and strength permit, best of kings, I will do in this war. With your kinsmen, witness it today! In the sight of all, singlehandedly I will contain the sons of Pandu as they lead their forces with all their kin. I will kill ten thousands of their men each day."

Thus addressed by Bhishma, your son has conches blown and drums beaten in joy. And the Pandavas also, hearing that loud uproar, blow their conches, and sound their drums and cymbals.'

CANTO 59

BHISHMA VADHA PARVA CONTINUED

Dhritarashtra says, 'After his dreadful vow made when stirred by the words of my son, what, Sanjaya, does Bhishma do to the sons of Pandu; what do the Panchalas do to the Pitamaha? Tell me all, O Sanjaya.'

Sanjaya says, 'After the passing of that morning, as the sun moves on his westward course, and after the high-souled Pandavas are victorious, Bhishma, knower of every nuance of dharma, protected by a vast force and by all your sons, rides on his ratha yoked to the swiftest horses towards the Pandava army.

As a result of your sinful policy, O king, a horrific battle breaks out between us and the Pandavas. The twang of bows and the flapping of bowstrings against leather gloves, unite to make a tumult like the cracking of mountains.

"Stay! Watch me! Know this one! Turn back! Stand! I await you—strike!" These roars resound everywhere. And the sounds of tumbling golden coats of mail, of crowns and diadems, and of standards, resemble the clatter of stones onto a great bed of rock. Heads and arms decked with

ornaments fall by the thousands upon the field of the awful sacrifice of living men.

Some warriors, with heads severed from their bodies, continue to stand, weapons in hand or armed with drawn bows. Soon a ghastly turbulent river of blood flows, choked with lifeless dismembered men and hewn limbs, and the corpses of elephants its jutting rocks. It flows from the bodies of horses, men, and elephants, delighting swarming raucous vultures and jackals, and it races towards the ocean of the next world. A war such as this one, Rajan, fought between your sons and the Pandavas, has never seen or heard before.

The bodies of slain soldiers render the field impassable for chariots. And dead elephants lying on the ground make Kurukshetra appear to be covered with the peaks of blue hills. And, ah, the battleground, strewn with multicoloured coats of mail and turbans, is also as beautiful as an autumn sky.

Some fighting men, though sorely wounded, can be seen charging joyfully and proudly against the enemy. Many fallen on the field, cry out, "O father, O brother, O friend, O kinsman, O companion, O uncle, do not abandon me!" Others shout, "Come! Come back! Why are you frightened? Where do you go? I stand firm in battle, do not be afraid."

In that deathly conflict, Bhishma, with bow drawn to a circle, looses astras like deadly snakes. Raining down a continuous tempest of arrows in all directions, that hero of rigid vows strikes the Pandava maharathas naming each one. Displaying his unearthly skill, and dancing as it were along the path of his chariot, he appears to be present everywhere, like an ubiquitous circle of fire.

The Pandavas, along with the Srinjayas, behold that lone Kshatriya as multiplied a thousand-fold; all who are there regard Bhishma as having multiplied himself with maya. Having seen him now in the east, the next moment they see him in the west. Having seen him in the north, the next instant they see him in the south. Thus the son of Ganga fights that war. None among the Pandavas is able to even gaze upon him. They see only the bankless, seamless blaze of arrows radiating from his bow.

Valiant warriors, seeing him butcher their ranks, lament loudly. And, kings in thousands attempt to face the Pitamaha, who seems to fly over the field in a superhuman way, falling into the fire, the conflagration that is the enraged Bhishma, like senseless insects that fly into a flame, only to be devoured.

Not a single shaft of that warrior is futile; each one claims a life, felling men, elephants and horses without favour. With a single arrow he kills a mighty tusker like a hill being riven by the Vajra. Another single shaft does to bring down two or three armoured elephant riders standing together.

Whoever approaches Bhishma, that tiger among tigers among men, is seen for but a moment before slumping to the ground. And being annihilated by Bhishma of incomparable prowess, that vast host of Yudhishtira Dharmaraja scatters in all directions. Assailed by Bhishma's simoom of arrows, the immense Pandava army trembles despite the presence of Krishna and Arjuna.

The gallant efforts of the heroic leaders of the Pandava army cannot check the flight of the maharathas afflicted by Bhishma's volleys; the prowess that routs this great legion equals that of Indra himself. Yudhishtira's army is so completely dispersed, that no two men can be seen together.

Chariots and elephants and horses are pierced all over, and standards and shafts of chariots strewn across the field. The Pandava forces cry out in anguish. The father strikes the son and the son strikes the father; and friend challenges the dearest of friends to battle to death as if goaded by destiny.

Many of the Pandava allies flee, dishevelled and distraught, flinging off their coats of mail. Loudly, dismally, the Pandava army wails and screams as it witnesses the best of its maharathas appearing as bewildered as a herd of cows lost in a terrible jungle.

Krishna, observing the rout of the army, stops the chariot and says to Arjuna, "The hour you awaited has arrived, Partha. Strike Bhishma now before you are lost. Remember, in an assembly of kings you said, 'I will slay all the warriors of Dhritarashtra's sons, headed by Bhishma and Drona; why, I will not leave a single man who fights against me alive.'

Son of Kunti, Parantapa, make those words true. Bibhatsu, look at your legions being routed on all sides. Seeing Bhishma looking like Rudra himself with open maw, watch how Yudhishtira's allies flee. Terrified they run, like weaker beasts on seeing the lion."

Arjuna replies, "Plunging through this sea of the hostile host, drive the horses to where Bhishma stands. I will overwhelm that invincible warrior, the revered Kuru Pitamaha."

Krishna drives his silvery horses to where Bhishma's chariot stands, chariot that shines like the sun, impossible to even gaze upon. Seeing Mahabaho Arjuna charging at Bhishma, the mighty army of Yudhishtira rallies for battle.

Bhishma, that foremost of Kuru warriors, roars like ten lions, and swiftly shrouds Arjuna's chariot with a gale of arrows. In a moment, that chariot, with standard and charioteer, becomes invisible. Patiently, fearlessly, Krishna guides his horses wounded by Bhishma's barbs. And Arjuna takes up his celestial bow, whose twang resembles the roar of thunderclouds, and cleaves Bhishma's bow with a clutch of jagged shafts.

The Pitamaha takes up another and strings it in a flash; with his two hands, he stretches that bow whose reverberation are like thunder. But Arjuna, excited with wrath, severs that bow as well.

The son of Shantanu applauds Arjuna, saying, "Excellent, Mahabaho, son of Pandu! Magnificent Dhananjaya, such a marvellous feat is truly worthy of you. I am pleased with you. Fight hard against me."

Having praised Arjuna, Bhishma seizes up another great bow and unleashes a fiercer storm on Arjuna's ratha. Krishna displays divine skill guiding that chariot in sharp, impossible circles, frustrating Bhishma's transcendent archery. But tireless Bhishma soon strikes both Krishna and Arjuna with subtle, whetted barbs. And pierced by those shafts, those two tigers among men look like two roaring bulls with the gashes of horns on their bodies.

In high dudgeon, Bhishma covers the two Krishnas from all sides with an unprecedented fusillade, which make Krishna shiver. Laughing loudly, Bhishma fills even blue Krishna with wonder.

Mahabaho Krishna contrasts the prowess of Bhishma with the mildness of Arjuna; he sees Bhishma loosing incessant firestorms of arrows, looking like the all-consuming sun himself in the midst of the two contending armies. And marking that that Kshatriya ancient was killing the best of Yudhishtira's warriors, bringing havoc to the legions as if Pralaya had arrived, Kesava of the fathomless soul, slayer of enemy hosts, thinking that Yudhishtira's army will be annihilated, cannot bear what he sees.

He thinks, "In a single day this Bhishma can kill all the Daityas and the Danavas. How easily then will he crush the sons of Pandu with their forces and allies. The vast Pandava army is again being scattered. And the Kauravas, seeing the Somakas routed, fight in high spirits, much to Bhishma's delight.

Protected by my kavacha, I will stop Bhishma today for the sake of the Pandavas. I will lighten their burden. As for Arjuna, though struck with keen shafts, he still hesitates, out of his reverence for Bhishma."

While Krishna thus reflects, Bhishma again looses a deep and violent swarm of arrows at Arjuna's chariot. All the cardinal directions are completely shrouded. And neither the sky nor the quarters nor the earth nor the brilliant sun can be seen. The gusts of winds that blow are mixed with smoke, and all the points of the compass are agitated.

And Drona, and Vikarna, and Jayadratha, and Bhurisrava, and Kritavarman, and Kripa, and Srutayush and the ruler of the Amvashtas and Vinda and Anuvinda, Sudakshina and the rulers of the western kingdoms, and the tribes of the Sauviras, the Vasatis, and the Kshudrakas, and the Malavas, swiftly advance towards Kiritin, at Bhishma's command.

The grandson of Sini sees that Arjuna is surrounded by hundreds of horses and footsoldiers, chariots and colossal elephants. Seeing both Krishna and Arjuna encircled, Satyaki rides swiftly forward. Coming to Arjuna's side like Vishnu to the aid of Indra, that noblest archer charges the gathered enemy.

In grand exhilaration, he addresses Yudhishtira's host of fighting men who, cowed by Bhishma, their elephants, steeds, chariots and standards slain, mangled and shattered, roaring, "Brave Kshatriyas, where do you go? This is not the dharma of the righteous as proclaimed by the ancients. Excellent heroes, do not break your vows. Keep your Kshatriya dharma!"

Unable to bear the flight of the army, marking the mildness with which Arjuna fights, and seeing Bhishma's forceful exertions, and the Kauravas rushing in from all sides, Krishna, younger brother of Vasava, and protector of all the Dasarhas, cries to the intrepid and famed Satyaki, saying, "O hero of Sini's race, let they who retreat go. And let they who remain, let them also flee.

I will fling Bhishma down from his chariot, and vanquish Drona, too, and all their followers. No one in the Kaurava legions will escape my wrath. I will kill Bhishma of high vows with my Sudarshana. Killing those two greatest of maharathas, Bhishma and Drona, and their forces, O my Satyaki, I will please Arjuna and Yudhishtira, and Bhima, and the twin Aswins. And killing all the sons of Dhritarashtra and all their allies, I will joyfully deliver unto king Ajatashatru a kingdom today."

Saying this, Vasudeva's son releases the reins of his horses, leaps off the chariot, and materialises over his right hand his beautiful chakra whirling, sharp as a razor, as radiant as the sun, with the force of a thousand thunderbolts. Making the earth tremble under his step, Krishna runs towards Bhishma.

And that Parantapa, the younger brother of Indra, charges Bhishma in the midst of his forces, like a lion wanting to kill a prince of elephants blinded with fury, proudly awaiting the attack. The fringes of Krishna's yellow pitambara robe flutter in the air like a lightning-charged cloud in the sky.

That lotus-like Sudarsana, having for its stalk the beautiful arm of Saurin, is as beautiful as the primeval lotus, bright as the morning sun, which springs from the navel of Vishnu Padmanabha. Krishna's anger is the morning sun that makes that lotus sway. And the exquisite leaves of that lotus are as sharp as a dagger's edge.

Krishna's body is the beautiful lake, and his right hand the stalk that, springing from it, holds the shining lotus. Seeing him, in wrath and roaring loudly, armed with that chakra, all creatures howl piercingly, thinking that the destruction of the Kauravas is imminent. With his chakra, Krishna looks like the Samvarta fire that appears at the end of the yuga to consume the world. And the preceptor of the universe blazes like a fierce comet risen to consume all creatures.

Seeing that Avatara advancing with the Sudarsana, Bhishma standing in his chariot, bow and arrow in hand, cries fearlessly, "Come, come, Lord of the Devas, you who dwell in all the universe! I bow to you, you who are armed with mace, sword and Saranga.

Lord of the universe, cast me down from this chariot, O you who are the refuge of all creatures in this war. Krishna, were I to be slain here by you, great will be my fortune both in this world and the next. You show me exalted regard, Lord of the Vrishnis and the Andhakas. My fame will be celebrated in all the three worlds.'"

Hearing Shantanu's son, Krishna charges him and says, "You are the cause of this great slaughter on earth. You will see Duryodhana killed today. A wise minister who walks the path of dharma must restrain a king addicted to the evil of gambling. That despicable one who transgresses dharma should be abandoned as one whose intelligence has been led astray by destiny."

Hearing this, the royal Bhishma says to the Lord of the Yadavas, "Destiny is all powerful. The Yadavas abandoned Kamsa for their own good. I said this to Dhritarashtra but he paid no heed. Destiny perverts the listener's understanding and, to his own detriment, he cannot receive good advice."

Meanwhile, leaping off his chariot, Mahabaho Arjuna runs towards Krishna and seizes him by his two hands. That supreme deity is incensed, and, though seized, he forcibly drags Jishnu after him, like a tempest bearing away a single tree. The high-souled Arjuna forcefully holds Krishna's feet, as he rushes towards Bhishma, and succeeds, Rajan, in stopping him with great difficulty at the tenth step.

And when Krishna halts, bedecked with a beautiful gold garland, Arjuna joyfully bows down to him and says, "Subdue your anger. You are the refuge of the Pandavas, O Kesava. I swear by my sons and my brothers that I will not retreat from what I have pledged myself to. Krishna, at your command I will annihilate the Kauravas."

Hearing Arjuna's vow, Krishna grows calm, he is gratified. And devoted to the cause of that most excellent Kuru, he once more mounts his chariot, still armed with his chakra. And that Parantapa takes up the abandoned reins, and blowing on his conch the Panchajanya, he fills all of the earth and the sky with its blast.

Seeing Krishna, decked with necklace and angada and earrings, with curling eyelashes coated with dust, and with teeth of perfect whiteness, take up his conch again, the Kuru heroes cry out stridently. The clash of cymbals and drums, and the thunder of chariot wheels and the clatter of smaller drums, mingle with those leonine shouts to become a fierce uproar. And the twang of Arjuna's Gandiva, like the roll of thunder, fills the sky and all the quarters of the earth. Its burning shafts flare out in all directions.

The Kaurava king, with a vast force, along with Bhishma and Bhurisravas, arrows in hand, resembling a comet risen to consume a constellation, dashes against him. Bhurisravas hurls seven spears with wings of gold at Arjuna, while Duryodhana flings a brutal lance; Salya launches a mace, and Bhishma looses an astra.

Arjuna stops Bhurisravas's spears with seven shafts, and cleaves the lance hurled by Duryodhana with another. He thwarts the blazing pike, as luminous as lightning, cast by Bhishma, and the mace of the ruler of the Madras, with two mighty arrows of his own.

Then drawing with both hands and with great energy his magnificent Gandiva, he invokes with fitting mantras the awesome Mahendra astra to appear in the sky. With it, that maharatha, decked with diadem and a garland of gold, produces an intense storm of flaming arrows that frustrates the Kaurava host.

Those shafts from Arjuna's bow sever arms, bows, standard-tops, and chariots; they pierce the bodies of the enemy kings and their imposing tuskers and horses. Arjuna fills the cardinal and subsidiary directions with his awe-inspiring arrows and makes the hearts of his adversaries tremble with the twang of Gandiva.

The blast of conches, the beat of drums and the sonorous rumbling of chariots are silenced by the resonance of the Gandiva. Following that reverberation, king Virata and other Kshatriyas, and the brave Drupada, the king of the Panchalas, all joyfully advance towards that Arjuna.

All your warriors are fearful and become rooted to where they stand when they hear the Gandiva. None dare to venture to the place from where the sound springs. In that terrific war of kings, valiant warriors are killed along with maharathas and their sarathies. And elephants with resplendent golden howdahs and beautiful standards, pierced with broad-headed shafts, fall dead, their bodies truncated by Arjuna.

Struck by Partha's winged wide shafts, the standards of many kings stationed at the heads of their yantras and Indrajalas are cut down. Hordes of footsoldiers and maharathas, and horses and elephants, fall rapidly on the battleground, their limbs paralysed, or themselves killed, by Arjuna's arrows.

Rajan, many fighting men have their armour and bodies perforated by the all-powerful Mahindra astra. And with his deadly shafts, Arjuna makes a vile river of blood course across the battlefield, formed by the twisted bodies of the warriors, with their fat as its froth. The bodies of slain elephants and horses form its banks.

Its mire consists of the entrails, the marrow, and the flesh of men, while Rakshasas are the majestic trees on its banks. And a profusion of human skulls, covered with hair, forms its floating morass; heaps of human bodies, forming its sandbanks, cause the current to flow in a thousand directions. The coats of mail strewn all over form its hard pebbles.

Its banks are infested with jackals and wolves, cranes and vultures, crowds of Rakshasas and Pisachas, and packs of hyenas. And they that are alive gaze upon that terrible river of fat, marrow and blood, caused by Arjuna's arrows, the river that embodies man's cruelty, like the great Vaitarani.

Seeing those outstanding warriors of the Kaurava army decimated by Phalguni, the Chedis, the Panchalas, the Karushas, the Matsyas, and all the Pandava allies roar jubilantly in unison to terrify the Kaurava fighting men. Their triumphant shouts proclaim the victory of Arjuna, who razes the Kaurava legions, though they are protected and led by the noblest men, the greatest maharathas, mighty leaders of aksauhinis; Arjuna terrifies them like a lion frightens herds of small animals.

And then the bearer of Gandiva himself and Krishna roar in delight. The Kauravas, with Bhishma, and Drona and Duryodhana and Bahlika, are savagely wounded by Arjuna's weapons. Watching the setting sun, and seeing the irresistible Aindrastra spread out as if to invite the end of the yuga, they withdraw their forces for the night and rest.

Famed for crushing his enemies, the victorious Arjuna, having achieved a great feat, seeing the sun turn red as dusk approaches, also retires with his brothers to their camp.

Then when darkness is about to descend, there arises a terrible lament in the Kaurava camp. And all cry, "In today's battle Arjuna has killed ten thousand maharathas and seven hundred elephants! All the forces of the western kingdoms, and all the tribes of the Sauviras, and the Kshudrakas and the Malavas, have been annihilated. Arjuna has achieved a mighty feat indeed. There is no other who could do this.

Srutayush, the ruler of the Amvashtas, and Durmarshana, and Chitrasena, and Drona, and Kripa, and the ruler of the Sindhus, and Bahlika, and Bhurisravas, and Salya, and Sala, and other warriors united in the hundreds, along with Bhishma himself, have been defeated today by the angry son of Pritha, Arjuna, that most wondrous of warriors."

Talking thus among themselves, Bhaarata, all your soldiers leave the battlefield and enter their tents. Petrified by Kiritin, your warriors enter their beautiful tents illuminated by countless torches and lamps.'

CANTO 60

BHISHMA VADHA PARVA CONTINUED

Sanjaya says, 'Next morning, the incensed Bhishma, supported by an enormous force, at the head of the Bhaarata army, advances against the enemy. And Drona and Duryodhana and Bahlika, and also Durmarshana and Chitrasena, the mighty Jayadratha, and other royal warriors, backed by massive legions, surround him on all sides. Protected by those magnificent maharathas, Bhishma shines forth like Indra in the midst of the Devas.

The colourful standards, red, yellow, black and brown, waving in the air, on the backs of the elephants in the vanguard, look beautiful. The entire army, with Bhishma and other chariot warriors, with their elephants and horses, glows, like a mass of clouds charged with lightning, or like dark thunderheads gathered in the sky during the monsoon.

The Kaurava army, ready for battle and led by Bhishma, charges towards Arjuna like the turbid current of the Ganga rushing towards the sea. Filled with many kinds of mighty forces, and having in its wings a profusion of elephants, horses, footsoldiers, and chariots, Arjuna, with the great Vanara on his banner, sees that vyuha like a dense mass of approaching clouds.

That Kshatriya mahatman, bull among men, upon his chariot furnished with a lofty standard, yoked to white horses, riding at the head of his own great army presses forward against the enemy.

Seeing the warrior with the wild Hanuman on his banner, lofty standard and chariot shaft wrapped in costly sheath, with Krishna Yadupumgava, his charioteer in battle, your sons and all the Kauravas are dismayed. Your army gazes upon that most excellent vyuha with four thousand elephants at each corner, protected by maharatha Arjuna with astras ready.

This vyuha of the Pandavas is as wonderful at the one formed just yesterday by Dharmaraja Yudhishtira, the like of which has never been seen or heard before by men.

Thousands of drums are pounded, and the deafening sound of conches, the blast of trumpets, and many leonine roars arise from every legion. The twang of countless bows stretched by noble warriors and the blowing of conches, silence that din of drums and cymbals.

The sky resounds with the booming of the conches and, diffused with an earthly dust, is awesome to behold; the sky looks as if it is a vast canopy is spread overhead. Seeing that canopy, the fighting men charge into battle.

Maharathas are overthrown by maharathas, with their sarathies, horses, chariots, and standards. Elephants fall to the ground, attacked by elephants, as do footsoldiers struck by other footsoldiers. Racing horsemen are felled by horsemen with spears and swords. And all this seems amazing.

Beautiful shields decked with golden stars and radiant like the sun lie smashed on the field, riven by battle-axes, lances and swords. Many maharathas, gored and mangled by the tusks and the trunks of elephants, collapse along with their charioteers; many are struck down by other chariot warriors. Hearing the cries of riders and footsoldiers pierced by the tusks or crushed by the massive legs of elephants as they charge in close ranks, other warriors fall senseless to the ground.

As the horsemen and foot-soldiers fall fast, and elephants, horses and chariots scatter in fear, Bhishma, surrounded by maharathas, glimpses him who has the mighty Vanara on his standard. The five Palmyra bannered warrior, attacks the diademed Arjuna, the Kiritin, whose chariot, because of the swift horses yoked to it, and the power of his mighty astras, blazes with energy like lightning.

And so against that son of Indra who was like Indra himself, advance many warriors headed by Drona and Kripa, and Salya and Vivimsati, and Duryodhana and Somadatta's son.

The gallant Abhimanyu, son of Arjuna, master of all weapons and protected by golden armour, attacks those warriors; and he of most wondrous feats, thwarts their mighty weapons, fiery like the adored Agni himself, on the sacrificial altar, invoked with mantras.

Bhishma of great tejas, letting a veritable river of the blood of his enemies, avoiding Subhadra's son, encounters Arjuna himself.

With sparkling coronet and bright garlands, with his Gandiva of wonderful mien and twang as loud as thunder, shooting cataracts of arrows, Arjuna foils the astras of Bhishma. And that invincible Kshatriya, with Hanuman on his banner, looses a towering gale of shafts upon the son of Shantanu.

Your troops watch that swarm of arrows shot by Arjuna dispersed by Bhishma like the maker of day dispelling the darkness of night. And the Kurus and the Srinjayas, and all the men there, behold that clash between those two supreme heroes, Bhishma and Dhananjaya, distinguished by the dreadful twanging of their bows.'

CANTO 61

BHISHMA VADHA PARVA CONTINUED

Sanjaya says, 'Drona's son, and Bhurisravas, and Chitrasena, and the son of Samyamani also, all attack Subhadra's son, who fights back single-handedly with great urjas against those five tigerish men, like a young lion against five tuskers. None among them equals Krishna's nephew in bravery, in lightness of hand or in the knowledge of astras.

Seeing his son, that Parantapa, displaying his prowess, Arjuna sets up a leonine roar. And seeing your grandson, Rajan, thus afflicting your army, your warriors encircle him. The valiant son of Subhadra, advances cheerfully against the Dhartarashtra host. His powerful and radiant bow is seen to be relentlessly stretched, always ready to strike.

Piercing the son of Drona with one shaft, and Salya with five, he overthrows the standard of Samyamani's son with eight. With another whetted arrow he cleaves the snakelike golden spear hurled at him by Somadatta's son. The heir of Arjuna cuts down his many deadly shafts and kills his four horses.

Bhurisravas, and Salya, and Drona's son and Samyamani, and Sala, terrified by this display of arms, cannot stand before him. Goaded by your son, the Trigartas and the Madras, with the Kekayas, numbering twenty-five thousand, all excellent men skilled in the science of weapons and unconquerable in war, surround Arjuna and his son to destroy them.

The Senapati of the Pandava army, the prince of the Panchalas, sees their chariots surrounded. Leading thousands of elephants and chariots, and hundreds of thousands of horsemen and footsoldiers, he stretches his bow in great wrath, and advances against that horde of the Madras and the Kekayas.

That division of the Pandava army, protected by this brilliant archer, and consisting of chariots, elephants, and horsemen, is so majestic as it advances. Moving towards Arjuna, that perpetuator of Panchala's race pierces Saradwat's son's shoulder with three keening arrows. He swiftly strikes the Madrakas with ten shafts, killing him who protects Kritavarman from the rear.

With a thick shaft, that Parantapa slays Damana, the heir of the high-souled Paurava. The son of Samyamani stabs the indomitable Panchala prince and his charioteer with ten arrows each. Though wounded, Dhrishtadyumna merely licks the corners of his mouth, resolutely, and cleaves his enemy's bow.

The prince of Panchala attacks his adversary with twenty-five arrows and kills his horses, and both the protectors of his flanks. Bharatarishabha, Samyamani's son, standing on that horseless chariot, looks intently at the son of the famed Drupada. Taking up a terrible sword of steel, Samyamani's son walks towards the Panchala prince who awaits him in his chariot.

The Pandavas, the soldiers and Dhrishtadyumna of Prishata's race watch him come like a surging wave, a snake falling from the skies. Dazzling like the sun, he whirls his sword and advances with the tread of an incensed elephant.

As Samyamani's son, sword and shield in hand, nears his enemy's chariot, the enraged prince of Panchala takes up a mace and smashes his head. The young warrior plunges to the ground, dribbling blood and brains, with his shining blade and shield loosened from his grasp.

And so, having killed his opponent, Dhrishtadyumna wins great glory.

Upon the slaying of that maharatha and most excellent archer, loud lamentations can be heard among your troops. Beside himself at seeing his son killed, Samyamani charges towards the invincible fire prince of Panchala. All the kings of both the Kaurava and the Pandava armies watch those two noble maharathas lock in battle.

The Parantapa Samyamani strikes down the scion of Prishata's race with three shafts much like a mahout of an elephant felling a mighty tusker with hooks. Thus does Salya, that jewel among kings, pierce the valiant son of Prishata in the chest. And another battle begins.'

CANTO 62

Bhishma Vadha Parva continued

Dhritarashtra says, 'I regard destiny to be superior to exertion, Sanjaya. This is clear to me as I watch my son's army being decimated by the Pandava host. You always describe my forces as being slaughtered, and you speak of the Pandavas as being unslain and cheerful. Indeed, you speak of mine as stripped of manliness, felled and falling, even as they fight uncompromisingly and strive hard for victory.

You portray the Pandavas as achieving victory and my sons as becoming progressively weaker. I incessantly hear of countless causes of unbearable and poignant sorrow caused by Duryodhana's deeds. I do not see, Sanjaya, the means by which the Pandavas may be diminished and my sons can triumph in this war.'

Sanjaya says, 'This great evil has ensued from you, Rajan. Listen now with patience to the annihilation of men, elephants, horses and maharathas. Dhrishtadyumna, wounded by Salya's nine shafts, pierces the ruler of Madras with many steely arrows. We watch the awesome prowess of Drupada's son as he swiftly impedes Salya.

The battle between them is brief, and they fight vigorously without rest. Salya rives Dhrishtadyumna's bow with a tempered shaft; he covers him with a deluge of arrows like a cloudburst on a mountain's breast during the monsoon. While Dhrishtadyumna is being attacked, Abhimanyu wrathfully charges towards the chariot of the ruler of the Madras. Nearing it, he stabs Artayani with three sizzling barbs.

To oppose Abhimanyu, your warriors quickly surround Artayani's chariot. And Duryodhana, and Vikarna, and Dussasana, and Vivimsati and Durmarshana, and Dussala, and Chitrasena, and Durmukha, and Satyavrata, and Purumitra position themselves to defend that chariot.

Incensed, Bhima, and Dhrishtadyumna, and the five sons of Draupadi one by each Pandava, and Abhimanyu, and the twin sons of Madri and Pandu attack the Dhritarashtra army with a rage of astras. They fight to kill one another, Rajan, as a result of your evil deeds.

When those ten enraged maharathas clash with the enemy ten, the other maharathas of both armies stand still like spectators, and gaze. Those powerful warriors bellow stridently and strike one another with myriad astras. With ever rising anger, they roar fiercely and challenge each other. They unite and fight the enemy with deadly, mighty weapons.

Choleric Duryodhana pierces Dhrishtadyumna with four shafts. Durmarshana pierces him with twenty, and Chitrasena with five, and Durmukha with nine; he shoots Dussaha with seven, and Vivimsati with five, and Dussasana with three barbs. Dhrishtadyumna resists each of them expertly with twenty-five arrows of his own.

Abhimanyu pierces Satyavrata and Purumitra each with ten shafts. The sons of Madri shroud their uncle with sheets of lean missiles. And all this appears wonderful. Salya attacks his nephews, those two excellent maharathas who want to counter their uncle's exploits; but the sons of Madri do not falter.

The mighty Bhima, seeing Duryodhana, and wanting to end the very war, takes up his mace. Beholding Mahabaho Bhima with raised mace and looking like the peak of Kailasa, your sons flee in terror. Duryodhana, incensed, goads the Magadha legion of ten thousand majestic tuskers to attack. Surrounded by that legion and placing the ruler of Magadha before him, Duryodhana rushes at Bhimasena.

Watching that legion of elephants coming towards him, Vrikodara, mace in hand, leaps down from his chariot with a lion's roar. Armed with that awesome mace, having the weight and strength of adamant, he charges like Siva himself with cavernous mouth agape.

Like a slayer of Vritra among the Danava host, Bhima ranges across the battleground killing elephants with his mace. With his frequent roars, that make the heart and mind tremble, the elephants cower and cannot move.

The sons of Draupadi, and the son of Subhadra, and Nakula and Sahadeva, and Dhrishtadyumna of Prishata's race, protecting Bhima's rear, move swiftly behind him, and stop all by loosing a barrage of arrows, truly like the very clouds pouring rain on a mountain's breast. From the backs of elephants, those Pandava warriors sever the heads of their adversaries with exquisite shafts.

The heads of elephant-riders, and arms decked with ornaments, and hands still holding iron-hooks, falling fast, resemble a downpour of strange rocks. The headless bodies of those riders on the necks of the beasts they rode look like crownless trees on mountain peaks. And we see mighty elephants felled and falling, killed by Dhrishtadyumna.

The ruler of the Magadhas goads his elephant which looks like Airavata himself towards the chariot of Subhadra's son. Parantapa Abhimanyu kills it with a single shaft. After killing his elephant, Abhimanyu cuts off that king's head with a silver-winged arrow.

Bhima penetrates that horde of elephants and meanders about, crushing those royal beasts around him like Indra crushing the mountains of yore. We watch Bhima kill those tuskers, each with but a single stroke of his mace, like hills riven by thunder. Numerous elephants as grand as hills perish, having their tusks broken, or temples, bones, backs, or frontal lobes shattered. Others lie dead, with foaming mouths. Many mighty elephants, with frontal lobes smashed, vomit streams of blood. And some, from fear, lie down on the ground side by side like a range of hills.

Smeared with their fat and blood, and almost bathed in their marrow, Bhima roams over the field like Siva himself; whirling his blood-soaked mace, he is terrible to behold, like Rudra armed with his Pinaka. Being crushed by the raging Bhima, those massive tuskers run wildly in pain, trampling their own warriors. All the while, the daring archers and maharathas, led by Subhadra's son, guard that awesome Kshatriya, whirling his gory mace, dripping the blood of elephants, like the Devas protecting Indra. Of terrible soul, Bhima now truly looks like none but Sankara.

Indeed, Bhaarata, displaying his strength on all sides, we see Bhima like Siva dancing his Tandava at the end of the yuga; his heavy and resounding mace resembles the club of Yama, it echoes with the sound of Indra's thunderbolt. His bloodthirsty mace, smeared with marrow and hair, seems to be the Pinaka annihilating all creatures during Rudra's rage.

As a herdsman chastises his herd of cattle with a goad, Bhima smites that elephant legion with his club. Slaughtered by Bhima and pierced with the arrows of the warriors who protect his rear, the elephants scatter, crushing your chariots. Driving away those great beasts from the field like a mighty wind great clouds, Bhima stands like the wielder of the Trisula on a cremation ground.'

CANTO 63

Bhishma Vadha Parva continued

Sanjaya says, 'When that elephant aksauhini is destroyed, your son Duryodhana rouses his entire army, commanding his warriors to kill Bhima. The whole awesome force rushes towards Vrikodara. That vast host, a challenge for the very Devas, impossible to cross like the surging sea at the full or new moon, teeming with chariots, elephants and horses, resounding with the blast of conches and the beating of drums, with countless footsoldiers and maharathas, and shrouded by the swirling dust it raises, that sea of hostile forces, is arrested by Bhima, like the shore containing the ocean. We are wonderstruck by Bhima's superhuman exploit.

With his mace, he fearlessly checks all those kings cholerically attacking him, with their steeds and chariots and elephants. Withstanding that vast force with his mace, Bhima stands in that fierce melee as unyielding as Meru.

And in that tremendous encounter, his brother and sons, and Dhrishtadyumna of Prishata's race, and the sons of Draupadi and Abhimanyu, and the undefeated Sikhandin do not cravenly abandon him. Taking up his hefty mace made of Saika iron, Bhima charges the warriors of your army like Mahadeva turned to ire. Grinding a multitude of chariots and throngs of horsemen into the earth, Bhima roves across the battleground like the fire consuming all at the end of the yuga.

Pandu's son of infinite prowess smashes a host of chariots just with his legs like iron and kills another host of your fighting men. He crushes your troops with such ease, like an elephant ploughing through a forest of reeds. Dragging down maharathas from their chariots, and horsemen from their horses, and footsoldiers as they stand their ground in your son's forces, Mahabaho Bhima demolishes them all with his mace like the mighty wind risen uprooting frail trees.

Slaughtering elephants and horses, smeared by now richly with fat, marrow, flesh and blood, his mace looks gruesome indeed. With the bodies of warriors and horsemen lying scattered, Kurukshetra appears like Yama's abode. Bhima's mace, that bludgeon of death with the brilliance of Indra's Vajra, is like the Pinaka of Rudra claiming all living creatures.

That swinging mace is fiercely resplendent like the Khatvanga of Siva at the end of the yuga. Seeing him routing that enormous force, your fighting men are dismal. Wherever Bhima casts his eye, there all the warriors seem to melt away.

Beholding Vrikodara consuming those legions, himself impregnable, Bhishma charges at him on his chariot radiant like the sun and with the sound of thunderous clouds, covering the sky with his gale of arrows like a misty rain-filled awning.

Seeing Bhishma charging him like another Rudra, Mahabaho Bhima attacks him fiercely. At that moment, that foremost Kshatriya of Sini's race, the matchless Satyaki, also assails the Pitamaha, killing so many of the enemy as he gloriously rides, filling your son's army with fear. Your warriors, Bhaarata, cannot stop or stand him at all, flying along with his silvery horses, spraying splendid winged shafts.

Only the Rakshasa Alambusha pierces him with ten shafts. Satyaki shoots Alambusha with four arrows and continues on his career. Watching that recalescent warrior whirl through his enemies, scything through the foremost of Kaurava fighting men, and roaring loudly all the while, your warriors shower him with clouds of arrows. But their deadly rain falls as onto a mountain's breast of rock. They cannot impede that gallant hero who looks like the noon-day sun in full glory.

Everyone is despondent, except for Somadatta's son, Bhurisravas, who, seeing the maharathas of his side dispersed, charges against Satyaki with his mighty bow.'

CANTO 64

BHISHMA VADHA PARVA CONTINUED

Sanjaya says, 'Bhurisravas, excited with great wrath, pierces Satyaki with nine arrows. Before the eyes of all, Satyaki stabs the Kaurava warrior with nine shafts of his own. Duryodhana and his brothers surround Somadatta's son as he fights passionately.

The Pandavas quickly encircle Satyaki, protecting him. Ever furious Bhima, mace raised, roars his challenge at all your sons led by Duryodhana. Supported by thousands of chariots, your son Nandaka attacks Bhima with arrows winged with the feathers of the kanka bird.

Duryodhana strikes Bhima in the chest with nine shafts. Mahabaho Bhima, standing in his chariot, says to his sarathy Vishoka, "These heroic and mighty sons of Dhritarashtra, all maharathas, are furious, and want to kill me. I will slaughter all of them today. So steer my horses carefully into battle."

O Dhritarashtra, saying this, Pritha's son strikes your son with a rash of gold decked arrows. And he pierces Nandaka with three barbs in his chest. Duryodhana stabs the mighty Bhima with six shafts and Vishoka with three. Duryodhana calmly cuts off Bhima's resplendent bow at its grasp with three arrows of incredible aim.

Bhima, bull among men, cannot bear to see Vishoka wounded by Duryodhana; he seizes another excellent bow to kill your son. Drawing a crescent-tipped winged arrow, he cleaves Duryodhana's bow in his hands. Roaring, your son discards it and plucks up a more robust one.

Aiming a fearful shaft blazing like Yama's danda, Duryodhana strikes Bhima. Deeply and painfully pierced in his chest, the mighty one drops down in his chariot and faints. Unable to endure seeing Bhima wounded, the illustrious maharathas of the Pandava army, led by Abhimanyu, with unwavering accuracy, loose a harmattan of arrows upon your sons.

Bhima regains consciousness and first covers Duryodhana with a hail of shafts. That gallant son of Pandu pierces Salya with twenty-five golden-winged barbs. Salya is carried off in a swoon from the battleground.

Your fourteen sons, Senapati, Sushena, Jalasandha, Sulochana, Ugra, Bhimaratha, Bhima, Virabahu, Aolupa, Durmukha, Dushpradarsha, Vivitsu, Vikata, and Sama, face Bhima. Unitedly they charge Bhima and with eyes red with anger wound him deeply with countless arrows.

Mahabaho Bhima, licking the corners of his mouth like a wolf amidst smaller creatures, falls upon them with the ferocity of Garuda. With a crescent-tipped shaft, Bhima decapitates Senapati. Exultant, laughing all the while, that towering Kshatriya kills Jalasandha with three arrows. Smiting Sushena, he dispatches him to Yama. And with a single barb he hacks away the stately head of Ugra, beautiful as the moon, decked with turban and adorned with ear-rings.

With seventy arrows, Bhima kills Virabahu and his horses, standard and charioteer. The smiling Bhima slays both the brothers Bhima and Bhimaratha. In that great war, Bhima also fells Sulochana. The rest of your sons, seeing indomitable Bhima roused like that, flee.

Bhishma addresses all the maharathas of his army saying, "Bhima, excited with wrath, can annihilate the mighty sons of Dhritarashtra and every other maharatha, all united together, regardless of their knowledge of weapons, and their valour. All of you must attack and kill that son of Pandu."

Hearing this, the vast legions of the Dhritarashtra army rush at Bhima. Bhagadatta, on his elephant of rent temples, dashes to where the massive Pandava stands. He mantles Bhima with countless arrows, like the clouds covering the sun.

But those intrepid maharathas of the Pandava army cannot bear seeing that shrouding of Bhima by the torrent of Bhagadatta's shafts, and they surround Bhagadatta, raining arrows on him. They also pierce his elephant with showers of barbs. Struck by the awesome shafts of those maharathas, that elephant of the ruler of the Pragjyotishas, with blood flowing down his body, appears as strikingly handsome as a mass of clouds stained by the sun's rays. With temporal juice pouring down, that elephant Supritika is goaded by Bhagadatta to race forward, shaking the earth with his tread.

The Pandava maharathas, gazing upon the beast's dreadful appearance, lose all courage. King Bhagadatta, lion among men, forcefully strikes Bhima in the chest with a straight shaft of great length. Bhima faints and falls to the floor of his chariot, holding onto his flagpole. Seeing the fear of the enemy maharathas and an unconscious Bhima, Bhagadatta roars exultantly.

Seeing his father Bhima fainted, the feral Rakshasa Ghatotkacha is incensed and vanishes from sight using maya. Creating a macabre illusion, he reappears the next moment in a form so prodigious and fierce as to fill the hearts of the timid with nameless dread. Riding on an Airavata created by his maya shakti, the other celebrated elephants, Anjana, Vamana, and Mahapadma, follow him.

Ridden by Rakshasas, those massive tuskers, with juice profusely trickling down in three lines, thunder into battle. Ghatotkacha spurs his own elephant forward to demolish Bhagadatta and his great beast. The other mastodons, each endowed with four tusks, goaded by huge and sinister Rakshasas, attack Bhagadatta's elephant from every side, goring him, shooting him with savage arrows.

Wounded by excruciating shafts, Supritika bellows boomingly as loud as Indra's thunder. Hearing those deafening cries, Bhishma says to Drona,

Suyodhana and all the kings, "The mighty Bhagadatta, battling the evil son of Hidimbi, is in distress. The Rakshasa is formidable, and the king beside himself with anger. They will slaughter each other. Loud shouts of the rejoicing Pandavas can be heard, as can the agonized cries of king Bhagadatta's terrified elephant.

Let us all ride to save the beleaguered king or he will be killed! Warriors of great urjas, do not delay. The battle becomes even fiercer, making one's hair stand on end. That legion's commander is of high varna, brave, and devoted to us. O my heroes of unfading glory, we must save him."

Hearing Bhishma's words, all the kings of the Kaurava army, led by Drona, charge towards Bhagadatta, sovereign of the Pragjyotishas. Seeing them come, the Panchalas with the Pandavas, led by Yudhishtira, pursue them. Ghatotkacha, mighty prince of Rakshasas, roars shatteringly as he sees the enemy legion press forward.

Hearing that roar and seeing those battle elephants, Bhishma says to Drona, "I do not wish to fight today with the evil son of Hidimbi. Mighty and vigorous, he is so well supported at the moment that even Indra could not vanquish him. He has a deadly aim. As for us, today our animals are tired. We have been crushed by the Panchalas and the Pandavas. I would not like a fresh encounter with them just now. Order our army to withdraw. Tomorrow we will fight anew."

Hearing these words of the Pitamaha, the Kauravas, terrified of Ghatotkacha and ready to use nightfall as a pretext, obey him promptly. After the Kauravas have withdrawn, the conquering Pandava lions roar and roar in victory, and their roars echo with the blast of conches and mingle with the notes of flutes. Bhaarata, in this way did the Kauravas and the Pandavas led by Ghatotkacha fight each other on that day.

The Kauravas, overcome with shame at being decimated and humiliated by the Pandavas, retire downcast to their tents. And those maharathas, the sons of Pandu, lacerated by arrows and wearied by the fighting, also retire to their camp led by Bhima and Ghatotkacha. Joyfully, they praise these two heroes. Their triumphant shouts mingle with the music of horns. Those sounds make the very earth tremble, carving the hearts of your sons.

Thus those Parantapas retreat into their tents. Duryodhana, stricken by the death of his brothers, is forlorn, overcome with grief and weeping. He passes the hours in meditation, anguish over the killing of his brothers burning him.'

CANTO 65

BHISHMA VADHA PARVA CONTINUED

Dhritarashtra says, 'Hearing of those feats of the Pandavas, before whom the very Devas appear powerless, my heart, Sanjaya, is filled with awe and fear. Hearing also of the humiliation of my sons, I dread the outcome of this war. Vidura's words trouble me. Everything that has occurred appears to be the will of fate.

The warriors of the Pandava army confront and annihilate our exceptional fighting men who are led by Bhishma and are so skilled in using every weapon. What ascetic penances have the high-souled and mighty sons of Pandu performed, what boon have they obtained, what science is known to them, that they do not diminish like stars in the sky? I cannot bear that my army is being slaughtered by them. This divine and cruel punishment has fallen on me alone.

Tell me everything truly, Sanjaya, that explains the invincibility of the Pandavas and the vulnerability of my sons. I am drowning in this ocean of anguish and cannot see the other shore. I am like a man thrashing to cross this vast ocean by just the strength of my two arms. I know that a great calamity has engulfed my sons. Certainly, Bhima will crush them. I do not see any hero who will be able to protect them. Their death, in this war, is assured.

I implore you, O Suta, to tell me everything about the true cause of all these events. Seeing his troops retreating from the melee, what does Duryodhana do? And what the respected Bhishma and Drona, and Kripa, and Subala's son, and Jayadratha, and that forceful archer, Drona's son, and mighty Vikarna? Wise Sanjaya, watching my sons withdraw, what do the Pandavas resolve to do?'

Sanjaya says, 'Listen carefully, Rajan, and having heard, understand this. Nothing is the result of a spell, or the outcome of chimera of any kind. Nor have the sons of Pandu created any new terrors. They are mighty, and fight fairly in this war. Seeking glory, the sons of Pritha always cleave to dharma, even when their own lives are at risk.

Having both great wealth and strength, they continue to battle, never straying from righteousness. And victory lies with the virtuous. This is why the sons of Pritha are unassailable and always victorious. Your sons are evil and sinful. They are cruel and shameful in what they do. This is why they are being diminished.

Your sons' actions towards the Pandavas have been devious and ruthless. The sons of Pandu have always disregarded these offences. On many occasions your sons have humiliated them. Let them now reap the terrible fruit, like poison, of that persistent course of sins. Rajan, you too will harvest that fruit, along with your sons and kinsmen, since you could not be persuaded to return to dharma despite the counsel of your well-wishers.

Repeatedly forbidden by Vidura, by Bhishma, by the high-souled Drona, and by me also, you would not understand, disregarding what we said for your good, like a sick man refusing medicine that would save him. Instead believing your sons' opinions, you considered the Pandavas already defeated. Again, listen to me about the true cause of the Pandava victory. Parantapa, I will tell you what I have heard.

Duryodhana asked the Pitamaha this very question. Seeing his brothers, all mighty chariot warriors, routed in battle, your grief-stricken son humbly goes to the wise Bhishma during the night and asks him this same thing. Rajan, I will tell you all about it.

Duryodhana says, "Drona and you, and Salya, and Kripa, and Drona's son, and Kritavarman the son of Hridika, and Sudakshina the ruler of the Kambojas, and Bhurisravas, and Vikarna, and Bhagadatta of exceeding prowess, are all deemed maharathas. All are dvija, and prepared to sacrifice their lives in battle.

It is my view that these are a match for even the hosts of the three worlds combined. All the warriors of the Pandava army jointly cannot oppose your prowess. A doubt has risen in my mind. Explain it to me. Whom do the Pandavas rely on to repeatedly subdue us?"

Bhishma says, "Listen to me, Suyodhana. I frequently advised you about this but you did not listen. Bharatarishabha, make peace with the Pandavas. This will benefit both the world and you. Enjoy this earth with your brothers and be happy, gratifying all your well-wishers and delighting your kinsmen.

Although I beseeched you, you did not heed my counsel. You have always scorned the sons of Pandu. The outcome has now overwhelmed you. Listen also to the reason why the tireless Pandavas cannot be slain.

There is not, was not, nor will be, in all the worlds a warrior who can overpower the sons of Pandu who are all protected by the wielder of the Saranga. Knowing dharma as you do, listen to that ancient history, itihasa, which was narrated to me by sages of restrained souls.

In olden days, all the Devas and the Rishis, united together, waited respectfully on the Pitamaha Brahma upon the mountains of Gandhamadana.

And the Lord of all creatures, seated in their midst, saw a wonderful luminous chariot in the sky. Having gained knowledge of it through dhyana, calmly joining his hands, Brahma, with delighted soul, greeted the highest Divine Being. The Rishis and the Devas, beholding this form in the sky, all stood up with folded hands, their eyes fixed on that wonder of wonders.

Worshipping him duly, Brahma, the Creator of the universe, aware of Brahman, conscious of the highest rectitude, spoke these noble words: 'With your form, you endow magnificence upon the universe. You are indeed the protector of the universe. O most Supreme One, the universe is your creation. You are Vasudeva. Therefore, I seek refuge in You who are the soul of yoga and the highest God. Victory to You who are the Supreme Deity!

Victory to You who personify all the good of the worlds. Victory to you, Lord of yoga, who are omnipotent. Victory to You who both precede and succeed yoga. With the lotus springing from your navel, and having all-embracing eyes, victory to You who are the Lord of the Devas. O Holy Being of the past, the present, and the future, victory to You, the embodiment of gentleness!

You are the sun of suns. The receptacle of countless attributes, the refuge of all things, may You triumph. You are Narayana, too deep to be fathomed. Wielder of the Saranga, may victory be yours.

Unsullied and blessed with every attribute, having the universe for your form, may you always prevail. Lord of the universe, Mahabaho, one who blesses the worlds, victory to You. O great Snake, mighty Varaha, O first Cause, with tawny hair, all-powerful One, may You always be victorious!

Saffron-robed Lord of the cardinal and the subsidiary directions, You, who pervade all the universe, are infinite and eternal, the manifest and the unmanifest. You that are the immeasurable Akasa, with all your senses under control, who attains what is good, You that are immeasurable, You who alone know your own nature, victory to You!

You are profound and vast; you grant all wishes, One without end, known as Brahman, You that are eternal, the Creator of all creatures, ever successful and wise, are familiar with dharma, the One who confers victory, You of mysterious Self, You are the soul of all yoga. You who cause everything to be born, who are the knowledge of the selves of all beings, Lord of the worlds, victory to you. Svayambhu, most blessed, you are also the veritable Destroyer.

Inspirer of all thoughts, dear to all conversant with Brahman, ever creating and destroying, controller of all wishes, Supreme Lord, the cause of amrita, You are all-existent, nityasya. You are the first to appear at the end of the yuga, guardian of victory, Divine Lord of the Lord of all creatures, from whose navel springs the lotus, mighty and, arisen from Yourself, embodying the great elements in their primeval state, You who are the soul of all rites and rituals, victory to You who grants everything!

Bhumi Devi represents your two feet, the cardinal and the subsidiary directions your arms, and the sky your head. I am your form, the Devas your limbs, and the sun and the moon are your two eyes. Tapasya and satya born of dharma and yagna are your strength. Agni is your energy, Vayu is your breath, and the waters have sprung from your sweat. The Aswins form your ears, and Saraswati is your tongue. The Vedas are your knowledge, and upon you rests this Brahmanda. Lord of yoga and yogins, we do not know your extent, your measure, your energy, your prowess, your power, your origin.

Vishnu, we worship you fervently, with vows and ceremonies, as the Supreme One, and depend upon you. The Rishis, the Devas, the Gandharvas, the Yakshas, the Rakshasas, the Pannagas, the Pisachas, the Manavas, animals and birds, were all created by me on Earth through your grace.

Krishna, with the lotus springing from your navel, O you of large expansive eyes, you dispel all despair and are the refuge and guide of all creatures. The Universe is your mouth and the Devas delight in your blessings. Through your grace the Earth is freed from terrors.

Therefore, take birth in the Yaduvamsa. Establish dharma, slay the sons of Diti, and uphold the universe. Vasudeva, I sing your supreme mystery through your own benevolence.

Having created the divine Sankarshana out of your own self by yourself, Krishna, you then made yourself as Pradyumna born of yourself. From Pradyumna you created Aniruddha known as the eternal Vishnu. And it was Aniruddha who created me as Brahma, the support of the universe. Created out of Vasudeva's essence I have, therefore, been created by you.

Krishna, dividing yourself into amsas, take birth among human beings. Slaughtering the Asuras there for the bliss of all the worlds, establishing virtue, and winning fame, You will again realise Yoga.

The regenerate Rishis on Earth and the Devas are devoted to you and sing of your wonder, pronouncing all your names. Mahabaho, all classes of creatures depend on you, having taken refuge in You who grants boons. The regenerate ones sing of you being Setu, the world's bridge to salvation, having no beginning, middle and end, possessing unlimited Yoga.""

CANTO 66

BHISHMA VADHA PARVA CONTINUED

Sanjaya says, 'Bhishma says, "Then the Lord of the worlds said to Brahma in a soft rumbling voice, 'Through Yoga, I know what you desire. It will be as you wish.'

And saying this, he disappeared. Then the Devas, Rishis and Gandharvas, filled with great wonder and curiosity asked Brahma, 'Who is that one that you worshipped with such humility and praised so highly? Tell us.'

The celebrated Pitamaha replied to all the Devas, the regenerate Rishis, and the Gandharvas, in sweet tones, 'He who is called TAT, He who is Supreme, He who exists now and for all time, He who is the highest Self, He who is the Soul of beings, and who is the great Lord, it was to Him that I spoke. I pleaded with the Lord of the universe, for the good of the universe, to take his birth among men in the family of Vasudeva.

I said to Him: Take birth in the world of men to slaughter the Asuras! Those fierce and strong Daityas and Rakshasas, killed in unworldly battle, have been born among men. Incarnating in a human womb, You will live on the Earth accompanied by Nara.

Those ancient and excellent Rishis, Nara and Narayana, cannot be defeated in battle by even all the Devas united. Of immense effulgence, those Rishis when born together in the world of men will not be recognised by fools.

He, from whose Self, I, Brahma, the Lord of the whole Universe, have sprung, that Vasudeva, that Supreme One, is worthy of your adoration. Imbued with great tejas, and holding the conch, the discus, and the mace, he should never be regarded as a mere man. He is the Unmatched Mystery, the Ultimate Refuge, the Supreme Brahman, and the Greatest Glory.

Unmanifest and eternal, he cannot perish. He has been praised as Purusha, though no one can understand him completely. The Creator has extolled him as the Supreme Energy, the Supreme Felicity, and the Supreme Truth.

Therefore, Vasudeva of vast capacities should never be considered as just a man, not by all the Asuras and the Devas led by Indra. Someone who speaks of Hrishikesa as only a man is a fool and a wretch.

People who disregard that Yogin of illustrious soul for entering into human form are blind. They labour under darkness who do not know that Divine luminary, that Soul of the mobile and the immobile creation, that one bearing the Srivatsa on his chest, that one of dazzling brilliance, that one from whose navel has sprung the primeval lotus.

He who disdains that high souled one, the wearer of the divine crown and the Kaustubha ruby, one who dispels his friends' fears, sinks into deep darkness. Vasudeva should be adored by all.'

Having said these words to those Devas and Rishis, the illustrious Brahma, dismissing them all, returned to his own abode. The Devas and the Gandharvas, and the Munis and the Apsaras, having heard those holy words of Brahma, were delighted and returned to Devaloka. I myself heard this about Krishna from Rishis of cultured souls speaking in their assembly.

You who know the Shastras well, I heard this from Rama, the son of Jamadagni, and Markandeya of great wisdom, and Vyasa and Narada. Having learnt all this and heard of the illustrious Vasudeva as the Eternal Lord, the Supreme God of all the worlds, and the great Master, from whom Brahma himself has sprung, I ask: why should not that Vasudeva be adored and worshipped by men?

You were forbidden by great sages who asked you never to go to war with that Vasudeva armed with his bow as also with the Pandavas. Your foolishness prevented you from comprehending what they said. I hence consider you a wicked Rakshasa. You are also enveloped in ignorance. It is for this reason that you hate Krishna and Arjuna, for who else among men would hate the divine Nara and Narayana?

It is for this, Duryodhana, that I say to you that this one is Eternal and Unfading, pervading the whole Universe, Unchanging, the Ruler, Creator and Upholder of all, and the truly Existent. He supports the three worlds. He is the Supreme Lord of all mobile and immobile creatures, and He is the great Master. He is warrior, He is Victory, He is Vanquisher, and He is the Lord of all nature.

He is full of goodness and without all the qualities of tamas and rajas, darkness and passion. Where Krishna is, there is righteousness; and where righteousness dwells, there is victory. It is by the Yoga of his Supreme Excellence, and the Yoga of his Self, that the sons of Pandu are supported. Therefore, they will surely triumph.

To the Pandavas he imparts understanding permeated with righteousness, and strength in battle; and He always protects them from danger. He is the Eternal God, pervading all beings, and ever blessed. Known as Vasudeva, he is humbly served by all, Brahmanas and Kshatriyas, Vaisyas and Sudras, who, fulfilling their own dharma, worship Him with restrained hearts.

Towards the close of the Dwapara Yuga and the beginning of the Kali Yuga, it is He who is praised with songs of devotion by believers. It is that Vasudeva who creates, yuga after yuga, the worlds of the Devas and Manushyas, all the cities encircled by the sea, and all the regions where men live.'"

CANTO 67

BHISHMA VADHA PARVA CONTINUED

Sanjaya says, 'Duryodhana says, "In all the worlds Vasudeva is known as the Supreme Being. Pitamaha, I want to understand his origin and glory."

Bhishma says, "Vasudeva is the Supreme Being. He is the God of all Gods. With eyes like lotus petals, there is none more exalted than him. Markandeya speaks of Govinda as the Most Wonderful and the Most High, as the All-being, as the All-soul, as the Highest soul, and as the Supreme Purusha.

He created Water, Wind, and Fire. That Divine Master created this Earth. That Supreme Being of illustrious soul and all kinds of Tejas laid himself down on the ocean and slept in Yoga. From his mouth He created Fire, and from his breath, the Wind. Of unfading glory, He created from his mouth Vak the Word and the Vedas.

It was thus that he created first the Worlds and also the Devas along with the many classes of Rishis. And he created the decay and death of all beings, as well as birth and maturity. He is Dharma itself. He grants us our boons and desires. He is the Actor and Action, and He is himself the Divine Guru.

He created the Past, the Present, and the Future; He is the Creator of the Universe. Of illustrious soul, He is the magnificent Preceptor. He created Sankarshana, the First-born of all creatures. He created the divine Sesha Ananta, who supports the Earth with all her creatures and mountains.

Of matchless Tejas, the regenerate ones know Him through Yoga. Sprung from the secretions of his ear, the fierce and merciless Asura Madhu, who intended to and almost destroyed Brahma, was slain by Vasudeva. And so the Devas and the Danavas, the Manavas and Rishis call Janardana the slayer of Madhu, Madhusudana.

The great Varaha, the great Narasimha, He is the Three-stepped Vamana. He is the Mother and the Father of all living creatures. There never was, nor will be, any more excellent than He of eyes like lotus petals.

He created the Brahmanas from His mouth and the Kshatriyas from His arms; from His thighs He fashioned the Vaisyas, and from His feet the Sudras. One who serves Him dutifully, observing vows with ascetic austerities on days of the full-moon and the new-moon, is sure to obtain the Divine Kesava, that refuge of all embodied creatures, that essence of Brahman and Yoga.

Kesava is the higher Energy, the ancestor of all the worlds. The sages call Him Hrishikesa. All should know Him as the Acharya and the Pitamaha. Him with whom Krishna is delighted, attains eternal regions of blessedness.

He who is fearful should seek Kesava's protection; and he who repeatedly reads this stuti, achieves happiness and prosperity. Those who attain Krishna are never deceived; Janardana always sustains those who are frightened.

Rajan, knowing this truly, Yudhishtira, has wholeheartedly sought refuge in Krishna, the Lord of Yoga, and the Lord of the Earth.'"

CANTO 68

BHISHMA VADHA PARVA CONTINUED

'Bhishma says, "I will recite this hymn that Brahma himself sang. In ancient times, this hymn was imparted by regenerate Rishis and the Devas to men:

'Narada described you as the Acharya and the Supreme Lord of the Devas and all the Sadhyas and the heavenly beings, and as one who knows the nature of Brahman. Markandeya spoke of you as the Past, the Present, and the Future, the sacrifice of sacrifices, and the austerity of austerities.

The celebrated Bhrigu said that you are the God of the gods and all creatures, the ancient form of Vishnu. Dwaipayana said that you are Vasudeva of the Vasus, who establishes Sakra. When mortals were being born, the sages described you as Daksha, the Father of creation.

Angiras said that you are the creator of all beings. Devala said that your body comprised the unmanifest, your mind the manifest, and that all the Devas are produced by your breath. The heavens are filled with your heads, and your arms support the Earth. In your stomach are the three worlds and you are the Eternal Being.

Even thus do men exalted by asceticism know you. You are the Sat of Sat, with Rishis gratified with sight of the Atman. With royal sages of liberal minds, resolute in battle and with ethical aims, you, destroyer of Madhu, are the only refuge.'

The Supreme Being, Hari, is thus adored and worshipped by Sanatkumara and other ascetic yogis. I have now described the truth about Kesava to you, both in brief and detail. Turn to him in love."'

Sanjaya continues, 'Hearing this sacred story, your son begins to revere both Kesava and the Pandava maharathas. Then, O Rajan, Bhishma says to Duryodhana, "You have now heard about Krishna's glory and about Nara. You also now know why Nara and Narayana have incarnated among men.

You have also been told why those heroes are invincible and have never been defeated in war, and why also no one can kill the sons of Pandu in war. Krishna greatly loves the sons of Pandu. And so I say: Make peace with the Pandavas. Curb your passions and enjoy the Earth with your mighty brothers. By disregarding the divine Nara and Narayana, you will be destroyed."

Having said these words, the Pitamaha becomes silent, and dismissing King Duryodhana, enters his tent. Duryodhana also returns to his tent, after paying his respects to Bhishma. And then, Bharatarishabha, he lies down to sleep.'

CANTO 69

BHISHMA VADHA PARVA CONTINUED

Sanjaya says, 'When the night passes and the sun rises, the two armies face each other again. Each side moves forward in united and furious ranks to overcome the other. And as a result of your evil deeds, the Pandavas and the Kauravas advance, encased in armour and in battle formation.

The vyuha that Bhishma protects from all sides is that of the Makara, the great crocodile. The Pandavas also form protect their vyuha. Maharatha Bhishma rides with a large aksauhini of chariots. Chariot warriors, footsoldiers, elephants, and horsemen, all follow him, positioned in assigned places.

Seeing them ready for battle, the Pandavas deploy their forces in the invincible Syena vyuha. On that vyuha's beak shines the formidable Bhima. The invincible Sikhandin and Dhrishtadyumna are its eyes. In its head is the heroic Satyaki of indomitable prowess.

On its neck stands Arjuna vibrating his Gandiva. Upon its left wing is the high-souled and blessed Drupada with his son supported by an aksauhini of all forces. And the king of the Kekayas, with an akshauhini, forms the right wing of that vyuha. On its back are the sons of Draupadi, and Subhadra's wonderful son. And at its tail is the heroic and excellent Yudhishtira himself, supported by Nakula and Sahadeva.

In the battle that ensues, Bhima penetrates the Kaurava vyuha of Makara through its mouth, and approaching Bhishma, covers him with stern arrows. Mighty Bhishma looses his deadly weapons, baffling the Pandava forces. And when the Pandava fighting men are thus confounded, Arjuna swiftly strikes Bhishma with a thousand shafts. Countering Bhishma's weapons, Arjuna, supported by his own spirited men, erupts into battle.

Maharatha Duryodhana, seeing the bloody carnage wreaked on his army and remembering the slaughter of his brothers, rushes up to Drona and says to him, "Acharya, ever my well-wisher, relying on you and on the Pitamaha, we hope to defeat the very Devas in battle, let alone the sons of Pandu who are floundering with neither energy nor prowess. O blessed one, fight today so that the Pandavas are annihilated."

At this, Drona plunges into the Pandava vyuha before Satyaki's very eyes, who quickly retaliates to stop the son of Bharadwaja. The battle that follows is pitched and fierce. Roused, the great Drona, smiling the while, pierces the grandson of Sini with ten shafts in his shoulder. Bhima shoots Drona with a rash of arrows, seeking to protect Satyaki. Infuriated, Drona, Bhishma and Salya shroud Bhima with their fire. Abhimanyu and the sons of Draupadi wound those armed warriors with their sharpest barbs.

In that brutal contention, the great archer Sikhandin charges against Bhishma and Drona who have fallen upon the Pandavas. Firmly grasping his bow, whose twang is the roar of clouds, that Kshatriya, obscuring the very sun with his volleys, ferociously attacks his adversaries. The Pitamaha, finding Sikhandin before him, avoids him, remembering his once womanhood.

Spurred on by your son, Drona, wanting to protect Bhishma, presses forward. Sikhandin quickly turns on Drona, avoiding the Pitamaha, fearing that warrior who is like fire that appears at the end of the yuga.

Duryodhana moves to protect Bhishma with a vast legion.

And the Pandavas, resolved on victory, also press forward, and the encounter between the two sides, both seeking fame and triumph, is breathtaking, indeed like the Devasura yuddha of old.'

CANTO 70

BHISHMA VADHA PARVA CONTINUED

Sanjaya says, 'Bhishma, son of Shantanu, fights awesomely to protect your sons from Bhima. The battle between the kings of the Kaurava and the Pandava armies is shocking and bloody, annihilating great Kshatriyas. From that war, a tumult rises, reaching the very heavens. Deafening is that bedlam, as tuskers scream and horse whinny, while conches blast and drums pound, and mighty enemies roar at one another like contending bulls in a cow-pen. Severed heads fall ceaselessly, like some grisly rain of weird rocks from the sky.

Bharatarishabha, countless heads lie strewn across the battlefield, with bright earrings and ornamented turbans. And the earth is covered over with limbs hacked away with broad-headed shafts, and bejewelled arms; with bodies sheathed in gleaming, red-stained armour, with braceleted arms, with moon-like faces and kohl-tinted eyes; limbs of elephants, horses and men lie everywhere. Dust swirls everywhere in a thick cloud, and bright weapons flash like lightning. The sound of all the weapons together is the roar of thunder.

The horrible war between the Kauravas and the Pandavas lets flow a bloody river, sprung from a million wounds made by the incessant tirade of arrows loosed by invincible Kshatriyas upon Kurukshetra. Bleeding from that gale of vicious barbs, the elephants of both armies shriek, and course furiously in all directions. Everything is hidden in the twang of virile bows and the mighty flapping of bowstrings against the leathern gloves of incensed and heroic fighting men.

On Kurukshetra, looking like a lake of blood, stand headless trunks, briefly; kings determined to kill their enemies charge reckless at them; mighty warriors, with club-like arms, slaughter one another with barbs, maces and swords; riderless horses and elephants, pierced with arrows, plunge wildly in all directions; many soldiers on both sides leap high and fall, heads stricken off.

In the battle between Bhima and Bhishma, ever-growing heaps of arms and heads, as also of bows and maces and spiked clubs, and hands and thighs, of legs, and jewels and bracelets, are strewn over the field. Across that dreadful field, Rajan, masses of unretreating elephants, horses and chariots can be seen. Kshatriya warriors, moved by destiny, decimate one another with maces, swords, spears, and arrows. Heroic and skilled fighting men contend with bare arms that resemble spiked iron clubs.

Other valiant men of your army fight the Pandava host, killing thousands with clenched fists and knees, slaps and blows. The fallen and falling warriors, and those lying on the ground wounded and in agony, make the fell field a horrible spectacle; maharathas, bereft of their chariots, still holding their swords, always eager to kill, attack one another in mad rage.

Surrounded by a large Kalinga aksauhini, with Bhishma at its van, Duryodhana charges the Pandavas. The Pandava warriors supporting Bhima ride wildly, intently against Bhishma with their fine horses and lumbering elephants.'

CANTO 71

BHISHMA VADHA PARVA CONTINUED

Sanjaya says, 'Seeing his brothers and the other kings battling Bhishma, Arjuna storms towards him, weapons raised. Hearing the blast of the Panchajanya and the twang of the Gandiva, and seeing his standard, we are terrified. That standard bears the emblem of a lion's tail and looks like a mountain blazing in the sky. Beautiful and of divine workmanship, it is flecked with many colours, looking like a rising comet on a horizon unobscured by any trees.

All the warriors see the Gandiva, chased with purest gold, as magnificent as a great flash of lightning amidst dense clouds in the sky. While razing the soldiers of your army, Arjuna's shouts are like the thunderous roars of Indra himself; the slaps of his palms are deafening.

Like a cloud mass charged with lightning, bolstered by a raging wind, Arjuna relentlessly looses his arrows on all sides, completely shrouding the ten points of the compass. He of the terrifying astras advances rapidly towards the Pitamaha. We that watch are struck senseless and cannot distinguish the East from the West.

Bharatarishabha, your men are bewildered and depressed, their animals tired, their horses slaughtered; huddling close to one another, together with your sons, they seek Bhishma's protection. And in that battle Bhishma becomes their protector.

Fearstricken maharathas leap from their chariots, horsemen from the backs of their steeds, and foot-soldiers fall where they stand. Hearing the thunder of the Gandiva, all your fighting men flee, shutting their ears.

With many swift horses of the Kamboja breed, surrounded by thousands of Gopas with a large Gopayana force, and supported by the Madras, the Sauviras, the Gandharas and the Trigartas, surrounded by all the principal Kalingas, along with king Jayadratha accompanied by all the kings, and supported by a large force of diverse races with Dussasana at their head, and fourteen thousand leading horsemen, spurred by your son, the great Kamboja king encircles Sakuni, son of Subala, to protect him.

All the sons of Pandu, united, again desiccate your forces from their chariots and animals. And the dust raised by maharathas, horses and foot-soldiers, flecked generously with spraying blood, renders Kurukshetra hideous, like a dark precinct of hell.

With a vast legion of elephants, horses and chariots, armed with spears, barbs and arrows, Bhishma fights Arjuna Kiritin. The king of Avanti engages the lord of the Kasis, and the ruler of the Sindhus, Bhima. With his sons and advisors, Yudhishtira battles Salya, his uncle, the famed ruler of the Madras. Vikarna engages with Sahadeva, and Chitrasena with Sikhandin. The Matsyas fight Duryodhana and Sakuni, while Drupada and Chekitana, and the maharatha Satyaki encounter the high-souled Drona and his son Aswatthaman. Kripa and Kritavarman both charge against Dhrishtadyumna.

Thus, all over the field, storming bodies of horses, elephants and chariots break upon each other. Although there are no clouds in the sky, flashes of lightning are seen on high. Every direction is darkened by flying clouds of dust raised by the hostile forces. Fierce meteors fail with loud reverberations. Violent winds blow swirling the dense dust everywhere. The sun is eclipsed by these. And all the warriors, wielding weapons, are choked by that dust and swoon.

The roar of weapons, discharged from the arms of the fearless, missiles which can cut through armour like knives through butter, rises to another tumult. Bharatarishabha, those weapons of stellar brightness, illuminate the sky. Dappled leather shields plated with gold are scattered all around. Heads and limbs are seen falling on all sides, cut down with radiant swords and spears. Their chariot wheels, axles and carriages smashed, their horses killed, valiant maharathas plunge to the ground, their proud standards toppling about them.

The horses of these slain chariot warriors, dragging their riderless chariots, mangled with weapons, finally crash to the ground. Some excellent horses, despite having their limbs mangled with arrows, continue to run, dragging their chariot yokes behind them. Maharathas, their sarathies and horses are all flattened like meat on a cook's board by powerful tuskers.

Many elephants, smelling the temporal juice of others, sniff the air repeatedly through wrinkled trunks. And the whole field is strewn with hilly corpses of these massive beasts, slaughtered by arrows, fallen along with their howdahs and mahouts. Many elephants, with their standards and riders, are trampled by others goaded on by their riders. Terror stalks Kurukshetra in every sinister guise.

Swinging thick trunks, the colossal war beasts, each one an Airavata, shatter chariot shafts all around; and many maharathas, with the jalas of their chariots cracked, are dragged by the bloodthirsty elephants from their rathas by their long hair, like branches of trees, and smashed again and again on the ground, crushed into shapeless heaps. Other enormous tuskers drag tangled chariots as if they were lotus stalks in lakes, and run bellowing in all directions.

And so we see that Kurukshetra grimly, copiously, adorned with the bodies of horse riders and foot-soldiers, maharathas and their standards.'

CANTO 72

BHISHMA VADHA PARVA CONTINUED

Sanjaya says, 'Sikhandin, with Virata the Matsya king, swiftly nears the invincible Bhishma. Arjuna encounters Drona and Kripa, and Vikarna and many other brave kings, all powerful archers; he also faces that mighty bowman, the ruler of the Sindhus, supported by his friends and kinsmen and many kings of the west and the south.

Bhima marches against your malicious son Duryodhana, and also against Dussaha. Sahadeva advances against those invincible warriors, Sakuni and the maharatha Uluka, those great archers, father and son. Maharatha Yudhishtira, so treacherously treated by your son, presses forward against the Kaurava aksauhini of elephants.

And that son of Pandu and Madri, the valiant Nakula, who can reduce any enemy to tears, faces the excellent Trigarta maharathas. Satyaki and Chekitana, indomitable, and the mighty son of Subhadra ride against Salya and the Kaikeyas. The unassailable Dhrishtaketu and the Rakshasa Ghatotkacha break upon your sons' chariots.

Maharatha Dhrishtadyumna, Senapati of the Pandavas, opposes fierce Drona. Thus those fearless and heroic archers of your army and the

Pandavas engage in battle.

When the sun is overhead and the sky brilliantly illuminated by his rays, the Kauravas and the Pandavas massacre one another. Beautiful chariots, draped in tiger skins, race across the field, their flags and pennants fluttering in the wind. Warriors let out leonine roars as they contend fiercely.

Furious and wonderful to watch is the encounter between the noble Srinjayas and the Kauravas. Arrows fly thickly in every direction, covering the sky, the sun and every point of the compass.

The splendour of polished barbs looking like blue lotuses, of bearded spears hurled like thunderbolts, of tempered swords, of flecked coats of mail, and of the ornaments worn by the fighting men, light up the sky and the earth with blinding radiance. And Kurukshetra shines with the brightness of embattled kings as if with the lustre of the sun and the moon. Brave maharathas, tigers among men, glow in that battle, Rajan, like the planets in the sky.

Maharatha Bhishma challenges the mighty Bhima before the eyes of all. Bhishma's golden-winged arrows strike Bhima. Bhima looses a serpentine astra at Bhishma, who cleaves that tangential weapon as it courses towards him with a flight of straight shafts. With another, he breaks Bhima's bow in two.

Satyaki flies up in his ratha and recklessly pierces Bhishma with a constellation of shimmering barbs shot from his bowstring drawn to his ear. Bhishma fells Satyaki's sarathy, while his horses bolt. Swift as the mind or a storm, they run wildly over the battleground.

Roars, yells, shouts and cries rise all around from the horrible melee: *Run, seize, check the horses, hurry!*

And this uproar follows Yuyudhana's chariot. Bhishma meanwhile begins to destroy the Pandava forces like Indra killing the Danavas. But the Panchalas and the Somakas, though suffering, courageously attack the Kuru grandsire. Other Pandava warriors, led by Dhrishtadyumna, determined to thin the ranks of your son's army, charge at Bhishma.

In this manner, the warriors of your army, headed by Bhishma and

Drona, fearlessly harry their enemies. Then the warriors ride away from their many contentions and other fresh battles begin.'

CANTO 73

BHISHMA VADHA PARVA CONTINUED

Sanjaya says, 'Virata pierces Bhishma with three shafts; he strikes his opponent's horses with three golden winged arrows. Aswatthaman, the deadly maharatha, shoots Arjuna through his chest with six whistling barbs. Arjuna rives Aswatthaman's bow and strikes him deep with five shafts. Incensed, Drona's son snatches another great bow and pierces Arjuna with ninety whetted arrows and Krishna with seventy.

Arjuna and Krishna breathe deeply and pause to take thought. Firmly grasping the Gandiva in his left-hand, Arjuna fits some vicious astras to his bowstring, and looses them at Aswatthaman. They plunge through the armour of Drona's son and drink his blood. But Aswatthaman does not flinch. With his heart set firm on protecting Bhishma, he unleashes his own robust volley back at Arjuna. And since he has faced the two Krishnas undaunted, the Kaurava legions roar his praises.

Aswatthaman has been taught the great astras by his father Drona, and he fights without fear.

"He is the son of my Acharya. He is Drona's beloved son. He is a Brahmana, and worthy of my respect," thinks Arjuna. And so he is lenient towards Drona's son. He avoids him, and instead decimates your other forces with terrible swiftness.

Duryodhana strikes Bhima with ten keen golden shafts winged with feathers of vultures. With a roar, Bhima seizes up a powerful bow which can despatch any enemy, and ten terrific arrows. He aims those shafts, draws his bowstring to his ear, and pierces the Kaurava king's wide chest. The pendant of Duryodhana's necklace, surrounded by those arrows, shines like the sun in the sky encircled by the planets.

Hissing like a beaten snake, Duryodhana responds in fury, covering Bhima with a rash of golden barbs. Thus your two mighty sons battle and draw blood from each other, looking like two Devas.

Abhimanyu assails Chitrasena with a haze of arrows and Purumitra with seven. Piercing Satyavrata with seventy shafts, Arjuna's son is like Indra himself in battle, as he seems to dance on the battleground drawing geysers of blood and sowing death all around.

Chitrasena attacks him with ten missiles, Satyavrata with nine, and Purumitra with seven. Abhimanyu is covered in blood, but he smashes Chitrasena's formidable bow, and strikes him deep through his breast with a potent shaft.

The wrathful kings of your army, magnificent maharathas, together stab Abhimanyu with barbs beyond count. And Abhimanyu, knower of the deadliest astras, shrouds them in supernal arrows. Seeing the splendid young Kshatriya consume your army like a blazing fire burning dry grass in summer, your sons surround him. As Abhimanyu devours your forces, he glows like a god on the profound and dreadful field of death.

Seeing him like that, Rajan, your grandson Lakshmana rounds on him. In a flash, Maharatha Abhimanyu pierces Lakshmana and his charioteer with six fleet shafts. Lakshmana responds with a flare of his own barbs. And this duel between the young princes is glorious.

Abhimanyu kills his four horses and his sarathy, and charges at Lakshmana, who looses a snakelike astra at Abhimanyu's chariot. Abhimanyu easily foils that ayudha, and Kripa rides up quickly to bear Lakshmana away from the field in full sight of all the warriors.

The fighting spreads like a dread disease, with men killing and dying thickly on every side. The great archers of your army and the maharathas of the Pandava host slaughter each other without pause, recklessly. Kurukshetra is a yawning portal to Yamaloka through with fervid hosts of warriors flow into death, in dark tide. With wild, dishevelled hair, deprived of armour and chariots, and their bows riven, the Srinjayas fight the Kauravas with their bare arms.

Mahabaho Bhishma continues to vigorously massacre the soldiers of the Pandava army with his divine weapons. And the earth is covered with the fallen bodies of elephants, horses, chariot warriors and horsemen.'

CANTO 74

BHISHMA VADHA PARVA CONTINUED

Sanjaya says, 'Mahabaho Satyaki takes up a fresh powerful bow and covers the field of Kurukshetra in a swathe of death. He is like a looming cloud of murder, as he draws his arrows, fits them to his bowstring and unleashes his bankless storms all round him in a seamless blur.

Seeing him blaze like a fire of the pralaya, Duryodhana sends ten thousand chariots against him. Satyaki is unmoved; he kills those maharathas in a flash flood with his divine weapons. He flares on towards Bhurisravas. Noble Bhurisravas, stricken to watch the decimation of the Dhartarashtra army, charges Satyaki in blind rage. Drawing his vast bow like Indra's, he looses a towering masterly salvo of thousands of shafts at the Vrishni. The warriors who follow Satyaki cannot endure that fulminant fire and scatter in all directions, abandoning their invincible leader.

Satyaki's mighty sons, celebrated maharathas all, cased in shining mail, bearing diverse weapons and flying fine standards, advance towards the great Bhurisravas, with his pennant with the emblem of a yupastamba, a sacrificial stake. They cry at him, "Kinsman of the Kauravas, come and fight us, jointly or separately. Either defeat us in battle and win fame, or be crushed by us and die!"

Proud of his strength, Bhurisravas roars back, "Kshatriyas, you speak nobly! Fight me jointly and vigilantly. For I will kill all of you in battle."

Those heroic archers energetically cover that lone Parantapa in a deluge of arrows. That majestic battle between Bhurisravas and those united against him is fought in the afternoon. The ten Kshatriyas, Satyaki's sons, rain unending storms on Bhurisravas, hiding him in a shroud of ferocious shafts. But none finds a mark on his leonine body, for he cuts them down with unworldly dazzling archery. All the while the Vrishni heroes press in on Bhurisravas, surrounding him, drawing nearer each moment. With incredible genius and prowess, whirling round and round in his ratha, he breaks their bows in their hands and sloughs off their handsome heads in scarlet explosions. And they plunge to the ground like majestic trees felled by thunder.

Seeing his mighty sons killed, Satyaki roars deafeningly and rushes at Bhurisravas. They thrust their chariots against each others. They destroy each other's horses. They leap down to the ground from their useless chariots. Taking up mighty swords and great shields they charge into each other, glow radiantly, those purushavyaghras. But then, armed with a mighty sword, Bhima streaks up to Satyaki and spirits him away in his chariot. And your son Duryodhana takes Bhurisravas into the safety of his chariot.

In that great war, the Pandavas fight vigorously, spiritedly against maharatha Bhishma. Near sunset, Arjuna massacres twenty five thousand maharathas. These had been sent by Duryodhana against him, but he destroys them entirely before they can even approach him, he burns them with astras like insects by a blazing fire.

The Matsyas and the Kekayas, all masters of astras, surround Arjuna and Abhimanyu to bolster them. Just then the sun disappears, and all the fighting men are exhausted.

His horses tired, Bhishma orders the withdrawal of the forces. And the armies of the Pandavas and the Kauravas, both anxious and shaken by the day's carnage, return to their camps. The two armies rest for the night in accordance with the laws laid down for war.'

CANTO 75

BHISHMA VADHA PARVA CONTINUED

Sanjaya says, 'Having rested the night, most sleeping only fitfully with nightmares of the dreadful day raging through their sleep, at dawn of the next morning, the Kauravas and the Pandavas emerge again for battle.

A deafening roar rises from fearless, still excited Kshatriya maharathas as they ready themselves to take the field. And great tuskers trumpet as they are readied for the day's conflict, and foot soldiers shout, at least to embolden themselves, as they wear their armour, and restless horses whinny, their eyes wild. The boom of conches and the beat of drums resound again across Kurukshetra.

King Yudhishtira addresses Dhrishtadyumna saying, "Mahabaho, deploy the forces in the Makara vyuha that will scorch the enemy," and maharatha Dhrishtadyumna arrays his rathikas in that formation of the great crocodile.

Drupada and Arjuna form the war beast's head, Sahadeva and Nakula its two eyes, and mighty Bhima is its snout. Subhadra's son and the sons of Draupadi and the Rakshasa Ghatotkacha, and Satyaki, and

Dharmaraja Yudhishtira are positioned at its neck. King Virata, with a large aksauhini, becomes its back, supported by Dhrishtadyumna and his vast force. The five Kekaya brothers comprise its left flank, and that tiger among men, Dhrishtaketu, and Chekitana of great prowess, are its right flank, to protect the vyuha.

The great reptile's two feet are formed by the maharathas Kuntibhoja and Satanika, solidly supported. And the illustrious Sikhandin, surrounded by the Somakas and Iravat, make up the tail of the Makara.

Having shaped this wondrous formation, the armoured Pandavas, Rajan, stand ready for battle at dawn. With elephants and horses, chariots and foot soldiers, with raised standards and unfurled parasols, with weapons gleaming, they march against the Kauravas.

Seeing the Pandava vyuha, Bhishma form a great Krauncha vyuha, formation of the crane. On its beak is Drona. Aswatthaman and Kripa form its two eyes. Kritavarman, most excellent archer, with the king of the Kambojas and with the Bahlikas is stationed on its head. In its neck are Surasena and your son Duryodhana, surrounded by many other kings.

The ruler of the Pragjyotishas, along with the Madras, the Sauviras, and the Kekayas, followed by a massive force, make up its chest. Susarman, king of Prasthala, with his legion forces, stands in full armour as the left wing. The Tusharas, the Yavanas and the Sakas, along with the Chulikas, form the right wing of that vyuha. And Srutayush and Satyatish and Somadatta's son stand in the rear protecting the others.

The Pandavas charge the Kauravas. The sun rises above the horizon as the battle begins. Elephants advance against elephants, horse riders against horsemen, chariot warriors against others like them, and also against war elephants in the war to end all others.

Maharathas attack riders of elephants, who bear down on horsemen. Foot soldiers engage with maharathas, horse riders with foot soldiers. All the fighting men storm against each other in battle.

The Pandava army, protected by Bhima and Arjuna and the twins, seem beautiful as the night spangled over with stars. And your army also, with Bhishma and Kripa, and Drona and Salya, and Duryodhana, shines like the sky sparkling with luminous planets.

Powerful Bhima, seeing Drona, wildly attacks the Acharya's aksauhini of swift horses. The spirited Drona pierces Bhima with nine iron arrows, deeply wounding his arms and legs. Bhima, roused, kills Drona's sarathy.

The adroit son of Bharadwaja, himself guiding his horses, begins to consume the Pandava army like fire consuming a stack of cotton. Slaughtered by Drona and Bhishma, the Srinjayas along with the Kekayas flee. Your troops also, mangled by Bhima and Arjuna, are benumbed and they stand still, like a magnificent lioness in her pride. In this war that annihilates Kshatriyas, both armies suffer grievously.

We are overwhelmed by the sight of men fighting frenziedly, unconcerned for their very lives. In this war, the Pandavas and the Kauravas oppose each other with all their energies and weapons.'

CANTO 76

BHISHMA VADHA PARVA CONTINUED

Dhritarashtra says, 'Our army is skilled, resourceful and has diverse forces. It is organised, deployed expertly and should be invincible. It is loyal to us. It is obedient, and free from the vices of drunkenness and licentiousness. Its abilities are proven. The soldiers are neither very old nor very young. They are neither thin nor fat. They are robust, muscular and healthy.

They are well armed and armoured. They are proficient in the use of all kinds of astras. They fight skilfully with swords, maces and even bare arms. They are well trained in the use of spears and arrows of many kinds.

The men are fit, adept in mounting and alighting from the backs of elephants, in marching forward, attacking and retreating, and in effectively striking the enemy. They have been often tested in their handling of elephants, horses and chariots. They are paid soldiers, hired not because of their lineage, or on the basis of their earlier associations with us; neither have we chosen them in order to favour them.

They are upright and honest; their kinsmen have been treated well by us in the past. We have esteemed them highly for their services. They

288 || THE COMPLETE MAHABHARATA: BHISHMA PARVA

are all eminent and capable men.

They are in turn led by many dynamic and famed warriors, rulers of the earth, celebrated all over the world. Countless illustrious Kshatriyas, who have freely allied with us, with their forces also protect them.

Our army is like the vast ocean filled with the water of a myriad rivers flowing from all directions. It has countless elephants, and its chariots, though wingless, fly even like birds. Warriors are the waters of that ocean, and the horses and other animals are its lashing, terrifying waves. Swords, maces, spears and arrows are the oars of our vast and numberless craft. Rich in emblems and jewels, adorned with cloth inlaid with gold and gems, the charging horses and elephants are the stormy winds that make that ocean surge.

Our host resembles the vast, shoreless, raging ocean. It is defended by Drona and Bhishma, and by Kritavarman and Kripa and Dussasana, and others headed by Jayadratha. It is also protected by Bhagadatta and Vikarna, by Drona's son, and Subala's son, and Bahlika, and by other mighty and high-souled Kshatriyas.

That our army is being destroyed is only due to Destiny, Sanjaya. Neither men nor highly blessed Rishis have ever before seen such preparations for war on earth. That such a vast and loyal force, deployed so scientifically, can be slaughtered in battle can only be the outcome of Destiny. All this appears strange and inexplicable.

Vidura had often given useful and wise advice. But my evil son Duryodhana would not accept it. I believe that Vidura foresaw all that is happening now; and hence he gave his counsel. Or it may be that all these, in every detail, has been predetermined by God, for that which is ordained by the Creator must happen and not otherwise.'

CANTO 77

Bhishma Vadha Parva continued

Sanjaya says, 'You are the victim of this calamity because of your own weakness. Bharatarishabha, you, and not Duryodhana, clearly saw that what was done to the Pandavas was wrong.

That the game of dice was ever played was your folly. And it is your fault that this war against the Pandavas has been fought. Having done wrong, you must now face the outcome. One reaps the fruit of one's own actions. You must now reap the fruit of your sins in this life and the next. Rajan, be calm and accept the unfolding tragedy; listen to my narration of the battle.

Having smashed your awesome vyuha with his shafts, Bhima advances upon Duryodhana's younger brothers. Mighty Bhima sees Dussasana and Durvisaha, Dussaha and Durmada and Jaya, Jayasena and Vikarna and Chitrasena and Sudarsana, and Charuchitra and Suvarman and Duskarna and Karna, and other maharathas of the Dhartarashtra host approach him; he attacks your vyuha protected by Bhishma.

Seeing him amidst them, these warriors cry, "Let us kill Bhima!" and Bhima is surrounded by his indomitable cousins. He resembles the burning sun encircled by the malevolent planets at the end of the yuga.

Though besieged in the very heart of the Kaurava vyuha, Bhima is fearless, like Indra surrounded by the Danavas in the ancient battle between the Devas and the Asuras. Thousands of maharathas engulf him with deadly arrows. Valiant Bhima ignores the sons of Dhritarashtra and slaughters many other mighty Kaurava warriors fighting from chariots and from the backs of elephants and horses.

Then, knowing that his cousins are determined to kill him, Bhima sets himself to exterminate them all. Leaping down from his chariot, mace in hand, he begins to destroy the enemy.

As he penetrates the Kaurava army, Dhrishtadyumna turns away from Drona whom he has been fighting and swiftly advances towards Subala's son Sakuni. Killing so many warriors of your army, he notices Bhima's empty chariot. He sees Bhima's sarathy Visoka, and is distraught.

Filled with sudden sorrow, and in a choking voice, he asks Visoka, "Where is Bhima who is as precious to me as life itself?"

Visoka replies humbly, "Bhima commanded me to wait here, while he strikes out alone into the heart of the Dhartarashtra host vast as the ocean. He cheerfully said to me, 'Wait here with my horses for some time, until I kill those who are determined to kill me.' Seeing him storm ahead, mace in hand, all our fighting men were elated. Bhima smashed through the enemy's mighty vyuha in his awesome way."

Hearing Visoka's words, Dhrishtadyumna says to him, "My life would be worthless if I deserted Bhima in battle. If I return without Bhima, what will the Kshatriyas say about me? What will they say when they know that while I was on the battlefield Bhima charged alone into the enemy vyuha?

The Devas led by Indra curse those who abandon their comrades in war and return unharmed themselves! Brave Bhima is my friend and kinsman. He is devoted to me, and I too love that Parantapa dearly. I will go where he has gone. Watch me raze the enemy like Vasava slaying the Danavas."

Dhrishtadyumna rides right through the enemy, along the path opened up by Bhima and marked by elephants crushed under his mace. He sees Bhima consuming the Kaurava host, felling Kshatriya warriors like a storm ravaging trees. Maharathas and horsemen, foot-soldiers and tuskers scream aloud as he slaughters them. Your men cry in anguish as he massacres them.

The Kaurava warriors surround Bhima and shower him relentlessly with their arrows. Dhrishtadyumna sees Bhima attacked from all sides; mangled with shafts, on foot, and vomiting the poison of his anger, mace in hand, he looks like Siva at the end of the yuga. Dhrishtadyumna moves towards him and takes him into his chariot; he plucks out the shafts from his body, and embraces him in the sight of the enemy.

Duryodhana, seeing this, says to his brothers, "Dhrishtadyumna has allied with Bhima. Let us attack and kill him. We must be on the offensive and not wait for the enemy to strike us."

Goaded by their eldest brother's command, the Dhartarashtras, with raised weapons, hurtle towards Dhrishtadyumna, looking like fierce comets at the hour of universal dissolution. Like clouds shrouding a mountain with torrential rain, these Kshatriyas loose a volley of arrows on him, wielding their beautiful bows, making the earth shiver with the twang of their bowstrings and the rattle of their chariot-wheels.

But Dhrishtadyumna, proficient in all kinds of warfare, does not falter for a moment. Seeing your sons ready to kill him, he uses the Pramohana astra against them, again looking for all the world like Indra facing the Danavas. The Pramohana of sleep instantly makes the Kaurava princes weak and they swoon. Seeing your sons faint, your forces flee in all directions, with their horses, elephants and chariots.

Drona advances towards Drupada and pierces him with three searing shafts. Drupada, remembering his earlier enmity with Drona, leaves the battlefield. Drona blows his conch triumphantly, and the Somakas are terrified on hearing that blast.

Wielder of weapons, Drona, full of tejas, now hears of your sons being overwhelmed by the Pramohana astra, and rides in a flash to where they struggle vainly to remain conscious. Drona sees Dhrishtadyumna and Bhima careering across the battleground. And the maharatha watches your sons rendered unconscious. He uses the Prajna astra to make powerless the Pramohana loosed by Dhrishtadyumna. Your sons recover and again storm ahead to fight Bhima and Dhrishtadyumna.

Yudhishtira says to his warriors, "Send twelve brave maharathas, led by Abhimanyu, to Bhima and Prishata's son. Let them find out about those two warriors. I am anxious."

Those Kshatriyas sally forth at mid-day. The Kaikeyas and the sons of Draupadi, and Dhrishtaketu, supported by a large force and with Abhimanyu at their head, form the Suchimukha vyuha and drive deep into the Dhartarashtra chariot aksauhini.

Your forces, already terrified by Bhima and Dhrishtadyumna, cannot withstand the charge of those maharathas led by Abhimanyu. They are weak like an unprotected woman.

With standards flecked with gold, the Pandava warriors cleave swiftly through the Kaurava ranks to rescue Dhrishtadyumna and Bhima. Seeing them approach, Bhima is elated and, with a glad roar, continues to demolish your soldiers.

The heroic Dhrishtadyumna sees the Acharya advance towards him, to protect your sons. He has the chariot of the king of the Kaikeyas take Bhima away, while he himself engages the superlative Drona.

With a broad-headed shaft Parantapa Drona cuts down Dhrishtadyumna's bow even as the Panchala prince rides recklessly towards him. Remembering his loyalty to Duryodhana, he also shoots hundreds of arrows after Prishata's son.

Dhrishtadyumna seizes another bow and pierces Drona with seventy whetted shafts, all golden winged. Drona again severs his bow and slaughters his four horses with four incredibly excellent barbs, and also kills his charioteer with a heavy shaft. Mahabaho Dhrishtadyumna leaps off his chariot and climbs onto Abhimanyu's colossal ratha. Right before of Bhima and Dhrishtadyumna, Drona makes the Pandava army with all its chariots, elephants and horses tremble in fear.

Seeing that army devastated by Drona, all its maharathas cannot to stop its flight. Slaughtered by Drona, that army heaves like a stormy sea. Seeing the Pandava army reduced, your forces are jubilant. Seeing the fiery Acharya consume the enemy, all your warriors roar loudly in praise of Drona.'

CANTO 78

BHISHMA VADHA PARVA CONTINUED

S anjaya says, 'On recovering, Duryodhana again looses a tide of arrows at Bhima. And again those maharathas, your sons, unite and bravely oppose the great Pandava. Mahabaho Bhima mounts his chariot and rides straight at your sons. He takes up a golden bow, with the power to overcome any enemy, and he covers your sons with his wrath.

Duryodhana strikes him deep with a spear. Roaring, Bhima draws his bow in a circle and pierces Duryodhana through his arms and his chest with three fierce barbs. But the king stands firm like a prince of mountains.

Seeing those great Kshatriyas fight, Duryodhana's younger brothers renew their resolve to kill Bhima and attack him again, prepared to die if they must. The mighty Bhima charges them like an elephant charging another. With untold power, Bhima strikes your son Chitrasena with a long arrow, and your other sons with many kinds of swift and golden-winged shafts.

Dharmaraja Yudhishtira meanwhile sends his twelve maharathas led by Abhimanyu to follow Bhima. These ride towards your sons. Looking at those Kshatriyas on their chariots, resembling the Sun himself or a radiant fire, beautiful and resplendent in their golden ornaments, your mighty sons turn away from Bhima. The Pandavas, however, are determined not to let them leave the battle alive.'

CANTO 79

BHISHMA VADHA PARVA CONTINUED

Sanjaya says, 'Abhimanyu, along with Bhima, hunts and dismays all your sons. The maharathas of your army, including Duryodhana, see Abhimanyu and Bhima united with Dhrishtadyumna in very middle of the Kaurava forces; they seize their bows and ride swiftly at those three warriors.

Ah, such a dreadful battle there is that afternoon, Rajan, between the two armies. Abhimanyu kills Vikarna's horses and pierces him with twenty-five fine arrows. Maharatha Vikarna abandons that chariot and mounts Chitrasena's shining one.

Abhimanyu envelops those two brothers of Kuru's race, standing together on one chariot, with a barrage of shafts. Durjaya and Vikarna stab Abhimanyu with five iron barbs. Abhimanyu stands firm like the mountain Meru.

Dussasana fights valiantly with the five Kekaya brothers. All these feats are more awesome than can be told. The Pandavas furiously round on Duryodhana and each of them pierces your son with three arrows. Your indomitable prince, too, shoots each of them with whetted shafts.

Thus pierced and drenched in blood, he glows like a mountain with rivers of muddy water running down its sides.

And the mighty Bhishma persists against the Pandava army like some herdsman belabouring his recalcitrant herd. The twang of the Gandiva is heard repeatedly as Arjuna slaughters his opponents on the right of the army. In that corner of the battlefield thousands of headless bodies of both sides can be seen still standing macabre among the living forces. And Kurukshetra resembles an ocean with blood for its water, with arrows as its currents. The elephants are its islands and horses its waves. Chariots form the boats that bold men use to cross that ocean. Thousands of brave warriors, with arms amputated, without armour, and hideously mutilated, lie on the ground.

With the bloody bodies of massacred elephants, the battleground looks as if scattered with hills. What a sight! Not a single warrior in both armies is less than eager to fight. And so they battle on: those daring warriors of both your army and that of the Pandavas, seeking victory and glory.'

CANTO 80

BHISHMA VADHA PARVA CONTINUED

Sanjaya says, 'At sunset, Duryodhana charges Bhima, always to kill him. Seeing him come with loathing in his heart, Bhima says, "The awaited hour has come. If you do not yield, I will kill you today.

By killing you I will dispel Kunti and Draupadi's sorrows, and all our anguish during our exile in the forests. You arrogantly humiliated the sons of Pandu. O son of Gandhari, you will reap the fruit of all your sins today.

You always listened to the vicious counsel of Karna and Subala's son, and dismissive of the Pandavas, you had treated us unjustly. You ignored Krishna who had pleaded with you for peace. Jubilantly you had sent haughty, mocking messages to us through Uluka. Today I will kill you and all your kinsmen, and avenge all the insults and suffering you inflicted on us."

Bhima stretches his bow, takes up many terrible shafts that shimmer like lightning, and looses thirty-six of them at Duryodhana. Flaming they fly at his cousin like thunderbolts. With two shafts, Bhima smashes Duryodhana's bow in his hands, and strikes his charioteer with two more.

With four shafts he kills Duryodhana's four horses; with another two he cuts down the king's royal parasol. With three others he fells the Kaurava's magnificent, jewel worked standard, which falls to the earth like a flash of lightning from the clouds. All the gathered rulers see that radiant Kaurava standard, bearing the emblem of a great tusker, adorned with precious stones, plunge to the ground, and Bhima roars triumphantly.

Smiling, maharatha Bhima stabs Duryodhana with ten shafts like a mahout piercing a colossal elephant with his hook. The mighty king of the Sindhus, with many brave warriors, swiftly sets himself at Duryodhana's flank, while maharatha Kripa quickly takes the seething Duryodhana onto his own chariot. The king, deeply wounded by Bhima and suffering, collapses on its platform.

Jayadratha surrounds Bhima with thousands of chariots to have his life. Dhrishtaketu and Abhimanyu, and the Kekayas, and the sons of Draupadi, all clash with your sons. And the high-souled Abhimanyu strikes each of them with five straight shafts that appear like dark lightning or guises of Yama.

They, in turn, unleash a storm of arrows at Abhimanyu, like black clouds pounding Meru with rain. But brilliant Abhimanyu makes your sons tremble like Indra did the mighty Asuras during the ancient Devasura yuddha. In a moment, he shoots fourteen broad-headed shafts like snakes at Vikarna; as if dancing in battle, Abhimanyu destroys Vikarna's standard and kills his charioteer and horses.

Subhadra's resplendent son covers every direction around him with astounding gales of arrows, shafts that can pierce the best armour. Plumed with feathers of the kanka bird, these barbs pass right through Vikarna's body and enter the ground like hissing snakes. And decked with gold, drenched in Vikarna's blood, they seem to vomit blood on the earth.

Seeing Vikarna wounded, his brothers charge the maharathas led by Abhimanyu and engage the heroes of the Pandava army, who shine like so many suns.

Durmukha pierces Srutakarman with five shafts, breaks his standard with a single shaft and strikes his sarathy with seven. Advancing, he butchers his enemy's horses, as swift as the wind and wearing bright armour, with six arrows, and kills his charioteer too.

Srutakarman stands firm on his horseless chariot and casts a meteor-like astra at Durmukha; that weapon cuts through Durmukha's kavacha and plunges into the ground behind him, glowing all the while. Sutasoma helps Srutakarman into his chariot, in plain sight of all the forces.

The heroic Srutakirti storms at Jayatsena. Your son severs Srutakirti's bow with a horse-shoe headed arrow. Seeing his brother's bow broken, brave Satanika rides up swiftly roaring like a lion. In a blink, Satanika pierces Jayatsena with ten shafts, and then bellows his victory like a wild elephant trumpeting.

Satanika stabs Jayatsena deeply in the chest; Dushkarna who is near his brother Jayatsena, breaks Satanika's bow. The mighty Satanika seizes another powerful bow and, roaring dreadfully, looses a tide of arrows at Dushkarna before Jayatsena arrests him with some serpentine nagapasas.

Recovering in a moment, Satanika destroys Dushkarna's bow with one fell barb, kills his charioteer with two more, and pierces Dushkarna himself with seven unerring astras. That flawless warrior slaughters all Dushkarna's swift glossy horses with twelve sharp shafts. Satanika strikes Dushkarna deeply through his chest and Dushkarna plunges to the ground like a tree felled by lightning.

To avenge Dushkarna's death, five maharathas surround Satanika determined to kill him. They attack him with dense volleys. The five Kekaya brothers press forward to protect Satanika. Seeing them advance, your sons fly at them like elephants thundering at other colossal tuskers.

Your sons Durmukha and Durjaya, and the youthful Durmarshana and Satranjaya and Satrusha, all celebrated warriors, plunge red-eyed at the five Kekaya brothers. They ride on splendid chariots that look like fortified cities, yoked to bejewelled horses and bearing beautiful coloured standards; those Kshatriyas carry formidable bows, and wearing beautiful coats of mail they penetrate the enemy force like lions entering one forest from another.

A pitched earthshaking battle erupts, in which chariots and elephants are shattered and mangled. With untold hatred, they fight until sunset; countless warriors on both sides are killed. Thousands of great chariot-warriors and horsemen are strewn over the battlefield, like rag dolls now, drenched in crimson.

In rage, Bhishma continues his massacre of the Pandava forces with banks and banks of straight shafts, streaming ceaselessly from his matchless bow. His arrows annihilate the Panchala fighting men. Having savagely reduced the ranks of the Pandavas, the Pitamaha withdraws his forces and retires to his camp.

And seeing Dhrishtadyumna and Bhima both safe, Yudhishtira is relieved and he also leaves the field and enters his tent.'

CANTO 81

BHISHMA VADHA PARVA CONTINUED

Sanjaya says, 'Those Kshatriyas return to their tents, blood-spattered and with the hatred and enmity in their hearts undimmed. They praise each other for their glorious feats of the day and spend the night, some in deep sleep, others tossing and turning in their beds from the dark and violent dreams which plunge through their sleep. The next morning find them again in full armour and ready for battle, which is now their very life to them; no other thought occupies their minds.

Duryodhana is anxious, and with blood still oozing from his wounds, asks his Pitamaha, "Our fierce forces carry countless standards. They are perfectly drilled and deployed. Yet the Pandava maharathas penetrate our vyuha, slaughter our men, and escape unharmed.

They humble us and win fame in battle. Smashing through our Makara vyuha, powerful as the Vajra, Bhima wounded me with terrible shafts each like a Yama danda. I was baffled by him. Even now I cannot regain my composure. Pitamaha only you can help me kill the sons of Pandu and achieve victory."

Foremost of all wielders of weapons, and imbued with great tejas,

Bhishma understands Duryodhana's anguish; though inwardly despondent, he cheerfully says, "My child, I truly exert myself wholeheartedly, to crush the Pandava forces and bring you victory and joy, O king. For your sake I do not hesitate.

The Pandava's allies in this war are many and magnificent. Celebrated maharathas, they are more than merely brave and great masters of astras. Tireless, they spew forth their righteous anger. They hate you, Suyodhana, and swelling with prowess, they will not be easily defeated. I will fight them with my whole soul, risking my life. For your sake, for your glory, I will stake my life.

For you, my child, I would consume all the worlds with the Devas and the Daityas, not just your enemies on this battleground. And I will fight the Pandavas, and do whatever pleases you."

Hearing these words, Duryodhana is reassured and filled with hope and joy. He cheerfully orders his forces, along with the allied kings, to advance. And his army of chariots, horses, foot-soldiers and elephants moves regally forward.

And sensing their king's fresh confidence, that vast force, armed with every kind of weapon, is also full of joy. It looks wonderful with its elephants, horses and foot-soldiers. And its colossal tuskers, brightly caparisoned, formed in massive aksauhinis, and skilfully goaded, look the most resplendent. Many royal Kshatriyas, all accomplished in the use of diverse weapons, are seen amidst your forces. And the dust, red as the morning sun, raised by the chariots and foot-soldiers and elephants and horses as they move across the field, is deeply beautiful, even as it swirls up to obscure the face of the sun.

And the vari-coloured banners on the chariots and elephants wave in the air and look like many-hued lightning in clouds in the sky. The din raised by the twang of stretched bows is like the roar of the ocean when the Devas and the Asuras churned it together during the Krita Yuga, to fetch up the Amrita.

The stately and accomplished army of your sons, consisting of a great variety of fighting men, roar and shout fiercely, looking like the clouds of the Pralaya that appear at the end of the yuga.'

CANTO 82

BHISHMA VADHA PARVA CONTINUED

Sanjaya says, 'O Bharatarishabha, Bhishma once again addresses your thoughtful son with these pleasing words:

"Drona and I, and Salya and Kritavarman of Satwata's race, and Aswatthaman and Vikarna, and Bhagadatta and Subala's son and Vinda and Anuvinda of Avanti, and Bahlika with the Bahlikas, and the mighty king of the Trigartas and the invincible ruler of the Magadhas, Brihadbala the king of the Kosalas, and Chitrasena and Vivimsati and thousands of maharathas with lofty standards, excellent horses mounted by superior riders, many incensed tuskers with the juice of rut trickling from their mouths and temples, and numberless brave foot-soldiers from many lands , are all prepared to fight for you.

These, and many others, are ready to lay down their lives for you, capable as they are of defeating the very gods in battle. I will however advise you again in your best interests.

The Pandavas are unconquerable even by the gods. With Krishna for an ally they are equal to Mahendra himself in prowess. As for myself, I am at your command. Either I shall crush the Pandavas or they will overcome me."

Saying this, Bhishma applies a poultice of medicinal herbs to Duryodhana's wounds and these heal instantly, magically.

At dawn, with a clear sky overhead, the valiant Bhishma, consummate master of vyuhas of all kinds, himself organises his fighting men in the Mandala vyuha, the formation of the Galaxy, bristling with weapons. And it still abounds in outstanding warriors, elephants and foot-soldiers.

It is protected on all sides by thousands of chariots, and with legions of horsemen armed with swords and spears. Near every elephant are seven chariots, and besides every chariot are seven horsemen. Behind every horseman are seven archers, and behind every archer are seven soldiers with shields. Thus, your army, assembled by mighty maharathas and protected by Bhishma, stands ready to fight.

Ten thousand horses, and as many elephants, and ten thousand chariots, and your sons, all covered in mail, the heroic Chitrasena and many others, all guard the Pitamaha. Thus Bhishma is protected by those intrepid princes, and they in turn are safeguarded by him. And Duryodhana in his coat of mail sits on his chariot, graceful and resplendent like Sakra himself.

Your sons let out thunderous shouts, and the clatter of chariots and the sound of musical instruments is deafening. The mighty and impenetrable Mandala vyuha of the Dhartarashtras created by Bhishma begins to move westwards. It is invincible and so beautiful to behold.

Seeing the Mandala vyuha, Yudhishtira himself arrays his forces in the Vajra vyuha. When all the aksauhinis of chariot-warriors and horsemen are suitably stationed, he roars like a most noble lion. The warriors of both armies advance; a thirst for battle, they want to destroy the other's vyuha, leaving not a single enemy alive.

Bharadwaja's son Drona rides against the king of the Matsyas, and his son, Aswatthaman, against Sikhandin. And king Duryodhana himself strikes out at the son of Prishata. Nakula and Sahadeva attack the king of the Madras.

And Vinda and Anuvinda of Avanti charge against Iravat. Many kings unite to oppose Arjuna. Bhima challenges the son of Hridika, while Abhimanyu faces your sons Chitrasena and Vikarna and Durmarshana.

Hidimba's son, Ghatotkacha, that prince of the Rakshasas, charges the mighty Bhagadatta, king of the Pragjyotishas, like one incensed elephant against another. The Rakshasa Alambusha, Rajan, with rising anger, battles the indomitable Satyaki surrounded by his Vrishni warriors. And Bhurisravas fights with vim against Dhrishtaketu.

Dharmaraja Yudhishtira advances against king Srutayush. Chekitana challenges Kripa. Other Kaurava fighting men confront maharatha Bhima. And thousands of other kings armed with spears, arrows, maces, and spiked clubs surround Arjuna.

Arjuna says to Krishna, "Behold, O Madhava, the Dhartarashtra troops, assembled by Bhishma conversant with every kind of vyuha. Look at these myriad daring warriors who seek to fight me. Kesava, look, there stands the lord of the Trigartas with his brothers. Today I shall kill them all, Janardana, before your eyes."

Saying this, Arjuna rubs his bowstring to warm it, pulls it to affright his foes and overwhelms that host of kings with his arrows. And those celebrated archers also cover him in gales of shafts, like monsoon clouds filling a lake with their torrents. Strident roars are heard in your army as the two Krishnas are mantled in a deluge of arrows. Seeing this from on high, the Devas, the celestial Rishis, and the Gandharvas with the Uragas are awestruck.

Arjuna, enraged, invokes the Aindra astra. We can only marvel at his impossible prowess, as he repels his enemies' scathing volleys, effortlessly. Thousands of kings, horses and elephants are direly wounded by Arjuna's unearthly archery; others are each pierced with two and three of his barbs and quickly flow blood.

The wounded warriors seek Bhishma's protection. The Pitamaha comes to their rescue them as they flounder in the bottomless ocean that is Arjuna's mystic archery. Rajan, as they scatter in fear and confusion and tangle with other warriors, your broken ranks appear like a sea heaving in a storm.'

CANTO 83

BHISHMA VADHA PARVA CONTINUED

Sanjaya says, 'When the battle rages on, after Susarman stops fighting, and the other valiant Kshatriyas of the Kaurava army are routed by the high-souled son of Pandu, indeed, after your army has been tossed like a slight fleet of boats upon a great and turbulent ocean, and Bhishma has charged swiftly against the chariot of Vijaya, Duryodhana, seeing Arjuna straddle Kurukshetra like Yama come hunting, rides up and speaks comfortingly to those belaboured, lacerated kings, and to the mighty Susarman in the vanguard.

Duryodhana says, "This Bhishma, the son of Shantanu, uncaring for his very life, will fight wholeheartedly against Arjuna. United, exert yourselves, and protect Bhishma as he forges at the enemy."

All the aksauhinis rally and follow the magnificent Pitamaha. Mighty Bhishma charges to confront Arjuna who also thunders towards him on his splendid chariot yoked to white horses, flying his standard bearing the fierce Vanara, who gives vent to the most bloodcurdling cries and roars.

Your entire army, seeing the diadem-decked Dhananjaya advancing into battle, cries out in terror. And your forces cannot gaze upon Krishna, as he stands, reins in hand, a fiery, magnificent sun.

The Pandavas also cannot look at Bhishma, who, with his white horses and gleaming bow, resembles Sukra rising in the sky. The son of Shantanu is ringed by the noble Trigarta warriors led by their king with his brothers and sons, and by many maharathas.

Drona strikes the king of the Matsyas with his winged shafts. He cuts down Virata's standard with a single arrow, and his bow with another. Virata, Senapati of a vast aksauhini, discards the cloven bow and swiftly takes up another that is strong and resilient. He seizes many blazing arrows resembling poisonous snakes, stabs Drona with three of these and his four horses with four. He fells Drona's standard with another barb, and his sarathy with five. Cracking Drona's bow in his hands with yet another shaft, he enrages that bull among Brahmanas.

Drona kills Virata's horses with eight long shafts, and then his charioteer with one. Virata has to leap down from his chariot whose horses have been slaughtered. Virata, that most excellent maharatha, mounts his son Sankha's chariot. Riding together, father and son powerfully resist Drona with a refulgent wrath of arrows.

In fury, Drona strikes Sankha with a missile like a serpent spitting venom. This shaft pierces Sankha's chest and he falls to the ground bathed in his own spraying gore. He plunges down from his chariot, before his father's eyes, his bow and arrows falling out of his grasp. Seeing his son killed, Virata flees howling in shock and terror, flees from the awful Drona who looks like Death with mouth agape.

Drona rapidly thwarts the vast Pandava host. Sikhandin strikes Drona's son in his forehead with three sharp darts. Aswatthaman glows like Meru with its three golden peaks. Incensed, in less than a blink of the eye, Aswatthaman overwhelms Sikhandin's charioteer and cuts down his standard, horses and weapons, covering them all in a swathe of arrows. Sikhandin, scorcher of enemies, leaps off his horseless chariot. Taking up a gleaming sword and shield, he moves as he wishes wrathfully and sharply like a hawk. Aswatthaman cannot kill Sikhandin and all are filled with wonder.

Aswatthaman looses thousands of arrows at his enemy but mighty Sikhandin wards them off with his whirling sword and shield, as if in another dimension of time. Drona's son shoots Sikhandin's radiant shield decked with a hundred moons into shards, and cuts his sword in two. He now stabs Sikhandin himself with a volley of winged arrows.

Sikhandin whirls the remaining length of his snake like blade, and hurls it at Aswatthaman like lightning. Drona's son shoots that blade into slivers even as it flies at him, brilliant like the fire that blazes at the end of the yuga. And he strikes Sikhandin himself with countless solid iron arrows. Deeply wounded and in agony, Sikhandin climbs onto Satyaki's chariot.

Satyaki pierces the feral Rakshasa Alambusha all over, on every side, deeply with his lusty arrows. That prince of Rakshasas shatters Satyaki's bow with a crescent-tipped shaft, then draws blood from Satyaki himself with countless other barbs. Using his Rakshasa's maya to create a formidable illusion, he shrouds Satyaki with torrents of fire and water, and storms of very real sharp missiles.

The grandson of Sini displays breathtaking prowess as he remains undaunted by that ferocious fusillade. The son of Vrishni's race intones a profound mantra and launches the Aindra astra, which he had from his guru Arjuna. The astra burns down that demonic illusion and envelops Alambusha in a torrid arrow storm. Wounded sorely by that exceptional Kshatriya, Alambusha flees to avoid facing Satyaki.

Defeating that prince of Rakshasas, unbeatable by Maghavat himself, the grandson of Sini flings back his handsome head and roars and roars before your stunned forces. The indomitable Satyaki now begins to decimate and scatter your fighting men at will.

Meanwhile, O Rajan, Dhrishtadyumna covers your son in a shroud of fire. Your royal Suyodhana stands rocklike and undaunted. He strikes Dhrishtadyumna with sixty shafts, and in a wink with thirty more. And all these feats seem amazing. The Pandava Senapati responds by smashing your son's bow in fury. That maharatha slaughters your son's four horses, and pierces him with seven finely-honed arrows.

Your son, so strong and vigorous, leaps from his horseless chariot, and runs straight at the son of Drupada wielding a raised sword. The mighty and loyal Sakuni quickly takes Duryodhana into his own chariot. Having routed their king, Drupada's fire prince begins to raze your forces like Indra killing the Asuras.

Kritavarman swathes maharatha Bhima with his shafts, overwhelming him like a mass of clouds hiding the sun. That nemesis of enemies, Bhima, only continues to furiously shoot arrow sat Kritavarman, laughing in glee. That atiratha of the Satwatavamsa, outshining everyone, boldly strikes Bhima with a ceaseless stream of lean missiles. The colossal Bhima kills Kritavarman's four horses and strikes down his sarathy and his beautiful standard; and masterful Bhima stabs Kritavarman with many kinds of arrows.

Pierced all over, his limbs mangled, Kritavarman runs to Vrishaka's chariot, in the sight of both Salya and your son. Fury unabated, Bhima begins to butcher your men all around. He beats them to pulp, like Siva with his mace.'

BHISHMA VADHA PARVA CONTINUED

Dhritarashtra says, 'I hear you speak of the countless awesome single contests between the Pandavas and my warriors. You do not mention, however, Sanjaya, the heroism or high spirits of anyone of my side. You talk of the cheerful and invincible sons of Pandu, and of mine as being listless, dejected and vulnerable in battle. Unquestionably, all this is Destiny.'

Sanjaya says, 'Bharatarishabha, your fighting men display strength and courage to their utmost. But just as the sweet waters of the celestial Ganga turn salty when they meet the sea, so is the valour of your sons rendered futile when they meet the heroic sons of Pandu in battle.

They exert themselves forcefully, and accomplish the most difficult feats: you should not censure your forces. It is your sins, and those of your sons, that have resulted in this horrific destruction of the world, all this shameful and bloody waste and ruin.

It does not befit you, Rajan, to mourn what you have caused. The duty of kings in this world is not merely to protect their lives. Wishing to win the realms of the righteous, they fight daily, thrusting into enemy aksauhinis, with the heavens alone as their aim.

In the bright morning, widespread carnage ensues, yes even like in the Devasura yuddha, the first of all wars. Hear of it with undivided attention.

The two lustrous princes of Avanti, those mighty archers, rush at Iravat. The battle that breaks out between them is brutal, making one's hair stand on end. The incensed Iravat strikes the divine brothers with a luminous and deadly volley, which they cut down in a shower of sparks. Hotly the three battle their only thought to have the enemy's life; so feverishly do they fight that they cannot be distinguished one from the others in the rage of arrows with which they darken earth and sky.

Iravat kills Anuvinda's four horses with four terrific shafts, and demolishes Anuvinda's bow and standard with another two, all of which pierce the general cloud of arrows all round. And this feat is truly wonderful.

Abandoning his chariot, Anuvinda leaps onto Vinda's. From that single ratha, the inspired brothers of Avanti unleash an elemental fury of missiles at the high-souled Iravat. Those golden arrows course through the air and cover the sky. Cut to the quick, Iravat creates a thunderhead of shafts in the sky and they lash down in a cataract on the two splendid maharathas and fell their sarathy.

When their charioteer falls dead to the ground, the unrestrained horses run amok, dragging the chariot wildly behind them. In some satisfaction, Iravat begins to consume your foot soldiers all around him. And the mighty Dhartarashtra host, thus slaughtered, reels like a man drunk on poison.

Mounted on his black ratha, its flag flying high, that prince of Rakshasas, Hidimbi's looming son Ghatotkacha charges Bhagadatta. The king of the Pragjyotishas rides his prince of elephants, Supritika, even like Indra did Airavata in the battle of antiquity provoked by Taraka's molestation.

The Devas, the Gandharvas, and the Rishis all assembled in the subtle akasa cannot distinguish between Ghatotkacha and Bhagadatta. As the infuriated king of the Devas once infused the Danavas with fear, so does Bhagadatta terrify the Pandava warriors. And stricken on all sides, they look around vainly for a protector among their ranks.

The son of Bhima stands valiant with darkly glimmering defiance on his chariot, while other maharathas melt away disheartened. When the Pandava forces rally, there rises a deafening roar among your fighting men. Ghatotkacha, O Rajan, pours down a thunder shower of arrows on Bhagadatta, as the clouds of the monsoon do on Meru's great summit. Bhagadatta foils every falling shaft from the Rakshasa's bow, and strikes Ghatotkacha deeply in all his marmas, the vital parts of his hulking body, lancing agony through him. That prince of the Rakshasas does not waver for a moment but stands still like a mountain pierced.

Rage mounting, the Pragjyotisha king hurls fourteen spears, all of which the magnificent Rakshasa cuts in slivers. Mahabaho Ghatotkacha stabs Bhagadatta with seventy keening shafts, each one like Indra's Vajra.

But laughing all the while, Bhagadatta slaughters the Rakshasa's four horses. Ghatotkacha remains steadfast on his ratha and launches a deadly javelin at Bhagadatta's elephant. The mountain king smashes that swift golden lance hurtling wildly towards him into three harmless stalks. Ghatotkacha flees terrified, like Namuchi, that foremost of the Daityas, did from Indra in the primordial battle.

Having defeated that daring Kshatriya, unassailable even by Yama himself or Varuna, king Bhagadatta with his elephant begins to crush the Pandava forces like a wild tusker trampling the lotuses in a lake.

Salya of the Madras fights his sister's sons, the twins. And he overwhelms them with salvos of arrows. Sahadeva shrouds his dead mother's splendid brother with arrows like clouds veiling the sun. Covered by these shafts, the king of the Madras is delighted, and the twins also are satisfied for their mother Madri's sake.

Maharatha Salya kills Nakula's four horses. Nakula leaps down from his own chariot and mounts his brother's. Standing on one ratha, the two brilliant Kshatriyas draw their bows in circles and pound Salya's chariot with a battery of arrows. That purushvyaghra remains unmoved as a mountain. Laughing, happy to see his nephews' prowess, he also inundates them with arrows.

Sahadeva charges at Salya, adroitly stabbing him with a powerful astra. Like Garuda's beak, the arrow pierces the Madra king and he falls in a faint in his chariot. Seeing him felled by the superb twins, and unconsciousness and prostrate, his sarathy steers him away to safety. Watching Salya's chariot leave the field, the Dhartarashtras are shocked, crestfallen, thinking he is dead.

Having bested their uncle, the twins blast their conches and roar triumphantly. They fly exultantly, Rajan, towards your forces like Indra and Upendra at the Daitya host.'

CANTO 85

BHISHMA VADHA PARVA CONTINUED

Sanjaya says, 'At noon, seeing Srutayush, Yudhishtira goads his horses at that Kshatriya. He attacks Srutayush, that chastiser of foes, striking him with nine keen shafts. Foiling those arrows, the illustrious Srutayush pierces Yudhishtira with seven barbs loosed in a single moment, which pierce his armour, spilling his blood and sapping the Dharmaraja's tejas.

Though painfully wounded, the son of Pandu shoots a missile formed like a boar's ear into Srutayush's breast and fells his standard from his chariot with another shaft. Seeing his proud standard destroyed, Srutayush strikes Yudhishtira with seven emerald arrows. The Dharmaraja is inflamed, and flares up like the fire that blazes at the end of the yuga consuming all creatures.

Seeing the son of Pandu's towering wrath, the Devas, the Gandharvas and the Rakshasas tremble on high, and the very universe is disturbed. And they fear that Yudhishtira will incinerate the three worlds that very day. And the Rishis and the Devas pray for peace. Still enraged and frequently licking the corners of his mouth, Yudhishtira looks like the sun that rises at the end of the yuga. Rajan, all your warriors fear for their lives.

With perfect composure, mighty Yudhishtira cleaves Srutayush's bow at its very grasp, and before the eyes of all the fighting men, he strikes Srutayush with a long arrow squarely though that king's chest. Summarily, the Pandava king despatches Srutayush's horses and his charioteer.

Srutayush abandons his horseless chariot and flees, and a wave of shame courses through Duryodhana's army. And now Yudhishtira begins to decimate your men at will, like Yama himself with mouth agape come hunting to Kurukshetra.

All see Chekitana of the Vrishnis cover maharatha Kripa Gautama with an extravagance of arrows. Cutting these down in flight, Kripa son of Saradwat shatters Chekitana's bow and fells his sarathy. Kripa kills Chekitana's horses, and the two warriors that protected his flanks.

Chekitana leaps down from his chariot with a mace in his hands. Dashing forward, he kills Kripa's horses and his charioteer with five sickening, bloody blows. Kripa, too, jumps down from his useless ratha and from the ground looses sixteen flashing arrows at Chekitana in the blink of an eye. Those barbs pierce cleanly through that noble Kshatriya and plough into the earth. Blossomed in blood flowers, in pain and enraged, Chekitana flings his mace at Kripa, like Purandara when he wanted to kill Vritra.

Gautama pulverises that gleaming gada coursing at him with a thousand arrows shot in an instant. Chekitana draws his sword and charges Gautama, who discards his bow, and drawing his own polished blade, also rushes towards his opponent. Both mighty warriors flay each other with their glinting weapons, sparks flying. Both bulls among men are wounded and fall onto the Earth, mother of all creatures. Exhausted, they faint.

Karakarsha, moved by friendship, rides up, and that invincible Kshatriya quickly lifts Chekitana into his chariot. And your brother-in-law, the intrepid Sakuni, swiftly helps maharatha Kripa onto his ratha.

Dhrishtaketu strikes the son of Somadatta in his chest with a blur of ninety shafts. And adorned with those arrows, Somadatta's son looks like Surya Deva with his burning rays.

Bhurisravas destroys maharatha Dhrishtaketu's chariot and kills his sarathy and his horses. Seeing him defenceless, Bhurisravas cloaks Dhrishtaketu with a veil of fine arrows. Dhrishtaketu abandons his chariot and mounts Satanika's. Encased in golden armour, maharathas Chitrasena, Vikarna and Durmarshana unite to attack the son of Subhadra. A fierce battle ensues between them and Abhimanyu, like the struggle of the body with vata, pitha and kapham, wind, bile, and phlegm.

Abhimanyu, tiger among men, smashes your sons' chariots, but does not kill them, remembering Bhima's vow to kill all the sons of Dhritarashtra himself. Arjuna sees Bhishma, invincible even against the Devas, advancing to save your sons from the terrible young Abhimanyu, already a maharatha among maharathas.

He addresses Krishna, "Urge your horses, Hrishikesa, to where those indomitable maharathas gather. Guide our horses so that the enemy does not annihilate our forces."

Krishna steers the chariot yoked to white horses into battle. Seeing Arjuna advance on your army, a loud clamour is heard among your fighting men. As he nears the kings protecting Bhishma, Arjuna addresses Susarman, "I acknowledge you both as excellent warriors and as our dire enemy. Today you will taste the harsh fruit of your sins. Today I will send you to the resting place of your ancestors."

That commander of chariot aksauhinis, Susarman, makes no reply to Arjuna's threat. Riding at Bibhatsu, with a large host of his allies, he surrounds him, and, supported by your sons, envelops him in a billowing gale of arrows, which hide the face of the sun.

Another dreadful battle breaks out between your army and that of the Pandavas, in which blood runs like water.'

CANTO 86

BHISHMA VADHA PARVA CONTINUED

Sanjaya says, 'Mighty Arjuna, pierced by Susarman and his host, inhales deeply and dissects the bows of those maharathas with his own arrow storm, he draws copious blood from all their bodies. Many of them fall bleeding on the ground. The limbs of some lie dissevered, and the heads of others roll, cut cleanly from their neck. Some die with bodies twisted and their coats of mail mangled. Struck by Arjuna's tremendous arrows, they plunge to gory death.

Seeing this carnage, Susarma, king of the Trigartas, yet advances on his chariot. And thirty-two other maharathas, who had been protecting the rear of those slain warriors, also attack Arjuna. Surrounding him, drawing their powerful bows in circles, they assail him relentlessly with deadly fire. Wounded by their deluge, Arjuna is incensed, and kills them all with six extraordinary shafts. Having slain sixty maharathas in moments and their legions in a few more, the glorious Kshatriya is exhilarated and he dashes ahead to kill Bhishma.

Seeing his allies overthrown, Susarman of the Trigartas still rushes at Arjuna with some other kings in his vanguard. Watching them press forward, the Pandava legion led by Sikhandin charges at them to protect Dhananjaya's chariot.

Arjuna turns and unleashes another arrow storm from the Gandiva at Susarman and his Samsaptakas. Eager to confront Bhishma, great Arjuna sees Duryodhana and some other kings led by the sovereign of the Sindhus, guarding the Kuru grandsire. Erupting into a grand inspiration of unearthly archery, sublimely thwarting the warriors who protect Bhishma, Arjuna who knows no fear adroitly avoids Duryodhana, Jayadratha and others, and forges on to engage the awesome son of Ganga.

Dharmaraja Yudhishtira also nimbly avoids the Madra king Salya, who has been assigned to harry him, and, along with Bhima and the sons of Madri, and rides furiously at Bhishma.

Dominating the field of war as ever, peerless Bhishma faces the unified onslaught of the sons of Pandu, never wavering. The dexterous Jayadratha takes careful aim and with gusto smashes the bows of all those Pandava maharathas. Always wrathful, Duryodhana strikes Yudhishtira, Bhima, Arjuna and the twins with a firetide of flaming shafts. Pierced roundly by Kripa and Sala and Chitrasena, Rajan, the Pandavas appear like the Devas attacked by the united Daitya hordes in ancient times.

Yudhishtira sees Sikhandin flee when Bhishma, with some disdain, consumes an astra loosed by the Panchala prince, and the Dharmaraja is stirred to anger. He cries at Sikhandin, "In the presence of your father, you had sworn to me that you would kill Bhishma. That was your solemn oath. Why do you not fulfil it now? O Kshatriya, do not neglect your vow. Defend your virtue, your noble race and your honour.

Look how Bhishma burns my troops with his fiery shafts, consuming them like Death himself. Your own bow is riven and you are repeatedly vanquished Shantanu's terrible son. Where do you go, deserting your kinsmen and brothers? This does not befit you.

Ah, you are terrified, and the colour fades from your face to watch indomitable Bhishma, and our army routed and in retreat. But you do not yet know that Arjuna has joined this dreadful fray. O celebrated

Kshatriya, why are you afraid of Bhishma today?"

Hearing Dharmaraja Yudhishtira, harshly though the Dharmaraja speaks, Sikhandin is quickly reassured, and turns back to fight, once more his sole and fervid purpose to destroy great Bhishma. As that prince rides back with verve into battle, Salya greets him with a flaming agneyastra. The son of Drupada, powerful as Indra himself, is undaunted, by that weapons, luminous as the fire that burns at the end of the yuga. Sikhandin stands firm, and invokes a Varunastra, and douses Salya's flames with a great tide of water in the sky. The Devas in the akasa and the kings of the earth all watch that awesome spectacle in wonder.

Meanwhile, the noble Bhishma breaks Yudhishtira's bow and cuts down his standard. Seeing Yudhishtira suddenly seized by fear, Bhima sets aside his bow and arrows, and, seizing a club, rushes roaring at Jayadratha on foot. Jayadratha riding in a circle pierces Bhima from all sides as the great Pandava runs at him, with five hundred whetted arrows each like a Yamadana. Calmly ignoring those barbs, the daring Vrikodara, incensed, turns his fury on Jayadratha's horses, foaled in Aratta, the kingdom of the Sindhus, and slaughters them all in explosions of blood.

Seeing Bhima fighting on foot, your son, the unrivalled Chitrasena, who, also, resembles the king of the Devas, swiftly attacks him from his chariot with astras. Mace in hand, Bhima bellows like ten wild bison and storms recklessly at your prince. Seeing Bhima's raised rod of Death, the Kauravas abandon your brave son and run like terrified boys.

In that fierce and bewildering fray, O Bhaarata, Chitrasena is undaunted as he watches that blood-dripping club flung by Bhima's tremendous hand course towards him through the air. Taking up a shining sword and shield, he leaps down from his chariot like a lion from the top of a cliff, to fight on foot. In that moment, falling on them like some meteor from the sky, Bhima's mace crushes Chitrasena's magnificent chariot, its horses and its sarathy. Watching your son's heroic and narrow escape, your forces are elated and shout triumphantly to applaud his deed.'

CANTO 87

BHISHMA VADHA PARVA CONTINUED

Sanjaya says, 'Your son Vikarna dashes up to Chitrasena and lifts him on to his own chariot. As the relentless war, fought at terror's very heart, continues, Bhishma attacks Yudhishtira. The Srinjayas, despite their chariots, elephants and horses, tremble to see the utterly frightening grandsire, and they believe Yudhishtira to be near his end.

Yudhishtira, accompanied by the twins, presses forward towards Bhishma, most illustrious archer, tiger among tigers among men. He shrouds Bhishma with thousands of arrows, clouds hiding the sun. And those countless arrows, so skilfully shot by Yudhishtira, reach the son of Ganga in distinct flights of hundreds and thousands.

And Bhishma responds by releasing a myriad shafts that are like dense locust swarms. In a flash, Bhishma mantles Kunti's son as in if several cerements of arrows which is looses in tide upon tide. Yudhishtira, stung, responds with an elongated nagapasa with venomous jade scales. Maharatha Bhishma destroys Yudhishtira's shaft in the air with a horse-shoe headed arrow.

Bhishma slaughters Yudhishtira's gold decked horses and the Pandava king abandons his horseless chariot and swiftly mounts Nakula's. Bhishma, conqueror of hostile cities, confronting the twins in battle, covers them entirely with his arrows. Seeing his afflicted brothers, Yudhishtira begins to seriously plot Bhishma's end.

He goads his friends and allies to the deed, crying, "Unite and kill Bhishma!" Hearing these words, the kings surround the Pitamaha with many chariots. But Bhishma, almost playfully, fells the maharathas, one after the other with his transcendent archery.

The Pandavas helplessly watch Bhishma thundering all over the battlefield, Bhishma like a young lion in a forest amidst a herd of deer. Roaring, he terrifies the bravest warriors; all the gathered Kshatriyas before him are like lesser animals before a lion. They see his swirling majestic movements in his chariot as being like a blazing wind-blown inferno devouring a heap of dry grass.

And Bhishma beheads maharathas like a forester felling ripe fruits from palmyra trees with stones. And those heads of helmeted soldiers fall upon the earth with the clatter of cascading rocks.

As that dreadful battle rages, utter chaos reigns among the armies. The carefully deployed legions of both armies fall into complete disarray. And the Kshatriyas challenge one another to individual combat.

Sikhandin charges at the Pitamaha, shouting to him to stop and fight. But Bhishma thinks of the princess Amba that Sikhandin once was, and disdaining him, advances against the Srinjayas who are delighted at seeing him approach. They cheer deafeningly and blast their conches.

Another bloodthirsty battle erupts in which chariots and elephants are mangled, and a thousand good fighting men die each moment. And the day passes as in a scarlet nightmare.

Dhrishtadyumna, prince of the Panchalas, and maharatha Satyaki are tormented by a barrage of arrows and spears aimed at them. With riptides of fire they begin to burn columns and columns of your warriors. Though under fiery siege, your forces do not retreat, but fight back bravely by now determined to die for honour if they must. Slaughtered by the illustrious son of Drupada, they cry out in anguish and fall in waves into the sea of blood which spreads everywhere and congeals upon sacred ground.

Hearing the desperate screams of those dying legions, maharathas Vinda and Anuvinda of Avanti ride in a froth at Dhrishtadyumna at his horrible sacrifice of living men. Abruptly killing his horses, they envelop him in deadly storms of dark arrows. The prince of the Panchalas leaps off his chariot and mounts that of the noble Satyaki.

King Yudhishtira, supported by a vast aksauhini, rides against the two enraged princes of Avanti. And your son surrounds them defensively.

Arjuna fights against many bulls of the Kshatriya race, like Indra against the Asuras. Drona, always ready to defend your son, begins to devour the Panchalas like fire consuming a heap of cotton. Your other sons, Rajan, loyal to Duryodhana, surround Bhishma, and confront the Pandavas.

When the evening sun turns red, Duryodhana says to your forces, "Hurry!" And as the sun sets behind the western hill, and the soldiers accomplish difficult feats, the ghastly river of blood flows and swells, infested by jackals.

And the battlefield turns hideous, full of spectres, and the jackals howl, portending further evil. Thousands of Rakshasas and Pisachas and other flesh eaters and blood drinkers are seen all round.

Having routed the kings led by Susarman and their soldiers, in the very midst of their aksauhini, Arjuna returns to his tent. And Yudhishtira and his brothers, followed by his men, withdraw to theirs.

Bhima, too, having brought deadly havoc among Duryodhana's warriors, returns to his tent. And Duryodhana, with his troops, after defending Bhishma successfully another savage day, turns back to his.

And Drona, and Drona's son, and Kripa, and Salya, and Kritavarman of the Satwata vamsa, all of the Dhartarashtra army, retire to their tents. Satyaki too and Dhrishtadyumna, the son of Prishata, shepherding their army, withdraw towards theirs.

Thus those fearless chastisers of enemies, your forces and the Pandavas, stop fighting at sunset. Both the Pandavas and the Kauravas enter their tents and praise one another.

Making arrangements for the protection of their fearless legions through the night, having their watch posts manned, they pluck out the day's arrows from their bodies and bathe in many kinds of water. And Brahmanas perform propitiatory rites for them, and poets sing their praises.

Those illustrious men amuse themselves with singing and instruments. And for a while the whole place resembles heaven itself! Those bulls among men do not speak of the war. And when both armies sleep, exhausted men and elephants and horses, they are serene and beautiful to watch.'

CANTO 88

BHISHMA VADHA PARVA CONTINUED

Sanjaya says, 'Having passed the night in sound sleep, at daybreak the Kauravas and the Pandavas once more advance into battle. As they come onto the battleground again, a great deep sound like the roar of the ocean is heard.

Duryodhana, and Chitrasena, and Vivimsati, and that most excellent maharatha Bhishma, and Drona, all united and in full armour, expertly array the Kaurava vyuha against the Pandavas. Fierce as the stormy sea, with horses and tuskers for its billows and current, the Pitamaha leads that dwindled but still vast army, supported by the Avantis and the Malavas, the people of the southern kingdoms.

Beside him is the noble son of Bharadwaja, with the Pulindas, the Paradas, and the Kshudraka-Malavas. The valiant and stalwart Bhagadatta is in your ranks, along with the Magadhas, the Kalingas, and the ghoulish Pisachas.

Behind Bhagadatta is Brihadbala king of the Kosalas with the Melakas, the Tripuras, and the Chichilas. Next to Brihadbala is the brave Trigarta, king of the Prasthala, surrounded by a vast number of the Kambojas, and by Yavanas in thousands.

Next to the lord of the Trigartas, Bhaarata, advances that mighty Kshatriya, Aswatthaman son of Drona, filling the earth with leonine roars. Alongside is king Duryodhana himself with his entire army, surrounded by his magnificent brothers. Behind Duryodhana rides Kripa the son of Saradwat.

Thus, that mighty vyuha, resembling the turbulent ocean, presses into battle. And standards and royal white parasols, beautiful bracelets and costly bows, shine radiantly. Watching the enemy advance, maharatha Yudhishtira says to Dhrishtadyumna, "Behold that oceanic vyuha! O son of Drupada, create another swiftly to contain and destroy it."

The gallant Dhrishtadyumna forms the Sringataka vyuha, which is known to raze all other vyuhas. At its horns are Bhima and Satyaki, with thousands of chariots, horsemen and foot soldiers. Near them is Arjuna, with his chariot yoked to white horses driven by Krishna. In the centre stand Yudhishtira and Madri's twin sons.

Other royal archers, all knowers of the vyuha shastra, with their forces, fill the remaining spaces. Abhimanyu, and Virata, the sons of Draupadi and the Rakshasa Ghatotkacha are told to bring up and defend the rear.

Having created this awesome vyuha, the noble Pandavas stand on the field, longing for battle and eager for victory. And the crashing of drums mingles with the blast of conches; the leonine roars of the soldiers and the slapping of their armpits are thunderous and fill every direction.

Those mighty warriors advance, and stare across Kurukshetra, field of dharma, chasmic field of death, unwinkingly. After a moment's perfect silence they erupt into fierce roars and yells, challenging each other, and attack! The war on the crack of the ages between your sons and their enemies, their cousins, resumes beneath its enveloping canopy of wrath.

Quickly lethal shafts fall like showers of serpents with mouths agape, and polished gleaming barbs rain down like gashes of lightning. Glittering maces loosed from bright slings fly up and whistle down over the enemy in batteries of thunder and blue swords and leather shields decked with a hundred moons look wondrous as they adorn the field of endless death.

The two hostile armies look at once awful and resplendent, like the Devas and Asuras fighting each other. In every direction they storm against one another, and the air is a thick hoarseness of roars and screams.

Celebrated maharathas crash violently into others, the yokes of their chariots tangling with those of their opponents. The friction of the tusks of elephants as they collide sets off flashes of fire and smoke.

Warriors on the backs of elephants, struck through with spears, fall like loosened rocks from hillsides. And the spectacle of foot-soldiers, fighting with bare arms or impaling one another with spears, is both magnificent and poignant.

With unending banks of arrows of every size and description, Kaurava and Pandava warriors mow each other down as if in some terrible game, a nightmare difficult to conceive. Bhishma charges the Pandavas, filling the air with the clatter of his chariot, while the twang of his bowstring petrifies his enemies all over again.

The resolute Pandava maharathas, led by Dhrishtadyumna, roar stridently and rush at him. This ignites a general battle between the foot soldiers, chariot warriors, and elephants of both sides, in which countless bright fighting men, old and young, killing and dying, become tangled with one another, their bodies and already written destinies.'

CANTO 89

BHISHMA VADHA PARVA CONTINUED

Sanjaya says, 'The Pandavas cannot even look upon Bhishma who rages over the battleground scorching every side like the Sun himself. The Pandava army, commanded by Yudhishtira, attacks the son of Ganga who destroys everything around him with blazing tides from his noble bow.

In elation, Bhishma razes the best of the Srinjaya and the Panchala archers. Yet the Panchalas and the Somakas continue to attack him with no thought for their lives. Bhishma severs the arms and heads of their maharathas. He smashes their chariots. And the heads of horsemen fall like eerie hail as they are hewn off in vermilion blasts.

We see countless war elephants, paralysed by Bhishma's astras, sprawled like hills on the ground, their riders crushed under them. None among the Pandavas can resist Bhishma, but only the formidable Bhima. Bhima rides to face his Pitamaha in battle, scything a bloody path through the Kaurava ranks, who roar or scream at him even as kills them. The jubilant Pandavas too roar like lions to see the carnage Bhima inflicts on the enemy.

Duryodhana, surrounded by his brothers, protects Bhishma. Inexorable Bhima still thunders up and beheads Bhishma's charioteer. Uncontrolled, his horses run wildly from the field, dragging their chariot behind them. Bhima decapitates Sunabha with horse-shoe headed arrow, so that son of yours falls out from his chariot. Seven of his brothers watch this cool brutal slaying and cannot bear it.

Adityaketu and Bahavasin, Kundadhara and Mahodara, and Aparajita, and Panditaka and the invincible Visalaksha, dressed in silver-flecked armour and carrying splendid weapons, attack Bhima in fury. Mahodara pierces Bhima with nine thunderbolt like arrows, quite like Indra assailing the great Asura Namuchi.

Adityaketu stabs him with seventy shafts and Bahavasin with five. Kundadhara strikes him with ninety barbs and Visalaksha with seven. And that conqueror of enemies, the maharatha Aparajita makes Bhima's mighty body a home for countless smoking barbs. And Panditaka also pierces him with three shafts.

Bhima does not flinch, he laughs, roars, instead in echoing peals and roars to make your sons' blood run cold. His bow firmly held in his left hand, Vrikodara of the cavernous appetites sloughs off your son Aparajita's most handsome head. And that head falls to the ground and rolls some way like some grisly ball.

While both armies watch transfixed, Bhima cuts your son Kundadhara's body in two with an exceptional sword-headed arrow. His next shaft, Rajan, is aimed at Panditaka and its rips through his armour so his heart bursts in a hot red font, and passing clean through your son's body, that irresistible barb burrows into the ground like a snake entering its hole after claiming its marked victim.

In great joy now, for he thinks of all the pain and shame your sons inflicted on him in the past, he cuts away Visalaksha's head. Bhima strikes the mighty Mahodara square through his chest with an interminable arrow which excoriates this next son of yours and your prince plunges lifeless to the ground. Slashing down Adityaketu's royal chatra with one light like shaft, he beheads this boy of yours as well with another.

Animated, roaring, roaring all the while, Bhima next kills Bahavasin in a bright red flash of gore.

Suddenly remembering the solemn oath that dreadful Bhima swore in the Kuru sabha, that he would kill every one of your sons, your other princes panic and flee from him. Stricken, sobbing, wailing to watch the brutal death of his brothers, Duryodhana roars at his forces, "There stands Bhima, preening. Destroy him!"

And your sons, those famed archers, seeing their brothers killed, painfully remember the wise and precious warning and counsel of the dignified and upright Vidura. For whatever nemesis he warned them of they now see unfolding before their eyes. Indeed, Rajan, everything that Vidura warned you of is coming to pass on Kurukshetra, field of dharma, field of death. But then you were blinded not just in your eyes, but your very heart by your greed, your foolishness and your inordinate love for your sons.

Ah, to watch that mahabahu decimating the Kauravas, it is amply clear that Bhima has undoubtedly been born to kill all your sons.

Overwhelmed by sorrow, Duryodhana rides up to Bhishma, and laments, "Bhima slaughters my brave brothers in battle like animals in a hunt. Our forces fight courageously, but they are failing. You seem to be an indifferent spectator, unconcerned about our fortunes. What terrible path have I taken? Ah, behold my evil destiny.'"

Sanjaya continues, 'Hearing Duryodhana's sad and cruel outburst, Bhishma's eyes fill with tears, and he says, "I said this before, as did Drona, Vidura, and the revered Gandhari. O my child, you did not understand it then. Parantapa, I have long ago determined that neither I nor Drona will leave this war alive.

But I also tell you this: Bhima will kill all whom he targets in this war. So muster your fortitude, and firmly resolved on battle, fight the sons of Pritha, making only Swarga your goal. As for the Pandavas, with Krishna on their side, they cannot be vanquished by the very Devas. Be resolute and brave; fight, O Bhaarata!'"

BHISHMA VADHA PARVA CONTINUED

Dhritarashtra says, 'Seeing so many of my sons killed by a single man, Sanjaya, how do Bhishma and Drona and Kripa respond? Day after day my sons are being slaughtered. Ah, I believe they are being overtaken by dark destiny; for they seem unable to find victory and always appear to face defeat. If my sons are being overcome despite Drona and Bhishma, and the high-souled Kripa, and Somadatta's gallant son, and Bhagadatta, Aswatthaman and other invincible heroes being with them, it can only be the will of fate.

Though reproached by me, Bhishma and Vidura, heinous Duryodhana paid no heed to what we said. Gandhari, too, warned him, but the dissolute Suyodhana did not realise his folly. And his folly now results in the death of my reckless sons at the hands of Bhima, day after day in battle.'

Sanjaya says, 'You yourself did not then understand Vidura's august words spoken for your good, but they have now come true. Vidura said, "Restrain your sons from gambling."

Like a man whose hour is come, refusing the remedy which can save him, you did not listen to the counsel of your well-wishers. The words of the righteous are being fulfilled and the Kauravas now perish for disregarding what the wise Vidura and Drona and Bhishma and other well-wishers warned them about. Why, O king, the dark omens portending the unthinkable tragedy which would ineluctably unfold were in evidence even when you refused to listen to their dire warnings.

It is far too late now and you cannot turn time back. So listen instead to my narration of the war exactly as it happens.

At noon, the battle turns even more savage and bloody. At the command of Dharma's son, the Pandava forces charge Bhishma yet again, always seeking to kill him. Dhrishtadyumna and Sikhandin, and maharatha Satyaki, with their spirited legions, ride at Bhishma as he stands alone like some great and unassailable column of light and death looming over Kurukshetra.

Maharathas Virata and Drupada, with all the Somakas, attack the solitary Bhishma. And the Kaikeyas, and Dhrishtaketu, and Kuntibhoja, armoured and bolstered by their forces, advance against the grandsire. Arjuna and the sons of Draupadi, and the fierce Chekitana press forward against all the kings commanded by Duryodhana who protect Bhishma. The noble Abhimanyu, terrible Ghatotkacha, and the smouldering Bhima fall upon the remaining Kauravas.

These three Pandava legions begin to slaughter the Kauravas, and the Kauravas also kill their enemy in ever mounting numbers. Drona assails the Somakas and the Srinjayas, meaning to raze them from the face of the earth. Shrill cries of anguish rise among the brave Srinjayas as they are mown down by Drona's remorseless tide of fire.

Countless Kshatriyas, struck by Drona, shudder and writhe in agony like men in the grip of some terrible disease. All over the field wounded men moan, some scream in pain, some groan hollowly like men dying of thirst or starvation.

And so also, like a second Yama, Bhima ravages the Kaurava forces. The river of blood swells and surges frothing across Kurukshetra and every moment hundreds of souls increase the population of Yama's kingdom. Bhima runs amok among the elephant aksauhini of the Kauravas, striking the great beasts down at will with arrows and mace, so their trumpeting rings horribly with the screams and mortal cries of dying men and their blood foams copiously into the ankle-deep lake of gore which spreads across the filed of horror.

Struck with Bhima's shafts, some of those tuskers plunge to the ground, some are paralysed and cannot move, some bellow in pain, while others run dementedly everywhere crushing men and chariots of both armies. Majestic elephants, their trunks cut off and limbs mangled, scream like cranes, and briefly pirouette ungainly before plummeting to the ground, shaking the earth.

Nakula and Sahadeva are at the Kaurava horsemen. Thousands of the finest horses, wearing garlands of gold on their heads and golden jewels on their necks and chests, are butchered by the radiant twins. The earth is strewn with handsome fallen steeds. Some have had their tongues cut away; some lying limbs askew with wild eyes, their flanks heaving; some whinny weakly in agony, while others are still, no movement or breath stirring in them and their noble spirits fled. The field of war presents a strange and unnerving sight, adorned with fallen horses of many breeds and colours.

The very earth looks fiercely resplendent, with the bodies of countless kings killed by Arjuna; and with broken chariots, slashed banners and brilliant parasols, with rent chamaras and fans, and mighty ayudhas smashed in pieces, with garlands and gold necklaces, with jewelled bracelets, with heads still decked with ear-rings, with crowns fallen from royal heads, with standards, with jutting bases of beautiful chariots ruined, O Rajan, and with traces and reins Bhumi Devi is as radiant as she is in spring when strewn with flowers. But with such a grim and eerie splendour.

Bhaarata, thus the Pandava host is devastated when Bhishma and Drona, and Aswatthaman, and Kripa and Kritavarman fight with their utmost ferocity, while your army also faces similar devastation when the Pandava heroes unleash their long withheld simmering rage and put forth their might.'

CANTO 91

BHISHMA VADHA PARVA CONTINUED

Sanjaya says, 'As that war greater and more horrible than any other continues to claim brave Kshatriyas all around, Sakuni charges the Pandavas. Hridika's son of the Satwata vamsa also rides at them.

Suddenly, joyfully, as if some hidden tide has turned in their favour, your warriors encircle the Pandava army; their horses are the best of the Kamboja breed and those born in the northern plains, those of Aratta and Mahi and Sindhu, Vanayu's white horses, and those of the mountain kingdoms. The Tittiri horses, swift as the winds, surround the Pandavas. And with swift, mail-covered horses, decked with gold, Parantapa Iravat, son of Arjuna, rides at the Kaurava legion.

Iravat is the son of Arjuna, born to the daughter of the king of the Nagas who was vulnerable and despondent when her husband was killed by Garuda. Childless, she was given to Arjuna by Airavat. Partha took her to be his wife for she desired him. Thus that son of Arjuna was born to the wife of another.

Abandoned by his uncle who hated Arjuna, he was raised among the Nagas, protected by his mother. He grew up handsome, strong and accomplished, with unassailable strength and many occult powers. Hearing that Arjuna had gone to Indraloka, he promptly went there. He approached his father and greeted him with folded hands. He introduced himself to Arjuna, saying, "I am Iravat. Blessed are you, and I am your son."

He reminded Arjuna of the circumstances of the Kshatriya's meeting with his mother. Arjuna embraced his son who was so like him in heroic deeds, and exulted. Mahabaho Iravat was then joyously commanded by Arjuna, "When the war begins, you shall fight for us." Agreeing happily, Iravat left.

And now at the hour of battle he presents himself, with many swift and beautifully coloured horses. Decked with gold ornaments, they glide across the field like swans on the surface of a lake. Those stallions dash headlong against yours and both fall to the ground with a reverberation like the swish of Garuda's wings. And the horse riders hack one another down. The riderless chargers of both sides break free and scatter wildly in every direction.

Their strength sapped by receiving so many arrows upon their splendid bodies, their horses killed under them, brave Kshatriya horsemen stagger exhaustedly on Kurukshetra and die. When those legions of horses diminish and only a few survive, the younger brothers of Sakuni ride out of the Kaurava vyuha to the front, mounted on fresh, rested, well trained chargers, neither old nor young, swift and forceful as a gale.

Those six powerful brothers, Gaya, Gavaksha, Vrishava, Charmavat, Aarjavam, and Suka storm out of the Kaurava vyuha. They are supported by Sakuni and by their ardent fighting men, all wearing armour. Breaking through the hitherto inviolable Pandava legion of horsemen, those indomitable and jubilant Gandhara warriors penetrate deep into it, longing for victory or death and the bliss of heaven.

Seeing these exhilarated warriors, Iravat says to his bejewelled Naga soldiers, "Destroy these, their astras and their beasts." And his uncanny fighters, many of them half human and half great serpents, begin to cold-bloodedly harvest the onrushing cavalry of spirited Dhartarashtra warriors.

Watching their horsemen being coolly erased by Iravat's nerveless legion, the distraught sons of Subala charge Iravat and surround him. Their forces to attack Iravat and his Naga cavalcade with spears, and gory pandemonium rules all Kurukshetra.

Pierced with deep spears and drenched in blood pouring free from his wounds, Iravat looks like an elephant repeatedly pierced with a hook. Though wounded deeply in his chest, back, and thighs, he faces his adversaries alone and never wavers, not for a moment, Arjuna's heroic son.

Iravat stuns his rivals with a tornado of arrows so they swoon. That parantapa rips out the spears from his body, and flings them back at the sons of Subala striking them deep. He charges them with sword and shield in hand to kill them. They recover consciousness and attack him ferociously. Undaunted, Iravat continues to run at them, blade upraised. So swiftly does he weave and run, that even on their fleet chargers they cannot accost him.

His enemies ring him round and try to capture him. But they near him that parantapa hacks off their arms in a flurry and hacks away the legs of some. Their ornamented arms and weapons fall, and Arjuna's terrifying Naga son cuts off their heads all around.

Only the wounded Vrishava, Rajan, escapes alive from Iravat. Seeing those valiant Kshatriyas killed in moments, Duryodhana says to the sinister Alambusha, master of maya, who loathes Bhima for having killed his brother Baka once, "Look how Iravat has slaughtered my troops. You, too, have maya at your command and can go anywhere at will. You loathe Arjuna. Now kill his son in battle."

Alambusha roars like a lion and, with the fiendish Rakshasa of his aksauhini, wielding weirdly shining spears, charge Iravat. With the remainder of the Kaurava horsemen, too, Alambusha rushes at the mighty Iravat, who covers him in blizzard of arrows in the twinkling of an eye. Immediately, the Rakshasa begins to uses sorcery again the Naga prince. He conjures illusory chargers ridden by Rakshasas armed with spears and axes.

Two thousand die in moments in the battle between Iravat and Alambusha, and the two of them quickly come face to face like Vasava and Vritra. As Alambusha closes on him, Iravat cleaves his bow with his sword, and, whirling like some dervish, cuts down the Rakshasa's arrows all round him.

Alambusha flies up into the air and flitting here and there, changing his form moment to moment, tries to confound Iravat with maya. But Iravat can also shift his shape at will, and baffles Alambusha with his chimeras, and swiftly hacks off the fiend's arms and legs, shredding them with lightning sword strokes.

But lo, Alambusha reappears in a wink, now with a youthful appearance. Making illusion is natural to rakshasas, and they can choose their age and form at will. The Rakshasa's severed limbs join magically together and are now darkly splendid and rippling with youth and vigour. With a howl, Iravat hacks at Alambusha with his axe, like a woodsman cutting down a tree, mangling him again so his blood flows in rills. Alambusha's horrible roaring echoes across the field entirely patinaed with a skin of blood.

Yet again, Alambusha's desiccated body rejoins miraculously and now assuming a more macabre form than any he yet has, he rushes forward to try to seize Iravat bodily. Arjuna's son never flees a battle. Quickly a great Naga a kinsman of his mother appears at his side, and through that uncle's maya, more, so Iravat is surrounded by his serpentine kin.

Surrounded by glimmering emerald-scaled Nagas, Iravat assumes a form as vast as Ananta himself. He then mantles monstrous Alambusha in a writhing mass of snakes. The Rakshasa reflects for only a moment and, assuming the form of Garuda, devours those snakes and Iravat's uncle with them. Seeing that Naga of his mother's line consumed through illusion, Iravat is momentarily confounded. In that moment, the Rakshasa kills him with his sword; Iravat's crowned head, lovely as a lotus, beautiful as the moon, rolls to the ground.

When Arjuna's noble son is slain by the Rakshasa, the Dhartarashtra legions erupt in celebration. Conches boom and drumrolls fill the air thick with ghosts of men and their beasts dying in thousands all the while, and hardly aware yet they have been killed.

What a bloodletting there is on both sides in the war on Kurukshetra. Horses and elephants and foot-soldiers are killed by rampaging tuskers, gored and trampled. And glossy steeds and countless elephants are felled by swarming foot-soldiers. Maharathas annihilate chariots and warriors in numbers that cannot be counted or told as death's hurricane swirls on, only mounting in savagery by the passing day, by the hour.

Unaware of his son's death, Arjuna continues to decimate the kings who shield Bhishma. The warriors of your army and the Srinjayas sacrifice their lives by the thousands as libations in the yagna fire of war. And having lost their swords and bows, many maharathas, with dishevelled hair, fight with their bare arms.

Bhishma kills so many maharathas with supernal astras of wind, fire and shafts of solid water and the Pandava forces tremble before him. He massacres horses, elephants, horsemen and chariot warriors without favour, the river of blood surging before him most of all. Surely, Bhishma's prowess appears equal to Sakra's.

The fearsome valour of Bhima and Parshata is no less than Bhishma's, and scintillating handsome Satyaki's no less than theirs. Yet on this day the Pandavas are most fearful when they see Drona put forth his might. They think: "Drona can destroy us and our forces singlehandedly. What can he not do when he has a legion of maharathas with him?" Even Arjuna thinks likes this and is afraid to watch his Acharya sow death all around him as casually as a farmer sowing seeds in a fertile, darkling field.

With every passing hour of war, the warriors of both sides become more ruthless and cruel, as a if demons possess them and impel them to commit every atrocity they can. Quickly the war, which began with noble covenants being made between both armies, degenerates in this horrible contention that is like a fell carnage between two Rakshasa hosts.'

CANTO 92

BHISHMA VADHA PARVA CONTINUED

Dhritarashtra says, 'Tell me, Sanjaya, how does Arjuna respond when the Pandavas learn that Iravat is dead?'

Sanjaya says, 'Seeing his cousin Iravat slain, the Rakshasa Ghatotkacha roars terribly again and again in anguish. And the earth, with her oceans and mountains and forests, trembles. The sky and the four quarters of the world shudder.

Hearing those roars, the legs and arms of warriors quiver, and they sweat profusely. Your army is terrified. Everywhere, your soldiers stand frozen, like a herd of tame elephants fearing the charging lion.

With shattering roar after roar, Ghatotkacha assumes a truly terrifying form; with a raised flaming spear, encircled by many fierce Rakshasas all wielding astras, he charges in wrath like Siva at the end of the yuga. Seeing him come like some plague and his own troops scatter in absolute panic, Duryodhana, roaring like a pride of lions, rides headlong at the wild Rakshasa loosing a rage of flaming arrows at Ghatotkacha. Behind Duryodhana rides the king of the Vangas, with ten thousand great tuskers with musth juice trickling down.

The sight of your son with a legion of elephants angers Ghatotkacha further and his slanted eyes seem to spew flames. A pitched battle, that makes the hair stand on end, breaks out between him and Duryodhana. Seeing the lumbering elephant force towering on the horizon, the infuriated Rakshasas rush at it, weapons in hand, thundering forward like clouds charged with lightning, with chilling cries and yells. With sword and arrow, spear and mallet and rough hewn axe, they begin to raze that elephant host.

They kill majestic tuskers with great rocks and uprooted trees. As the Rakshasas demolish the elephants, we see some of the mighty beasts with their frontal globes smashed, some bathed entirely in their own blood, others with their limbs mangled or trunks sliced off leaving blood spraying hollow stumps whistling.

As his elephant host is laid waste, Duryodhana charges the Rakshasa horde recklessly. He looses cataracts of arrows at Ghatotkacha's legion of night, killing any number of those dark and excellent warriors. Inflamed, Suyodhana strikes four of the best and most dangerous Rakshasas, Vegavat, Maharudra, Vidyujihva and Pramathin, with four particularly deadly arrows and swathes the entire fell force in a calorific mantle of arrows. Many handsome and magnificent Rakshasas perish.

Bhima's wild son blazes up at your son's success. He draws his resplendent bow and charges Duryodhana. But your son is unperturbed at seeing Ghatotkacha storming towards him like Yama at Siva's bidding.

With fiery eyes, Ghatotkacha says to Duryodhana, "Today I will be released from my debt to my elders, and my mother; they were exiled by your vile game of dice. You dragged Drupada's daughter Krishnaa, in her period and clad in a single garment, into the Kuru sabha and humiliated her. Your persecution did not end there, and at your command, Jayadratha of the Sindhus tried to ravish her in the forest. Wretched Duryodhana, if you do not surrender, I will avenge all those injuries today!"

With that, Hidimbi's son bites his lower lip with his fangs, and licking the corners of his mouth with his long sharp tongue, covers Duryodhana in a scathing tide of arrows.'

CANTO 93

Bhishma Vadha Parva continued

S anjaya says, 'Duryodhana calmly bears that storm of arrows, hard even for the Danavas to withstand, like a bull elephant, lord of his herd, enduring the rains. Bharatarishabha, your son is in grave danger, but heedless of it he looses twenty five keen arrows, which flash to strike great Ghatotkacha, like poisonous snakes on the chest of Gandhamadana. Pierced by those shafts, blood trickles down the Rakshasa's body and he looks like an elephant with rent temples and juices flowing down.

Ghatotkacha turns his attention on Duryodhana, to kill your son no less. He seizes up an enormous spear, which could rive even a mountain. He chants an arcane mantra over it and it begins to blaze with light, like a comet, like a streak of lightning in his awesome hands. The Rakshasa raises it high above his head to cast it at Duryodhana, certainly impaling him, having his life.

Even as the recondite and dreadful thing burns and fizzes in Ghatotkacha's hand, Bhagadatta king of the Vangas, riding an elephant taller than any other, the peerless Supritika, thunders and sets himself squarely between Suyodhana and the Rakshasa, shielding your son completely.

Ghatotkacha fumes to see his intention foiled and casts his incendiary lance at Bhagadatta's elephant instead. Supritika give a most abysmal bellow as the fiery ayudha strikes him with a huge explosion, blasting a gaping hole in his side, blowing his great heart to shreds, and slowly, his eyes screaming a legend of grief and pain that lord of all mountain elephants buckles at his knees and falls over dead, shaking the earth. Bhagadatta leaps down to save his life, with a heartbroken roar to see his beloved beast die.

Duryodhana is anguished to see that prince among elephants killed and his troops give way to the wave of despair that sweeps over them and they run is dismay in every direction. But steadfast himself, cleaving to his Kshatriya dharma and his dignity, and full of fresh wrath, the Kaurava king unleashes an astra seemingly made of the flames of the pralaya at Ghatotkacha.

With alacrity, Ghatotkacha thwarts that burning shaft in flight. He seems to grow even taller with the mahima siddhi he commands and looming like some great shadow over the cowering Kaurava legions, his eyes shining crimson red with rage, he give a roar truly like a thundercloud's, so your warriors stand rooted and trembling before him. Again and again, Ghatotkacha roars and all Kurukshetra quakes to hear him.

Hearing him, Bhishma rides up to Drona and says, "Hidimbi's son is battling Duryodhana and no creature on earth can quell Ghatotkacha. O blessed one, go and protect the king or the Rakshasa will have his life today. Hurry Drona, and all your parantapas, this is our highest dharma!"

Drona and the other maharathas rush towards where the king of the Kauravas stands facing the roaring Rakshasa. They meet Duryodhana and Somadatta, Bahlika and Jayadratha, Kripa and Bhurisravas and Salya, and the two princes of Avanti, along with Brihadbala, Aswatthaman and Vikarna, Chitrasena and Vivimsati, all in the thick of the wheeling, whirling, blood spraying battle.

Thousands of other maharathas and their legions press forward to defend your son who is being cornered. Seeing those invincible forces dash towards him, Ghatotkacha stands unyielding as the Mainaka mountain, bow in hand, surrounded by his fiendish kinsmen armed with clubs and mallets and many astras.

The Rakshasas on one side and the best of Duryodhana's aksauhinis on the other launch into a mortifying battle. The twang of bows everywhere is like the ear-splitting cracks of burning bamboos cracking at their knots. The clatter of weapons falling upon coats of mail is as deafening as mountains shattering. Spears hurled by noble arms course through the sky like snakes.

Ghatotkacha raises his enormous bow, roars like a pride of lions, and cleaves Drona's bow with a strange, curved arrow. He fells Somadatta's standard with another broad-headed one. He pierces Bahlika with three shafts through his chest. He strikes Kripa with one arrow and Chitrasena with three. With another swift one from his fully stretched bow, he strikes Vikarna in the shoulder. Spouting blood, Vikarna falls to the floor of his chariot.

The Rakshasa vigorously drives fifteen shafts into Bhurisravas; they pierce through his armour and flesh and enter the earth. He smashes the chariots of Vivimsati and Aswatthaman. They drop the reins of their horses, and fall to the ground.

With another crescent-tipped arrow he fells Jayadratha's standard bearing the emblem of a golden boar; with a shaft he rives thee Sindhu king's bow. In frightful rage, he kills the king of Avanti's four horses with four unerring barbs. With another well tempered shaft, he stabs king Brihadbala deep, and the wounded king stumbles in his chariot. Never pausing, Ghatotkacha looses a clutch of serpentine narachas, which pierce the celebrated Salya.'

CANTO 94

BHISHMA VADHA PARVA CONTINUED

Sanjaya says, 'Having scattered all your warriors, the rampant Rakshasa attacks Duryodhana, at which many indomitable warriors of your army rise up to kill Ghatotkacha.

Those maharathas draw their mighty bows and charge at him, roaring like a countless lions. Surrounding him, they lash him with arrows like clouds belabouring a mountain with torrential rain. Deeply struck and in agony Ghatotkacha is like an elephant pierced repeatedly with a cruel hook. Then, like Garuda, he soars up into the sky, from where he thunders like stormclouds, and his fierce roaring resounds in every direction.

Hearing the Rakshasa's roars, Yudhishtira says to Bhima, "Listen to Ghatotkacha! For certain he is battling the maharathas of the Dhartarashtra army. The Pitamaha stands always ready to slaughter the Panchalas and Arjuna fights to protect them. Mahabaho, both these tasks demand your immediate attention; go and support Hidimbi's son who is in grave danger."

Bhima advances swiftly, terrifying the enemy with his tigerish roars that sound like the ocean at full moon. The valiant Satyadhriti and Sauchiti, and Srenimat and Vasudana, and the powerful son of the king of Kasi, all follow Bhima Vrikodara. Countless other rathikas led by Abhimanyu, and by the sons of Draupadi, and the bold Kshatradeva, and Kshatradharman, and Nila follow these. To protect Ghatotkacha they encircle him with a great force of chariots and six thousand war elephants.

Their loud shouts and roars, the thunder of their horses' hooves and the clatter of their chariot wheels make the earth shudder. Hearing that tumult, your anxious forces, ever fearing Bhima, turn ashen. Leaving Ghatotkacha, they flee. An unrelenting battle breaks out between those high-souled warriors and yours. Maharathas unleash astras at each other.

The war makes the brave exult and strikes terror into the hearts of the timid, as horsemen and elephant warriors face each other, and foot-soldiers and maharathikas. Absolutely possessed by the spirit of battle and bloodlust, they fight blindly, in rage.

In that seething ferment of chariots, horses, elephants, and foot-soldiers, a pall of dust rises from chariot wheels and the running feet of men and animals. Impenetrable, like red smoke, it obscures Kurukshetra. The warriors cannot distinguish friend from enemy. The father does not recognise the son, nor the son the father, in that vicious, unfeeling war which makes one's hair stand on end.

The ceaseless ominous whine of coursing weapons and the roars and screams of fighting men are like the howls of dead souls in torment. The blood of men and their beasts flows in frothing rivers; warriors' hair upon dissevered heads form its ghastly weeds and moss. Indeed, severed heads fall like hail on Kurukshetra. The earth is scattered with headless corpses of men, alongside mangled bodies of elephants and hacked limbs and bodies of horses.

Maharathas pursue each other and loose elemental astras to consume the enemy. Chargers, goaded by their riders, dash against others and fall down dead, their wild eyes glazing over in death. And men with burning, mad eyes, who have lost their weapons, dash against each other breastplate on breastplate, helmet on helmet, and fall stunned. Cruelly prodded by their mahouts, elephants gore other elephants disembowelling one another. Covered with bleeding wounds, their backs decked with standards, they are seen locked horribly, inextricably into each other like clouds charged with ivory lightning.

Some lie on top of others; some have their frontal lobes split with spears; they run wildly thundering like roaring clouds. Some, with their trunks lopped off, others with mangled limbs, plunge to the ground like mountains shorn of their wings of old by Indra. Other majestic tuskers bleed copiously, their sides ripped open; they look like mountains with red muddy streams gushing down their sides after a cloudburst. Others, riderless and pierced with arrows and spears, are like mountains shorn of their peaks.

Some of the great beasts are blind with fury, with juice streaming down their temples and cheeks and over their maddened eyes; no longer guided or restrained by any goad, for their riders have fallen, they trample hundreds of chariots, horses and foot-soldiers.

Horses, attacked by horsemen with bearded arrows and spears, whinnying in pain and rage and helplessness, careen at their assailants, disturbing all the points of the compass. Noble maharathas, encountering others, all fight without fear, recklessly. All those that fight on that abysmal field seek earthly glory or eternal life as they hew and smite and loose coruscating tumults of arrows.

Then, their spirits suddenly broken by the primeval brutality of it all, the Dhartarashtra troops quit the battle and flee the field.'

CANTO 95

BHISHMA VADHA PARVA CONTINUED

S anjaya says, 'Duryodhana is incensed on seeing his forces decimated and he charges Bhima. With his bow luminous as lightning, he envelops Pandu's son with a wither of arrows. He cleaves Bhima's bow with a crescent-moon-tipped winged shaft. He ruptures his detested enemy's chest with a missile with the power to split mountains. Pain screaming through him in a flash, yet Bhima remains tenacious, clasping his golden flag pole.

Seeing his father spurting blood, Ghatotkacha blazes up like a wrathful inferno. With booming shouts, a swarm of Pandava maharathas, led by Abhimanyu, attacks Duryodhana.

Seeing them, Drona says to your maharathas, "The Pandava maharathas, with Bhima at their head, hem Duryodhana in. They terrify our own warriors with squalls of fire. The king is in mortal peril, fly to protect him!"

Led by Somadatta your rathikas fall upon the Pandava ranks. Kripa and Bhurisravas and Salya, and Drona's son and Vivimsati, and Chitrasena and Vikarna, and Jayadratha, and Brihadbala, and the two princes of

Avanti, encircle Bhima in a ring of protection. The Pandavas and the Dhartarashtras encounter each other a mere twenty paces apart.

Mahabaho Drona bends his colossal bow and strikes Bhima with twenty six shafts. He bedevils Vrikodara with a luciferous volley like a cloudburst upon a mountain. Mighty Bhima swiftly pierces his Acharya with ten barbs through his left side. Frail with age, and tormented by pain, Drona faints on to the floor of his chariot. Roaring, Duryodhana dashes at Bhima with Aswatthaman beside him.

Seeing them come, each like a Yama at the end of the yuga, Bhima seizes a mace, and, leaping off his chariot, he stands like a hill on the field, unyielding. Why, he is like the imposing Kailasa, as Aswatthaman and Duryodhana attack him fervidly. Bhima, who knows no fear, runs straight toward them mace aloft. So terrible is his face that the Kaurava aim great astras at him to stop him somehow. Led by Drona, they harangue him from every side. Such is the immediate danger to his life and such his disdain for it, that the host of Pandava maharathas, led by Abhimanyu, dash forward, all of them ready to sacrifice their lives to save him.

Looking like a mass of blue clouds, heroic Nila charges Aswatthaman. A famed archer himself, he had long desired a duel with Drona's son. He strikes Aswatthaman with an irruption of winged shafts, even like Sakra who chastised Viprachitti, the Danava who once terrified the Devas and the three worlds.

Blood drenched in moments, infuriated, Aswatthaman draws his bowstring and, with a twanging as loud as Indra's thunder, unleashes a refulgence of flaming barbs at Nila. He fells Nila's standard and four horses with six rutilant shafts. With a seventh, he find Nila's chest and Nila, gushing blood, slumps down in his chariot.

Seeing Nila swoon, Ghatotkacha, with his invincible Rakshasas, falls upon Aswatthaman, who turns calmly to ride directly at his assailants. Quick as light, deadly as venom spitting king cobra, Drona's son despatches a host of Rakshasas in Ghatotkacha's vanguard. His anger stoked, Ghatotkacha uses powerful maya to create a great and demonic illusion. Aswatthaman stands bewildered and momentarily afraid. Your men run from that hellish vision, as part of which they see one another, though alive and breathing, lying dead, convulsed by death's spasms on the field of all horrors.

Drona and Duryodhana, Salya and Aswatthaman, and other noble Kaurava archers scatter before Ghatotkacha's fell sorcery. In his hallucinatory illusion, all your maharathas appear as being already routed, and all your allied kings slain. Meanwhile, the Pandava maharathas raze thousands of your horses and horsemen. Wailing, your legions escape to the safety of their tents.

Bhishma and I cry out to them, "Fight, do not run away! This is merely Rakshasa maya conjured up by Ghatotkacha."

Panic stricken, they pay no attention to us, they do not stop. Watching this flight, the Pandavas regard themselves victorious. Along with Ghatotkacha they roar like lions. The air resounds with their shouts, the blast of their conches, and the throbbing of their drums.

By dusk, your entire army has been routed and scattered by Ghatotkacha.'

CANTO 96

BHISHMA VADHA PARVA CONTINUED

Sanjaya says, 'After that rout, Duryodhana approaches Bhishma and, with a humble salutation, tells him about the defeat at the hands of Ghatotkacha.

Dejectedly he says to the Pitamaha, "O sire, relying on you, just as the Pandavas rely on Krishna, I began a fierce war with the Pandavas. Parantapa, I and my eleven aksauhinis obey your command. Despite this, I have been routed in battle by the Pandavas drawing on the powers of Ghatotkacha.

Ah, this consumes my limbs like a fire burning down a dry tree. O Parantapa, with your support and blessings, I want to crush Ghatotkacha myself. It befits you to fulfil my desire."

Bhishma says to Duryodhana, "O king, you should always conduct yourself suitably. Protect yourself in battle under every circumstance. Fight against Dharmaraja Yudhishtira, or with Arjuna, or with the twins, or with Bhima. In accordance with varnadharma, a Kshatriya must only contend with another Kshatriya.

Myself, and Drona, and Kripa, and Drona's son, and Kritavarman of the Satwata race, and Salya, and Somadatta's son, and that maharatha Vikarna, and your valiant brothers led by Dussasana, will all combine to fight the Rakshasa. Or if you are inconsolable at the carnage he brought to your legions, let Bhagadatta, who is equal to Purandara himself in war, fight Ghatotkacha."

And Bhishma says to Bhagadatta, "Advance swiftly, Rajan, against the son of Hidimbi. Engage that savage Rakshasa with caution, like Indra in ancient times did Taraka. You have divine weapons; your prowess is great. You, who have vanquished many Asuras in the past, are a true match for Ghatotkacha on the field. Backed by your vast forces, kill that bull among Rakshasas."

Hearing Bhishma's words, Bhagadatta advances towards the enemy, roaring like a lion. Seeing him approach like a storm of thunderheads, many Pandava maharathas furiously move against him: Bhima, Abhimanyu and Ghatotkacha, the sons of Draupadi, and Satyadhriti, and Kshatradeva, and the rulers of the Chedis, and Vasudana, and the king of the Dasarnas.

Mounted on his great new elephant, Bhagadatta charges into battle. A truculent encounter erupts. Forceful shafts, shot by maharathas, fall on elephants and chariots. Majestic trained tuskers with rent temples fall upon one another. Blind with rage, with temporal juice trickling down their bodies, they gore one another with column-like tusks.

Regal horses, ridden by warriors armed with spears, are goaded to fearlessly fly at each other. And thousands of foot-soldiers, attacked by legions of foot-soldiers with spikes and arrows, plunge to the ground, their legion spirits quitting their carved and mangled bodies in thick swarms. Roaring maharathas slaughter their daring adversaries with livid coruscations of barbed arrows.

In that battle which makes one's hair stand on end, the famed Bhagadatta, mounted on his elephant of rent temples with juice trickling down in seven streams, which makes him look like a mountain with seven rivers gushing down after heavy rain, like Indra himself riding Airavata, attacks Bhima in fury. Riding on the head of his massive beast, he looses a fulmination of arrows on the hulking Pandava.

King Bhagadatta unleashes that volley on Bhima like clouds lashing rain on to a mountain at the end of summer. Incensed, Bhima kills more than a hundred fighting men that protected Bhagadatta's rear and flanks in a sanguinary flash.

Wrath surges up in Bhagadatta and he goads his elephant straight at Bhima's chariot, why, even like some unimaginable arrow from a great god's bow! Bhima leads a host of Pandava maharathas directly at the attacking elephant. These warriors are the five Kekaya princes and Abhimanyu, the five sons of Draupadi and the ruler of the Dasarnas, Kshatradeva and the ruler of the Chedis, and Chitraketu. They wield divine astras with consummate skill and prowess, and they quickly surround their opponent's elephant.

That majestic tusker, stabbed with many arrows, streams blood from his wounds, and looks resplendent like a mountain plastered with red mud after the rains. The ruler of the Dasarnas rides his elephant out towards Bhagadatta. Bhagadatta's beast contains the attack like a continent the surging sea. Seeing this remarkable resistance, even the Pandava troops applaud and marvel.

The ruler of the Pragjyotishas is enraged and casts fourteen spears at the Dasarna king's regal mammoth. Like snakes entering anthills, these pierce the tusker's gold-decked armour. Deeply pierced and sorely wounded, that elephant's fury subsides and it swiftly retreats. As it flees, it mows down the Pandava host of its own side like a gale smashing down young trees.

With their elephant defeated, the maharathas of the Pandava army roar like lions and setting Bhima at their head, storm at Bhagadatta loosing all manner of arrows and astras at him. Bhagadatta is unmoved by these weapons and the legion that surges roaring at him; instead, he goads his great prince among elephants at them, prodding it with his hook and spurred boots. That elephant provoked with hook and spur seems to assume the form of the Samvarta fire that destroys everything at the end of the yuga.

Crushing hordes of chariots, elephants and horses with their riders, it thunders about in every direction, pounding down foot-soldiers by the thousands. The vast legions of the Pandavas shrink like leather exposed to fire.

As Bhagadatta thins the Pandava vyuha, Ghatotkacha, with fiery eyes and blazing face, charges towards him. Assuming a terrible form alight with rage, he seizes a bright lance that can penetrate a mountain and hurls the flaming thing at Bhagadatta's elephant. Seeing it course towards him, the ruler of the Pragjyotishas cuts it in two with a crescent-headed arrow, and the golden spear plunges into the earth like Indra's thunderbolt.

With a shout, Bhagadatta takes a glittering spear and in a fluid blur casts it at Ghatotkacha, who leaps up into the air and seizes it in his hand. The Rakshasa snaps it like a twig it against his knee before the eyes of the assembled kings. All this appears awesome. The Devas, the Gandharvas and the Munis are wonderstruck. And the Pandava warriors, led by Bhima, also cry out their praises at what Ghatotkacha incredibly does.

Bhagadatta cannot endure these exultations. He roars, draws his radiant bow, and shoots a scintillation of fire shafts at all the Pandava maharathas. He strikes Bhima with one arrow and Ghatotkacha with nine. He shoots Abhimanyu with three, and the Kekaya brothers with five. With his bow drawn in a circle, he pierces Kshatradeva's right arm deeply so that Kshatriya's bow falls from his hand.

Bhagadatta strikes the five sons of Draupadi with five arrows; he kills Bhima's horses; with three feathered shafts, he cuts down Bhima's standard bearing the lion emblem. And with three more searing arrows he pierces Bhima's charioteer Visoka, who plunges to the floor of his chariot in agony. Bhima leaps down from his chariot with his mace. All your forces are terrified, watching him with gada upraised, looking like a mountain peak.

As Bhima and Ghatotkacha are battling the ruler of the Pragjyotishas, Arjuna appears, slaying the enemy on all sides. He sees his embattled brothers and radiates tides of fire in every direction. Duryodhana swiftly moves his legion of chariots and elephants. Arjuna charges that Kaurava aksauhini on his chariot of white horses.

Riding his elephant, Bhagadatta crushes the Pandava ranks, and storms towards Yudhishtira. A fierce battle begins between Bhagadatta and the Panchalas, the Srinjayas and the Kekayas. Bhima narrates the details of the slaughter of Iravat to Krishna and Arjuna.'

CANTO 97

BHISHMA VADHA PARVA CONTINUED

Sanjaya says, 'Hearing of his son Iravat's death, Arjuna's eyes glisten with tears and he sighs deeply. He says to Krishna, "Ah, the wise Vidura Mahatman surely saw this terrible destruction of the Kauravas and Pandavas clearly with his mind's eye. And so did he warn Dhritarashtra repeatedly.

Krishna, the Kauravas have killed so many of our heroes, and we have killed many of theirs. What contemptible deeds have been done in the pursuit of kingdom and wealth! I curse these that have led to such slaughter of kinsmen.

For him who is penniless, even death would be better than acquiring a fortune by killing his relatives. Krishna, what will we gain by destroying our own blood and lineage? Duryodhana, Sakuni and Karna are to blame for the extermination of the very Kshatriya race.

I now understand, Mahabaho, that Yudhishtira was wise to ask Suyodhana for only half the kingdom, indeed for only five villages. And even that was not given. Seeing so many brave warriors lying dead on the field, I curse myself and curse the dharma of a Kshatriya.

I continue to fight only so that I am not called weak and cowardly. Otherwise, this war repulses me. Ah, drive the horses forward towards the Dhartarashtra army; let me continue with this bloodthirsty sacrifice. There is no time to lose."

And Krishna goads those fleet white horses forward, while your troops are disturbed like the stormy ocean at high tide. The battle between Bhishma and the Pandavas is dreadful and deafening like thunder.

Your sons surround Drona like the Vasus surrounding Vasava, and storm into battle against Bhima. Bhishma and maharathas Kripa, Bhagadatta and Susarman advance against Arjuna. Kritavarman and Bahlika attack Satyaki. And king Amvashta sets himself before Abhimanyu. Other great chariot-warriors clash with each other. On every side, the war is ever more fierce and gruesome.

Bhima is a fire that blazes up with offerings of ghee. Your sons shroud him with arrows, but that Kshatriya, his body and litheness like a tiger's, licks the corners of his mouth in savage glee. Bhima kills your son Vyudoroska with a horseshoe-headed arrow; with another keen shaft, he blows Kundalin's heart to shreds like a great lion killing a small cub. He covers your other sons who are close in gusts of fire, killing Anadhriti, and Kundabhedin, and Virata, and Dirghalochana, and Dirghabahu, and Subahu, and Kanykadhyaja, who topple lifeless from their chariots, Bharatarishabha, looking like mango trees sprouted with red blossoms in spring.

Your other sons flee from Bhima as if from Yama himself. Drona envelops him in a shroud of arrows. But Bhima is irresistible, his prowess astounding as he continues to massacre your sons in the face of Drona's best efforts to thwart him. Bhima laughing aloud wildly, magnificently foils Drona's intense volleys, while he continues to feed the blood and corpses of your sons to yawning thirsty Kurukshetra. He sports among your sons like a tiger among a herd of deer. Like some mythic wolf, Vrikodara terrifies your sons and kills them one after the other.

Meanwhile, Bhishma, Bhagadatta and Kripa oppose the daring Arjuna. Dhananjaya thwarts the astras of his adversaries with his own, and kills many leading warriors of your army.

Abhimanyu decimates king Amvashta's of his chariot with a flurry of arrows. Amvashta leaps out of his ruined ratha in shame, hurling his sword at the high-souled Abhimanyu. And he hastily mounts the chariot of Hridika's son, while Abhimanyu shatters his sword in the air. The Pandava warriors marvel at the inspired archery of Subhadra's son and cheer loudly. Others led by Dhrishtadyumna continue to raze your forces, which still stand valiant, fighting on, facing death squarely.

With great feats of daring, the war swells and plunges on, claiming thousands of lives across grisly Kurukshetra every moment. Brave fighting men seize one another by the hair, fight with their nails and teeth, fists and knees, heads and hands and swords, and strapping arms. With frightening vigour they slaughter each other.

Father and son kill one another. The soldiers fight desperately using all their limbs. Beautiful bows with golden arrows slip from the hands of fallen warriors, and precious jewels and gleaming feathered shafts lie scattered thickly across the killing field; glistening arrows resemble snakes with shed skins.

Golden swords with ivory handles, and shields dappled with gold, lie fallen on the field, blood slicked, glistening under the hazy sun. Arrows, axes, swords and spears, many decked with gold, beautiful coats of mail, and heavy and spiked clubs, and howdahs of elephants, and yak tails, and fans, are strewn everywhere.

Lifeless maharathas, still clasping their weapons, look as if they are still alive, biting bloodied lips. Their arms and legs shattered with maces and heads smashed with clubs, or crushed by elephants, horses and chariots, footsoldiers lie like broken puppets on the crimsoned earth. The earth laden thickly with the corpses of horses, men and elephants, looks beautiful, Rajan, as if dotted with hills great and small. How copiously Kurukshetra of the terrible blood sacrifice is covered with arrows, axes, swords, spears, cudgels, satagnis and mangled bodies.

Bleeding profusely, warriors lie with limbs askew, some silent in death, others moaning in anguish. What a sight the Earth presents! Smeared with sandalwood paste and wearing fine leather gloves and golden armlets, severed arms of powerful warriors are to be seen everywhere one looks; also mighty, shapely thighs like the trunks of elephants, and fallen bejewelled turbaned heads– and all their fill the field of dread with strange and poignant beauty.

The field of the Kurus, stained with blood, covered with bloodied coats of armour and radiant ornaments, looks as if on fire. Like a beautiful woman adorned with jewels, Bhumi appears eerily lovely with scattered ornaments, bows, arrows with golden wings, smashed chariots with silvery bells, and horses with tongues lolling out, with standards, quivers, banners and great conches of heroes, and elephants with severed trunks – with all these.

Wounded elephants groan in agony and appear like shifting mountains. Colourful mantles and finely wrought hooks studded with stones of lapis lazuli, and bells, flecked cloths and deerskin, neck-chains and golden girdles that once adorned majestic tuskers, are spread across the ground as if in some great and bizarre exhibition.

Various devices lie broken by golden darts, and embroidered saddles of horses, caked with mud. The hacked arms of horsemen, decked with bracelets, are everywhere, along with shining spears and swords, and turbans fallen off noble heads.

The earth looks like the star-strewn sky with crescent-headed arrows, crushed saddles of ranku deer skin, and glistening jewels from the coronets of kings. It glows with the resplendent parasols, yak tails and fans, and with faces, bright as the lotus or the moon, of daring Kshatriyas, with gleaming ear-rings and elegant beards, who lie lifeless.

Thus the two armies annihilate each other in the fight. The warriors are exhausted in body and spirit; the events and sights of the day have been splendid and horrifying beyond imagining; until, dark night sets in and nothing can be seen. The Kauravas and the Pandavas withdraw their armies. Retiring to their tents, they rest for the night.'

CANTO 98

BHISHMA VADHA PARVA CONTINUED

Sanjaya says, 'Duryodhana, Sakuni, Dussasana and the invincible Karna sit together and evaluate their situation. How can the sons of Pandu and their allies be defeated? This is the subject of their discussion.

Duryodhana says to them, "Drona, Bhishma and Kripa, and Salya and Somadatta's son do not challenge the Pandavas. I do not know why. Unopposed, they are destroying my forces. Karna, I am being weakened and my weapons exhausted. I am baffled by my adversaries; I feel that even the Devas cannot vanquish them. My mind is filled with doubt; how can I quell the Pandavas in battle?"

Karna replies, "Do not be distressed, O lord of the Bhaaratas, for I will achieve the end you desire. Let Bhishma withdraw from the great war. When he puts down his weapons, I will kill the Parthas and the Somakas, before Bhishma's eyes.

I swear I will do this. Indeed, Bhishma shows mercy towards the Pandavas everyday. He cannot defeat those maharathas. Bhishma is proud in battle. He enjoys the fight. Why would he subdue the Pandavas, for then the war itself will end?

Go to Bhishma's tent, and ask the revered Pitamaha to set aside his weapons. When he does this, consider the Pandavas dead, slain along with all their supporters and kinsmen by me alone."

Thus addressed by Karna, Duryodhana says to his brothers, "Dussasana, get ready to accompany me." He says to Karna, "Parantapa, I will persuade Bhishma to consent to what you ask, and then promptly come to you. After Bhishma retires from the fight, you will destroy the enemy."

Accompanied by his brothers, your son sets out like He of a hundred sacrifices accompanied by the Devas. Dussasana makes him mount on his horse. Adorned with bracelets, with a crown on his head, and ornaments on his arms, he shines brilliantly as he goes forth. Smeared with fragrant sandalwood-paste, bright as the burnished gold of the bhandi flower, wearing spotless garments, Duryodhana goes forth like a great lion, looking like the glowing sun in the sky.

And as that tiger among men goes towards Bhishma's tent, many celebrated archers follow him. His brothers also accompany him, like the Devas walking behind Vasava. Other gallant men, riding on horses, elephants and chariots, go with him.

Like the Devas surrounding Sakra, his well-wishers assemble in hordes to protect him. Adored by all the Kauravas, Duryodhana rides slowly, regally towards Bhishma's tent.

He raises his right arm, like an elephant's trunk with which he can crush all enemies, and accepts the homage paid to him by the bystanders who stand with folded hands raised above their heads. As he canters along, he hears the sweet voices of the people of many lands. He is praised by their bards and poets. That great king responds with equal respect to all.

Many high-souled men stand around him with golden lamps burning with perfumed oil. Duryodhana looks radiant like the moon surrounded by blazing planets. Attendants with head-gear decked with gold, with canes and jhariharas in hand, gently part the crowd.

The king reaches Bhishma's tent and dismounts from his horse. He greets the Pitamaha and sits on a golden seat covered with an ornate cloth.

With hands folded, tearful eyes, and in a grieving voice, he says to Bhishma, "Parantapa, under your protection, we could defeat the very Devas and Asuras led by Indra. What can I say, then, of the gallant Pandavas, their kinsmen and friends?

Son of Ganga, be merciful. Kill the sons of Pandu like Mahendra destroying the Danavas. *I will slay all the Somakas and the Panchalas, and the Karushas along with the Kekayas*: these were your words to me. Stand by those words.

Kill the Parthas, and the Somakas. Honour your promise. If your love for the Pandavas, or loathing towards me, sways you to spare them, then allow Karna to fight. He will put a swift end to them along with their allies and kinsmen."

Having said this to Bhishma, your son Duryodhana falls silent.'

CANTO 99

BHISHMA VADHA PARVA CONTINUED

Sanjaya says, 'Bhishma is saddened by your son's dagger like words. But he does not reply with a single harsh word. He is overwhelmed with grief and anger, sighs deeply and reflects silently for a long time.

Looking up, as if angrily swallowing the world with the Devas, Asuras, and Gandharvas, Bhishma speaks calmly to Duryodhana, "Why do you stab me with such sharp words? I always try hard to achieve your interests. For this I am prepared to sacrifice my life in this battle.

The Pandavas cannot be defeated. This is clear ever since the brave son of Pandu pleased Agni in the Khandava vana, after vanquishing Sakra himself in battle. O Parantapa, Arjuna rescued you when you were captured by the Gandharvas; even that was a clear sign.

On that occasion, your brave brothers fled, as did Radha's son. What Arjuna did even then clearly revealed his prowess. In Virata's city, he single-handedly subdued us all. That was a sufficient indication.

He defeated and disrobed both Drona and me. That was ample evidence. When the cows were stolen, he overcame Aswatthaman and

Saradwat. This surely should have shown you what he is.

Having easily quelled Karna, who boasted loudly of his manliness, Arjuna took his robes and gave them to Uttara. That should have been unmistakable proof for you. Arjuna defeated the Nivatakavachas who were invincible even to Vasava. How much clearer could it be, Suyodhana?

Who can hope to defeat such a hero, and besides one protected by the Protector of the Universe armed with sankha, chakra and gada? Krishna has infinite power, and is the Destroyer of the Universe. He is the highest Lord of all, the God of Devas, the eternal Paramatman. He is eulogised by Narada and other great Rishis.

But, ah, you are foolish and do not know what should be said and what should not. To a man on the point of death, all trees appear to be made of gold. Son of Gandhari, you see everything as being the opposite of what they truly are. Having provoked war with the Pandavas and the Srinjayas, fight them now. Let us see you not moan and whine like a boy, but fight like a man.

As for me, I will bring death to the Somakas and the Panchalas, avoiding only Sikhandin. If killed, I will go to Yama's abode; if I kill them, I will give you joy.

Once, Sikhandin was born in Drupada's palace as a woman. Upon receiving a boon, she became a man. She is Sikhandini. I cannot kill him even to save myself. She is the same Sikhandini created by Brahma. Sleep peacefully tonight. Tomorrow I will fight so fiercely that men will remember the battle as long as the world lasts."

Duryodhana comes away with these words. He bows to the Pitamaha and returns to his own tent. He dismisses his attendants. He enters his tent and sleeps. At dawn he rises, and orders the royal warriors, "Gather our forces. Today Bhishma will slay all the Somakas."

Bhishma regards Duryodhana's lamentations as commands to himself. Saddened, and deploring his servile position, he thinks carefully about a possible duel with Arjuna.

Duryodhana anticipates Bhishma's plan and commands Dussasana, "Deploy the chariots to defend Bhishma. Press all our twenty two legions into battle formation. The moment that we have been thinking about for years, the slaughter of the Pandava army and seizing the whole kingdom, has arrived.

For this, our first duty is to protect Bhishma. Well guarded, he will protect us and kill the Parthas in battle.

Bhishma said to me, 'I will not kill Sikhandini, for he was a woman once and I will not face him in battle. The world knows that, to honour my father, I gave up a vast kingdom. I will not kill any woman or anyone who was once a woman. This is the truth by which I live and the dharma I will never break.

Sikhandin was first born a woman. You have heard that story as I have narrated it to you before the war began. Killing herself first and taking birth as a daughter, she who was once the princess Amba of Kasi has become a man. She will fight me, but I will never aim an arrow at her.

Other Kshatriyas who fight for the victory of the Pandavas, I will consume them all with devastras.' These were the wise Bhishma's words to me.

Our first and last duty is to protect the son of Ganga. If a lion is left unprotected in the jungle, he can be killed even by a wolf. We cannot allow the Pitamaha to be slain by Sikhandin like the lion by the wolf. Let Sakuni and Salya, Kripa and Drona, and Vivimsati safeguard Bhishma. If he is safe, our victory is assured."

Hearing Duryodhana, all surround Bhishma with a majestic legion of chariots. Your sons position themselves around him and ride into battle. As they advance the earth and the sky shudder and strike fear into the hearts of the Pandavas.

The Kaurava maharathas stand around Bhishma, in full armour, backed by that resplendent chariot force and by their elephants. They hold their positions to protect the Pitamaha even like the Devas watching over Indra in the war against the Asuras.

Duryodhana says to his brother, "Yudhamanyu protects the left wheel of Arjuna's chariot, and Uttamaujas his right wheel. Arjuna in turn protects Sikhandin. Dussasana, see that Bhishma is never left unprotected for even a moment so that Sikhandin might attack him."

With his surging forces, Dussasana rides with Bhishma in the vanguard of the Kaurava army. Seeing Bhishma encircled by so many chariots, Arjuna says to Dhrishtadyumna, "Prince of Panchala, place Sikhandin before Bhishma today, and I myself will be your brother's protector.'"

CANTO 100

Bhishma Vadha Parva continued

S anjaya says, 'Bhishma advances with his forces. He ranges them in the sweeping, encompassing Sarvatobhadra vyuha. Kripa and Kritavarman, and maharatha Saibya, and Sakuni, and Jayadratha of the Sindhus, and Sudakshina king of the Kambojas take their positions at the forefront of the army and the vyuha, along with Bhishma and your sons.

Drona and Bhurisravas, and Salya and Bhagadatta, guard the vyuha's right flank. Aswatthaman and Somadatta, and those maharathas, the two princes of Avanti, with a vast host, protect the left. Surrounded by the Trigartas, Duryodhana places himself in the middle, ready for the Pandavas. Maharathas Alambusha and Srutayush, position themselves behind that vyuha and the whole army.

Your mail-clad warriors form this enveloping vyuha and they look like flames upon Kurukshetra.

Yudhishtira and Bhima, Nakula and Sahadeva, in glistening armour, position themselves in the vanguard of their vyuha, in front of all their fighting men. Dhrishtadyumna and Virata, and maharatha Satyaki stand ready, hungry for battle. Sikhandin and Arjuna, the Rakshasa Ghatotkacha, Mahabaho Chekitana, and the valiant Kuntibhoja, all encircled by their forces, stand prepared. Abhimanyu and Drupada, and the five Kaikeya brothers, all in their chariots, are splendid to behold, weapons at the ready.

Having formed their mighty vyuha, the Pandavas serenely wait for the conches to boom, the drums to roll and the day's fighting to begin. Today, the kings in your vyuha and their warriors set Bhishma at their head and with a tumult of blaring sankhas and deafening roars, they charge out against the Parthas. The Pandavas, led by Bhimasena, rush out against Bhishma seeking victory.

Roaring and shouting, blowing their krakachas and cow-horns, beating their drums and cymbals, the Pandavas forge into battle. We respond to their call with the pounding of our drums, and clash of cymbals and conches; roaring like lions, we attack our enemies furiously.

Those sounds from both armies mingle like two surging seas and the warriors of the two armies charge wildly into the ranks of the enemy, so that in moments there are no longer two great forces facing each other but a single throng of men all intent on killing one another as brutally as they can. The earth shudders with the clamour of that vast collision.

Birds scream and wheel in the sky. The radiant sun dims. Fierce winds blow, portending ever greater terrors. Jackals roam howling, foretelling another horrible carnage. All corners of the earth seem to be on fire, and dust rains down.

A rain of hewn limbs and spurting, splashing blood falls on to the earth. And tears fall from the eyes of weeping animals. In their distress they urinate and defecate. The cries of the Rakshasas drown every other roar and shout of the battle. Jackals and vultures, and crows and dogs wheel at the perimeter of the holocaust and also in the air above the canopy of arrows and spears that quickly covers Kurukshetra.

Ominous meteors collide against the sun and fall to the earth, foreboding incomprehensible tragedy. The blast of conches and drums shake the Pandava and the Dhartarashtra hosts like forests in a hurricane.

The uproar of the two armies, kings, elephants and horses, which face each other in that malevolent hour, resembles that of a raging ocean.'

CANTO 101

Bhishma Vadha Parva continued

Sanjaya says, 'Riding his tawny horses, the dashing Abhimanyu charges Duryodhana's host, his bow flaring arrows. Bharatarishabha, your warriors cannot withstand him, as he plunges into the sea of Kaurava hordes with his wealth of astras.

Subhadra's son kills many Kshatriyas with deadly shafts that are like venom-spitting cobras and rods of death. Phalguni's son truncates maharathas and their chariots, horses and riders, elephant-warriors and their tuskers. The kings of the earth are delighted, and laud these feats and those who achieve them, regardless of whether they are ally or enemy.

Abhimanyu tosses those Kaurava legions about like a storm that scatters a heap of cotton in every direction. Like elephants stuck in mire, your men flounder without a protector. Having routed them, Abhimanyu stands like a fire which blazes pure and smokeless. Like insects drawn irresistibly to a fire but consumed by it, your warriors cannot endure that Parantapa. Abhimanyu looks like Vasava himself armed with his Vajra.

His gold inlaid bow flashes like lightning amidst clouds as it courses through the enemy in its magnificent archer's hand, loosing endless shafts like swarms of from trees blossoming in the forest. No one is able to strike or contain Abhimanyu, as he careers over Kurukshetra in his golden chariot. Riding swift as the wind, the sublime youth baffles Kripa and Drona, Aswatthaman and Jayadratha. He consumes your forces, his bow always bent in a circle, his chariot also wheeling in a circle, resembling the bright halo sometimes seen around the sun.

Seeing him lustily decimating the enemy, brave Kshatriyas think that the world contains two Arjunas. The vast host of the Bhaaratas reel under that golden prince's onslaught like a drunken woman. He routs them everywhere, terrifying maharathas and delighting his friends, like Vasava who pleased the Devas when he vanquished Mayaa.

Your warriors roar in anguish even like thunderclouds. Hearing that awful wail like the turbulent sea raging at full tide when lashed by violent winds, Duryodhana says to Rishyasringa's Rakshasa son Alambusha, "Abhimanyu single-handedly destroys my army like Vritra routing Indra's legions. You, who know war so well, must challenge him for it seems none else can. Ride swiftly, Alambusha, and kill the preening sons of Arjuna. And led by Bhishma and Drona, we will kill Arjuna himself."

That dreadful Rakshasa charges into the fray, his roars like thunderclouds rumbling, and the Pandava host trembles. Why, many warriors are so terrified by those roars that they fall dead. Jubilant, dancing in glee, it appears, in his chariot, Alambusha advances towards Abhimanyu with bow drawn round. On reaching Arjuna's son he begins to despatch his supporters. Alambusha dwindles the Pandava legion, like Balasura once did the divine host.

Carnage and rivers of blood flow once more when the Rakshasa assails the Pandava force with thousands of immaculate arrows. Terror-stricken, the Pandava army flees his slaughter. Ravaging the enemy like an elephant trampling lotus-stalks, Alambusha now rides at the Pandavas themselves. The five sons of Draupadi attack the Rakshasa like five planets plunging at the Sun. They torment him as the five planets afflict the Moon at the end of the yuga.

Prativindhya pierces the Rakshasa with shafts as heavy and sharp as battle-axes, which can cleave any armour, drawing geysers of blood from the Rakshasa, who looks like clouds stabbed by the sun's rays. Lacerated by golden-winged shafts, he looks like a mountain with peaks ablaze.

The Pandavas wound him grievously with gusts of arrows that look like angry snakes. Alambusha is enraged like the king of the Nagas himself. Pierced all over by those maharathas, he faints and remains unconscious for a long time. Awakening, he jumps up with a fulminant roar and using the mahima siddhi grows to twice his size, and in fury carves up their bows, arrows and standards. Baring great fangs in a hideous smile, he shoots them each with five seething shafts.

Wild Alambusha dances in his chariot, and kills their horses and sarathies. Burning, he stabs them with thousands of every kind of fell barb. That night ranges dashes forward now to kill the beleaguered sons of Pandu. Seeing them tormented by the Rakshasa, Abhimanyu attacks him. The battle between him and the Rakshasa compares with that between Vritra and Vasava. The maharathas of both armies witness that encounter. Their eyes bloodshot, both warriors seem to be aflame with wrath, and regard each other as the fire that burns at the end of the yuga.

The duel between them is like the ancient one between Sakra and Sambara in the war between the Devas and Asuras.'

CANTO 102

BHISHMA VADHA PARVA CONTINUED

Dhritarashtra says, 'Sanjaya, how does Alambusha resist Abhimanyu who so imperiously dominates our maharathas? How does the son of Subhadra face Rishyasringa's son? Tell me all this in detail, exactly as it happened. How do Bhima, and Ghatotkacha, Nakula and Sahadeva, and maharatha Satyaki, and Arjuna confront my forces? You are a master narrator, Sanjaya; tell me everything.'

Sanjaya says, 'I will describe the merciless, tumultuary duel between Alambusha and Abhimanyu. I will also describe Arjuna's prowess in battle, and the marvellous feats of Bhima, Nakula and Sahadeva, and the achievements of your warriors led by Bhishma and Drona.

Alambusha roars at Abhimanyu to stand and fight and then charges him. Abhimanyu whirls around to face his father's sworn enemy. Mounted on their chariots, like Deva and Danava, man and Rakshasa confront each other. Alambusha owns the hermetic powers of maya, while Abhimanyu is accomplished in the use of divine astras.

Abhimanyu strikes the Rakshasa with three sizzling shafts, and yet again with five. Alambusha pierces Abhimanyu's chest with nine barbs like a mahout goading his elephant with his hook. In a wink, he looses a scathing volley of a thousand shafts at Arjuna's superb son. Incensed Abhimanyu makes a bloody home in the Rakshasa's hirsute breast for nine steely arrows, which delve deep into Alambusha's innards. The bloodied Rakshasa looks like a mountain lush with flowering kinsukas. The Rakshasa bears those golden-winged shafts and glows like a mountain on fire.

Alambusha shrouds Abhimanyu, equal to Mahendra himself, in clouds of smoking arrows. Like Yama dandas these pass through Abhimanyu into the earth. Abhimanyu's golden shafts plunge through the Rakshasa and also enter the ground. Alambusha retreats before the prince's scintillating barrage of arrows, like Mayaa repulsed by Sakra. Quickly the Rakshasa invokes sorcery, mantling the field in perfect darkness using maya. All the warriors on Kurukshetra are lost in that blind night. Abhimanyu is hidden by it, and friend and enemy cannot be distinguished.

Abhimanyu calls forth the blazing Suryastra and Alambusha's illusional night is dispelled in a moment, and everything is visible again. With renewed ferocity Abhimanyu covers the Rakshasa with a solid swath of brilliant arrows.

Now Alambusha creates a slew of magical illusions, hunts of sinister beasts and monsters bound at Arjuna's son from every side. Abhimanyu dissipates them all with knowing astras. His every sorcery pierced and made impotent, and bleeding from countless wound mouths that Abhimanyu opens all over his devilish body, Alambusha flees in terror from the lustrous prince.

After routing the devious Rakshasa, Abhimanyu begins to demolish your forces, truly like a maddened tusker wading into a lake of lotuses. Seeing the field being richly strewn with his warriors' corpses, Bhishma looses a tremendous volley at Abhimanyu, shrouding him in a wave of arrows.

Swiftly, numerous maharathas of the Dhartarashtra army encircle that angelic and terrible young Kshatriya and strike him repeatedly. So resembling his father and equal to Krishna in profound valour, Abhimanyu demonstrates his stunning genius worthy of both his vamsas. He astounds his gathered enemies with archery not yet seen on Kurukshetra.

Seeing his precious magnificent son hemmed in, Arjuna arrives at the place where Abhimanyu continues to raze your warriors with breathtaking ease. Immediately Bhishma rides at Arjuna, like Rahu approaching the Sun. Supported by chariots, elephants, and horses, your sons surround the Pitamaha as he comes. And the Pandavas ride with Arjuna and a feverish battle breaks out.

Kripa stabs Arjuna with twenty-five arrows, as Dhananjaya engages Bhishma. Like a tiger attacking an elephant, Satyaki pierces Kripa with countless whetted shafts. Enraged, Gautama bloodies his chest with nine arrows like time. Sini's grandson draws his bow round and looses a deadly astra him at Kripa, but fiery Aswatthaman cuts it down as it flames at the old Acharya. Satyaki leaves Kripa and charges Drona's son like Rahu flying to devour the Moon. Aswatthaman rives Satyaki's bow in two, and launches a fury of barbs at the bright Vrishni.

Satyaki seizes up another colossal bow and strikes Aswatthaman with six searing arrows through his chest and arms, drawing a howl of pain from him. Aswatthaman faints and falls to the floor of his chariot, clinging on to its flagpole. Regaining his senses in a moment, he looses a long shaft at Satyaki, which passes right through the handsome body of Sini's grandson, and plunges into the earth like a young snake entering its hole after the end of winter.

Another arrow shatters Satyaki's standard. Drona's son roars like five lions and covers his adversary in a rain of arrows as the clouds do the sun at the onset of the monsoon. Like the sun from behind clouds, Satyaki emerges undimmed, and shrouds the son of Drona with twisting sheets of arrows, vicious windings. Aswatthaman unravels them unscathed. Anger mounting, with a roar,, Satyaki unleashes a thousand arrows in a moment, a deadly relucent torrent of shafts. Seeing his son afflicted like the Moon by Rahu, Drona storms at Satyaki, striking him deep with a streak of lightning from his great bow.

Satyaki turns away from Aswatthaman and pierces Drona with a scourge of twenty stinging barbs. Immediately, Arjuna rushes at Drona, and these two, guru and sishya, assail each other like the planets Budha and Sukra in the sky.'

BHISHMA VADHA PARVA CONTINUED

Dhritarashtra says, 'How do those famed warriors, Drona and Arjuna, face each other in battle? The son of Pandu is as dear as a son to Drona. Arjuna worships the Acharya. Both maharathas delight in war, and both are awesomely powerful. How do they battle each other?'

Sanjaya says, 'In battle Drona remains distant from his love of Arjuna. Arjuna focuses on his dharma as a Kshatriya and does not recognise his teacher but only an enemy. Kshatriyas never turn away from battle. They are detached, and fight their fathers and brothers.

Arjuna stabs Drona with three scalding shafts. Drona remains unperturbed. Arjuna covers the Acharya in a mantle of arrows. Drona blazes up in anger at the heart of the dreadful war, like a fire in a dense forest. Drona covers Arjuna with myriad arrows. Duryodhana sends Susarman to protect Drona's flank. The king of the Trigartas swathes Arjuna in countless iron-tipped missiles, beautiful like cranes flying through the sky. They pierce Arjuna like birds vanishing into a fruit laden tree. Arjuna roars and savages Susarman and his son with riptides from the Gandiva.

Despite the towering attack, and quite ready to die, they do not retreat. They target Arjuna's chariot and the Pandava faces their onslaught like a mountain receiving a cloudburst. Partha's prodigious archery is superhuman as, almost with disdain, he scatters his enemies' combined, virile flurries of fire, cutting down their storms of arrows as if he were facing some boys in battle, why like a high wind scattering fleecy clouds. The Devas and Danavas congregated in the firmament acclaim his feat.

Arjuna invokes the Vayavya astra against the Trigarta legion. A mighty gale sweeps across Kurukshetra, shaking the sky, felling trees, and blowing away enemy chariots and soldiers like bits of straw. Drona looses the Sailastra, which makes Arjuna's squall abate and calm returns to all quarters. But, fearing Arjuna now that they have seen some part of his actual prowess, the Trigarta maharathas are despondent and leave the battlefield.

Duryodhana and Kripa, and Aswatthaman, and Salya, and Sudakshina, the king of the Kambojas, and Vinda and Anuvinda of Avanti, and Bahlika supported by the Bahlikas, surround Arjuna with their chariots. Bhagadatta and the mighty Srutayush encircle Bhima with an aksauhini of elephants. And Bhurisravas, and Sala, and Subala's son attack the twins with luminous whetted arrows. Along with your sons, Bhishma rides to surround Yudhishtira.

Bhima watches that legion advance and licks the corners of his mouth like a hungry lion. He seizes his mace, leaps off his chariot again, terrifying your warriors. The elephant-warriors besiege him from all sides. At the very heart of your sons' forces, Bhima looks like the sun in the midst of dark clouds. And like the wind that scatters those clouds, the Vayuputra swings his mace all around him in scarlet eruptions to slaughter your son's elephant legion. The shrill trumpeting of those tuskers and Bhima's dreadful roars shake the very earth; covered with gashes inflicted by the tusks of the elephants, Bhima blossoms in blood like a flowering kinsuka.

Seizing some of the elephants by their tusks, he rips them out and then with those tusks smashes other elephants on their round foreheads and kills them like Siva himself. Like Rudra, his body and mace are drenched in blood. A few surviving tuskers run in every direction, crushing their own ranks as they blunder away from the fearful Bhima. Duryodhana's frantic forces quit the field any way they can.'

CANTO 104

Bhishma Vadha Parva continued

S anjaya says, 'At high noon a bloody battle breaks out between Bhishma and the Somakas. Bhishma denudes the Pandava ranks with thousands of immaculate arrows, every one claiming a life. He crushes them like a herd of bulls grinding paddy clumps under their hooves.

Dhrishtadyumna and Sikhandin, and Virata and Drupada attack maharatha Bhishma with a torment of arrows. Bhishma pierces Dhrishtadyumna and Virata each with three exquisite barbs, and aims a long lance at Drupada. Wounded, shamed by Parantapa Bhishma, those maharathas are like snakes stamped upon. Sikhandin darts within range and besieges the Pitamaha with countless arrows. Bhishma does not shoot back, still regarding his enemy as a woman.

Dhrishtadyumna skewers Bhishma with three lean shafts through his arms and chest. Drupada pierces him with twenty-five barbs, Virata with ten, and Sikhandin with another twenty-five. Bhishma is covered in blood, and looks quite magnificent like an ashoka in full carmine bloom. Bhishma shoots them each with three arrows. He cracks Drupada's bow with a broad-headed shaft. Drupada seizes another bow and strikes his adversary with five barbs quick as one. He stabs Bhishma's sarathy with three shafts.

Draupadi's five sons, the five Kaikeya brothers and Satyaki, all led by Yudhishtira, charge Ganga's son to protect the Panchalas and Dhrishtadyumna. All your warriors attack the Pandava host to defend Bhishma.

Another pitched battle ensues, resulting in another carnage. Maharathas kill maharathas. Soldiers, elephant-riders and horse-riders kill others with inhuman, heartless projectiles. Riderless chariots are hauled wildly across death's abysmal field. Careening blindly, these crush countless men and mow horses down; they dash everywhere like the wind strewing cloud forms across a sunset sky, bathing it in stains of blood.

With sparkling ear-rings, bright garlands and bracelets, handsome as the sons of Devas, surpassing Vaisravana in wealth and Brihaspati in intelligence, great rulers of vast kingdoms, brave maharathas left without their chariots, run like ordinary men in every direction.

Mighty tuskers, their skilled riders slain, crush friendly ranks and run wildly until they fall. These mammoths, their armour cut away by arrows and spears, flowing blood from all over their massive bodies, roar like clouds and scatter in all directions. The chamaras and dappled standards, their golden parasols, and the dazzling spears of their riders lie in ruins everywhere.

Elephant-riders of both armies, their mounts slain, run on foot in that awful melee. Thousands of horses with golden ornaments gallop away from death's field. Armed with swords, but without horses, horsemen run from their assailants.

Elephants continue to dash against other elephants, crushing foot-soldiers and horses on their way. They smash countless chariots; chariots ride tilting over fallen horses lying in their path. Horses trample footsoldiers under their hooves. Thus, O Rajan, they massacre one another and mercy has fled this war entirely.

The river of blood swells every hour, frothing across Kurukshetra with a hundred tributary streams. Fallen bows obstruct its straight course, and the hair of dead warriors forms its moss. Smashed chariots are its islands, and arrows beyond count create its eddies. Horses make up its fish; heads of tuskers its boulders; butchered elephants are the river's crocodiles. And coats of mail and helmets form its froth.

Bows still clutched by fallen warriors regulate its swift current and swords are its tortoises. Banners and emblems stand like forlorn trees on its banks. And bodies of men are its banks relentlessly consumed by the russet river. Countless carnivores are its swans, drinking thirstily of its sanguine waters.

That river swells not the ocean but Yama's kingdom. Noble and fearless maharathas try to cross that river with their chariots, elephants, and horses for rafts and boats. Like the river Vaitarani bears the dead to Yama's realm, so does that bloody river on Kurukshetra sweep along diffident and unconscious men.

The Kshatriyas look upon that horrible carnage and exclaim, "Alas, the very race of Kshatriyas will perish from Duryodhana's sin. Deluded by greed, why, O Dhritarashtra, was he so envious of the virtuous Pandavas?"

Such cries are accompanied by others that praise the sons of Pandu. Hearing these reproaches, Duryodhana says to Bhishma and Drona and Kripa and Salya, "Fight without pride. Why do you delay?"

The murderous war caused by a game of dice, resumes between the Kauravas and the Pandavas.

Son of Vichitravirya, you see now the dreadful outcome of disdaining the advice of your true friends. Neither the Pandavas nor their forces and allies, nor the Kauravas, fear for their lives in this war. And for this very reason, Rajan, of savage Kshatriya dharma, such a terrible destruction of kinsmen is underway on Kurukshetra, ah, caused either by Destiny or your wicked design.'

BHISHMA VADHA PARVA CONTINUED

S anjaya says, 'With banks of razor like arrows Arjuna kills the warriors who ride with Susarman. Susarman strikes Arjuna with an angry volley. He pierces Krishna with seventy barbs and Arjuna again with nine. Serenely, Arjuna continues to kill Susarman's men.

Those maharathas flee from Arjuna as if Death himself had come to hunt them at the end of the yuga, for indeed the Dwapara Yuga is drawing to its end and the Kali , age of wrath, is rising near. Some of the Trigartas jump down from their horses, some from their chariots, others clamber down from their elephants and flee. Others swiftly escape on their very mounts and chariots. Foot-soldiers throw away their weapons in panic, and run helter-skelter with no thought for their comrades. Though stridently forbidden by Susarman and other noble kings, they desert their armies.

Seeing this rout, Duryodhana, together with Bhishma, mounts a driving attack against Arjuna to protect Susarman. While his men take to their heels all around him, Duryodhana is unyielding and, surrounded by his brothers, continues to engage the enemy with undiminished vigour.

To protect Arjuna, the other Pandavas advance on Bhishma. Aware of Phalguni's prowess, they still dash forward roaring, and the Pitamaha relentlessly dwindles the Pandavas army with every moment, his every arrow a killer. At noon, absolute, bloody, chaos reigns on Kurukshetra so it seems unclear whether the war between cousins is being fought in the realm of the living or the dead, whether on Bhumi or in Yamaloka. Striking Kritavarman with five arrows, the triumphal Satyaki kills thousands of Dhartarashtra men with uncanny archery so like his master Arjuna's. King Drupada, having already drawn blood from his old and hated enemy, his boyhood friend Drona, strikes the Acharya with seventy shafts, all loosed in a moment, and Drona's sarathy with another nine.

Bhima roars like some mythic tiger after wounding his great granduncle, king Bahlika. Chitrasena wounds Abhimanyu deep with a brace of torrid shafts, and the luminous Abhimanyu adorns Chitrasena's broad breast with three perfect barbs. Locked in battle, the two are as glorious on the field as Venus and Saturn in the sky. Then, in a flash, Abhimanyu kills his noble adversary's horses and charioteer and maharatha Chitrasena leaps off his chariot and mounts Durmukha's.

Drona repeatedly carves slivers off Drupada's ratha, and remembering their enmity of such long standing, the Panchala king retreats with his swift horses.

Bhima kills Bahlika's horses and sarathy. Finding himself in grave danger, Bahlika jumps down from his chariot and mounts Lakshmana's and they ride away from dreadful Bhima.

Satyaki thwarts Kritavarman, who fights for Duryodhana, and looses a plethora of every kind of barb upon the Pitamaha whom Kritavarman protects. Piercing Bhishma with sixty whetted feathered shafts, the ebullient Satyaki seems to dance on his chariot, brandishing his bow. Bhishma shoots an extraordinary iron arrow at the Vrishni, flecked with gold, serpentine and beautiful as a Naga woman.

But Satyaki intercepts it with another astra and both exceptional weapons explode into flames and lunge harmless to the ground like extinguished meteors. Satyaki seizes up a shimmering golden spear and casts it like a streak of lightning at Bhishma. It flies at the Kuru ancient like his very death coming to claim a doomed man. Quicker than seeing, Bhishma trisects it with two lean horse-shoe-headed arrows and it falls to the ground in three strips, undone.

Possessed by the murderous spirit of war, yet smiling the while, Parantapa Bhishma strikes Satyaki through his chest with nine arrows in an incredibly close and neat cluster. With their chariots, elephants and horses, the Pandava warriors besiege Bhishma form every side to rescue Satyaki.

Yet another general fray, always more bloody than the ones gone before, breaks out between the Pandava and the Kaurava hosts, both seeking glory, both wanting victory more than life itself.'

CANTO 106

BHISHMA VADHA PARVA CONTINUED

Sanjaya says, 'Seeing Bhishma seethe upon Kurukshetra, encircled by the Pandavas, like the sun in the sky by monsoon clouds, Duryodhana says to Dussasana, "Parantapa Bhishma is surrounded by the Pandavas. Your only charge is to protect him. If we guard him well, our Pitamaha will destroy the Panchalas and the Pandavas. Defending Bhishma is our first and highest dharma, for he is our protector and our main hope. Surround him with your legions, Dussasana, and make sure he comes to no harm!"

Dussasana surrounds Bhishma with a vast force and stands ready to fight anyone who threatens his grandsire. With thousands of horsemen carrying shining spears, swords and standards, forming a confident legion, together with twice as many proficient foot-soldiers, Subala's son Sakuni assails Nakula, Sahadeva and Yudhishtira.

Duryodhana sends ten thousand horsemen to attack the Pandavas. As they fly like so many Garudas, the earth trembles and groans under their horse hooves, the din of which resounds like a bamboo forest on fire. They raise a cloud of dust as they hurtle across the battlefield, obscuring the sun. They unnerve the Pandava host like a flight of swans that disturbs a lake while descending on it. Nothing can be heard above their loud neighing.

Yudhishtira and the sons of Madri contain their charge like the shore the surging sea at high tide. Those three maharathas mow down line after line of horsemen with tides of arrows. Themselves wheeling across the battleground, the three Pandava brothers display some incredible archery in concert as they decapitate those onrushing lines of horsemen while never so much as scratching any other part of their bodies.

Felled with swords and arrows, heads drop like fruits from tall trees. Everywhere riders and their horses fall dead to the ground. Many horses bolt in fear like deer on seeing lions. And the Pandavas blow their conches and beat their drums in triumph.

Duryodhana is crestfallen to see his forces demolished again and says to Salya, king of the Madras, "Before your eyes, Yudhishtira and the twins have routed our army. Mahabaho, you are powerful and irresistible. Stop Yudhishtira, like the continent that resists the ocean."

Salya rides at Yudhishtira with a legion of chariots. As he rushes at Yudhishtira like a tidal wave, the Pandava calmly strikes Salya through his chest with ten thudding shafts. Nakula and Sahadeva assail him with seven more. Salya, whose very name means to menace, to harry, pierces them each with three arrows, and further stabs Yudhishtira with sixty keen darts. Enraged, he makes the twins bleed with two shafts each. Parantapa Bhima sees Yudhishtira within Salya's reach, as in the jaws of Death, and rushes to his defence.

And as the sun begins to set, one more dark and destructive battle begins.'

CANTO 107

BHISHMA VADHA PARVA CONTINUED

Sanjaya says, 'Bhishma bestrides the yawning field and his great bow radiates arrows in every direction, every shaft claiming an enemy soldier's life or drawing blood from a Pandava maharatha. Yet he fights without rancour even with deep sadness in his aged heart, and even for this is more terrible. He strikes Bhima with twelve arrows and Satyaki with nine. Stabbing Nakula with three barbs, he shoots Sahadeva with seven. Yudhishtira he pierces through his arms and chest with twelve faultless shafts. Lacerating Dhrishtadyumna with a flat flight of barbs, that mighty old lion roars deafeningly.

Nakula stabs him with twelve arrows and Satyaki with three. Dhrishtadyumna shoots him with seventy shafts and Bhima with seven. Yudhishtira pierces the Pitamaha with twelve barbs. Drona attacks Satyaki and Bhima at once, stabbing them each with five whetted arrows like Yama dandas. Bhima and Satyaki retaliate without a moment's pause.

Rulers of the eastern, western and northern regions, the Sauviras, the Kitavas, the Malavas, the Abhishahas, the Surasenas, the Sibis, and the Vasatis, vigorously assail Bhishma despite his endless barrage of arrows.

Other kings of various realms loose many astras of fire, water and air at the Pandavas themselves.

The Pandavas surround the Pitamaha. Encircled and doubly defiant, the aged lion blazes like a forest fire, continuing to raze the enemy army with transcendent archery. His chariot is his fire-chamber; his bow its flames; swords, arrows and maces are his fuel; his shafts are sparks; and Bhishma himself becomes the fire that consumes his adversaries.

Bhishma shrouds the Pandava hosts with golden-winged shafts decked with the feathers of vultures, with nalikas, and dirghastras, elongated barbs. He fells elephants and chariot-warriors. He makes the Pandava legion of chariots look like a forest of palmyras shorn of their leafy heads. He decimates riders of horses, elephants and chariots without favour. Hearing the thunder of his bow-string and the thunderclaps of his palms as he looses his tirades of fire, all the soldiers tremble.

His arrows shot from his bow pierce through armour like through butter. And again, endlessly, we see riderless chariots dragged across the battlefield by their yoked horses. Fourteen thousand celebrated and noble maharathas, with golden standards, of the Chedis, the Kasi, and the Karushas, stand firm and ready to sacrifice their lives; they do not retreat, and are swiftly despatched, in blasts of gore, along with their horses and elephants, by Bhishma like Siva with mouth agape.

We see thousands of chariots with smashed axles, terraces and wheels. The ground is covered with wrecked chariots, arrows, axes, ruined coats of mail and the mighty bodies of maharathas, which seem to glow on even after life has left them. Maces and arrows, quivers and bows, swords, and jewelled severed heads lie scattered in profusion; as do gloves and felled standards, and riven bows.

Riderless elephants and horse-riders lie dead as if they are mere clods of earth, so plentiful are they. The most valiant efforts of the Pandavas cannot any more rally their maharathas who lose their nerve and flee before Bhishma's relentless arrow storms. By himself the Kuru Pitamaha disperses that teeming force of fighting men with the ageless energy of Indra. With its chariots, elephants, horses and standards felled, the

Pandava army in disarray laments loudly and scatters. Driven by ruthless destiny, fathers, sons and friends kill one another, on and on.

The Pandava warriors tear off their armour and run dementedly in all directions, like terrified bulls lowing in despair, and running wild and unrestrained from the great terror which is Bhishma.

Seeing the Pandava army disbanding, Krishna reins in Arjuna's chariot, and says to his warrior, "The awaited hour has arrived. Strike now, O tiger among men, or you will be lost. You said, in Sanjaya's presence, in the assembly of kings in Virata's city, 'I will kill all Duryodhana's warriors and their followers, including Bhishma and Drona, if they oppose me in battle.' Son of Kunti, O Parantapa, honour your words now. Remember your Kshatriya dharma; fight fearlessly."

Arjuna, troubled and unsure, says, "I can seize the kingdom, slaughtering the innocent, or accept exile in the forest. These are my choices. Which of these should I strive for? Spur the horses on, Krishna; I will obey you. I will kill the invincible Bhishma." Krishna goads the silvery white horses to where Bhishma stands dazzling like the sun.

Seeing Arjuna riding at Bhishma, Yudhishtira's host rallies to the fight. Roaring, the Pitamaha shrouds Arjuna's chariot in an opacity of arrows so it is hidden from view. Krishna adroitly urges the wounded horses on. Arjuna raises the Gandiva and slashes Bhishma's bow into pieces. Bhishma promptly strings another bow. Arjuna breaks this one as well too. Bhishma cries out in some delight, "Wonderful, Mahabaho! Well done, son of Kunti."

Bhishma takes up another beautiful bow and looses a crescendo of arrows at Arjuna's chariot. Krishna skilfully manoeuvres his horses and avoids the searing volley. Yet some shafts find their mark, and those two tigers among men look like two angry bulls gored by horns in a fight.

Meanwhile, yet again, Krishna sees that while Bhishma, positioned between the two armies, unleashes his firestorms of arrows, scorching everything like the Sun himself, and killing Yudhishtira's warriors relentlessly, proclaiming, as it were, the end of the yuga, Arjuna still hesitates and turns mild when faced with his grandsire.

Leaving Arjuna's horses, Krishna leaps off the chariot in fury. His eyes crimson, his body burning with terrible light, and the whip in his hand his only weapons, the Lord of the universe runs straight at Bhishma, like some great lion, his strides appearing to cleave the earth, and his heart set on killing the Kuru ancient.

All the assembled warriors can only watch, rooted and stunned as they see Krishna rush Bhishma. "Bhishma is dead!" they cry. Their shouts of dismay are loud and fearful.

Dark as lapis lazuli, clad in yellow silk, Krishna streaks towards Bhishma, like a thunderhead charged with lightning. Like a lion at an elephant, or a great bull thundering at another, Krishna roars as he storms at Bhishma.

Seeing the Dark One come with cosmic fury on his brow and in his eyes, Bhishma stands perfectly calm and fearlessly draws his great bow. Serenely he says to Krishna, "Come, O you with eyes like lotus petals. O Lord of the Devas, I bow to you. O best of the Satwatas, kill me today in this great war, for, Govinda, I will be blessed in every way if I die by your hand in battle. Krishna, the honour in the three worlds is mine today. Kill me as you please, for I am your slave."

But Arjuna has leapt down from his chariot and running after Krishna, seizes the Blue God in his arms, restraining him. Krishna hardly seems to notice Arjuna and drags him along as if he were not there at all. At the tenth step, Arjuna falls to the ground and stops Krishna by clinging to his legs.

Arjuna cries in despair to the terrifying Lord, "Stop, Krishna! You must not break your vow that you will not fight or men will say that Krishna is a liar. This burden is mine and I will kill the Pitamaha. I swear by my weapons, by truth, and my punya that I will do everything in my power to destroy all my enemies. Watch me now and I will effortlessly quell this great maharatha, even like the crescent moon being extinguished at the end of the yuga, at the moment of final destruction."

Krishna's brow is still like thunder, but he remains silent and allows Arjuna to lead him back to their chariot. The moment of absolute dread passes and the universe breathes again!

Bhishma once more envelops the two Krishnas in a cloud of arrows, while continuing to consume the Pandava ranks like the sun sapping the life force of all things in summer. The Pitamaha kills two Pandava soldiers for every life that the sons of Pandu claim from his own army. Without being able to even look upon him who blazes like the noonday sun, thousands of helpless dispirited warriors perish at Bhishma hands.

Fearful and grown timid, the Pandavas themselves are powerless before Bhishma's super-human feats in war. Unprotected, their forces flee like a herd of cows swarmed by an army of ants, his millions of arrows.

The Pandavas, too, cannot bear to look upon that maharatha who turns his fire on Yudhishtira, their king. As the sun sets ever so slowly for the decimated Pandava army, and too swiftly for the triumphant Kauravas, the exhausted soldiers withdraw from the battlefield.'

BHISHMA VADHA PARVA CONTINUED

Sanjaya says, 'Even while they fight like figures in a nightmare scathed by the many flares of Bhishma, the sun sets and in the deep twilight nothing can be seen, not the corpses now past all count with which the awesome grandsire has strewn Kurukshetra. Yudhishtira sees the remnants of his devastated forces throw down their weapons and eagerly quit the battlefield before the conches have been sounded for the day's slaughtering to end. But Bhishma stands still blazing in the gloom of dusk, still unleashing his arrow storms all around him. The shaken Pandava king orders the conches to be blown for the armies to withdraw.

In honour, Bhishma also withdraws his legions, and all the wounded and weary maharathas, those left alive, return to their tents.

As they have their wounds inflicted by Bhishma tended, the Pandavas reflect on how entirely terrible and invincible their Pitamaha had been through the day he has won so resoundingly for the Kauravas, and they are deeply distraught. Across the darkling field on which numberless corpses lie under the stars, Duryodhana and the Kauravas eulogise Bhishma's exploits as the old lion makes his way to his tent with some satisfaction surrounded by your jubilant sons.

Night, that quietens all creatures, sets in. In that intense hour, the Pandavas, the Vrishnis and the Srinjayas confer. Those noble one, experienced in deliberations, discuss the courses that lie before them.

Yudhishtira says sombrely to Krishna, "Ah, look how the Pitamaha savaged our men like an elephant trampling a forest of reeds. We dare not even look at him, while he consumes my army like a raging fire. He is grown as fierce as the poisonous Takshaka. Yama can be defeated, even Indra armed with the Vajra, or Varuna, noose in hand, or the Lord of the Yakshas with his mace. But Bhishma cannot be killed.

Krishna, I am helpless, and drown in anguish, when I face Bhishma in battle. I will go into the forest and take sannyasa. That would benefit me. I do not want to fight this hopeless war any more. Bhishma conquers us always. Riding against him, I am like an insect that flies into a fire only to meet certain death. By foolishly fighting for a kingdom, I am being destroyed.

My brave brothers have all been wounded, looked how they still bleed. Out of their love for me, their eldest brother, they lost their kingdom and followed me into exile. For my sake, Krishna, you also suffer. Life is so precious and now even that is threatened. If I survive this war, I will devote the rest of my days to the performance of penance and good deeds. If you bear us good will, Krishna, tell me what I should do, without forsaking the duties of my varna, my Kshatriya dharma."

Krishna speaks kind, comforting words to Yudhishtira, "Son of Dharma, you are unwavering in your commitment to truth; do not be sad, blessed as you are with Parantapas for brothers. Arjuna and Bhima are imbued with the energy of the Wind and Fire. The twin sons of Madri are as valiant as the king of the Devas.

Honour our friendship; use me and achieve victory. I will fight with Bhishma myself. Only command me and I will show you my prowess in war. If Arjuna will not, I will challenge Bhishma and kill him, in the very sight of the Dhartarashtras. If you think that killing noble Bhishma will help you triumph, I will singlehandedly destroy the Pitamaha. My prowess is equal to Indra's in battle. I will overpower that Kshatriya of great weapons.

He, who is an enemy of the Pandavas, is also my enemy; and my detractors are yours. Your brother Arjuna is my friend, kinsman, and devotee. I will cut off my flesh and sacrifice it for Arjuna's sake. He, too, will give up his life for me. This is our sacred bond, and we will protect each other.

So command me: how should I fight? At Upaplavya, Arjuna vowed that he would kill Bhishma. Now he must honour his words with deeds. If he asks me to, I will fulfil what he swore he would do, unquestioningly. Otherwise, he must accomplish the task himself. It is not difficult for him, he can kill Bhishma easily, for this Arjuna can achieve feats that others cannot.

He can annihilate the very Devas, along with the Daityas and the Danavas. What then of Bhishma? Bhishma is old now, dull, his strength reduced by his years, and he cannot stand against Arjuna, if Arjuna once decided that he will indeed bring Bhishma down."

Yudhishtira says, "It is as you say, Mahabaho. When you both are united, not Bhishma or all the Kaurava maharathas together can stand before you. Krishna, with you by my side I am certain to have victory and everything that I might wish for. With you as my defender, I can overcome the very Devas with Indra at their head. And Bhishma, though he is the greatest maharatha, can also be vanquished. But, Krishna, for my own honour and truth, I cannot let you break your vow that you would not actually fight. Give me the support you promised, but without actually fighting yourself. Bhishma said to me, 'I am obliged to fight for Duryodhana and against you. But you can always come to me for advice.'

Krishna, Bhishma might still help me regain my kingdom by telling me what I should do. Taking you with us, we will all go to the Pitamaha once again and ask him how he can be killed. Let us go to him even now and I will do whatever he tells me to in battle. He is honourable and a man of unswerving dharma. His heart lies with us and he will tell me how I can win this war."

Yudhishtira's eyes are moist and his voice is low as he says, "We were orphans, mere children, and our Pitamaha raised us with his love. Ah, how cruel this Kshatriya dharma is that today I must go and ask my grandfather how I can kill him."

Krishna says to Yudhishtira, "Wise king, I approve of what you say. Bhishma is an unrivalled maharatha, the greatest master of astras. He can kill an enemy with just a look from his eyes. Yes, let us go to him and ask him how he himself can be killed. He will answer truthfully, especially if you are the one that asks this question. Let us go to him even now and ask him how we can win this war." The Pandavas and Krishna set aside their armour and weapons and go towards Bhishma's tent; they enter, and bow to him. The Pandavas pay him obeisance and worship, and ask for his blessings.

The Pitamaha, Mahabaho Bhishma, says warmly to them, "You are welcome, my sons. Welcome to you Arjuna. Welcome Yudhishtira Dharmatma, and you also, my Bhima. Welcome Nakula and Sahadeva. Tell me why you have come to me at this hour. What can I do for you? Let it be anything, however demanding, and I will do it wholeheartedly."

His head bowed, Yudhishtira replies, "Pitamaha, wise Bhishma, tell us how we can win this war and have our kingdom back. Tell us how we can end this terrible slaughter of men. You, great Kshatriya, are invincible on the field of battle, you leave no chink through which an enemy might strike you down. As long as you live, we can never hope to win this war. O Pitamaha, tell us how you can be killed!"

You bow is always drawn and streams tides of arrows razing my army. Day after day, we see you, Parantapa, mounted on your chariot, blazing like a second sun, as you consume our chariots and horses, men and elephants.

Bharatarishabha, there is no man who can defeat you, and you wreak destruction on us with your arrows. Pitamaha, tell me how we can triumph against you in battle, regain what is rightfully ours, and prevent any more bloodshed."

Bhishma says to Yudhishtira, "'As long as I live, you cannot win.

This is the simple truth. Sons of Pandu, only if you vanquish me can victory be yours. Indeed, if you want to win this war, you must kill me immediately otherwise your cause will be lost. I gladly give you leave to strike down me in any way. Why, I would be the happiest one if you did so for I hate this war in which I must fight against you. After you kill me, the others can all be slain. I do not ask you to do this, I, your Pitamaha, command it."

Yudhishtira says, "Tell us how we can defeat you in battle, you who are like the mace wielding Siva himself. Indra, Varuna, or Yama may be quelled, but not the Devas and Asuras united under Indra's command can overcome you."

Bhishma says, "What you say is true, Mahabaho. As long as I fight with my bow and my astras, I cannot be defeated by the Devas and Asuras led by Indra. But if I lay down my weapons, these brothers of yours, these maharathas can surely kill me. I never fight against one who has discarded his weapons, who has fallen, who has lost his armour, whose standard has collapsed, or who is fleeing from battle; nor will I confront anyone who is afraid, who humbles himself before me, or one who is weak and vulnerable, or a man who has only one son, or a vulgar lowly man. And I will never bear arms against a woman or a man who bears a woman's name.

This is my old resolve. I will never fight if I see an inauspicious sign. Sikhandin, son of Drupada, brave and tenacious in war, fights on your side; he was once a woman, a royal princess, before he became a man. We all know how this happened and the reasons for it.

Let Arjuna set Sikhandin in front of him, and then attack me. When I see that inauspicious sight, that ill omen in the form of a prince who was once a woman, I will never attack him. I will put down my bow and Arjuna must seize that moment to strike me down me with his arrows, piercing me through every limb and organ, from every side.

Even if I lay my weapons down, other than Krishna and Arjuna, there is nobody from any of the three worlds who can kill me in battle. Setting Sikhandin before him, let Arjuna, with his Gandiva and every astra, strike me down from my chariot. Then, and only then, will your victory be assured. Do as I have told you, Rajan, and after I have fallen you will surely kill all the Dhartarashtras."

The Pandavas listen numbly to what their grandsire says. They can only bow in silence to acknowledge the terrible counsel he gives them. Taking the dust from his feet, they return grimly to their tents.

Arjuna hears Bhishma's awful advice, he sees how his beloved Pitamaha is ready, so eager to die, and he is filled with shame and anguish. He cries to Krishna, "Krishna, how can I do what Bhishma asks me to? How can I kill our Pitamaha, who is so great and wise, and the eldest of our race?

In my childhood, I would climb onto his lap and playfully smear his face and body with dust. He is my father Pandu's father. As a child I once called him father as I clambered on his lap; and he said: I am not your father, but your father's father. That was his reply.

How can I kill someone who said those words to me? Ah, let my army perish and let me also die. I do not care if we lose this war, but I will never fight my Pitamaha. And how can I even think of killing him in the cowardly, shameful way that he commands me to? Ah Krishna, save me from this sea of grief in which I am drowning. Tell me what you think!"

Krishna says, "Having once sworn to kill Bhishma, how can you now break your solemn vow, without violating your sacred dharma as a Kshatriya? Arjuna, you must strike Bhishma down, for you cannot win this war unless you kill Ganga's invincible son. And he has told you the only way by which he can be sent to Yama's realm, and you are the only one who can do this thing.

The Devas decided this a long time ago and what is destined to happen must happen. It cannot be otherwise. You alone, not even Indra, can conquer Bhishma, who is like Siva with mouth agape. Fearlessly kill the Kuru Pitamaha.

My words are but those that Brihaspati said to Sakra. One should kill even an old person, however meritorious and revered, if he comes as an enemy, indeed one must kill anyone who comes to destroy you. Arjuna, this is the eternal dharma of Kshatriyas; they must fight, protect their subjects, and perform sacrifices, without hatred."

Arjuna says, "Sikhandin will certainly become the cause of Bhishma's death, for as soon as he sees the prince of the Panchalas my Pitamaha will put down his bow. We will keep Sikhandin in front of us, I will thwart the other archers who surround him and thus we will vanquish Bhishma. Sikhandin will fight Bhishma alone. I know that he will not strike Sikhandin, for he was once a woman."

Yet again, Krishna gives Arjuna the courage he needs for the great and violent deed. Having decided on their course, at Bhishma's own counsel and with his leave and blessings, the Pandavas feel relieved and hopeful again. And past midnight, these bulls among men retire to sleep.'

CANTO 109

BHISHMA VADHA PARVA CONTINUED

Dhritarashtra says, 'How did Sikhandin ride against Bhishma, and how did Bhishma press forward against the Pandavas? Tell me everything, Sanjaya.'

Sanjaya says, 'At dawn, to the beating of drums and the clash cymbals, and the blare of milk white conches, the Pandavas advance into battle, setting Sikhandin before them. They form a daunting vyuha.

Sikhandin is positioned in the vanguard. Bhima and Arjuna defend his chariot wheels. The sons of Draupadi and Abhimanyu ride behind the Panchala prince. In turn, Maharathas Satyaki and Chekitana guard them. Behind them is Dhrishtadyumna surround by the Panchalas. Behind Dhrishtadyumna ride Yudhishtira and the twins, filling the air with roars. They are followed by Virata, surrounded by his troops.

Alongside Virata is Drupada. And the five Kaikeya brothers and the valiant Dhrishtaketu protect the rear of the Pandava army. Having prepared their vyuha, the Pandavas, taking their lives in their hands, charge your army by first light.

The Kauravas place maharatha Bhishma at the head of their army and advance against the Pandavas. That indomitable Kshatriya is protected by your mighty sons. Behind him are Drona and Aswatthaman.

Bhishma is followed by Bhagadatta surrounded by his elephant aksauhini. Behind Bhagadatta are Kripa and Kritavarman. Behind them are Sudakshina of the Kambojas, and Jayatsena of the Magadhas, and Sakuni and Brihadbala. Countless other kings, all great archers, protect the rear of your army.

Every day, Bhishma forms vyuhas, sometimes like those of the Asuras, sometimes similar to those of Pisachas, at other times comparable to ones of the Rakshasas. The battle between the two forces begins yet again; sweeping into each other, both forces recommence the great slaughtering, the blood sacrifice on Kurukshetra.

The Parthas with Arjuna leading them place Sikhandin before them all, and attack Bhishma with every kind of arrow and astra maiming and killing your warriors in waves. Nakula, Sahadeva and maharatha Satyaki vigorously annihilate your forces.

Such is the carnage the Pandavas bring to your warriors this day, from every side, that it does not take them long to scatter and flee from the rampaging maharathas. Felled by the whetted arrows of the Pandavas and the Srinjayas, your troops cannot defend themselves.'

Dhritarashtra says, 'Tell me, Sanjaya, what does Bhishma do when he sees my army afflicted by the Parthas? How does that greatest Kshatriya, that Parantapa, storm the Pandavas and slaughter the Somakas?'

Sanjaya says, 'I will tell you what Bhishma does when attacked by the Pandavas and the Srinjayas. In great heart after the night's secret meeting with Bhishma, the Pandavas assail your son's forces, slaughtering all in their path. Seeing their inexorable, bloody advance, seeing his men, elephants and horses razed at will, Bhishma blazes up in wrath.

Uncaring of his life, that greatest maharatha unleashes a tornado of every kind of shaft at the enemy, elongated arrows, calf-toothed and crescent-headed ones, and many others. He covers the five mighty Pandavas in sheets of fire, holding them up; countless elephants and horses he kills; and that bull among men unseats so many maharathas from their chariots, riders from their horses, elephant-warriors from the backs of their beasts, and strikes fear into the hearts of the enemy.

All together, the Pandava warriors charge maharatha Bhishma, like the Asuras assailing Indra in unison. He brings them up sharply with a storm of stone-whetted arrows, each like Indra's thunderbolt, and so fierce his very countenance, that the enemy quails to look at him. Like Sakra himself, his vast bow is always drawn in a circle, and arrows flare from it in tide.

Watching their Pitamaha, your sons are awestruck and humbled. The Pandavas are as shaken as they look at Bhishma dominate Kurukshetra as he pleases as the Devas were dejected by the feats of the Asura Viprachitti. They have neither the nerve nor the prowess to face that Kshatriya who looks like Siva with mouth agape.

On that tenth day of the great Mahabharata yuddha, the day on which the Dwapara Yuga ends and the Kali Yuga actually rises over the world, Bhishma devours Sikhandin's aksauhini like a fire burning down a dry forest. Resembling an angry Naga, or indeed Siva goaded by Yama himself, Sikhandin pierces the flaming Kuru grandsire squarely through his breast with three sizzling shafts. The surprised, wounded Bhishma sees that it is Sikhandin who has struck him.

Incensed, yet Bhishma laughs and says, "Whether you attack me or not, I will never fight with you. You remain the same Sikhandini, the princess Amba whom the Creator first made."

Sikhandin's eyes turn red, and licking the corners of his mouth he says to Bhishma in a ringing voice, "I know you, Parantapa, to be the exterminator of the race of Kshatriyas. I have also heard of your battle against your guru, Jamadagni's son. I have heard a great deal about your superhuman prowess. Despite all that I have heard, I will fight you today.

What satisfies the Pandavas is also what I want; Parantapa, I will not only fight you but surely kill you today. I solemnly swear this. You have heard me now; do whatever you must. Whether you resist me or not, you will not escape alive. O mighty, ever-triumphant Bhishma, look at this world for the last time."

Having loosed these word barbs, Sikhandin pierces Bhishma with five straight shafts. Arjuna urges the Panchala prince on, "Sikhandin, I am behind you, and the enemy will not stand before my arrows. Attack Bhishma and kill him now!

If you return without killing Bhishma today, you will be ridiculed by all. Kill him now, so that we may not be mocked in this great war. I will protect you from the Kaurava maharathas. Kill Bhishma, O Sikhandin!

I will contain Drona and his son, and Kripa, and Suyodhana, and Chitrasena, and Vikarna, and Jayadratha of the Sindhus, Vinda and Anuvinda of Avanti, and Sudakshina of the Kambojas, and the mighty Bhagadatta, and Salya of the Magadhas, and Somadatta's son, and Rishyasringa's son Alambusha and his fierce Rakshasas, and Susarman and the Trigartas, and all the other Kaurava maharathas.

I will contain them all like a continent does the surging sea. Destroy the Pitamaha even now!'"

CANTO 110

BHISHMA VADHA PARVA CONTINUED

Dhritarashtra says, 'How does Sikhandin attack the noble and righteous Bhishma? Which Pandava maharathas, armed with astras and seeking victory, protect Sikhandin? On the tenth day of the war, how does Bhishma fight the Pandavas and the Srinjayas? I cannot bear the thought of Sikhandin meeting Bhishma in battle. When Sikhandin attacks Bhishma what happens to the Pitamaha's chariot and to his bow?'

Sanjaya says, 'Neither Bhishma's bow nor his chariot is in the least damaged in that battle. He continues to mow down the enemy with deadly banks of arrows. Thousands of your maharathas and elephants and horses, led by the Pitamaha, advance into battle. Bhishma fulfils his word given to Suyodhana to massacre the Pandava forces. The Panchalas and the Pandavas can in no way withstand the magnificent Kshatriya and he destroys their forces as he likes.

On the tenth day, Bhishma scythes through the enemy with his countless shafts. Rajan, the sons of Pandu cannot remotely contain him for he is truly like Siva with his flaming trident come to Kurukshetra.

Then Arjuna, with Krishna at his chariot head, appears and the perfectly ambidextrous Savyasachin is at your maharathas like some dreadful plague.

Roaring like a lion now, the greatest of them all, he seems to be everywhere, so prodigious is Krishna's chariotry, and the Pandava's bow, the peerless Gandiva, appears to have life of its own for it seems to hang in the air, always drawn in a round of flames, so one cannot see that awesome archer's hands or any apparent movement from them, while firetides of unearthly arrows flare in seamless spate from his chariot, incinerating the enemy all around him wherever he goes. Your warriors are petrified, and either stand rooted while this Kshatriya like one they have never seen the like of before, while this bowman like Yama strews the field with their corpses, reduces them to ashes, or they flee like small animals at the growl of the lion.

Duryodhana, alarmed, cries to Bhishma, "Look at Arjuna, white horses yoked to his chariot, driven by Krishna, consuming your army like a flame of the pralaya burning a forest. O great Kshatriya, see how he devours our men, thinning our army by a thousand lives every moment.

My maharathas are as hard pressed as some cowherds in the jungle trying to control their stampeding herd attacked by a two great lions. From every side Arjuna and Bhima beset my legions and my men are butchered, and those that still live are terrified, their spirits broken. Satyaki, and Chekitana, and the twin sons of Madri, and the terrific Abhimanyu hunt with Arjuna and Bhima, and panic sweeps through my legions and they flee as they can.

Dhrishtadyumna and Ghatotkacha also put my men to rout so their blood flows again in rills. Ah, in this carnage, I see no one other than you, with your divine powers, who can prevent the Pandava maharathas from winning this war within the hour. Pitamaha, save us or we are lost!"

Bhishma ponders these words, and says slowly to your son, "Duryodhana, listen calmly to what I say. I vowed that I would kill ten thousand noble Kshatriyas every day, and return triumphant from the battlefield. I have fulfilled that vow!

Even today I will achieve a great feat as you watch me. I will either kill the Pandavas or die. Tiger among men, today I will free myself from my debt to you by sacrificing myself while leading your army." And Bhishma attacks the Pandava host.

The Pandavas oppose the son of Ganga who stands at the heart his forces seething like an angry snake. He annihilates thousands of warriors on that tenth day of the war. Like the sun sucking the earth dry of her moisture, he exhausts the regal ranks of the Panchala maharathas. He kills ten thousand spirited elephants, ten thousand horses with their riders, and two hundred thousand foot-soldiers; like a smokeless fire, Bhishma blazes like a flame which burns at its brightest just before being extinguished.

And none among the Pandavas can even look at him who is like the sun fixed in the northern solstice. The heroic Pandavas and the Srinjaya maharathas still storm at him in waves. Battling the countless warriors who surround him, Bhishma looks like Meru's steep slopes covered by dense clouds.

Your sons surround Bhishma with a vast protective force. Another fierce battle between the Kauravas and the Pandavas ensues.'

CANTO 111

BHISHMA VADHA PARVA CONTINUED

Sanjaya says, 'Watching Bhishma ablaze, more fearsome than he has yet been, Arjuna says to Sikhandin, "Ride towards the Pitamaha. Do not fear him today. For it is I who ride behind you and I who will strike him down from his chariot today."

Sikhandin charges Bhishma, and Dhrishtadyumna and the radiant Abhimanyu ride with him, their bows streaming many fires. Splendid in their armour, old Virata and Drupada, and Kuntibhoja also attack Bhishma before your son's eyes. And Nakula, Sahadeva, and Yudhishtira too, along with the other warriors ride at only Bhishma.

As for your Kshatriyas, listen, O Rajan, as I speak of them who advance so bravely, united against the Pandava army. Like a young tiger attacking a bull, Chitrasena charges Chekitana who is harrying Bhishma. Kritavarman holds up Dhrishtadyumna who is threateningly close to the Kuru Pitamaha. Somadatta's son fearlessly attacks Bhima who is also furiously trying to make Bhishma's great frame a home for his powerful arrows. Vikarna creates a magical wall of shafts between Nakula's gales of barbs and the grandsire.

Kripa prevents Sahadeva from approaching Bhishma's chariot. Durmukha storms against the mighty Ghatotkacha who also wants to kill just the son of Ganga. Duryodhana stops Satyaki from advancing. Sudakshina, king of the Kamabojas, engages and holds up Abhimanyu as he nears Bhishma's chariot. And Aswatthaman foils both Virata and Drupada.

Drona somewhat easily contains Yudhishtira who also is bent just on having Bhishma's life today. Showing incredible skill today, Dussasana thwarts Arjuna himself who, with Sikhandin before him, is dashing towards Bhishma, lighting up the ten quarters of the world with his shining astras.

Other warriors of your army clash with the Pandava maharathas advancing against Ganga's majestic son.

Dhrishtadyumna rides at Bhishma alone, crying to his forces, "Look at Arjuna storming at Bhishma. Be without fear today and attack just the son of Ganga. Bhishma will be helpless to harm you today. Why, Vasava himself cannot face Arjuna in battle, then what to say of Bhishma who, though he great indeed and courage incarnate, is also old and weak?"

Hearing this from their Senapati, the Pandava maharathas are jubilant and rush all together towards Bhishma's chariot. Many excellent men of your army spiritedly resist those Kshatriyas hurtling hungrily towards Bhishma.

To shield him from the hunting Arjuna, Dussasana fearlessly attacks the Pandava. The other sons of Pandu assail your mighty sons who surround Bhishma's chariot. It is wonderful to see Arjuna stopped short by Dussasana. As the shore contains the surging sea, your son Dussasana holds up the storming son of Pandu.

Both of them are excellent maharathas. Both are invincible. Both magnificent to behold, they resemble the sun and the moon. Both are incensed, and both want to kill the other. They fight like Mayaa and Sakra in olden days.

Dussasana stabs Arjuna with three shafts and Krishna with twenty. Enraged to see Krishna bleed, Arjuna looses a hundred shafts at

Dussasana, which flash through his armour and draw spouts of blood. Dussasana strikes Arjuna in the chest with five barbs, and upon his brow with three whetted shafts. These project from his head, making him look like Meru with lofty peaks. Looking like a radiant kinsuka, your son harangues Arjuna in that duel.

Inflamed like Rahu on a full moon night, Arjuna unleashes a flurry of arrows winged with the feathers of the kanka bird, and wounds Dussasana deeply. Arjuna cleaves Dusasana's bow and smashes his chariot with three shafts, and looses countless arrows like barbs of death at your son. But splendid Dussasana swiftly thwarts them in flight. All this appears so marvellous.

Dussasana strikes Arjuna with a hundred shafts and the angry Partha replies with flocks of searing arrows that plunge into Dusasana's body like swans diving into a lake. Covered in his own blood and staggering from the wounds of Arjuna, your son now runs towards Bhishma's chariot. He seeks Bhishma out like a drowning man clings to an island.

Finding refuge, your heroic Dussasana once more rains arrows at Arjuna, even like Purandara resisting Vritra. Though he is so mighty and powerful, his best efforts to vanquish Arjuna are in vain.'

CANTO 112

BHISHMA VADHA PARVA CONTINUED

S anjaya says, 'Alambusha thwarts Satyaki and rides towards Bhishma to offer his protection. The incensed Satyaki strikes the Rakshasa with nine dire arrows. Alambusha responds with nine shafts as well. Satyaki unleashes a storm of arrows at the Rakshasa, who, roaring dreadfully, responds in kind. Deeply injured by Alambusha, Satyaki laughs off his wounds. Bhagadatta stabs him with more keenly whetted shafts like a mahout piercing a tusker with his hook.

Satyaki turns away from Alambusha to vent his wrath upon Bhagadatta, who calmly breaks the shining Vrishni's hero's massive bow in his hands. Satyaki Yuyudhana seizes another and pierces Bhagadatta deeply, drawing small fonts of blood from his great frame. Bhagadatta licks the corners of his mouth and flings a most deadly iron spear, shimmering with gold and lapis lazuli, fierce like Yama's rod, at his enemy.

Satyaki cuts down that coursing shaft even as it flies at him, and it falls lustreless, like a burnt out meteor. Duryodhana surrounds Satyaki with many chariots.

He says to his brothers, "Kauravas, ensure that Satyaki does not escape from this encirclement. If he is killed, consider the vast host of the Pandavas also destroyed." Before Bhishma's eyes, those Kaurava maharathas attack Satyaki all together.

The king of the Kambojas sees Abhimanyu sweeping towards Bhishma and rides to bar his way. In a flash, Arjuna's son strikes Sudakshina with sixty four shafts. The Kamboja pierces Abhimanyu with five arrows and his charioteer with nine, to defend Bhishma. The duel between these two is ferocious and wonderful.

Meanwhile, Sikhandin continues to advance towards the Pitamaha. Destroying the teeming Kaurava army, maharathas Virata and Drupada also press their way towards Bhishma but they are confronted by an infuriated Aswatthaman.

Virata strikes Drona's son, that ornament of battle, sharply, as he dashes at them, and Drupada pierces him with three heavy shafts. Aswatthaman looses a fuming volley at the twain. With awesome archery the two old warriors serenely thwart Aswatthama's arrow storm.

Like an incensed elephant charging another in a forest, Kripa rides at Sahadeva who is also advancing upon Bhishma. He strikes Sahadeva with seventy golden shafts. The son of Madri cleaves Kripa's bow in his hands and pierces his first acharya with nine barbs.

Seizing another great bow, Kripa shoots ten immaculate barbs at Sahadeva in the space of a wish. Possessed by the single thought of killing Bhishma, annoyed at being thus held up, Sahadeva unleashes an altogether more savage clutch of missiles at his aged master's chest. And another zealous duel begins.

Parantapa Vikarna, also wanting to protect Bhishma, strikes Nakula with sixty shafts and Nakula replies with a hot salvo of seventy-seven barbs. Quickly, those purushavyaghras battle like two bulls in a herd over a cow. For Bhishma's sake, too, your son Durmukha whirls at Ghatotkacha who is slaughtering your army as he also rides at Bhishma. Hidimbi's son opens a deep gash in Durmukha's breast with one arrow like time. Durmukha only roars at the wound, even in elation, and stabs Ghatotkacha with sixty keen darts.

Dhrishtadyumna, also, sweeping down on Bhishma and Hridika's son Kritavarman, obstructs him. Drupada's fire prince looses a sear of five molten shafts at Kritavarman and strikes him with another fifty iron barbs in his chest, most of which glance off his mail. Dhrishtadyumna swift as the mind shoots nine more burning arrows, winged with the feathers of the kanka bird at the Yadava prince.

They battle impassionedly for Bhishma's sake, as fiercely as Vritra and Vasava. Bhurisravas assails Bhima who is also advances ever nearer the mighty Bhishma. That grand Kuru warrior pierces Bhima's commodious chest with a telling golden-winged arrow; so awesome does Bhima look as dramatic as the Krauncha mountain did of old when it bore Lord Skanda's barb. Ablaze, the two Kshatriyas, Purusharishabhas both, loose livid rivers of missiles, bright as sunflares, at each other. Bhima fights, longing for Bhishma's death, while Somadatta does to secure Bhishma's victory, and each matches the other's stunning feats.

Drona arrests the careen of Yudhishtira storming towards Bhishma. The Prabhadrakas tremble hearing the roar of Drona's chariot that is like the rumble of massed thunderheads, and that vast Pandava host cannot advance even a step because of Bharadwaja's formidable son.

Your tenacious son Chitrasena impedes the fierce Chekitana, also riding at Bhishma. Chekitana attacks him vigorously, and scintillating is the duel between these two. Though Dussasana powerfully obstructs Arjuna's path to Bhishma, that irresistible Pandava overwhelms him and forces your son to retreat. Arjuna strews the field with Kaurava corpses at his majestic, inexorable will, and the other Pandava maharathas also decimate your legions which try to keep Bhishma safe.'

CANTO 113

BHISHMA VADHA PARVA CONTINUED

Sanjaya says, 'Like an incensed elephant, Drona penetrates the Pandava ranks, and mows them down on every side with his godlike archery.

Drona, knowing interpreter of omens, sees the signs of an age ending and another rising all around him and says to Aswatthaman who also ravages the enemy on every side, "This is that day on which Arjuna will put forth all his prowess to have Bhishma's life.

My arrows leap out from their quiver by themselves. My bow seems to yawn. My astra seems unwilling to obey me, and I feel a great despondence. Animals and birds cry relentlessly in fearful voices. Vultures fly down and vanish under the feet of the Bhaarata forces.

The Sun appears dull. The four quarters are on fire. Everywhere the Earth seems to wail and tremble in some great fear. Kankas, vultures and cranes cry out repeatedly warning of some dreadful evil. Jackals scream and wheel in inauspicious apradakshina also predicting grave danger.

Immense meteors seem to flare down from the heart of the Sun. The Parigha constellation appears around Surya Deva, shrouding his light.

The Sun and Moon look threatening, foretelling a massacre of Kshatriyas. The statues in the temples of the Kauravas tremble and laugh and dance and weep, as if they have gone mad. The glowing crescent moon rises with horns turned down. The bodies of the kings in the Kaurava army appear pale, and though clad in armour, they are strangely dull.

The blast of Panchajanya and the twang of Gandiva resound all around both armies, above every other sound. Today, bearing all his astras, Arjuna will surely mow his way through all our maharathas and mount his attack on Bhishma.

The pores of my body contract, and all my hope drains from me, when I think of the coming battle between Bhishma and Arjuna. Ah, look! Keeping the deceitful Panchala prince before him, even now Arjuna rides at the Pitamaha. Bhishma has said that he will not kill Sikhandin because this prince was born a woman, and only later became a man.

That mighty son of Yajnasena is himself the most inauspicious omen. Bhishma will never fight with such an unnatural one. Ah, my son, fear grips my heat in a vice knowing that every moment Arjuna draws nearer the revered Pitamaha.

Yudhishtira's anger, which has been restrained so long, the very thought of Arjuna fighting his beloved grandsire, and me, a Brahmana taking to arms in a war, all portend the gravest tragedy. Arjuna is imbued with untold tejas; he is powerful, brave, and a great master of weapons. Apart from loosing his arrows farther and more powerfully than any other man, he too is a sure reader of omens.

So strong, intelligent and tireless is Arjuna that not the Devas with Vasava at their head can defeat him in battle. He has the most virulent astras and he is called Vijaya because he never loses a battle but always triumphs in war. Avoid him, my son, and ride to defend Bhishma from this terrible son of Pandu.

Today we shall see such carnage that not even this war among all wars has yet shown us. The beautiful golden armour of heroic Kshatriyas will be riven by his arrows, and Arjuna will cut down their flags, and bearded javelins in flight, and bows, and bright pointed spears, and glittering arrows, and the standards on the backs of their elephants.

O my son, this is not the time to care for our lives. Focussed on heaven, fame and victory, go and fight. There, the Vanara-bannered Arjuna crosses the treacherous river of battle in his chariot, the river that has blood for its currents and shattered chariots, dead elephants, and horses for its islets.

Regard for Brahmanas, self-restraint, liberality, asceticism, and noble conduct are to be found in Yudhishtira alone; for his brothers he has Arjuna, the mighty Bhima, and the twin sons of Madri by Pandu; and he has Krishna of the Vrishni vamsa for his protector.

His body has been purified by the flames of tapasya, and Yudhishtira's anger, born of grief, is directed at the black-souled son of Dhritarashtra and this righteous anger is what destroys the Bhaarata host.

There comes Arjuna; with Krishna as his sarathy and refuge he advances irresistibly and lays waste the entire Dhartarashtra army. Look, he terrifies our host like a great whale stirring up an ocean with towering waves. Listen to the frantic sad cries of our army.

Charge against the heir of the Panchala king. I will ride against Yudhishtira. The heart of his vyuha is difficult to penetrate. Inaccessible as the depths of the sea, it is guarded on all sides by Atirathas. Satyaki, and Abhimanyu and Dhrishtadyumna, and Bhima, and the twins, all protect Yudhishtira.

Dark as the younger brother of Indra, and standing like a tall sala tree, behold Abhimanyu storming ahead at the head of the Pandava host, like a second Arjuna! Seize your mighty weapons, and with your great bow ride against Sikhandin and Bhima.

Who doesn't want their son to live long? However, I now observe the dharma of a Kshatriya, and I assign this task to you. Ah, look where Bhishma also razes the swarming Pandava host. O son, the Kuru Pitamaha is equal to Yama or Varuna himself in battle.'''

CANTO 114

BHISHMA VADHA PARVA CONTINUED

Sanjaya says, 'Hearing what Drona says, Bhagadatta and Kripa and Salya and Kritavarman, and Vinda and Anuvinda of Avanti, and Jayadratha of the Sindhus, and Chitrasena and Vikarna and Durmarshana, these ten warriors of your army, supported by a legion of diverse soldiers, boldly face Bhima, wanting to win fame in the war for Bhishma's sake.

Salya strikes Bhima with nine arrows, and Kritavarman stabs him with three, and Kripa with nine. And Chitrasena and Vikarna and Bhagadatta, each pierce him with ten barbs. Jayadratha strikes him with three, and Vinda and Anuvinda of Avanti each with five shafts.

Duryodhana attacks him with twenty arrows. In return Bhima relentlessly pierces each one of those kings, those maharathas of the Dhartarashtra army. He shoots Salya with seven arrows and Kritavarman with eight. And he cleaves Kripa's bow in two. He pierces Kripa once more with seven shafts. And he strikes Vinda and Anuvinda with three barbs each.

Bhima strikes Durmarshana deep with twenty arrows, Chitrasena with five, Vikarna with ten, and Jayadratha with five; and once more flaying the king of the Sindhus with three astras, Bhimasena roars loudly with delight.

Kripa, maharatha, angrily stabs Bhima with ten polished shafts. Pierced like an elephant by a goad, Bhima's eyes turn red in a moment and he looses a vicious salvo at Kripa, drawing founts of blood from his old master. Splendid as Yama, as he appears at the end of the yuga, Bhima kills Jayadratha's horses with three scarlet explosions, and also his charioteer. Maharatha Jayadratha leaps down from his horseless chariot and looses a squall of keen shafts at Bhima.

Bhima destroys Jayadratha's bow with two broad-headed arrows. His bow broken, his chariot stranded, his horses and sarathy killed, Jayadratha mounts Chitrasena's chariot. Triumphant Bhima draws blood from all the maharathas before him; celebrant, he smashes Jayadratha's chariot into pieces in the very sight of all the Kaurava army. Watching Bhima's dreadful feats, Salya roars out a challenge to him; he looses a gale of gleaming barbs at the monumental Pandava.

Kripa and Kritavarman and the valiant Bhagadatta, and Vinda and Anuvinda of Avanti, and Chitrasena, and Durmarshana, and Vikarna, and Jayadratha all attack Bhima in concert. Irrepressible Bhima stabs each of them with hot clutches of arrows, five for each one. And he harries Salya with seventy shafts loosed in the twinkling of an eye, and again with ten more. Salya drives nine steaming arrows through him, and then five more. With another broad one he pierces Bhima's charioteer deep.

Seeing his charioteer Visoka wounded deep, with a terrible cry, Bhima drills three searing shafts into the arms and chest of the Madra king; he riddles the other maharathas each with three perfectly straight arrows and, throwing back his massive head, lets out a deafening, lion's roar.

Those mighty archers gore Bhima, probing his very vitals. Wounded, he yet remains still, like a mountain drenched by lashing rain clouds. That Pandava maharatha, that celebrated Kshatriya, wrathfully reams the ruler of the Madras with three light like arrows; he punishes the ruler of the Pragjyotishas with a hundred.

He castigates Kripa with countless barbs and, with astounding dexterity, cleaves Kritavarman's bow with a single shaft – all this in a breathtaking instant. Kritavarman, parantapa, scourge of his enemies, takes up another bow and strikes Bhima right between his eyes with a fine long arrow.

Having pierced Salya with nine iron arrows, and Bhagadatta with three, and Kritavarman with eight, Bhima chastens the others led by Kripa, each with two shafts. These warriors reply with calid flurries, making blood flowers sprout on great Bhima. They scathe him with diverse astras, but Bhima remains nonchalant and courses effortlessly across the battleground, spraying Kurukshetra liberally with enemies' blood. Hundreds of thousands of arrows rain down on him from ever side.

Bhagadatta casts a fierce golden javelin spear at him; the Sindhu king, Mahabaho, flings both a javelin and a battle-axe at Bhima in wrath, to remember the humiliation this Pandava inflicted on him once in the forest. Kripa unleashes a satagni of a hundred flames at Bhima, and Salya a single arrow as fulgurant. The other archers each aim five punitive shafts at him.

The son of Vayu cleaves Bhagadatta's missile along its deadly length; he pulverises Jayadratha's axe as if were a stem of sesame. He douses the satagni with five occult shafts winged with the feathers of the kanka bird, blows Salya's one arrow of dread into dust. Proud Bhima, who knows neither doubt nor fear, cuts every other arrow flying at him in three. And he strikes each of those illustrious archers who attacked him with blinding archery that rivals, why, now exceeds, his brother Arjuna's.

As the war burns on, Arjuna sees Bhima devouring the enemy on all sides like Yama and rides towards him on his chariot. The warriors of your army watch those two enkindled sons of Pandu come together, and their spirits tremble.

Arjuna has only a single intention today - to kill Bhishma. Setting Sikhandin before him, he nears Bhima who has been battling the ten Kaurava maharathas by himself; Arjuna descends on those fierce ten like some dreadful plague. In a wink he strikes all of them with arrows that fling them back in their chariots or strike them down.

In some alarm, Duryodhana cries to Susarman, the Trigarta king, "Great Susarman, fly taking your Trigarta host with you. Let the earth drink the blood of Pandu's sons Dhananjaya and Vrikodara today!"

Roaring, his host of sterling archers riding with him, Susarman, king of the Trigartas, lord of Prasthala, swoops on Bhima and Arjuna and surrounds them with thousands of chariots. A stupendous duel spumes up between him and Arjuna.'

CANTO 115

BHISHMA VADHA PARVA CONTINUED

Sanjaya says, 'With shafts of fierce precision, Arjuna envelops maharatha Salya who fights him gallantly. Arjuna pierces Susarman and Kripa with three arrows each.

Atiratha Arjuna torments your army all around him; he adorns Bhagadatta and Jayadratha, and Chitrasena, and Vikarna, and Kritavarman, and Durmarshana, and those two maharathas, the princes of Avanti, each with three barbs winged with the feathers of the kanka and the peacock.

Jayadratha, whom Siva blessed, putting forth his best fight, pierces Arjuna and also Bhima from Chitrasena's chariot. Salya and Kripa both strike Arjuna with diverse arrows, which burrow deeply into his virile form. Your sons led by Chitrasena, Rajan, each pierce Arjuna and Bhima with five arrows like daggers.

Kunti's two prodigious sons, both maharathas without compare, Bhima and Arjuna, begin to pound the mighty Trigarta host. Then Susarman looses nine extraordinary arrows at Arjuna, all of which find their mark, and roaring loudly terrifies the Pandava forces.

Other noble Kshatriyas rack Bhima and Dhananjaya with many

whetted golden winged shafts. Standing amidst them, those two bulls of the Bharata vamsa only ever more look magnificent and they seem to tantalise their opponents like two furious lions hunting in a herd of cows.

The two peerless Kshatriyas cleave their most valiant adversaries' bows and barbs and fell the heads of countless warriors. Innumerable chariots they smash, hundreds of horses they kill, and so many elephants, along with their riders, in that tumultuary and dreadful battle. Chariot warriors and untold numbers of horsemen and elephant-riders are slain outright or seen convulsing in death's final spasms all over Kurukshetra. And the earth is covered with the corpses of elephants, horses and foot-soldiers, and chariots destroyed in many ways.

Arjuna's prowess is wonderful to behold, as he thwarts his enemies and slaughters them in droves. Kripa, and Kritavarman, and Jayadratha, and Vinda and Anuvinda of Avanti remain resolute. And as if inspired at being opposed by any, Bhima and Arjuna appear to raise the level of their archery and where hundreds died at their hands each moment now thousands perish and the rout of the fierce Kaurava host swells exponentially. The enemy kings loose millions of arrows with peacock feathers at Arjuna's chariot. Dazzling, thought-swift Arjuna cuts all these missiles down as in some dream and in the same moment, it seems, annihilates his challengers.

Inflamed to watch this, Salya strikes Arjuna in his chest with some broad headed shafts. With five startling barbs, Arjuna breaks Salya's bow and shreds his leather gloves, and pierces him deep in his body. Snatching up another powerful bow, the Madra king furiously attacks Arjuna with three arrows and Krishna with five. He gores Bhima in the arms and the chest with nine shafts.

At Duryodhana's urgent command, Drona and the Magadha king ride swiftly to where Arjuna and Bhima massacre the mighty Kaurava army at will. As his rides up, Jayatsena pierces Bhima of terrible weapons with eight serrated arrows. Bhima looses a flash of fifteen searing shafts at him. With another broad-headed arrow he fells Jayatsena's charioteer from his chariot head, and the Magadhan's unrestrained horses dash wildly away and carry him out of battle in the sight of all the troops.

Drona, seeing an opening, stabs Bhima with eight unusual barbs with heads like a frog's mouth. Bhima, always delighting in battle, wheels round and strikes the Acharya with five heavy arrows, and O Bhaarata, with sixty more fleet ones.

Arjuna looses countless iron barbs at Susarman himself, while also demolishes his Trigarta forces like a high wind dispersing massed clouds. Bhishma and Duryodhana, and Brihadbala, king of the Kosalas, wrathfully advance upon Bhima and Dhananjaya. At this, the gallant Pandava warriors and Dhrishtadyumna charge against Bhishma who is pressing forward like Yama with mouth agape.

Sikhandin sees the Pitamaha of the Bhaaratas; he charges fearlessly and jubilantly towards that greatest maharatha. All the Parthas with Yudhishtira at their head, uniting with the Srinjayas and setting Sikhandin in their van, come hunting Bhishma. With Bhishma at their head, all the warriors of your army confront all the Pandava legions with Sikhandin in their van. That pitched battle between the Kauravas and the Pandavas, fought for Bhishma's victory or his death, is the fiercest and most terrifying one yet.

Indeed, on that fateful tenth day, first of the fell Kali Yuga, age of vileness and wrath, in that brutal game of war, being played out on sacred, bloodied Kurukshetra, field of dharma, Bhishma becomes the stake wagered, his life the precious thing on which the success or defeat of your army depends.

Dhrishtadyumna roars his command at all his men, "Charge against the son of Ganga. Be fearless, O you wonderful maharathas!"

Hearing their Senapati's call to the moment of a great reckoning, the Pandava host swarms towards Bhishma, themselves roaring, ready to lay down their lives to achieve holy, priceless victory. Great Jaya! Maharatha Bhishma receives that storming host like a continent withstanding the surging sea.'

CANTO 116

Bhishma Vadha Parva continued

Dhritarashtra says, 'Sanjaya, how does mighty Bhishma fight the Pandavas and the Srinjayas on the tenth day of the war? How do the Kauravas oppose the Pandavas? Describe the great endeavour of, that jewel of battle.'

Sanjaya says, 'I will tell of how the Kauravas fight the Pandavas, and the details of their battle. Day after day, Arjuna Kiritin obliterates countless maharathas of your vast army with his astras. The triumphal Bhishma also wreaks great carnage upon the Pandavas. O Parantapa, seeing Bhishma ablaze at the head of the Kurus, and Arjuna at that of the Panchalas, it is hard to say who will be victorious.

On the tenth day, when Bhishma and Arjuna face each other, there is an unprecedented bloodbath on Kurukshetra. Bhishma slaughters thousands of unknown but heroic warriors, all resolute in battle. Scorching the Pandava army for ten days, Mahabaho Bhishma fights without the slightest care for his life, and magnificently, yet with sorrow in his noble heart. And on this day of moment, he wishes fervently that he may not take any more noble lives discharging his terrible Kshatriya dharma, and he wishes for his own death.

Seeing Yudhishthira near him, he says, "Wise Yudhishtira, listen to my righteous words. I no longer want to save my body. I have already killed countless great warriors. If you want to truly please me, your Pitamaha, set Arjuna with the Panchalas and the Srinjayas in your van, and exert yourself to the utmost to take my life."

Understanding him, Yudhishtira presses forward with the Srinjayas. Also having heard what Bhishma said, Dhrishtadyumna goads his legions forward.

Yudhishtira cries with as much rage as grief, "Fly at Bhishma and kill him even now! Arjuna will protect you, as will Dhrishtadyumna and Bhima. Srinjayas, do not fear Bhishma today. With Sikhandin before us, we will surely vanquish the Pitamaha."

Determined to either triumph or die, led by Sikhandin and Arjuna, the Pandava host essays at Bhishma giving their all and with nothing to lose. Many powerful kings, urged on by your son Suyodhana, along with Drona and his son and a vast force, with Dussasana at the head of all his brothers, also fly toward Bhishma at the very heart of all the unspeakable and resplendent butchery.

Keeping Bhishma at their head, your legions spiritedly engage with the Pandavas led by Sikhandin. Supported by the Chedis and the Panchalas, the Vanara-bannered Arjuna, keeps Sikhandin before him, and storms at his Pitamaha. Satyaki clashes first with Drona's son, and Dhrishtaketu with Puru's descendant; Yudhamanyu grimly fights Duryodhana and his legion. Virata leads his heroes against Jayadratha's.

Parantapa, Vardhakshatra's heir encounters Chitrasena of the most excellent bow. And Yudhishtira faces the haranguing Salya at the head of his forces. Bhima, purest, mightiest and most unalloyed of all Kshatriyas in spirit, roaring, always roaring in exultation at being in battle at last, storms yet against the Kaurava elephants.

Dhrishtadyumna, fire prince of Panchala, along with his brothers, furiously attacks the unconquerable Drona, foremost of all wielders of weapons. Parantapa Brihadbala, who flies the lion on his standard, hurtles at Abhimanyu whose standard bears the karnikara flower. With countless kings going with them, your sons advance upon Sikhandin and Arjuna. When these warriors clash, the earth trembles.

Seeing Bhishma approach, both armies fall into disarray and become hopelessly entangled, flailing out with sword and spear, covering the air with a single dense cloud of arrows. Great is the commotion they make, those warriors inflamed with rage charge madly, bloodthirstily at one another. The tumult rings all around, a ceaseless deafening din, shattering the eardrums of warriors so blood oozes down their necks before those necks are hewn.

The blast of conches and the tigerish roars of fighting men form what appears to be an unending bellow of pain from the wounded earth's very womb. The radiance of the bracelets and crowns of all the heroic kings, equal to that of the sun or the moon, is dimmed by the dust raised by flying hooves, thundering elephants' charges, the running feet of millions of footsoldiers, the whirling swerving wheels of numberless chariots; against this dark thunderhead of dust and smoke, the flash of weapons everywhere is like braids and streaks of lighting.

The twanging bows, the stentorian hum of arrows like that of black bee swarms beyond count disturbed, the booming conches, the pounding drums, and the dementedly barbarous clatter of chariot-wheels, of both the armies, is numbing. And the sky darkens deeper by the moment with rich flights of bearded barbs, spears, swords wildly flung and the ceaseless rain of fell astras.

Maharathas and horsemen cut each other down as if offering rivers of noble blood to the earth in some ghastly sacrifice in that awesome war, at once so abominable and so irresistibly beautiful. And elephants gore down elephants, and foot-soldiers butcher foot-soldiers. And the war on that tenth day, being fought for Bhishma's life, between the Kauravas and the Pandavas assumes an incrementally hideous aspect, while it is also like a fight two hawks for a fine piece of flesh. The crimson river of death foams ever higher and darker on bleeding, incomparable Kurukshetra.'

CANTO 117

BHISHMA VADHA PARVA CONTINUED

S anjaya says, 'Abhimanyu displays his prowess before Bhishma, and challenges your mighty eldest son. Duryodhana strikes Abhimanyu through his chest with nine straight arrows, and in a flash with three. Arjuna's son hurls a fierce and strange lance resembling Yama's rod at Duryodhana's chariot. Your son cleaves it along its length as it courses towards him. Seeing his spear plummet, Abhimanyu seizes his bow and strikes Duryodhana deep with three shafts through his arms and breast. Quicker than the eye sees, that scintillating young maharatha stabs the Kaurava king with a blur of ten barbs making a neat feathered circle of quivering arrows on his wide chest.

And the duel between those two Kshatriyas, one fighting to kill Bhishma and the other to vanquish Arjuna, is brutal and breathtaking to watch, and gratifying to the senses; it is praised by all the kings.

The son of Drona, that bull among Brahmanas and chastiser of enemies, bloodies Satyaki's chest with a salient arrow. The grandson of Sini also pierces all his vital limbs with nine signal shafts winged with the feathers of the kanka bird. Aswatthaman stabs Satyaki's arms and breast with nine horned barbs, and then with thirty significant shafts more. That celebrated bowman of the Satwatavamsa returns the fire cardinally, covering Aswatthaman in blood.

Maharatha Paurava swathes Dhrishtaketu with his remarkable volleys and fairly mangles him. But the formidable Dhrishtaketu is unmoved and looses a jagged volley of lightning bolts at Paurava. Paurava smashes Dhrishtaketu's bow, and roaring loudly, strikes him repeatedly with a clutch of keen arrows. Dhrishtaketu seizes another bow and gouges Paurava with an astonishing salvo of seventy-three shafts all shot in the heart of a moment.

Those two illustrious archers cover each other with arrows. Each shatters the other's bow, and each kills the other's horses. They face each other with gleaming swords drawn, and bull's hide shields, one adorned with a hundred moons and the other with a hundred stars. They run at each other like two lions in the forest, over a lioness in heat. They wheel around in elegant circles, advance and retreat, and display other dancelike movements, all the while looking for an opening to strike the adversary.

Growing impatient, Paurava roars at Dhrishtaketu to stop and fight, and swiftly strikes him on his mail-covered collar bone, a mighty blow. Not flinching, the Chedi king fetches Paurava a powerful stroke on his shoulder, so some blood flies from the wound. In a blink, they rain a dreadful flurry of cuts, thrusts and wild swings on each other, so that both fall to the ground. Your son Jayatsena takes Paurava into his chariot and bears his away from the field, while Sahadeva bears Dhrishtaketu away.

Chitrasena, having already pierced Susarman with manifold arrows, looses a fresh salvo of sixty-nine burning shafts at him. The incensed Susarman wounds your son all over his body with hundreds of barbs. Chitrasena, infuriated, retaliates with thirty penetrating shafts, and Susarman strikes Chitrasena again.

In that battle for Bhishma's life, Subhadra's son further swells his fame and honour when he flays Brihadbala, drawing that maharatha away from Arjuna, and then marching towards Bhishma. The Kosala king attacks Abhimanyu with five heavy iron shafts, and then with twenty more. Abhimanyu stabs Brihadbala with eight similar missiles, which Brihadbala only shrugs off and Arjuna's son lifts his archery to rive Brihadbala's bow in his hands, and strikes him again thirty barbs swifter than light. Brihadbala takes up another bow and covers the brilliant youth of just sixteen summers in fire.

Both Kshatriyas, one so young and the other seasoned and mature, are such masters of war, that the duel between them is surely reminiscent of the contention between Indra and Bali during the Devasura yuddha in time out of mind.

Bhima, wild and bloody amongst the elephants, looks as resplendent as thunderous Sakra after splitting lofty mountains. The screams and dismal bellows of the great beasts, big as cliff, that he strikes down as he pleases fill the world. Hillocks of antimony, the tuskers lying dead across Kurukshetra with their round temples cloven by terrible Bhima are like mountains scattered over the earth.

Well protected, Yudhishtira attacks Salya, king of the Madras, who loses no time turning on his assailant. Jayadratha of the Sindhus strikes Virata with nine keen arrows, and seamlessly with thirty more. Commanding a vast legion, Virata makes a home in Jayadratha's chest for thirty polished shafts. And radiant are those two, the lord of the Matsyas and the ruler of the Sindhus, both armed with beautiful bows, swords and other weapons, wearing dazzling armour, and flying brilliant pennants.

Drona encounters Dhrishtadyumna and mounts a ferocious attack on the prince sworn, why, born to kill him. Smashing Drupada's son's bow, Drona excoriates him with a hum of fifty barbs. That parantapa raises another bow and vents his wrath on the Acharya with a fiery volley. Maharatha Drona slices those arrows along their length even as they flare at him, and looses five keening barbs at his old enemy Drupada's prince. Dhrishtadyumna, roaring, hurls a knobbed golden mace at the Brahmana warrior and Drona nervelessly shatters it with fifty arrows loosed in a blink.

Dhrishtadyumna launches a most refined astra at Drona, who effortlessly foils it with a clutch of nine smoking barbs, unsettling the Pandava Senapati. Rajan, thus they fight, master and disciple, both inspired to draw upon their deepest skills, during this duel fought for the life of Bhishma.

Arjuna, meanwhile rushes towards Bhishma like one king elephant at another, showering ceaseless fire over his Pitamaha. Bhagadatta arrests Arjuna's dangerous careen, setting his massive Supratika between the marauding Pandava and the Kuru grandsire and lashing down a gale of arrows from his height. Arjuna storms straight at Bhagadatta, unleashing a fury of silver shafts at his towering beast, so that Bhagadatta quickly turns away and thunders down upon Drupada's chariot.

Again, Arjuna sets Sikhandin before him and courses on towards Bhishma, who is all he sees before him, his only real target. With loud yells and roars, hordes of your brave fighting men assail Arjuna, who so calmly sows death all around him, in a carmine flash flood. And, ah, all this appears wonderful.

Like the high wind scattering fleecy clouds in a summer sky Arjuna disperses your son's aksauhinis, all the while thinning them, thinning them dreadfully. Each moment, Sikhandin of the single obsession that has possessed him through two strangest lives, heralding his advent with an endless stream of wooden arrows, plunges ever nearer Bhishma.

As for Bhishma, his chariot is his fire-chamber. His bow is the flame of that fire. And swords, shafts and maces are its fuel. The arrows he shoots are the blazing sparks that consume Kshatriyas in that grisly war. As a raging fire rolling across a field of dry grass with the wind, Bhishma burns gloriously as he unleashes his divine astras.

And he decimates the Somakas that follow Arjuna into battle; that effulgent maharatha attenuates the other Pandava legions that ride with Arjuna with swarms of golden-winged shafts. Bhishma fills all the directions, with his leonine roaring, and endlessly strews the awful field of dharma with corpses of chariot warriors and horses with their riders. He reduces the massed chariots to look like palm forests with their leafy heads severed. He strips horses, elephants and chariots of their riders, a thousand each moment.

Hearing the twang of his bow and the slap of his palms against his bowstring, like rolling thunder, terror sweeps through the Pandava ranks; even your own fighting men are affrighted. Not an arrow shot by the daunting Pitamaha misses its mark. They do not just pierce or slay his numberless victims; his barbs plough right through their armoured bodies in bright red eruptions and enter the earth behind them. What count is there of chariots careering across the field of death, with riders and sarathies slain and yoked horses dragging them on all sides with the speed of the wind?

Fourteen thousand noble maharathas, all ready to sacrifice their lives, with gold-worked standards, great warriors belonging to the Chedis, the Kasis, and the Karushas, attack Bhishma, Kshatriya who can only be Siva himself with mouth agape; in moments they are destroyed along with their horses, chariots and elephants.

Rajan, not a single maharatha of the Somakas returns alive from that encounter with Bhishma. Seeing his prowess, all know that none who dares ride against Bhishma this day will escape with his life. And indeed, after the massacre of the Somakasa, no rathika will approach Bhishma anymore, but only Arjuna Swetavahana of the white horses, with Krishna as his charioteer, and Sikhandin, prince of Panchala.'

CANTO 118

BHISHMA VADHA PARVA CONTINUED

Sanjaya says, 'Sikhandin storms within range of Bhishma and strikes him squarely through his chest with ten broad-headed arrows. The son of Ganga merely looks at Sikhandin as if to kill him with withering disdain. Bhishma will not shoot back at Sikhandin.

Sikhandin pauses, bemused. Arjuna cries at the Panchala prince, "Do not hesitate, Sikhandin. Destroy Maharatha Bhishma, for you alone can. This is the truth. Kill him, Purushavyaghra, kill him now!"

Like a dreamer waking, Sikhandin covers Bhishma in a tirade of every kind of arrow. Ignoring these, Bhishma only looses his own shafts at Arjuna; he also razes the Pandava ranks behind these two. Like grim clouds occluding the sun, the Pandavas, with their vast hosts, push forward to engulf Bhishma.

Bharatarishabha, though surrounded on all sides, that Kshatriya without equal continues to consume the advancing legions like the forest fire does countless trees. Dusasana's shining prowess is wonderful to see as he battles Arjuna to protect the Pitamaha. Even his enemies laud his sheer courage as he fights alone and gloriously against all the Pandavas, and they cannot resist him.

Dussasana smashes the chariots of so many maharathas. With deadly salvos he fells mighty archers from horseback, powerful rathikas and elephants. The great beasts thunder away from the terror and pain of the incandescent Dussasana; flowing blood from the wounds he inflicts on them they scatter in all directions.

Like a fire that blazes more fiercely when fuelled, so does your son rage against the Pandava host. And no Pandava maharathika dares to advance against him as he is then, other than Arjuna with his white horses and Krishna for his sarathy. And, watched by all the warriors, Arjuna, the Vijaya, ineluctably quells the flaming Dussasana and flashes past him towards Bhishma. Though beaten, your son, still relying upon Bhishma's invincible might, comforts his forces and continues to fight fiercely against the Pandavas. Arjuna is radiant; his body seems to blaze with light as he scythes through his enemies.

Sikhandin pierces the Pitamaha with many arrows deadly as lightning and fatal as a snake's venom. But all the Panchala prince's missiles have little impact as Bhishma receives them smiling, as if with delight. Even as a man whose body is fevered by summer heat welcomes torrential rain so does awesome Bhishma seem to welcome Sikhandin's arrows.

All the assembled Kshatriyas behold Bhishma as a great and fierce being, more than merely a man, who relentlessly devastates the Pandava warriors. Duryodhana says to his troops, "Attack Arjuna from all sides. Bhishma will protect you."

The Kaurava forces shed their fears and charge the Pandavas. Duryodhana says again to them, "With his lofty standard with the golden palmyra, Bhishma stands resolute, protecting the honour and the power of all the Dhartarashtra warriors. The very Devas cannot defeat him. What then to say about the Pandavas who are mere mortals? Kshatriyas, do not flee when you face Arjuna. I myself will fight the Pandavas, and be your support."

Hearing your son's words, Rajan, enraged warriors of the Videhas, the Kalingas, and the many tribes of the Daserkas fall upon Phalguni. And many belonging to the Nishadas, the Sauviras, the Bahlikas, the Daradas, the western and northern kingdoms, the Malavas, the Abhighatas, the Surasenas, the Sibis, the Vasatis, the Salwas, the Sakas, the Trigartas, the Ambashtha, and the Kekayas, also swoop down on Arjuna, like swarms of insects upon a fire.

Arjuna aims his devastras at the maharathas leading their aksauhinis; he makes ashes of them, like a fire swallowing insects. As he creates thousands upon thousands of arrows with his astras, his Gandiva dazzles.

Wounded by those arrows, their grand standards torn, those Kshatriyas, even united, cannot so much as draw near Arjuna. Assailed by Kiritin's shafts, rathikas fall with their standards, horsemen with their horses, and elephant riders with their elephants. Soon the earth is covered with the fleeing forces of those kings, routed by Arjuna's arrows.

Having crushed the Kaurava army, Arjuna looses a storm of arrows at Dusasana. The iron shafts pierce through him, and enter the earth like snakes through ant-hills. Arjuna kills Dusasana's horses and his charioteer.

With twenty barbs he smashes Vivimsati's chariot, then strikes that prince with five straight shafts. Attacking Kripa and Vikarna and Salya with a terrific volley, he demolishes their chariots. Defeated, they flee, along with Dussasana and Vikarna and Vivimsati.

Victorious over those maharathas, Arjuna blazes like a god on Kurukshetra. Unleashing waves of arrows on every side, even like the sun streaming rays, Partha overcomes many other kings. Bhaarata, killing them disdainfully with his unearthly archery, he makes another bloody river flow between the Kaurava and Pandava hosts.

Elephants and horses and maharathikas are slaughtered by chariot warriors. And many chariot warriors are trampled by elephants, and many horses are butchered by foot soldiers. The bodies of elephant-riders and horsemen and chariot warriors are hacked to pieces, which, along with their heads, tumble to the ground.

And the field of the dread war, Rajan, is strewn with the corpses of princes, maharathikas all falling or fallen, decked with ear-rings and bracelets. The bodies of warriors bisected by chariot wheels, or crushed by elephants, also lie scattered. And footsoldiers and horse riders flee.

Elephants and maharathikas plunge to the earth on all sides. Numerous chariots, with their wheels, yokes and standards smashed, lie strewn across Kurukshetra, as if by some vengeful god's hand. Dyed with the gore of numerous elephants, horses and chariot warriors, the earth looks beautiful like a red cloud in the sky.

Dogs, crows and vultures, wolves and jackals, and other terrifying beasts and birds howl and screech, hungering for dead flesh. Many fell winds blow from all sides. And Rakshasas and Pisachas can be seen with monstrous and ghoulish visages roaring fiercely. Golden strings and costly banners flap in the unnatural wind. Thousands of royal parasols and lofty chariots with splendid standards lie ruined on the ground.

Before all the archers, Bhishma invokes an agneyastra and aims it at Arjuna. His kavacha glittering, Sikhandin rides between the Kuru ancient and Arjuna and attacks Bhishma fiercely. Bhishma promptly withdraws the blinding astra of flames. Arjuna of the white steeds continues to raze your forces, letting ever more streams of blood, while Bhishma is a helpless spectator to the massacre of his army.'

CANTO 119

BHISHMA VADHA PARVA CONTINUED

Sanjaya says, 'Resolved to fight to the death, the teeming legions of both armies are ranged against each other, tenacious Kshatriyas ranged in vyuhas which have long since been violated. And no more, as had been agreed before the war began, do rathikas exclusively fight other chariot warriors, or foot-soldiers against foot-soldiers, or horsemen face other horsemen, or elephant-warriors other elephant-warriors. Instead, possessed completely by the feral spirit of war they attack each other wildly, chaotically, like men gone mad.

Ghastly devastation sweeps both armies, as elephants and men fight each other without distinction.

Then Salya and Kripa, and Chitrasena, and Dussasana, and Vikarna, mounted on their shining chariots, bring swift terror to the Pandava host. Savaged by those great Kshatriyas, the Pandava army reels and lurches like a boat tossed on the ocean by the wind. Like the biting cold that chills ther blood of soft cows, Bhishma ploughs through the forces of sons of Pandu.

Immaculate and absolute mayhem rules Kurukshetra. Celebrated

Arjuna fells your mighty tuskers like bulging clouds; his arrows drink the blood and claim the lives of great rathikas by now past all count. Struck by tempests of arrows and spears, whole elephant legions fall trumpeting. And oh, the battlefield looks eerily magnificent with the lifeless bodies and heads of warriors still adorned with sparkling ornaments.

Watching the Pitamaha exert himself against the storming Arjuna, your sons draw near him and surround him with their forces. Wanting to give up their lives and attain swarga this very day, they ride fearlessly at the Pandavas. Remembering all the insults and injuries inflicted upon them by you and your son, the noble Pandavas, eager for revenge and victory, joyfully engage your sons and their army.

The Pandava Senapati Dhrishtadyumna roars to his men, "Somakas and Srinjayas, attack Bhishma!" And though wounded by innumerable arrows, they charge at the son of Ganga. Himself in the grip of the fury of battle, the Pitamaha turns on the Srinjayas. When he was a boy, Bhishma learnt the astra shastra from great Parasurama, who imparted to him knowledge of mighty devastras which could consume hostile armies. Using that knowledge now, the Kuru ancient wreaks havoc on the enemy ranks, killing ten thousand great warriors every day.

Bharatarishabha, on the tenth day, Bhishma single-handedly slaughters ten thousand elephants. He kills seven famed maharathikas of the Matsyas and the Panchalas; he kills five thousand foot-soldiers, one thousand tuskers, and ten thousand horses and horsemen.

Having razed the troops of all the kings who have come to war for the Pandavas, he kills Satanika, Virata's beloved brother. The incomparable Bhishma annihilates a thousand Kshatriyas with his broad-headed inexorable shafts. He cuts a russet swathe through the Kshatriyas of the Pandava army as they advance towards him following Arjuna.

Enveloping the Pandava host with dense barrages of arrows, with fire, water and wind of awesome devastras, Bhishma stands imperious at the head of the Kaurava forces. On the tenth day of the war, he stands between the two armies, bow in hand, and none of the kings can even look at him, for he burns like the mid-day sun in the summer sky. As

Sakra scorched the Daitya host in battle, even so does Bhishma sear the Pandava army.

Seeing the Kuru Pitamaha's torrid prowess, Krishna says blithely to Arjuna, "'There between the two armies stands Bhishma, the son of Shantanu, devouring our ranks. Only you can withstand Bhishma's arrows. Only you can bring him down. Kill Bhishma today, Arjuna, or this war will be lost."

The Vanara bannered Arjuna lifts his archery and shrouds Bhishma, his chariot, horses and standard with his blistering arrow storm. But serenely Bhishma cuts Arjuna's every shaft down.

Dhrishtaketu, Bhima, Dhrishtadyumna, Nakula and Sahadeva, Chekitana, and the five Kaikaya brothers, and Mahabaho Satyaki and Subhadra's son, and Ghatotkacha, and the five sons of Draupadi, and Sikhandin, and the valiant Kuntibhoja, and Susarman, and Virata, and countless powerful Pandava warriors have been wounded by Bhishma's arrows, and they all seem plunged in an ocean of despair, until Arjuna arrives to rescue them.

Protected by Arjuna, Sikhandin seizes a mighty astra and charges toward Bhishma alone. The indomitable Arjuna makes short and bloody work of those who surround and follow Bhishma, and then himself attacks the Pitamaha. Satyaki, and Chekitana, and Dhrishtadyumna, and Virata, and Drupada, and Madri's twin sons, all led and shielded by Arjuna, attack Bhishma. And Abhimanyu, and the five sons of Draupadi, with raised weapons, also storm against him.

All those unwavering maharathas pierce various parts of great Bhishma's body with deadly barbs. Disregarding them entirely, Bhishma plunges ahead into the Pandava ranks with undimmed assurance. Effortlessly he thwarts all the arrows they rain down upon him and strikes them with terror and death.

Glancing frequently at Sikhandin, always with a mocking smile, always remembering this prince was born a woman, he does not aim a single arrow at him. Instead he kills seven maharathikas of Drupada's aksauhini. Confused and despairing shouts arise amongst the Matsyas, the Panchalas, and the Chedis, who unitedly attack that preternatural Kshatriya. With vast numbers of foot-soldiers and horses and chariots, and with unending volleys of arrows, they engulf Bhishma, son of Bhagirathi, that devourer of his enemies, like clouds hiding the sun.

Truly now, the war is turned as awesome as the Devasura yuddha of old at its most brutal, and Arjuna Kiritin sets Sikhandin before him and strikes Bhishma repeatedly with transcendent archery, with terrible fusillades.'

CANTO 120

BHISHMA VADHA PARVA CONTINUED

Sanjaya says, 'Keeping Sikhandin in front, the Pandavas surround Bhishma and rain wave upon wave of arrows at him. All the Srinjayas unite to strike him with hundred-flamed satagnis, with spiked maces and battle-axes, clubs and bearded barbs, golden winged shafts and spears and Kampana, arrows with heads shaped like the calf-tooth and myriad other missiles.

His coat of mail is pierced all over; he is wounded in every vital part and blood gushes from all him limbs; but Bhishma feels no pain. And to his enemies, he looks like the fire that blazes at the end of the yuga. His bow and arrows are the apocalyptic flames of that fire. The flight of his astras is like the winds of the pralaya. The clatter of his chariot wheels is its heat, and his weapons are its blinding brilliance. His beautiful bow forms its fierce tongue and the bodies of heroic warriors he slays is the source of its energy.

Bhishma blasts his scarlet way through hosts of chariots that encircle him and emerges triumphant from the welter of that seething throng. Ignoring the king of the Panchalas and Dhrishtaketu, he penetrates deep into the Pandava army. He stabs the six Pandava maharathas, Satyaki and Bhima, Arjuna and Drupada, Virata and Dhrishtadyumna, with a many headed dragon of arrows which can melt any armour on earth.

Those maharathas foil Bhishma's beast of barbs and strike him forcefully with ten barbs, always closing in on him still. Sikhandin continues to pierce great Bhishma's body with his golden winged arrows, and Bhishma never offers him any response. And protected by Sikhandin, Arjuna dashes at Bhishma and smashes his bow in his hands.

The seven maharathas, Drona and Kritavarman, Jayadratha and Bhurisravas, Sala and Salya, and Bhagadatta cannot bear to watch this affront. Inflamed, they assail Arjuna; they cover him with elemental devastras and the thousands of shafts that these divine weapons spew. As they charge Arjuna's chariot, their roaring is like that of the raging ocean at the end of the yuga: *kill, bring up our forces, take, pierce, hack them down!* These shouts resound all around.

Hearing that tumult, the Pandava maharathas fly up to defend Arjuna. Satyaki, and Bhima, and Dhrishtadyumna of Prishata's race, and Virata and Drupada, and the Rakshasa Ghatotkacha, and the wrathful Abhimanyu: enraged, and bearing mighty bows, they advance like seven storms. And the battle that breaks out between them and the Kaurava warriors makes one's hair stand on end, even on this tenth blood-soaked day of the war, for it is like the battle of the Devas against the Danavas.

Guarded by Arjuna, the Kiritin, Sikhandin strikes Bhishma with ten deep arrows after the Pitamaha's bow was broken. He strikes Bhishma's charioteer with another volley, and fells his standard with yet another.

Bhishma takes up another colossal bow. That too is riven by Arjuna with three barbs. Bhishma seizes up another, quick as thinking, but ambidextrous Arjuna, switching the Gandiva from hand to hand, breaks that one as well, and, indeed, every other bow which his Pitamaha picks up.

Bhishma licks the corners of his mouth and takes up a spear charged with an astra which can split a mountain. He hurls it furiously at Arjuna's chariot. Watching it course towards him like lightning, Partha looses five thick arrows swift as the mind and shatters Bhishma's recondite missile into five pieces. And it plummets, extinguished, like a flash of lightning separated from a mass of clouds.

Bhishma flares up in anger. That Kshatriya, that conqueror of enemy cities, now says to himself, "With a single bow I could kill all the Pandavas, if they were not protected by Mahavishnu himself.

But I will not fight them for two reasons: because they cannot be slain and because Sikhandin is a woman. When my father married Kali, he granted me two boons: that no one could kill me in war, and that I could choose the time of my death. I believe that this is the fitting hour, and I should now wish my own death."

Knowing Bhishma's resolve, the Rishis and the Vasus in the sky say, "We commend your decision, O son! Do as you have resolved and withdraw your heart from battle." As they finish speaking, a fragrantly moist and auspicious breeze blows along a natural direction. Heavenly cymbals clash and a shower of bright unearthly flowers rains down upon Bhishma.

Only Bhishma hears the words spoken by the Rishis and the Vasus. And I hear them through the power given to me by the Muni. The hearts of the Devas are full of anguish at the thought of Bhishma, that favourite son of all the worlds, falling from his chariot.

Having heard those divine words, though deeply pierced already, Bhishma of great tapasya attacks Arjuna more violently than ever. Incensed, Sikhandin strikes the Pitamaha in the chest with nine sharp arrows. Bleeding profusely, yet Bhishma remains fearless, and unyielding as a mountain during an earthquake. With a ferocious laugh, Arjuna draws his Gandiva, strikes the son of Ganga with twenty five barbs, and then roaring he pierces him through every limb and vital organ with a fiery sermon of hundreds of arrows.

Maharatha Bhishma remains unmoved and returns Arjuna's mighty fire, shaft for shaft. As for Sikhandin's whetted arrows with golden wings, they make not the least impression on the Kuru grandsire.

Still keeping Sikhandin before him, and his rage quickening each moment, even as if he finds himself hurtling, now helplessly, toward some great and fateful moment in time, Arjuna continues to advance towards Bhishma and once more breaks the bow in his hands. Striking Bhishma with ten punitive arrows, he cleaves the Pitamaha's standard with another. Pounding Bhishma's chariot with ten explosive shafts, he makes him shudder.

The son of Ganga takes up an even greater bow. But no sooner does he heft it than Arjuna slices it into three slivers with a trinity of broad-headed shafts. And thus the son of Pandu destroys all Bhishma's bows in that duel.

Suddenly the last vestige of resistance within Bhishma, the pure Kshatriya, gives way and with it Bhishma no longer wants to fight Arjuna. Arjuna strikes him with another tremendous volley of twenty five thudding shafts. Dripping blood, down his noble face and his magnificent body, Bhishma says to Dussasana, "Behold Arjuna, this magnificent Pandava maharathika, who has singlehandedly pierced me with countless arrows. Not even Indra can vanquish Arjuna in battle. As for me, even united, the Devas, Danavas and Rakshasas cannot quell me. What then of maharathas among men?"

Even while Bhishma is speaking, Arjuna, still with Sikhandin before him, continues to attack his Pitamaha.

Deeply wounded by Arjuna's unearthly shafts, Bhishma says to Dussasana with a smile, "These arrows coursing at me in a straight line, whose touch is like lightning, are not Sikhandin's but Arjuna's. They plunge easily through my impenetrable armour, strike me with the force of mushalas and shake me with their ferocity. These shafts are not Sikhandin's.

Hard as the Brahmana's rod of punishment and with an irresistible force like lightning, these arrows ravage my very prana. These are not Sikhandin's. Each as forceful as a mace or a jagged club, these arrows destroy my strength like messengers sent by Yama himself. These are not Sikhandin's. Like angry serpents, flicking their tongues, these barbs eat into my vitals. These are not Sikhandin's - these that cut through me like the biting cold of winter that kills cows.

Other than the valorous wielder of Gandiva, the Vanara-bannered Jishnu, all other kings, even united, cannot harm me in the least."

And then, once more Kshatriya fire blazes up in the old warrior, like a lamp burning high just before it is put out, and Bhishma unleashes a terrible astra at Arjuna as if to destroy all the Pandavas with that single weapon. Before all the great warriors of your army, Arjuna truncates the incendiary shaft with three light like arrows, and it falls harmlessly to the ground. Ready for either death or victory, Bhishma takes up a sword and a golden shield. Before he can even alight from his chariot, Arjuna shatters that shield into a hundred pieces. All this, my lord, is breathtaking.

Yudhishtira goads his forces on crying, "Charge at Ganga's son. Do not be afraid!" And roaring all together, as if in some god's gigantic voice, they attack that solitary warrior from all sides with bearded shafts and long spears, axes and swords, with calf-toothed and thick arrows.

Longing for Bhishma's triumph, your sons surround him also roaring like lions. On that tenth day of the great war, when Bhishma and Arjuna face each other in that final contention, the two armies, with everything at stake this momentous day, fight a battle like none yet seen, inundating Kurukshetra with noble warriors' gore. An abysmal whirlpool of killing and dying rises and spins wildly where the two armies collide, even like the vortex that occurs where the Ganga meets the ocean. And the bloody Earth assumes a fierce form. Her even and rough surfaces can no longer be distinguished; the swollen tide of blood covers them.

Although pierced in all his limbs and vital organs, Bhishma stands serene, having annihilated ten thousand warriors. At the head of his forces, Arjuna breaks through the very heart of the Kaurava legions. With white horses yoked to his whirling chariot, he terrifies us with his astras, and your men flee from the nightmared field.

The Sauviras, the Kitavas, the kings of the eastern, western and northern regions, the Malavas, the Abhishahas, the Surasenas, the Sibis, the Vasatis, the Salwas, the Sayas, the Trigartas, the Ambashthas, the

Kaikeyas, and many other illustrious warriors, all mutilated by implacable, paramount Arjuna, desert Bhishma and flee.

The Pandava hosts encircle Bhishma and overwhelm the Kauravas that protect him. *Kill, hack them to pieces, show no mercy, drink his blood, off with their heads!* These are the unmitigated roars and yells which ring out around Bhishma's chariot.

Having killed so many thousands, now every inch of Bhishma's body is pierced by arrows, most of them Arjuna's keen shafts. And then, with a final echoing roar, with his head to the east, just before sunset, before your sons' very eyes, mighty, mighty Devavrata falls out of his chariot and onto to the waiting, grieving earth.

When Bhishma falls, the sky is rent with the sad cries of the Devas and of earthly kings. Seeing the high-souled Pitamaha fall, our hearts fall with him. That greatest of all maharathas, that Mahabaho, plunges to the ground like Indra's standard cut down, and the earth shakes.

With arrows protruding from him all over, his body never touches the ground. O Bharatarishabha, at that awful moment a miracle reveals him lying on a bed of arrows all plunged deep into his own body! Cloud scud into the sky at that twilight hour and bathe his resplendent, bleeding form with a soft, cool, fragrant shower; and Bhumi Devi trembles.

Fallen Bhishma observes that the sun is in the southern solstice, and he does not allow himself to die, for it is Dakshinayana still and an inauspicious time. The very sky is full of divine voices saying, "Why does Ganga's son, that foremost of all men, give up his life during the southern declension?"

Hearing them, Bhishma replies, "I am alive!"

Although fallen, Bhishma waits for Uttarayana, the northern declension, to die. Learning of his resolve, Ganga, the daughter of Himavat, sends some great Rishis to him. They come as swans who dwell on the Manasa lake, and fly down together to Bhishma, where he lies on his bed of arrows.

Those Rishis alight from the sky and walk around him in pradakshina. Knowing well that it still Dakshinayana, while the Sun is on his southern journey, they say to one another, "Being such a Mahatman, why should Bhishma pass from the world during the southern declension?"

Having said this, they fly up and towards the southern direction. Knowing Bhishma sees them and reflects for a moment. And he says to them, "I will not leave this world as long as the sun is in the southern solstice. I will die when the Sun resumes his northern journey, during Uttarayana. O swans, I swear this to you. I will keep my breath in this broken body until the northern declension.

I can choose the hour of my death, it was my father's boon to me and let his boon be proved true. I will stay alive, and die only when the Sun resumes his northern course during Uttarayana. I will hold life within this body and I have the power to decide the time of my death." Having said these words to the swans, Bhishma continues to lie upon his bed of arrows.

The Pandavas and the Srinjayas rejoice when they see Bhishma fall, and your son is aghast when the Pitamaha is overthrown. All the Kauravas are stricken, benumbed. Led by Kripa and Duryodhana they stand transfixed, tears leaking from their disbelieving eyes. Overcome, they remain motionless for a long time; as if frozen in that abyssal moment, they no longer fight the Pandavas.

When the unslayable Bhishma of untold tejas is felled, all the Kauravas think that the destruction of the Kuru king is now certain. Routed by Arjuna, in the midst of their fallen heroes, themselves mangled, they are all bemused, not moving a muscle, not knowing what to do.

The daring Pandavas, raise massive arms that look like spiked maces, and exult in their victory and blow their great conches. And the Somakas and the Panchalas rejoice. Thousands of trumpets are blown, and the mighty Bhima slaps his arm-pits and roars and roars above the shocked silence, peals of thunder.

When Bhishma falls, the warriors of both armies put down their weapons. Some then scream loudly and some flee, while others faint. Some condemn the ways of the Kshatriya varna while others praise the fallen Bhishma.

The Rishis and the Pitris all extol Bhishma of lofty vows; the departed ancestors of the Bhaaratas also honour Bhishma. Meanwhile, wise Bhishma himself, the noble son of Shantanu who knows the final Yoga, the communion described in the Vedanta, prays silently. He is quiet, and awaits his hour.'

CANTO 121

BHISHMA VADHA PARVA CONTINUED

Dhritarashtra says, 'Alas, deprived of Bhishma, god-like Brahmacharin, what is the state of my warriors, O Sanjaya? The very moment that Bhishma did not attack Sikhandin, even though he despised him, I knew that the Kurus would soon be vanquished by the Pandavas.

Ah, I am dejected to hear of the Pitamaha's fall. What can be a heavier sorrow than this? My heart must surely be made of stone that it does not break into a hundred pieces on hearing of Bhishma's end! Tell me of his achievements for, alas, the war has claimed even he who was invincible.

I cannot bear that Devavrata should be killed in battle. He who could not be overcome by Jamadagni's son himself, even with divine astras, alas, he is now felled by Drupada's son Sikhandin, that paltry prince of Panchala.'

Sanjaya says, 'Overpowered in the twilight hour, the Pitamaha Bhishma dismays the Dhartarashtras and delights the Panchalas. Falling onto the lap of the Earth, he lies on his bed of arrows without his body touching the ground.

When he plunges from his chariot, despondent cries are heard among all creatures. When that great tree of shelter of the Kurus, the ever victorious Bhishma, plummets, the Kshatriyas of both armies are astounded. Seeing Bhishma overthrown with his standard, his armour desiccated, the Kauravas and the Pandavas are both grief-stricken. And the sky darkens and the Sun himself is dimmed. The Earth seems to cry out when Bhishma is cut down.

This one is the foremost of those with knowledge of the Vedas! He is unsurpassed in this learning! This is what all men say of that Purusharishabha as he lies on his bed of a thousand arrows.

Once, discovering that his father Shantanu had been struck by Kama, he resolved to draw up his vital seed and to remain a brahmacharin throughout his life—this is what the Rishis, Siddhas and the Charanas say of Bhishma as he lies on his bed of arrows.

When Bhishma, the Pitamaha of the Bhaaratas, is struck down, your sons stand as if in a nightmare, bewildered, disbelieving, not knowing what to do next. Their hearts and faces are suffused with sadness. Their splendid appearances are dull. They hang their heads low in shame.

The victorious Pandavas, on the other hand, stand jubilantly at the head of their forces; and they blow their golden conches. As thousands of trumpets blast celebrantly, we see the mighty Bhima, drenched in blood, looking like some gory phantasm, prancing about, dancing, roaring, even singing in delight, having himself slaughtered countless enemy maharathas, among them many of your sons.

The Kauravas are crippled in spirit. Karna and Duryodhana sigh deeply. When Bhishma falls, cries of anguish and dismay are heard all around, and great confusion sweeps your son's ranks.

Seeing Bhishma fall, your son Dussasana swiftly rides into Drona's aksauhini. Duryodhana had given charge of protecting Bhishma's life to his younger brother, with his legion. Dussasana is now surrounded by a sea of abject, shocked fighting men. The Kauravas surround him wanting to hear what he has to say.

Dussasana gives Drona the grave tidings, and the Acharya staggers as if struck by an astra and falls down in a dead faint. When he recovers, he stops the Kuru army from continuing the battle. Seeing the Kauravas hold back, the Pandavas send messengers on horseback to forbid their forces also from fighting on. The kings of both armies remove their armour and move towards Bhishma.

Thousands of other warriors too put down their weapons and advance towards the high-souled Bhishma, like the Devas towards Indra. The Pandavas and Kauravas approach Bhishma, lying on his bed of arrows, and bow reverently to him.

Bhishma speaks to the Pandavas and the Kurus who stand sorrowing and silent before him. He says, "Welcome to you, blessed ones! Welcome to you, maharathas! I am pleased to see you, who are the equals of the very Devas." His head lolls back awkwardly unsupported. Bhishma says, "My head need a pillow, fetch me one."

The assembled kings rush away and bring back many soft and fine pillows. The Pitamaha refuses them all. That purushavyaghra says with a laugh, "These are not fitting for a Kshatriya's bed." Seeing the world's greatest maharatha, Arjuna, he says "Dhananjaya, Mahabaho, my head hangs back. Give me a pillow that you regard fitting."'

BHISHMA VADHA PARVA CONTINUED

Sanjaya says, 'Stringing the Gandiva and bowing, Arjuna, with tear-filled eyes, says, "Command me, you invincible one, greatest of all Kshatriyas, O foremost among the Kurus, for I am your slave! What should I do, Pitamaha?"

Bhishma says, "My head droops. O Phalguna, quickly get me a pillow for my bed. You are the most outstanding archer. You know Kshatriya dharma, and you are both wise and noble."

Arjuna says, "So be it," and sets himself to the task. He raises the Gandiva and, with Bhishma's leave and chanting mantras, drills three arrows into the ground beneath the Pitamaha's head, to be its support! Bhishma is satisfied and he praises Arjuna.

Looking at all the Bhaaratas there, he says to Dhanajaya, "Son of Pandu, you have given me a fitting pillow for a fallen Kshatriya. Had you done otherwise, I would have cursed you. Mahabaho, a Kshatriya should sleep on the battlefield on even such a bed of arrows."

Bhishma then says to the gathered kings and princes, "Look at the pillow that Arjuna has given me. I will lie on this worthy bed until the sun turns north again at Uttarayana. Those kings who come to see me then will watch me die. When the Sun moves towards Vaisravana on his swift chariot yoked to seven horses, only then will I leave my body even like the dearest friend.

Dig a ditch around me, O kings. Lying upon these hundreds of arrows, I will worship the Sun. As for you, forsake your enmity and stop fighting.'"

Sanjaya continues, 'Now some physicians and men skilled in drawing out arrows, bring the tools of their trade. Seeing them, Bhishma says to your son, "Dismiss these physicians with gifts, after paying proper respect to them. I have no need for them now. I have won the highest and most praiseworthy state ordained for Kshatriyas!

Lying on this bed of arrows, it is not proper for me to accept any treatment. I should be burnt with these arrows in my body." Duryodhana honours and dismisses the physicians. The rulers of different realms who witness this display of great Bhishma's steadfast virtue are moved to wonder.

The Pandavas and the Kauravas together draw near Bhishma Mahatman lying on his magnificent bed. They pay him worship and circumambulate him three times in pradakshina; posting guards around him, those Kshatriyas, with bodies drenched in blood, retire to their tents in anguish, reflecting on what they have seen this dreadful day, the first of the Kali Yuga.

Krishna comes to the Pandavas, as those maharathas sit together both elated and grief-stricken at the fall of Bhishma, and says to Yudhishtira, "Your victory is the outcome of your good fortune. Through good fortune alone the indomitable Bhishma has fallen. Or perhaps it is destiny that he who was a master of every weapon found you, O king of dharma, as his enemy and has been consumed by your wrathful eye!"

Dharmaraja Yudhishtira replies feelingly, "Krishna, through your grace comes victory, and through your fury defeat! You dispel the fears of those who worship you. You are our refuge. It is no surprise that they whom you have always protected in battle, in whose welfare you have always been engaged, Kesava, should triumph. With you as our protector, I do not regard anything as surprising, fortunate or wonderful!"

Krishna answers with a smile, "O best of kings, only you can speak such words!"'

CANTO 123

BHISHMA VADHA PARVA CONTINUED

" anjaya says, 'The next morning, all the kings, the Pandavas and the Dhartarashtras go again to the Pitamaha. They worship that incomparable Kshatriya, lying on his hero's bed, and stand before him with folded hands. Thousands of maidens shower powdered sandalwood, cooked rice grains over him; they drape auspicious garlands of flowers on him.

And women and old men and children, and countless other spectators to the gruesome war, all approach Bhishma like earthly creatures wanting to gaze at the setting sun. Hundreds of thousands of conches boom and trumpets resound, and actors, mimes, and skilled craftsmen draw near the aged Pitamaha to pay homage.

The war pauses, as the Pandavas and the Kauravas put aside their armour and weapons and together come to that Parantapa. And once more, as in earlier times, they stand there together, kinsmen and enemies, and speak to each other amiably. That assemblage of hundreds of Bhaarata kings, adorned by Bhishma in their very midst, is glorious like a gathering of the Devas in Swarga. And they honour him like the

Devas adore Brahma.

Though his body is broken by the very arrows on which he now lies, and they sear pain through him like burning fire, Bhishma shows hardly any sign of agony. Almost unconscious because of his wounds, Bhishma looks at the kings and asks for water. Those Kshatriyas bring him many beautiful jars of cool, crystalline water, and other exquisite drinks besides.

Seeing all that sweet water and wine, Bhishma says curtly, "I am now distanced from worldly pleasures and this fine water and wine is of no use to me. I am lying on a bed of arrows, waiting for the return of the Moon and the Sun!" Thus reproaching the kings in a low voice, he says, "I want to see Arjuna."

Mahabaho Arjuna comes forward, stands with folded hands, and says, "What shall I do?"

The righteous Bhishma says to him, "My body burns with your shafts and I am in agony. My mouth is parched. Give me water, O Arjuna. You are a great archer, and only you can give me water to quench my thirst."

Arjuna says, "I will, Pitamaha."

He mounts his chariot, and stretches the Gandiva. Hearing the twang of his bow and the slap of his palms like a thunderclap against his bowstring terrifies the armies and the kings. That maharatha mounts his chariot and circles the fallen Pitamaha. Before both vast hosts, chanting mantras to invoke the Parjanyastra, Arjuna shoots a candescent arrow into the ground, slightly south of where Bhishma lies.

Nectar-like in scent and taste, a spring of pure, auspicious and cool water gushes out of the earth and up into Bhishma's lips. And with that jet of water Arjuna slakes the thirst of Bhishma, that bull among the Kurus, of godlike deeds and prowess.

Watching that Sakra-like feat of Arjuna's, all the kings are amazed; and seeing his superhuman ability, the Kurus tremble like cows shivering in the cold. The gathered sovereigns of the world wave their pennants in admiration. And the deafening blast of conches and the pounding of drums are heard all over the battlefield.

His thirst quenched, Bhishma praises Arjuna before all the kings saying, "O Mahabaho, this is not as amazing as it seems, O son of Kuru's race, for, you of immeasurable effulgence, even Narada spoke of you as the ancient Rishi Nara!

With Krishna for your ally, you will accomplish things that even Indra may not try to achieve. Those who know such things recognise you as the destroyer of the entire race of Kshatriyas. You are the supreme archer. You are the most superior man. Just as humans are the best of all animals, and as Garuda is the foremost of all avians; as the Ocean is the best among all water bodies, and the cow foremost among all quadrupeds; as the sun is the most brilliant among all luminous bodies and Himavat among all mountains; as the Brahmana is among all varnas, you are the greatest archer!

Duryodhana did not listen to what Vidura and Drona and Rama and Janardana and I, and also Sanjaya repeatedly said to him. Rashly, foolishly, he ignored our most earnest advice. Beyond all counsel, he will die at the hands of Bhima!"

Hearing these words, Duryodhana is plunged in dejection. Bhishma says, "Listen to me, O king, and at least now discard your anger. You have seen how Arjuna created this spring of water like amrita for me. No one else on earth can achieve such a feat.

The weapons of Agni, Varuna, Soma, Vayu, and Vishnu, those of Indra, Pasupati, and Paramesthi, and those of Prajapati, Dhatri, Tashtri, Savitri, and Vivaswat – in this world of men, all these are known only to Arjuna. Yes, Krishna also knows them. But there is no one else.

Not even if the Devas and Asuras unite can they defeat this son of Pandu in battle. His powers are more than superhuman. Make peace with this mighty warrior, this ornament of battle. Before great Krishna is moved to complete wrath, king of the Kurus, it is dharma for you make peace with the heroic sons of Pandu. As long as a few of your brothers still remain unslain, let peace, O Rajan, be struck. Before Yudhishtira, with eyes blazing fury, entirely annihilates your forces, let peace be made. Before Nakula, and Sahadeva, and Bhima exterminate your army, you must befriend the Pandavas again.

Let this war end today with my death. Make peace with the Pandavas; listen to me, Anagha, and do as I say! Only this can still save you, and indeed the entire Kuru vamsa. Put aside your rage and make peace with your cousins.

What Arjuna has achieved is enough. Let Bhishma's death renew love between the sons of Dhritarashtra and those of Pandu. Let the surviving warriors live. Relent, O Rajan! Give half the kingdom to the Pandavas. Let Dharmaraja Yudhishtira go to Indraprastha. Do not be small-minded or incite further bloodshed; this will only bring you eternal disgrace among the kings of the earth.

With my death, let peace come to all. Let all the rulers of the earth embrace and mingle joyfully with one another. Let father be united with son; let sister's son join his uncle. Ah Suyodhana, if ignorance and foolishness keep you from listening to me, you will repent greatly. This is the truth. Stop this war now!"

Having said this kindly to Duryodhana in the midst of the gathered kings, Bhishma falls silent. The arrows burn his body and, withdrawing his mind from the pain with dhyana, he applies himself to yoga.

Your son disregards what Bhishma has told him, those words of dharma which might still have saved him, like a dying man refusing medicine.'"

CANTO 124

BHISHMA VADHA PARVA CONTINUED

"Sanjaya says, 'After Bhishma shuts his eyes and falls silent, all the assembled kings return to their encampments. When he hears that Bhishma's has been struck down, Radha's son Karna comes alone to him, in some fear. He sees that most illustrious Kshatriya lying on his bed of reeds.

With eyes closed, he approaches Bhishma and falls at his feet. His voice choking, Karna says, "O Lord of the Kurus, I am Radha's son, whom you always looked upon with hate whenever I was near."

Bhishma opens his failing eyes, asks the guards around to withdraw, and suddenly he embraces Karna with one arm, like a father holding his son, and speaks to him lovingly. "Come, come near me. You are my adversary who always challenges me. If you had not come to me, I would have been sad indeed.

You are Kunti's son, not Radha's. Adhiratha is not your father. Mahabaho, I heard this from Narada and from Krishna. And it is true. Ah Karna, I do not bear you any grudge. I only spoke harshly to you to weaken your resolve.

You of excellent vows, you speak ill of the Pandavas for no reason. You were born out of wedlock and that is why you have said and done whatever you have. Through pride, and keeping the company of base men, you have come to hate men of worth. And so I spoke unkindly about you in the Kaurava camp.

I know too well that your prowess in battle is irresistible. I also know of your deep reverence for Brahmanas, your courage, and your charity. You are like a Deva and there is none like you among men. I wanted to prevent this war between brothers and that is why I always spoke cruelly and contemptuously about you, for I knew that Duryodhana depended on you to win this war for him. And, my child, as a warrior and an archer you are Arjuna's equal in battle, why, even Krishna's peer!

O Karna, you rode by yourself to Kasi with your bow and vanquished all the kings there singlehandedly to get a bride for Duryodhana. The invincible Jarasandha, who always boasted of his great prowess, was no match for you in battle and you quelled him.

You are devoted to Brahmanas; you always fight fairly. In strength and vigour, you are equal to a child of the Devas and superior to all men. I have never felt any true anger towards you and that which I showed is now dispelled. For I have learnt that men's best efforts cannot prevent Destiny from taken its course, having its way.

O Parantapa, the valiant sons of Pandu are your brothers. Mahabaho, if you want to gratify me, your Pitamaha, join them. O Suryaputra, let this war end with me. Even today let all the kings of the Earth who remain alive be freed from danger!"

Karna says, "I know this, Mahabaho! It is as you say. I know I am Kunti's son, and not the son of a Suta. But I was abandoned by Kunti, and I have been raised by a Suta. Having enjoyed the wealth and friendship of Duryodhana, I cannot betray his trust now. Like Krishna who fights resolutely for the Pandavas, I too am willing to sacrifice my possessions, my body itself, my children, and my wife, for Duryodhana's sake. It is fitting for a Kshatriya to die on the battlefield, and not from disease or old age!

Relying upon Suyodhana I have always chosen to oppose the Pandavas. This choice will run its full course. It cannot be changed. Who dares, O Bhishma, to challenge Destiny? Who can prevail against what is written in the stars before we are even born?

Pitamaha, you saw and spoke of various signs and omens which portended the destruction of the world. I know only too well that Arjuna and Krishna cannot be conquered in battle. Still we will fight them. And I will overcome Arjuna in war! This I am determined to do. I cannot put aside this hatred I have for the Pandavas. Readily and unwaveringly, I will face Arjuna in battle. I am firm in my resolve, so give me your leave to go to war.

Now that you have fallen, I will fight. This is my only wish. Ah Pitamaha, forgive me any cruel words that I may have spoken to you, or any angry or callous deed which I might have directed against you."

Bhishma says, "I allow you to fight, Karna, if you cannot root out this loathing in your heart. Fight, moved by the wish to attain Swarga! Without anger and spite, serve your king righteously with all your power and courage.

You have my leave, Karna! Achieve what you seek. Through Arjuna you will attain what is possible by fulfilling the dharma of a Kshatriya. Free of pride, fight vigorously and well, for a Kshatriya's source of happiness lies in a just war. For a long time I tried to make peace between the sons of Pandu and the sons of Dhritarashtra. But, Karna, I failed. This is the truth.'"

Sanjaya says, 'Having obtained Bhishma's forgiveness and his blessing, Karna takes the dust from his Pitamaha's feet, bows deeply to him, mounts his chariot and rides towards Duryodhana's tent.'"

End of Bhishma Parva

Appendix for The Bhagavad Gita

1. Samkhya

Notes directly quoted from Sanskrit-English dictionary of Vaman Shivram Apte:

1. Relating to numbers. 2. Calculating, enumerating. 3. Discriminative. 4. Deliberating, reasoning, a reasoner. 5. Of one of the 6 systems of Hindu philosophy, attributed to the Sage Kapila. The philosophy is so called because it enumerates 25 tattvas or true principles; its chief objective is to enter the final emancipation of the 25th tattva, the Purusha or Soul, from the bonds of this worldly existence—the fetters of phenomenal creation—by conveying a correct knowledge of the 24 other Tattvas and by properly discriminating the Soul from them. It regards the whole universe to be a development of an inanimate principle called Prakriti q.v., while the Purusha is altogether passive and simply an onlooker. Samkhya agrees with the Vedanta in being synthetical and thus differs from the analytical Nyaya or Vaiseshika; but its great point of divergence from the Vedanta is that it maintains two principles that Vedanta denies, and it does not admit God as the creator of the universe, which the Vedanta affirms.

2. Yoga

Also from the dictionary of Vaman Shivram Apte:

1. Joining, uniting. 2. Union, conjunction. 3. Deep and abstract meditation, contemplation with the Supreme Spirit. 4. The system of philosophy established by Patanjali, which is considered to be the second division of the Samkhya philosophy, but is practically reckoned as a separate system. The chief aim of the Yoga philosophy is to teach the means by which the human soul may be completely united with the Supreme Spirit and thus secure absolution; and deep abstract meditation is laid down as the chief means to securing this end, elaborate rules being given for the proper practice of such Yoga or concentration of mind.

3. For further details on Samkhya and Yoga philosophy, see:
    a. Online article 'Samkhya and Yoga: two classical Hindu 'paths of insight', by Professor Russell Kirkland, University of Georgia.
    b. Samkhya and Yoga, Encyclopaedia Britannica article.
    c. Samkhya and Yoga, Wikipedia.
    d. Classical Samkhya and Yoga: the metaphysics of experience. Mikel Burley (Routledge. July, 2006).

4. Kalpa

A NOTE ON HINDU TIME

'365 human years make one year of the Devas and Pitrs, the Gods and the manes.

Four are the ages in the land of Bharata¾the krita, the treta, the dwapara and the kali. The krita yuga lasts 4800 divine years, the treta 3600, the dwapara 2400, and the kali 1200; and then, another krita yuga begins.

The krita or satya yuga is the age of purity; it is sinless. Dharma, righteousness, is perfect and walks on four feet in the krita. But in the treta yuga, adharma, evil, enters the world and the very fabric of time begins to decay. Finally, the kali yuga, the fourth age, is almost entirely corrupt, with dharma barely surviving, hobbling on one foot.

A chaturyuga, a cycle of four ages, is 12,000 divine years, or 365 x 12,000 human years long. 71 chaturyugas make a manvantara; fourteen manvantaras, a kalpa. A kalpa of 1000 chaturyugas, 12 million divine years, is one day of Brahma, the Creator.

8,000 Brahma years make one Brahma yuga, 1,000 Brahma yugas make a savana, and Brahma's life is 3,003 savanas long.

One day of Mahavishnu is the lifetime of Brahma.'

www.ingramcontent.com/pod-product-compliance
Lightning Source LLC
Chambersburg PA
CBHW030421100426
42812CB00028B/3049/J